THE ULTIMATE
TV TRIVIA
BOOK

THE ULTIMATE TV TRIVIA BOOK

Vincent Terrace

FABER AND FABER
BOSTON AND LONDON

Terrace, Vincent
   The ultimate TV trivia book / Vincent Terrace.
      p.   cm.
   ISBN 0-571-12913-7
   1. Television programs—United States—Miscellanea.   I. Title.
PN1992.9.T48   1991
791.45'75'0973—dc20   90-44098
                                                                  CIP

Cover design by Don Leeper

Printed in the United States of America

CONTENTS

INTRODUCTION

From the first known TV film broadcast (a Charles Jenkins experiment) in 1925 to the program you watched just last night, there has always been one aspect of television that has been neglected: its trivia (addresses, phone numbers, names of pets and so forth). These facts have become the lost information of television. *The Ultimate TV Trivia Book* is the first attempt to find that lost information and present it in an entertaining and accessible way. As you read through these pages you may find information that you had long forgotten or become acquainted with facts you never knew existed. *The Ultimate TV Trivia Book* is a collection of over 10,000 TV trivia facts, nostalgic information that is completely based on the most reliable source—the actual episodes of the series. This is not a book of opinions; the information is culled from the screen—characters' lives, hometowns, relatives, jobs, pets, hobbies, etc. It is a world of information that, for the most part, has never before appeared in print.

Because a book of this nature has not been attempted, it presented a number of problems, the biggest of which was acquiring series episodes. The selection of programs for inclusion in this edition was based on what shows could be had at the time. Not all entries are created equal; some are chock-full of information (e.g., "Dobie Gillis"), others have less (e.g., "Nancy") and some not enough to qualify as an entry (e.g., "Meet Corliss Archer"). Many types of series were watched, but the situation comedy proved to be best suited to a book on TV trivia. While the sit-com accounts for a good portion of this book, series of other genres are also included: adventure, police and detective dramas, early 1950s Saturday kid shows, mysteries, animations, science fiction and westerns. (Since this book was completed, many new series have been acquired. If your favorite show is not listed here, there is a good chance it will appear in the sequel.)

Due to the varying amounts of trivia, and to make longer entries clear, entries have been set up in two ways: divided under headings for programs with considerable amounts of information; simple paragraph entries for those that offered less information. Where possible, unaired pilot information has been included with appropriate series (for example, "How to Marry a Millionaire," "That Girl," "Mr. Terrific" and "Diana").

While all the basic information about a represented series will be found here, the concentration is on episode trivia—not production credits, producers, writers or directors. The cast listings are principal regulars only (those involved with the trivia or related to a cast regular); hence, some minor performers who may be listed in other TV history or reference books may not be listed here. However, in addition to the principal cast listing, the relatives, flashbacks and flash forwards listings make each cast listing the most extensive ever published for a particular series (even not-seen, but mentioned relations are listed).

From Cadet Happy's "Holy Smokin' Rockets" catch phrase on "Space Patrol" to the names of Alice's pet flies on "This Is Alice" to the Tanners' address and phone number on "ALF," all the information you have been searching for but could never find is here for the first time in *The Ultimate TV Trivia Book*—the first book about TV to be based totally on what you saw on TV.

A note on spellings: Because the trivia information presented here is based entirely on actual shows, spellings of place and character names not shown onscreen or given in the credits are as close as possible to what is heard. They are not necessarily definitive.

ACKNOWLEDGMENTS

The author would like to thank the following people
for their help in making this book possible:

Steve Eberly
Lloyd Friedman
Barry Gilliam
Laura Stuart

THE ULTIMATE
TV TRIVIA
BOOK

THE SHOWS

THE ABBOTT AND COSTELLO SHOW

Syndicated, 1952 to 1954

Principal Cast: Bud Abbott, Lou Costello, Hillary Brooke and Sidney Fields (*as themselves*), Gordon Jones (*Mike Kelly*), Joe Besser (*Stinky Davis*), Joe Kirk (*Mr. Bachagalupe*)

Trivia: The series, set in and around the Fields Rooming House at 214 Brookline Avenue in Hollywood, California, focuses on the antics of several of its tenants.

Bud Abbott and Lou Costello are former movie and radio stars who are now down on their luck. Even with rent costing only $7.00 a week, they are constantly behind seven to eight weeks and are desperate for any jobs that come along. Most notable of these: delivery boys for the Susquehanna Hat Company on Flugel Street; selling discount roller skates ("Abbott and Costello Cheap Skates"); and door-to-door salesmen selling "No Peddlars Allowed" signs. In one episode they have their own business ("Abbott and Costello Pest Exterminators"); in another, they try to win money by appearing on a "Beat the Clock" type of game show called "Hold That Cuckoo" (in which Lou holds that cuckoo and wins the grand prize—a box of bubble gum).

In one episode, Bud mentions he is a professional loafer (one who makes bread) and a member of the loafers union. Lou, who thought Bud meant he got paid for sitting around and doing nothing, is a junior detective, a graduate of the Acme Detective School correspondence course. Lou also mentioned that he helps support his sister and three nieces in his hometown of Paterson, New Jersey.

Bud and Lou's phone number is given as Alexander 4444 (also Alexander 2222) and Lou's pet chimpanzee is Bingo the Chimp (whom Lou adopted when working in the Fields Pet Shop). Bingo dresses like Lou, and eats watermelon for breakfast and 50 pounds of bananas a week. His mother is traveling with a circus and his father is in Africa.

Hillary Brooke, the only female regular, most often plays Lou's girlfriend. While it is clear that she works, her exact job is never revealed. In one episode she moves to Texas to take over the B-Bar-B Ranch when she inherits it from a late relative; in another she appears as "the beautiful blonde stranger" who asks for an ice cream sundae at the Fields Drug Store where Lou works as a soda jerk; in still another, she inherits a haunted castle at Goblins Knob from her late uncle, Montague Brooke.

Sidney Fields, the cigar-smoking, often exasperated and easily fooled landlord, is the owner of the rooming house. In many episodes, Sidney plays his own relatives—from druggists to ice cream vendors to lawyers (e.g., Professor Melonhead, an instructor at the police academy when Bud and Lou tried to become cops; Lawyer Fields, who defended Lou for shooting holes in Mrs. Crumbcake's bucket; and Dr. Fields, who tried to cure Lou's insomnia).

Other Tenants: Mike "Mike the Cop" Kelly, the not-too-bright Los Angeles cop who is constantly plagued by Lou's antics; Stinky Davis, the mischievous 30-year-old "kid" who plays games with Lou (e.g., jump rope, cops and robbers, and hopscotch. They "get" each other by pinching each other on the shoulder); and Mr. Bachagalupe, the enterprising businessman (e.g., owner of an ice cream wagon, a sidewalk café and a fruit and vegetable stand where bananas are five cents each or three for a quarter).

Second season episodes feature Joan Shawlee in various roles and an unnamed and uncredited girl is seen each week placing a large card in front of Lou's face to introduce the guest stars.

Theme: "The Theme from The Abbott and Costello Show," by Raoul Kraushaar

Note: In "The Abbott and Costello Cartoon Show" (syndicated in 1966), Bud Abbott provided his own voice; Stan Irwin was the voice of Lou.

THE ABSENT-MINDED PROFESSOR

NBC, 11.27.88 (Episode 1)
2.26.89 (Episode 2)

An adaptation of the Disney film about Henry Crawford (Harry Anderson), a Medfield College physics professor who invents Flubber, a green rubbery substance that generates its own energy. Ellen Whitley (Mary Page Keller) is Henry's girlfriend, an English teacher at Medfield.

Henry, who has a dog named Newton (after Sir Isaac Newton) and a computer named Albert (after Albert Einstein), derived the name Flubber from his invention, Flying Rubber. The voice of Albert is provided by Jay Johnson and Harry Anderson. Tom Scott composed the theme, "The Absent-Minded Professor."

ADAM'S RIB

ABC, 9.14.73 to 12.28.73

A romantic comedy based on the film of the same name about Adam Bonner (Ken Howard), a Los Angeles D.A., and his wife, Amanda (Blythe Danner), a prosecuting attorney who is often pitted against Adam in court. Amanda, a lawyer with the firm of Kipple, Kipple and Smith, is nicknamed Pinkie, and Adam is nicknamed Pinky. The theme, "Two People," was written by Perry Botkin Jr. and Gil Garfield.

THE ADDAMS FAMILY

ABC, 9.18.64 to 9.2.66

Principal Cast: John Astin (*Gomez Addams*), Carolyn Jones (*Morticia Addams*), Jackie Coogan (*Uncle Fester*), Lisa Loring (*Wednesday Addams*), Ken Weatherwax (*Pugsley Addams*), Ted Cassidy (*Lurch*), Blossom Rock (*Grandmama Addams*)

Trivia: "They're creepy and they're kooky, mysterious and spooky . . . So get a witch's shawl on, a broomstick you can crawl on, we're gonna pay a call on the Addams Family." Deadly nightshade, poison sumac and weeds grow in their backyard. Quicksand and a swamp can also be found there. The Addams family enjoys thunderstorms, gloomy weather, moonbathing and exploring caves. Their address is 000 Cemetery Lane in the town of Cemetery Ridge.

Gomez Addams, the father, enjoys running Lionel "O-Gauge" electric trains (for the thrill of collisions and explosions), dabbles in the stock market (his favorite stock is Consolidated Fuzz), owns an elephant herd in Africa and a nut plantation in Brazil. His favorite person in history is Ivan the Terrible; when his wife, Morticia, speaks French, it drives him wild (it also cleared up a sinus condition that he had for 22 years.).

Gomez and the former Morticia Frump met and married when they were each 22 years old. They both like fried eyes of newt, fried yak, and barbecued turtle tips. Blue-eyed Morticia, whose favorite color is black ("It's so soothing and mysterious"), always wears the same black dress (on their wedding day, Gomez was driven wild by it; "I'll never wear another," Morticia told him). Morticia, who loves to paint, smokes (literally) and has a pet plant (an African Strangler) named Cleopatra. The plant bites and loves zebra burger. As a child, Morticia had a doll named Anne Boleyn. Gomez still has his childhood companion, a human right hand named Thing (played by Ted Cassidy and Jack Volgelin). Thing lives in a box and acts as a family servant. The Addams' favorite holiday is Halloween.

Gomez's pet names for Morticia are "Cara mia" and "Caita."

Their children, Wednesday and Pugsley, attend the Sherwood Elementary School. Wednesday has a doll named Marie Antoinette (who is missing her head, of course) and a pet spider named Homer; Pugsley has an octopus named Aristotle. Their favorite bedtime story is Edgar Allan Poe's "Murders in the Rue Morgue."

Other Family Members: Morticia's Uncle Fester (his favorite story is "Dr. Jekyll and Mr. Hyde" and he once worked as an advice-to-the-lovelorn columnist until everybody started suing him. He thrives on electricity and cures headaches by forcing the pain out with vises); Lurch (the zombie-like butler who loves to play the harpsichord. When he is summoned by a gong, he responds, "You rang?"); Grandmama Addams (Gomez's mother, who attended Swamp Town High School); Ophelia Frump (Morticia's sister, who cooks all day so she can do dishes. "She loves to do dishes. She loves water. She is forever jumping into fountains and brooks, even tubs and sinks"); Cousin Itt (the family intellectual who speaks in a language all his own. He is a ladies' man, is covered with hair and his favorite nook is up the chimney or in the broom closet. When Gomez asked Itt what was under all that hair, Itt replied, "Roots.").

The family pet is Kit Kat (a lion), and in one episode, Thing fell in love with Lady Fingers, a left human hand who serves as the handmaiden of Gomez's Aunt Millicent.

Relatives: Felix Silla (*Cousin Itt*), Don McArt (*Cousin Cackle*), Carolyn Jones (Morticia's sister, *Ophelia Frump*), Margaret Hamilton (Morticia's mother, *Esther Frump*), Ellen Corby (*Mother Lurch*), Elvia Allman (Gomez's aunt, *Princess Millicent*). Roger Arravo also played Cousin Itt and Nat Perrin provided Itt's voice.

Unseen Relatives: Morticia's Uncle Droop and Aunt Drip, Morticia's Uncle Tick (who has two left feet) and Aunt Phobia (who has two right feet), Gomez's Aunt Trivia, Grandmama's Great Grandfather Blob

Theme: "The Addams Family," by Vic Mizzy

Note: In "The Addams Family" cartoon series (NBC, 9.8.73 to 8.30.75), voices are by Lennie Weinrib (Gomez), Janet Waldo (Morticia and Grandmama), Cindy Henderson (Wednesday), Jodie Foster (Pugsley), Jackie Coogan (Uncle Fester) and Ted Cassidy (Lurch).

In the TV movie, *Halloween with the Addams Family* (NBC, 10.30.77), all of the original cast members, with the exception of Blossom Rock, reprised their roles. (Jane Rose portrayed Grandmama, and Henry Darrow appeared as Gomez's brother, Pancho Addams.) The series and its spin-offs are based on characters created by cartoonist Charles Addams.

ADDERLY
CBS, 9.24.86 to 9.11.87
Government agent V. H. Adderly (Winston Reckert) is assigned to the Bureau of Miscellaneous Affairs—an ostensibly useless agency—after being injured on assignment. Adderly, whose code name is Beauty One, was originally assigned to the International Security and Intelligence Agency. Dixie Seatle plays the agency receptionist, Mona; and Jonathan Welsh, V. H.'s superior, Melville Greenspan. Larry Reynolds and Kay Hawtrey appear as V. H.'s parents, Mr. and Mrs. Adderly. Micky Erbe and Maribeth Solomon composed the theme.

THE ADVENTURES OF RIN TIN TIN
ABC, 10.15.54 to 9.29.57
Corporal Rusty (Lee Aaker), the sole survivor of an Apache wagon train raid, and his dog, Rin Tin Tin, are with the Fighting Blue Devils of the 101st Cavalry, stationed at Arizona's Fort Apache during the 1880s. James L. Brown plays Lieutenant Ripley "Rip" Masters, Rusty's guardian, and Joe Sawyer plays Sergeant Aloysius "Biff" O'Hara. In 1975, the se-

ries was resyndicated in sepia tint with new opening and closing segments that were filmed in color. James L. Brown, as Lieutenant Masters, appeared in Fort Apache to relate stories of Rusty and Rin Tin Tin to a group of children visiting the fort.

THE ADVENTURES OF SUPERMAN

Syndicated, 1953 to 1957

Principal Cast: George Reeves (*Clark Kent/Superman*), Phyllis Coates (*Lois Lane,* 1953–54), Noel Neill (*Lois Lane,* 1954–57), Jack Larson (*Jimmy Olson*), John Hamilton (*Perry White*), Robert Shayne (*Inspector Bill Henderson*), Phillips Tead (*Professor J. J. Pepperwinkle*)

Trivia: Moments before the planet Krypton, which is being drawn closer to its sun, explodes, the scientist Jor-El places his infant son, Kal-El, in an experimental rocket ship he programs to head for the planet Earth. When Krypton explodes, it scatters millions of particles of Kryptonite, the only substance that can harm Kal-El, into the universe. The rocket crash-lands near the Jones farm in Smallville, U.S.A., on April 10, 1926. Sarah and Eben Kent, a farm couple who witnessed the landing, rescue Kal-El from the rocket. The baby, wrapped in red and blue blankets, is miraculously unharmed, and the rocket, which explodes seconds later, destroys all evidence of ever having been there.

Realizing that no one would ever believe their fantastic story, the Kents decide to raise the baby as their own son, whom they name Clark. As the years pass, Clark develops amazing powers (for example, X-ray vision, super strength, the ability to fly). Twenty-five years later, following Eben's death from a heart attack, Sarah moves in with her cousin Edith. Clark, who has decided to use his great abilities to help mankind, moves to the city of Metropolis—and thus the legend begins.

Clark, who is a reporter for the Metropolis *Daily Planet*, lives in Apartment 5-H of the Standish Arms Hotel (phone number West 3–0963). Lois, the reporter who always seems to be in a jam, lives in Apartment 6-A of an unnamed building; she was born in the small town of Clifton-by-the-Sea. Jimmy Olson, the young cub reporter whose middle name is Bartholomew, lives with his mother (address not given) and constantly annoys editor Perry White by calling him "Chief" ("Don't call me 'Chief'!"). Perry (mobile car phone number MX 31962) was a top-notch reporter before he became editor. He is also a member of the Amateur Magician's Society. When angered, Perry exclaims "Great Caesar's Ghost!" Inspector Bill Henderson is with the Robbery Division of the Metropolis Police Department. The mischievous Professor J. J. Pepperwinkle lives at 64 Hope Street (phone number Greenleaf 8975).

The telephone number at the *Daily Planet* is Metropolis 6–0500 and the building seen in the opening theme is actually Los Angeles City Hall. The diesel locomotive in the opening theme is owned by the Southern Pacific Railroad. In the episode, "The Face and the Voice," George Reeves also played Bolder, an evil Clark Kent/Superman double (thanks to plastic surgery), who was part of a plan to rob an armored car. Jack Larson played Jimmy's mobster double, Kid Collins, in the episode "Jimmy the Kid," in which he sought documents in Kent's office. Never explained was how Sarah Kent was able to cut and sew the indestructible red and blue blankets that became Clark's Superman costume. The series is based on the comic strip by Jerry Siegel and Joe Shuster.

Leon Klatzkin wrote the theme.

Relatives: Robert Rockwell (Clark's Krypton father, *Jor-El*), Aline Towne (Clark's Krypton mother, *Lara*), Tom Fadden (Clark's Earth father, *Eben Kent*), Dina Nolan (Clark's Earth Mother, *Sarah Kent*), Sarah Padden (Jimmy's aunt, *Louisa Horne*), Mabel Albertson (Perry's sister, *Kate White*), Lane Bradford (Perry's nephew, *Chris White*). Stuart Randall played Clark as a boy (flashbacks).

Spinoffs (excluding animation):

"Superpup." An unsold and never-aired 1958 pilot that portrayed characters in costume as dogs. Billy Curtis played Bark Bent, reporter for the *Daily Beagle*; Ruth Delfino played reporter Pamela Poodle; Angelo Rositto portrayed editor Perry Bite; and Harry Monty played the villain, Professor Sheepdip.

"Superboy." Another unaired pilot attempt to bring the basic concept back to TV in 1961. This version dealt with the exploits of Clark Kent as a teenager (attending Smallville High School), battling crime as Superboy. Johnny Rockwell played Clark and Superboy; Bonny Henning was his girlfriend, Lana Lang; and Monty Margetts was Martha Kent.

"Superboy." Syndicated 10.8.88 to .John Haymes Newton (first season) and Gerard Christopher as Clark Kent in stories that find Clark as a journalism student at Shuster University (and writer for the school newspaper, the *Herald*) who battles crime as Superboy.

Other roles include: Stacy Haiduk (as *Lana Lang*), Jim Calvert (*T. J. White*), Stuart Whitman (Clark's father, *Jonathan Kent*) and Salome Jens (Clark's mother, *Martha Kent*).

AIRWOLF

CBS, 1.22.84 to 7.23.86

Principal Cast: Jan-Michael Vincent (*Stringfellow Hawke*), Ernest Borgnine (*Dominic Santini*), Jean Bruce Scott (*Caitlin O'Shaughnessy*), Alex Cord (*Michael Coldsmith Briggs III; a.k.a. Michael Archangel*)

Trivia: When an awesome attack helicopter called Airwolf is stolen by its creator, Dr. Moffet (David Hemmings), Michael Archangel of the government agency The Firm asks former employee Stringfellow Hawke to retrieve it. In return, the government promises it will look for Hawke's brother, Saint John, who is listed as missing in Vietnam. When Hawke accomplishes his mission, he decides to keep Airwolf and force the government to keep its promise. (In the meantime,

Hawke uses Airwolf to help Michael when the need arises.)

Stringfellow Hawke, 34, a one-time pilot for The Firm, served in the 328 AHC in Vietnam. Orphaned at age 12, he was raised by his brother Saint John and his friend, Dominic Santini (for whom he now works). Hawke, who lives in a remote, wooded area of California, has a dog named Tet and has hidden Airwolf deep in "The Valley of the Gods" (a secret location in the California desert).

Dominic Santini runs the Santini Air Charter Service from the Van Nuys Airport (also given as the Municipal Airport) in California. Dom, who was born on the island of San Remo, calls Airwolf "The Lady." Dom's jeep license plate: 1-BOX-070; his station wagon license plate: IDT 0406; the Santini Air Gas Truck license plate: 2G 15626.

Caitlin O'Shaughnessy, a pilot for Santini Air, was originally a deputy with the Texas Highway Patrol, Aerial Division (helicopter pilot). Caitlin was also a member of the Kappa Lambda Chi Sorority in college. Jean Bruce Scott based Caitlin on the character Sarah Stickney, played by Caitlin O'Heaney in the series "Tales of the Gold Monkey."

Michael Archangel, the head of The Firm, had several gorgeous female assistants throughout the series run. They were: Belinda Bauer (as *Gabrielle* in the pilot), Deborah Pratt (*Gabrielle*, series), Sandra Kronemeyer (*Lydia*), Kandace Kuehl (*Amanda*) and Leigh Walsh (*Rhoda*). His limo license plate is FIRM-1.

Airwolf: Airwolf, U.S. Government file A56-7W, is a black with white underbellied Bell 222 helicopter with a cruising speed of 300 knots and a maximum speed of six mach (662-plus miles per hour with the main rudder disengaged). In some episodes the top speed is mentioned as 250 knots without turbo thrust. The Airwolf's Coast Guard code is Ranger 276.

Airwolf Armaments:
Four 30mm chain guns
Two 40mm wing cannons
Six Hellfire missiles (short-range, air-to-surface)

Twelve Redeye missiles (short-range, air-to-air)

~~Six Copperhead missiles (long-range, air-to-surface)~~

Air-to-Air missiles: Sidewinder, Sparrow (radar-homing), Phoenix (programmable, radar-homing)

Air-to-Surface missiles: Hellfire (laser-homing), Maverick (infrared radio-imaging), Shrike (electromagnetic-homing)

Warheads: Bullpup (radio-command), Harpoon (radio-homing, anti-sky)

Relatives: Christopher Connelly (Hawke's Brother, *Saint John*), Richard Harrah III (Hawke's nephew, *Le Van Hawke*), Barbara Howard (Dom's niece, *Holly Matthews*), Diane McBain (Dom's ex-wife, *Lila Morgan*). Not seen was Dom's daughter, Sally Ann, who died from a drug overdose.

Theme: "Airwolf," by Sylvester Levay

Theme Narration: Lance LeGault (network version only; cut from syndicated version)

Note: For information on the cable-TV version of "Airwolf," see the following entry.

AIRWOLF

USA, 1.23.87 to 7.15.88

Principal Cast: Barry Van Dyke (*Saint John Hawke*), Michele Scarabelli (*Jo Anne "Jo" Santini*), Geraint Wyn Davies (*Mike Rivers*), Anthony Sherwood (*Jason Locke*)

Trivia: A revised version of "Airwolf" which begins by introducing a new employee—Dom's niece Jo—to Santini Air. We are informed that Michael Archangel has been transferred to the Far East, and Jason Locke now heads The Company (not The Firm as in the previous series).

Stringfellow Hawke acquires positive proof that Saint John is alive, but before Hawke can effect a rescue, he is seriously injured in a helicopter explosion that kills Dom. As Jo readies Airwolf for a rescue attempt, she is surprised by two strangers in the copter's hideout—Jason Locke and U.S. Air Force pilot Mike

Rivers (who tracked Airwolf through high-resolution photography). When Jason is told about Saint John, he allows Jo to proceed with the rescue. With Saint John rescued, Jason decides to keep Airwolf a secret and forms a new Airwolf team—Jo, Saint John, Mike and Jason. (Jason fears the copter may fall into the wrong hands if it is returned to the government). Episodes relate the team's dangerous missions for the government.

Company officials call Jo "Little Lady"; the team's code for Airwolf's hideout is Wolf, although they call it "The Company Store"; their code for Santini Air is Cubs (e.g., "Wolf to Cubs"); and during assignments, Saint John often uses "Plan B" (make it up as you go along). Donnelly Rhodes played Jo's father, Tony Santini.

Theme: "Airwolf," by Sylvester Levay, adapted by Dan Milner for this series

ALF

NBC, 9.22.86 to 6.18.90

Principal Cast: Max Wright (*Willie Tanner*), Anne Schedeen (*Kate Tanner*), Andrea Elson (*Lynn Tanner*), Benji Gregory (*Brian Tanner*), J. R. and Charles Nickerson (*Eric Tanner*), Paul Fusco (*voice of ALF*)

Trivia: Just as Willie Tanner begins operating his ham radio, an alien's spaceship guidance system malfunctions—the frequencies interfere with each other. Unable to control his ship, the alien crashes into the Tanners' garage. Lacking parts vital to repairing his craft, the marooned alien becomes the Tanners' permanent house guest.

ALF, which stands for Alien Life Form, was born Gordon Shumway on the planet Melmac (since destroyed by an explosion) 229 years ago. In one episode he mentions he was born on the 28th of Nathanganger; in another episode, he mentions he was born to parents Biff, Bob and Flo on August 12th and October 2nd, 1757. ALF has a body temperature of 425 degrees, eight stomachs and a craving for cats. He attended Melmac High School for 122 years and Melmac State College for two years (he holds degrees in Pedestrian Crossing and Software). On Melmac, ALF, who was known as Mr. Science, was employed as the bearded lady in a circus, as a TV show host, as a car dealer and as an Orbit Guard. At age 150 ALF became a male model; later he co-captained the Bouillabaisseball Team (the Codsters) on Melmac for three years (played like Earth's baseball with the exception of the ball—fish parts are used; fish gills are sold at the concession stand). Their "baisseball" cards feature such players as Mickey Mackerel and come in packages with tabby- and Persian-flavored gum.

Upon moving in with the Tanners, ALF lived in a laundry basket next to the washing machine; later he resides in the attic.

ALF, whose god on Melmac was named Barry, has a passion for eating (as do all Melmacians), and his favorite meal is "everything with everything on it." On Melmac, ALF preferred Siamese cats. Although the furry little alien (burnt sienna color with off-black eyes) has many strange qualities, the most bizarre of them is brought out when he diets. When ALF goes without food, he becomes Wolf, a primitive Melmacian hunting machine (crash diets cause a change in his body chemistry and send him howling back to a wolf-like state).

Melmac: The motto of the planet is "Are you going to finish that sandwich?" and its good luck charms are a mouse and a Tupperware lid. On Melmac, the monetary system is based on foam and the term "stupid" translates as slang for a rich person. The motto of the Orbit Guards (of which ALF was a member) was "To Guard the Orbits—Whether They Want It or Not."

The Tanners: Parents Willie and Kate, and their children Lynn, Brian and Eric, live at 167 Hemdale Street in San Francisco, California, though the locale is also given as Los Angeles. Their phone number is given as 555–8531, 555–4044 and 555–7787. Willie, whose ham radio call letters are KC276XAA, works for the Los Angeles Department of Social Services. He majored in social science in college, while Kate majored in art history. Willie and Kate married on July 11, 1967 and honeymooned at the Duke of Mist Hotel in Niagara Falls. Lynn attends an unnamed high school, and Brian attends Franklin Elementary School. (Their third child, Eric, is an infant.) When Lynn felt she was not as pretty as the other girls in her class, ALF entered her in the Miss Southland Beauty Pageant to boost her confidence. (He listed her talent as clog dancing.) Though prettier than some of the other 32 contestants, she came in last. (On Melmac, the judges wear swimsuits in beauty pageants and the contestants judge the judges.)

Lucky, the cat, is the original family pet who passes away and is succeeded by Lucky II (whom ALF calls Flipper).

Relatives: Anne Meara (Kate's mother, *Dorothy Halligan*), JM J. Bullock (Willie's brother, *Neal Tanner*), Elisha Cook Jr. (Willie's *Uncle Albert*), Allyce Beasley (Neal's ex-wife, *Barbara*), Lisa Buckley (ALF's girlfriend, *Rhonda*), Bob Fappiano (ALF's friend, *Skip*)

Flash Forwards: Andrea Elson (*adult Lynn*), Edward Edwards (*adult Brian*), Mark Blankfield (*adult Eric*)

Theme: "ALF," by Alf Clausen

ALIAS SMITH AND JONES

ABC, 1.21.71 to 1.13.73

In the 1890s, Kansas-based outlaws Jed "Kid" Curry (Ben Murphy) and Hannibal Hayes (Peter Deuel; later Roger Davis) adopt the aliases Thaddeus Jones (Curry) and Joshua Smith (Hayes) in an attempt to begin new lives and end their criminal past (as leaders of the Devil Hole Gang). J. D. Cannon appears as Harry Briscoe, the Betterman Detective seeking to apprehend them. Billy Goldenberg composed the "Alias Smith and Jones" theme.

ALICE

CBS, 9.29.76 to 3.19.85

Principal Cast: Linda Lavin (*Alice Spevack Hyatt*), Vic Tayback (*Mel Sharples*), Beth

Howland (*Vera Gorman*), Philip McKeon (*Tommy Hyatt*), Polly Holliday (*Flo Castleberry*), Diane Ladd (*Belle DuPree*), Celia Weston (*Jolene Hunnicutt*)

Trivia: Shortly after the death of her husband, Donald, Alice Hyatt and her son Tommy move to Arizona to start over. Hoping to become a singer but unable to find a gig, Alice takes a waitress job at Mel's Diner, a less than fashionable roadside eatery that is owned by Mel Emory Sharples, an always-yelling cheapskate who is also the diner's only cook (purportedly famous for his special dish, Mel's Chili). Episodes relate Alice's experiences as well as those of Vera Gorman, Flo Castleberry, Belle DuPree, and Jolene Hunnicutt, Alice's fellow waitresses.

The address of Mel's Diner is 1030 Bush Highway in Phoenix, Arizona; Alice's address is given as both the Desert Sun Apartment House and Apartment 108 of the Phoenix Arms. The waitresses, in cute pink uniforms, earn $2.90 an hour. Vera has a pet cat named Mel, and two hamsters named Mitzi and Harold. Her middle name is Louise. Flo (Florence Jean), famous for her comeback, "Kiss my grits," eventually leaves Mel's Diner to run her own bar, Flo's Golden Rose, in her hometown of Cowtown, Texas, in the series "Flo" (CBS, 3.24.80 to 7.21.81).

In the last episode of "Alice" ("Th-Th-Th-Th-That's All, Folks"), Mel, who has owned the diner for 27 years, sells it to the Ferguson Brothers (who plan to tear it down); Alice, who does sing a number of times on the show, finally gets her big break and moves to Nashville to sing with Travis Marsh; Vera, who has married police officer Elliott Novack (Charles Levin), discovers she is pregnant at the same time Elliott gets a promotion; and Jolene, who has inherited money from her grandmother, plans to open a beauty salon.

In the original pilot (CBS, 8.31.76), Alfred Lutter played the role of Tommy Hyatt. Though not in the pilot, character actor Marvin Kaplan appears almost regularly as Henry, the ever-complaining, henpecked customer. (He works for the phone company, and his wife's name is Chloe.)

Relatives: Doris Roberts (Alice's mother, *Mona Spevack*), Eileen Heckart (Alice's mother-in-law, *Rose Hyatt*), Martha Raye (Mel's mother, *Carrie Sharples*), David Rounds (Mel's *Cousin Wendel*), Merie Earle (Mel's *Grandma Sharples*), Forrest Tucker (Flo's father, *Edsel Jarvis Castleberry*), Mildred Natwick (Vera's *Aunt Agatha*), Art Carney (Vera's cousin, *Art Carney*), Gregory Walcott (Jolene's father, *Big Jake Hunnicutt*), Trevor Henley (Jolene's brother, *Jesse*), Kent Perkins (Jolene's brother, *Jasper*), Grant Wilson (Jolene's brother, *Jeremy*), Robin Eurich (Jolene's brother, *Jimmy*), Steve McGriff (Jolene's brother, *Jake Jr.*), Gurich Koock (Jolene's brother, *Jonas*), Natalie Masters (Jolene's *Granny Gumms*), Ruth Buzzi (Henry's wife, *Chloe*)

Theme: "There's a New Girl in Town," vocal by Linda Lavin

ALIEN NATION: THE SERIES

Fox, 9.18.89 to 9.17.90

Principal Cast: Gary Graham (*Matthew Sikes*), Eric Pierpont (*George Francisco*), Michele Scarabelli (*Susan Francisco*), Terri Treas (*Cathy Frankel*), Lauren Woodland (*Emily Francisco*), Sean Six (*Buck Francisco*)

Trivia: In 1990, a slave ship from another galaxy lands in the Mojave Desert. The occupants, 250,000 workers bred to survive in any environment, are assimilated into Los Angeles society when they cannot return to their own planet (Tencton). The series, set in 1995, follows the life of one such family, the Franciscos: George, a Los Angeles Police Department detective, his wife Susan, and their children Emily, Buck and Vessna (an infant).

The Aliens (called the Newcomers; also Slags), have two hearts, and require U.V. (Ultra Violet) light for energy. Infant aliens require "The Touch" to be comforted (administered to the temples, through which love flows). The Newcomers fear salt water, which burns, and cannot eat earth foods made from meat or animal fat. Their favorite holiday, the Day of Descent, celebrates the day they landed on Earth. They speak the Tenctonese language. The backs of their knees are especially sensitive; a female's ear valley that forms the shape of the letter "S" is most sexy to male aliens. When a TV station broadcasts an emergency broadcast system test, the piercing tone you hear – F sharp above high C – sexually arouses Newcomer women. A Binon (special mating alien) and a husband and wife are needed for the male to have a child. The Palace Theater shows American films dubbed in Tenctonese; in the opening theme, theater marquees show *Rambo 6* and *Back to the Future 5*.

George and his Earth partner, Matthew Sikes, are with the Central Homicide Division of the L.A.P.D. Their car code is 1-William-52. Matthew, whose car license plate number is 2IMU684, lives in Apartment 203 of an unnamed building (he is the president of the tenants' association); his neighbor, the beautiful alien Cathy Frankel, lives in Apartment 204. Matthew buys three scratch-off lottery tickets in search of the three pineapples and $25,000 each day; he has spent $750 since he has known George, and only won $25.

George, who lives in a house numbered 1377 in an area called Little Tencton, is the first Newcomer to be made a detective second grade (he earns $100 a week more than Matthew). George also won the Kareem Abdul-Jabbar Standing-Tall Citizenship Award. His alien name is Neemo. Cathy, whose alien name is Gelana, is a biochemist and works at the Newcomers' Behavioral Center. James Greene appears as George's Uncle Moodri. The series is based on the 1988 feature film.

Theme: "Alien Nation," by Joe Harnell

ALL IN THE FAMILY

CBS, 1.21.71 to 9.16.79

Principal Cast: Carroll O'Connor (*Archie Bunker*), Jean Stapleton (*Edith Bunker*), Sally Struthers (*Gloria Bunker Stivic*), Rob Reiner (*Mike Stivic*), Danielle Brisebois (*Stephanie Mills*), Allan Melvin (*Barney Hefner*), Liz Torres (*Teresa Betancourt*), Corey and Jason Drager (*Joey Stivic*)

Trivia: The bigoted, uncouth and conservative Archie Bunker; his dim-witted wife, Edith; their liberal daughter, Gloria, and Gloria's husband Mike (a.k.a. "Meathead") live at 704 Hauser Street in Queens ("the only house on the block with a paid-up mortgage") – Archie and Edith have lived there for 25 years.

Archie and Edith first met at the Puritan Maid Ice Cream Parlor. During "The Big One" (World War II), Archie was first stationed at Fort Riley, Kansas; he later served 22 months in Italy, where he received a Purple Heart, the good conduct medal, and "a butt full of shrapnel" – which is why he "ain't danced with his wife for 30 years." In 1944, when Gloria was born, the hospital bill for her delivery was $131.50. With the advent of TV in 1948, Archie and Edith, who couldn't afford a set, would watch "Milton Berle" in the window of Tupperman's Department Store. Two years later they got their first set – a console with a six-inch screen.

Archie works as a dock foreman for the Prendergast Tool and Die Company. After being laid off, he buys his favorite hangout – Kelsey's Bar – and turns it into Archie Bunker's Place (a bar-restaurant in Astoria, Queens). Adding spice to life at the bar is Mildred "Boom-Boom" Turner (Gloria LeRoy), the well-endowed (44D-32-40) waitress who appeared in several episodes before being written out.

Archie, whose blood pressure fluctuates between 178/90 and 168/95, drinks Schlitz beer and is a member of the Royal Brotherhood of the Kings of Queens Lodge (phone number 555-4378). As a kid, Archie was called "Shoebootie" (he once wore one shoe and one bootie when his Depression-poor family couldn't afford to buy him a new pair of shoes). As a child of six, Edith committed her most "despicable act" – she stole a five-cent O'Henry bar from the candy counter at F. W. Woolworth (she later went back to make restitution – but had to pay a dime as the price had gone up).

Although Archie calls Edith "Dingbat," he loves her very much and only strays once to nearly have an affair with a woman named Denise (Janis Paige). Archie considers the day Sammy Davis Jr. came to his house to be the greatest thing that ever happened to him (he even let Sammy sit in his favorite easy chair by the TV—a privilege few can claim).

Edith, whose maiden name is Baines, is a simple housewife who takes life as it comes. Her favorite TV soap opera is "As the World Turns," she buys her meat at Klemer's Butcher Shop, and she serves as a Sunshine Lady at the Sunshine Home for the Elderly (she earns $2.65 an hour and once received the Citizen of the Week Award for saving the life of an elderly man). At the First Friendly Bank of Queens, Archie and Edith have joint checking and savings accounts. In addition, Edith has three accounts of her own (that total $78.00): the Magic Potato Cutter account, a Christmas Club account and Joey's Education account.

Gloria, a perfume salesgirl at Kresler's Department Store, earns $80.00 a week. Her husband, Mike, is first a college student and later a college teacher (the schools are not named). After the birth of their son, Joey, Mike moves his family to California when a better-paying job comes his way. (Before Joey's birth, Mike and Gloria planned to name him Stanislaus—but Archie objected and put up a fuss: "Kids are mean. They're gonna call him Louse.") When Mike and Gloria moved to California, the spinoff series "Gloria" (CBS, 9.26.82 to 9.21.83) evolved.

In the "Gloria Comes Home" episode of "Archie Bunker's Place" (2.28.82), Gloria returns to Queens with Joey (Christian Jacobs) when Mike deserts them and moves to a commune in Humboldt, California. Shortly after, Gloria finds a job in Fox Ridge (Duchess County, N.Y.) as the assistant to Dr. Willard Adams (Burgess Meredith), an aging veterinarian. Joey, played by Christopher Johnston in the pilot, has a dog named Archie and a pet turtle named Murphy.

Stephanie Mills, Archie's ward, is a daughter of Edith's "no-good" cousin, Floyd Mills (with whom she went to live after her mother was killed in a car acci-

dent). She became a member of the family when Edith took pity on her and gave her an opportunity to grow up in a decent environment. She is Jewish and a member of the Temple Beth Shalom (Edith is Episcopalian; Archie only mentions that he is a Christian).

Teresa Betancourt, the nurse who comes to live with the Bunkers (in Gloria's old room) calls Archie "Mr. Bunkers" (with her Spanish accent it comes out "Mr. Bonkers"), and pays $100 a month rent.

Relatives: Richard McKenzie (Archie's brother, *Fred Bunker*), Bea Arthur (Edith's cousin, *Maude Findlay*), Bill Macy (Maude's husband, *Walter Findlay*), Marcia Rodd (Maude's daughter, *Carol Findlay*), Nedra Volz (Edith's *Aunt Iola*), Elizabeth Wilson (Edith's *Cousin Amelia*), Tim O'Connor (Edith's *Cousin Roy*), Ruth Manning (Edith's *Aunt Clara*), Marty Brill (Stephanie's father, *Floyd Mills*), Michael Conrad (Mike's father, *Casimir Stivic*), Estelle Parsons (Barney's wife, *Blanche*)

Theme: "Those Were the Days" (vocal by Carroll O'Connor and Jean Stapleton), written by Lee Adams and Charles Strouse

Spinoffs: "Archie Bunker's Place" and "The Jeffersons" (see separate entries). Information on "Gloria" appears above in this entry. "Maude" aired on CBS (9.12.72 to 8.29.78) and dealt with an outspoken liberal named Maude Findlay (Bea Arthur), her husband Walter (Bill Macy), and her daughter, Carol (Adrienne Barbeau), all of whom live in Tuckahoe, New York.

Note: Two unaired pilots were made prior to the series that evolved into "All in the Family." In "Those Were the Days," produced in 1968, Kelly Jean Peters played Gloria and Tim McIntire was Mike. The second pilot, taped in February 1969, had Candace Azzara as Gloria and Chip Oliver as Mike. In both pilots, based on the British series, "Till Death Do Us Part," Carroll O'Connor and Jean Stapleton were Archie and Edith.

ALL IS FORGIVEN

NBC, 3.20.86 to 6.2.86

Paula Winters Russell (Bess Armstrong) produces the TV soap opera "All Is Forgiven" (the network is assumed to be NBC, although it is not actually stated). Her husband, Matt Russell (Terence Knox), whom she married the day she got the job as producer, owns the Ying Yang Donut Company.

Matt's pretty but somewhat rebellious daughter, Sonia (Shawnee Smith), has a difficult time accepting Paula as her new mother. Nicollette Bingham (Carol Kane) is the show's temperamental writer. Actresses Cecile Porter-Lindsay (Judith-Marie Bergan) and Sharry Levy (Debi Richter) play Selena and Coral on the serial.

Lorraine Elder (Valerie Landsburg) is the station's receptionist, and Deborah Harmon played Matt's ex-wife, Sharon, in one episode. Robert Kraft composed the theme.

In the unaired pilot version, Gary Sandy played the role of Matt Russell.

AMANDA'S

ABC, 1.10.83 to 5.26.83

Principal Cast: Bea Arthur (*Amanda Cartwright*), Kevin McCarthy (*Zachary Cartwright*), Fred McCarren (*Marty Cartwright*), Simone Griffeth (*Arlene Cartwright*), Tony Rosato (*Aldo*), Michael Constantine (*Avril Krinsky*)

Trivia: Since the British series "Fawlty Towers" (see separate entry) first appeared here in 1977, it has become a challenge to produce an American version of the series. The first response was a failed pilot called "Snavely" (ABC, 6.24.78), in which Harvey Korman played Henry Snavely, the inept proprietor of Snavely Manor, and Betty White portrayed his wife, Gladys. "Amanda's" was the second attempt; it ran for nine episodes. In it, Amanda Cartwright owns a hotel called Amanda's-by-the-Sea. Despite its charm and million-dollar view of the Pacific Ocean, the hotel is fraught with prob-

lems. At first, Amanda is assisted by her son Marty and his wife, Arlene. When this fails, Amanda's brother-in-law, Zachary, becomes her new assistant. Avril Krinsky, who owns the nearby Hotel Casa Krinsky, wants to buy Amanda's hotel. Like "Fawlty Towers," "Amanda's" has its own muddled-mouth bellboy, Aldo.

A third unsuccessful attempt to adapt the British series was "The Nutt House" (NBC, 9.20.89 to 10.25.89), in which Harvey Korman plays Reginald J. Tarkington, manager of the Nutt House, a once-prosperous New York hotel that has fallen on hard times. Cloris Leachman, in a dual role, plays the head housekeeper, Mrs. Frick, as well as the elderly hotel owner, Edwina Nutt.

THE AMAZING SPIDER-MAN

CBS, 4.5.78 to 7.6.79

Principal Cast: Nicholas Hammond (*Peter Parker/Spider-Man*), Robert F. Simon (*J. Jonah Jameson*), Ellen Bry (*Julie Masters*), Michael Pataki (*Police Captain Barbera*), Chip Fields (*Rita Conway*)

Trivia: When Peter Parker, a graduate student at Empire State University in New York City, is bitten by a radioactive spider, he absorbs the proportionate power and abilities of a spider. In light of his newfound powers, Peter creates a special red and blue costume to conceal his true identity. To best learn of troublesome situations in a hurry, he becomes a photographer for the *Daily Bugle*, a local newspaper whose editor is J. Jonah Jameson. In stunt sequences, Fred Waugh plays Spider-Man; Irene Tedrow appears as Peter's Aunt May. (In the original pilot [CBS, 9.14.77] David White played Jameson and Jeff Donnell, Aunt May Parker.) The series is based on the comic strip by Stan Lee.

In 1969, ABC presented the animated adventures of "Spider-Man" (8.30.69 to 9.9.72) in the first TV adaptation of the Marvel comic book character. In this series, Peter Parker (voice by Peter Soles) is a student at Central High School; later he is a reporter for the *Bugle*.

Not forgetting women, ABC later aired the animated "Spider-Woman" (9.22.79 to 3.1.80). In it, Jessica Drew (voice by Joan Van Ark), daughter of a famous scientist, is bitten by a poisonous spider. To save his daughter's life, Dr. Drew injects her with an experimental spider serum. The serum saves Jessica's life and endows her with amazing spider-like abilities. Jessica, who publishes *Justice* magazine, creates a red and blue costume to conceal her true identity when she battles crime.

AMERICA 2-NIGHT

Syndicated, 10.3.77 to 7.4.78

On "Fernwood Tonight" (7.4.77 to 9.30.77), the summer replacement for and spin-off of "Mary Hartman, Mary Hartman" (see entry), Barth Gimble (Martin Mull) was the host of "Fernwood Tonight," a mythical talk show produced by Channel 6 in Fernwood, Ohio. Gimble interviewed the most grotesque people imaginable.

When he is unable to raise the money he needs to continue broadcasting his show, Barth moves to Alta Coma, California, to become the host of "America 2-Night," a variety show that spoofs other talk-variety shows. The program airs on the mythical UBS (United Broadcasting System) network. The network's slogan is, "The network that puts U before the BS." Alta Coma is famous for being the shoelace capital of the world. Jerry Hubbard (Fred Willard) plays Barth's dim-witted announcer, and Happy Kyne (Frank DeVol) plays the leader of the Mirth Makers Orchestra.

Recurring guests are Jim Varney as daredevil Virgil Simms (who does death-defying stunts in a mobile home), Bill Kirchenbauer as Tony Roletti (an awful lounge-singer) and Ken Mars as William W. B. "Bud" Prize, a talent scout who represents people with little or no talent. Sisters Michelle and Tanya Della Fave are the show's dancers, Michelle and Tanya. Frank DeVol composed the theme.

THE AMERICAN GIRLS

CBS, 9.23.78 to 11.10.78

Seasoned reporter Rebecca Tompkins (Priscilla Barnes), formerly the anchor of KSF-TV Channel 6's "10 O'Clock News Hour" in San Francisco, and newcomer Amy Waddell (Debra Clinger), a former general assignment reporter for WREF-TV, Channel 36 in Washington, D.C., are now roving reporters for the "The American Report," a TV newsmagazine. (Presumably the series airs on CBS.) Their mobile phone number is 456–2114 (later 555–2114).

Francis X. Casey (David Spielberg) produces the show; Jason Cook (William Prince) is the show's host. In a flashback sequence, Lisa Lyke plays Amy as a young girl. Jerrold Immel composed the theme.

THE AMOS 'N' ANDY SHOW

CBS, 6.28.51 to 6.11.53

Principal Cast: Alvin Childress (*Amos Jones*), Spencer Williams Jr. (*Andrew Halt Brown*), Tim Moore (*George "Kingfish" Stevens*), Jane Adams (*Ruby Taylor Jones*), Ernestine Wade (*Sapphire Stevens*), Amanda Randolph (*Mama*), Lillian Randolph (*Madame Queen*), Johnny Lee (*Algonquin J. Calhoun*), Nick O'Demus (*Lightnin'*)

Trivia: "Out of the library of American Folklore, those treasured stories such as 'Huck Finn,' 'Paul Bunyon' and 'Rip Van Winkle,' come the warm and lovable tales of 'Amos 'n' Andy.' Created by Freeman Gosden and Charles Correll and presented by the Blatz Brewing Company of Milwaukee, Wisconsin . . . " Shortly after arriving in New York City from Marietta, Georgia, Amos Jones and his friend, the not-too-bright Andrew Halt Brown, rent an apartment at 134th Street and Lenox Avenue. It is Andy who first meets the fabulous but inept con-artist, George "Kingfish" Stevens.

While watching the construction of a skyscraper in Manhattan, Andy catches Kingfish attempting to pick his pocket. As George explains that one of his "solid gold cufflinks" must have gotten caught on Andy's jacket sleeve, he learns that Andy has $340 to invest in a business. That's all George needs to hear. Before he knows it, Andy has himself a cab—and a company to go with it. He and Amos choose the name Fresh Air Taxi Cab Company of America, Inc.

While all three men are married, it is Amos, who met Ruby Taylor after a Sunday mass, who has the most stable marriage. Andy, who has many girlfriends, is perhaps most famous for his romantic involvement with the fabulous Madame Queen, who steals Andy's heart then sues him for breach of contract when she catches Andy with another woman.

George, the "Kingfish" of the Mystic Knights of the Sea Lodge, is married to the constantly nagging Sapphire. Complicating George's life are Sapphire's mother, Mama, who lives with them, and Sapphire's brother, Leroy (not credited), who George thinks is a jinx and calls "Goofy." Sapphire, treasurer of the Women's Club (a gathering of her neighborhood friends), and George have been married for 20 years.

The address of the Mystic Knights of the Sea Lodge is given as 127th Street and Lenox Avenue. George lived at 134 East 145th Street (on Lenox Avenue) and, after Amos married, Andy took his own apartment on 134th Street.

Andy's net worth, taking into account his life insurance policy, investments, Christmas Club, savings and checking accounts, amounts to $9.00. The Kingfish and Andy often eat their lunch at The Beanery, next to the Lodge Hall. Andy smokes two-cent cigars (he is hoping one day to be able to afford five-cent ones). Both Andy and George do their banking at the Lenox Savings Bank and the New Amsterdam Savings Bank. George, who has many money-making schemes, sells Superfine Brushes door-to-door and becomes partners with Andy in a disastrous parking-lot business.

Other characters include the inept lawyer Algonquin J. Calhoun and Lightnin', the agonizingly slow cab company janitor. George's interest in money began at an early age when, as a boy in Georgia, he attended a christening and noticed that his Uncle Clarence gave $500 to the parents when a baby was born into the family. Watching other people acquire Uncle Clarence's money, George figured he, too, could acquire other people's money by being clever. (The actors playing Uncle Clarence and young George were not given screen credit.)

Theme: "The Perfect Song," by Clarence Lucas and Joseph Breil

Note: Variations on both the Amos and Andy characters appeared in the animated series, "Calvin and the Colonel" (ABC, 10.3.61 to 9.22.62), which dealt with a cunning Southern fox, Montgomery J. Klaxon (voice of Freeman Gosden), Calvin Burnside (voice of Charles Correll), a not-too-bright bear; Maggie Bell (voice of Virginia Gregg), Klaxon's wife; and lawyer Oliver Wendell Clutch (voice of Paul Frees).

THE ANDY GRIFFITH SHOW

CBS, 10.3.60 to 9.16.68

Principal Cast: Andy Griffith (*Sheriff Andy Taylor*), Ronny Howard (*Opie Taylor*), Don Knotts (*Deputy Barney Fife*), Frances Bavier (*Aunt Bee Taylor*), Betty Lynn (*Thelma Lou*), Aneta Corsaut (*Helen Crump*), Jim Nabors (*Gomer Pyle*), George Lindsey (*Goober Pyle*), Jack Burns (*Deputy Warren Ferguson*), Ken Berry (*Sam Jones*), Hal Smith (*Otis Campbell*), Jack Dodson (*Howard Sprague*), Howard McNear (*Floyd Lawson*), Paul Hartman (*Emmett Clark*), Arlene Golonka (*Millie Swanson*), Buddy Foster (*Mike Jones*)

Trivia: The sleepy little town of Mayberry, North Carolina, is a virtually crime-free community where Sheriff Andrew Jackson "Andy" Taylor and Deputy Bernard Milton "Barney" Fife uphold the law (which consists basically of handing out parking tickets, helping children across the street and replacing lids on garbage cans). Although Mayberry's sheriff's office is a bit behind the times—no tear gas or submachine guns—it does boast five rifles on the wall rack (in some episodes seven rifles) and some emergency equipment—a rake and a shovel—that Andy carries in the trunk of his squad car (license plate number JL 327).

Although Andy does not carry a gun (he is referred to as "the sheriff without a gun" in the national sheriffs' magazine), he does allow Barney to carry a gun—but only one bullet (which he is not to use unless there is a real need for it). In one episode, Floyd, proprietor of Floyd's Barber Shop, was deputized so he could carry the flag in the Veteran's Day Parade. Goober, who works with Gomer at Wally's Filling Station, is also deputized yearly to guard the cannon in the park on Halloween to prevent kids from putting "orange peels, 'taters, and rotten tomatoes in it."

Andy and Barney, 1945 graduates of Mayfield Union High School (the school colors are orange and blue) are actually cousins. Barney has only been a deputy for five of the twelve years Andy has been sheriff. While Barney's address was only given as 411 Elm Street, Andy's was given as both 322 Maple Road and 14 Maple Street. Andy goes hunting twice a year with Ed Crumpacker (not seen). Andy and Barney, whose birthstone is the ruby, eat at the Junction Café (the always talked about waitress, Juanita Beasley, is not seen). Raleigh and Mt. Pilot are mentioned as Mayberry's neighboring towns. Barney left in 1965 for a job in State Traffic with the Raleigh Police Department. He was replaced by Warren Ferguson.

Opie is Andy's young son; Helen, Andy's girlfriend (whom he later marries), is the town's schoolteacher. Other characters include Betty Lou, Barney's longtime girlfriend; Sam Jones, a widowed farmer who becomes a city councilman; Millie Swanson, Sam's girlfriend; and Mike, Sam's son. Emmett owns Emmett's Fix-It Shop. Otis, the town drunk, has jail privileges—he locks himself up when he gets intoxicated and lets himself out when he is sober once again. The town's notary public is Mary Pleasant (who works in the bank, but is not seen). In the opening theme, Andy and Opie head for their fa-

vorite fishing hole at Meyer's Lake. The original pilot aired on "The Danny Thomas Show" on February 15, 1960.

In the TV movie, *Return to Mayberry* (NBC, 4.13.86), Mayberry and its citizens remain virtually unchanged. Andy, who has married Helen Crump, moved away in 1968, but returns to run for sheriff—without knowing the race is against Barney Fife, the acting sheriff (who, after 25 years, is still engaged to Thelma Lou). Opie has married a girl named Eunice (Karlene Crocket) and is now the editor of the Mayberry *Gazette*; Gomer and Goober own the G&G Garage. (The movie ends with Andy becoming sheriff and Barney his deputy.)

Relatives: Candace Howard (Bee's niece, *Martha*), Joe Connell (Martha's husband, *Darryl*), Mary Lansing (Emmett's wife, *Martha Clark*), Mabel Albertson (Howard's mother, *Mrs. Sprague*), Dub Taylor (Emmett's brother-in-law, *Ben*), Elizabeth Harrower (*Millie's mother*), Steve Pendleton (*Millie's father*), Jan Shutan (Andy's cousin, *Gloria*), Mary Ann Durkin (Helen's niece, *Cynthia*)

Theme: "Theme from the Andy Griffith Show," by Earle Hagen

Spinoffs: "Gomer Pyle, U.S.M.C." (CBS, 9.25.64 to 9.19.69), in which Gomer joins Marine Company B at Camp Pendleton; and "Mayberry, R.F.D." (CBS, 9.23.68 to 9.6.71), in which Sam Jones becomes a city councilman in Mayberry.

ANGIE
ABC, 2.8.79 to 10.23.80

The rags-to-riches story of Angie Falco (Donna Pescow), a poor waitress who marries a wealthy doctor named Brad Benson (Robert Hays). Angie, who worked at the Liberty Coffee Shop in Philadelphia, now owns the diner. Her sister, Marie Falco (Debralee Scott), and mother, Theresa Falco (Doris Roberts), live at 4221 Vermont Street (Apartment 1). They originally ran the Falco Newsstand; later Theresa purchases a beauty salon called Rose's House of Beauty.

Brad's divorced sister, Joyce Benson

(Sharon Spelman), objects to the marriage, while their father, Randall Benson (John Randolph), is delighted to have Angie as a daughter-in-law. Tammy Lauren is Joyce's pretty daughter, Hilary; Carlo Imperato is Angie's cousin, Pete Fortunato; and Danny DeVito appeared as Angie's uncle. Maureen McGovern sings the theme, "Different Worlds."

ANN JILLIAN

NBC, 11.30.89 to 1.20.90
8.5.90 to 8.19.90

Principal Cast: Ann Jillian (*Ann McNeil*), Lisa Rieffel (*Lucy McNeil*), Amy Lynne (*Robin Walker*), Chantal Rivera-Batisse (*Melissa Santos*), Cynthia Harris (*Sheila Hufnagel*), Zachary Rosencrantz (*Kaz Sumner*), Noble Willingham (*Duke*)

Trivia: After her husband Eddie, a fireman, is killed in the line of duty, Ann McNeil, an ex-Radio City Music Hall Rockette, moves with her daughter Lucy from Queens, New York, to Marvel, California, to begin a new life. There Ann, who has a bank account at Fidelity Mutual, secures employment as manager of Aunt Betty's Coffee and Bean Shop, a quaint eatery owned by Sheila Hufnagel.

Lucy, who attended St. Michael's School in New York, now attends Marvel High School. The 15-year-old eats Dipples Potato Chips as a bedtime snack. She has a dog named Corky, a mischievous animal Ann nicknamed "the puppy from hell."

Robin Walker is Lucy's schoolmate and Ann's not-too-bright assistant. Melissa Santos, a conceited high-school bombshell, is a beauty pageant winner who holds the titles "Miss Teenage Tomato" and "Miss Teen Avocado." Kaz Sumner is Ann's neighbor, the kid next door who apparently lives with his grandfather, Duke.

Ann and her husband first met as teenagers. On their first date, they saw a play and took a hansom cab ride through Central Park. To neck, they used to go to Montague Point "to watch for Halley's Comet—which wasn't due for 30 years." (In Marvel, the make-out spot is Paradise Point—where the kids go "to watch for UFO's.") Before a date, Ann used to hang upside down to get color in her cheeks. Thunderstorms still frighten Ann; to feel secure, she snuggles up in bed with Lucy.

Theme: "Ann Jillian," vocal by Ann Jillian and Stan Harris

Note: In the original (unaired) 1989 pilot ("The Ann Jillian Show"), Ann and Lucy's last name was Morgan.

The August 19, 1990 episode introduced a new format in an effort to save the series. When Ann makes a pastry delivery from Aunt Betty's Coffee and Bean Shop to Marsh Pearson, president of the Merchants Association of the Marvel Mall, she suggests a way to improve the mall—make it a happy place. Marsh finds the idea terrific and hires Ann as its activities director.

Ann's license plate is given as 2DDL 274: There are 317 mannequins in the mall. The town of Marvel was founded by Jacob Sweeney in 1921. (While driving to San Francisco, Jacob's Model-T Ford had a flat tire. Rather than fix the flat, he decided to stay where he was.)

The revised-format cast added Bruce Kirby as Marsh Pearson; Adam Biesk as Tad Pearson, Marsh's son and Ann's assistant; and James Henriksen as Russ, the security guard. Only the above episode aired.

THE ANN SOTHERN SHOW

CBS, 10.6.58 to 9.25.61

Principal Cast: Ann Sothern (*Kathleen "Katy" O'Connor*), Ernest Truex (*Jason Maculey*), Reta Shaw (*Flora Maculey*), Don Porter (*James Devery*), Ann Tyrrell (*Olive Smith*), Kathleen Freeman (*Mrs. Bennett*), Louis Nye (*Dr. Delbert Gray*), Ken Berry (*Woodrow "Woody" Hamilton*), Jack Mullavey (*Johnny Wallace*), Lester Matthews (*Tom Bartley Sr.*)

Trivia: Katy O'Connor is the assistant manager of the Bartley House Hotel (owned by Tom Bartley Sr.) in New York City. She and her secretary, Olive Smith, are roommates and share apartment 3-B at East 10th Street in Greenwich Village (address also given as 15 Greenwich Place). Mrs. Bennett is their landlady.

Jason Maculey first managed the hotel (1958–59) but was replaced by James Devery in 1959 (until 1961) when Jason was transferred to the Calcutta Bartley House. The henpecked Jason, who calls Katy "the best darned assistant manager" he ever had, is married to the overbearing Flora. James Devery, whose middle name is given as both Aloysius and Arlington, was born on August 23, 1916, in Ohio. He graduated from Harvard in 1938 and then became a bellboy for the Bartley chain. Other hotel regulars are bellboys Woody Hamilton and Johnny Wallace, and the hotel dentist, Dr. Delbert Gray.

Relatives: Cecil Kellaway (Katy's *Uncle Sean*), Terrence De Marney (Katy's *Uncle Terence*), Frederick Ford (Tom's son, *Tom Jr.*), Christine White (Tom's niece, *Margaret Finchley*), Gladys Hurlbut (Delbert's mother, *Dr. Gray*—also a dentist), Frances Bavier (Johnny's mother, *Mrs. Wallace*). Mentioned, but not seen, were Katy's father, Patrick, and his four other brothers: Timothy, Thomas, Michael and James.

Theme: "Katy," by Ann Sothern and Bonny Lake

ANNIE OAKLEY

Syndicated, 1.54 to 2.57

Principal Cast: Gail Davis (*Annie Oakley*), Brad Johnson (*Deputy Lofty Craig*), Jimmy Hawkins (*Tagg Oakley*)

Trivia: Expert sharpshooter Annie Oakley and Deputy Lofty Craig uphold the law in Diablo County, Arizona, during the early 1900s. In the opening theme, Annie, who was orphaned and now takes care of her kid brother, Tagg, shoots a hole in the center spade of the nine of spades playing card. Her horses were Target and (later) Daisy. Tagg, whose horse is named Pixie, has a pet frog named Hector.

Judy Nugent appears as Lofty's niece, Penny; Nan Martin, a remarkable Gail Davis lookalike, plays Annie's outlaw double, Alias-Annie Oakley. Fess Parker (as Tom Conrad) plays the editor of the Diablo *Courier* (the position is later played by Stanley Andrews as Chet Osgood). In the original (unaired) pilot, called "Bull's Eye," Billy Gray played Tagg.

Theme: "Annie Oakley," by Ben Weisman and Fred Wise. Gail Davis sang the theme on a record album called *Hooray for Cowboys*.

ANYTHING BUT LOVE

ABC, 3.7.89 to 4.11.89
9.27.89 to 3.28.90

Principal Cast: Jamie Lee Curtis (*Hannah Miller*), Richard Lewis (*Marty Gold*), Louis Giambalvo (*Norman Kiel*), Ann Magnuson (*Catherine Hughes*)

Trivia: The series centers around the platonic relationship between Hannah Miller, a former Los Angeles schoolteacher turned researcher, then writer, for *Chicago Monthly* magazine, and Marty Gold, who is the magazine's top writer, formerly a reporter for the Chicago *Tribune*. Originally, the magazine's editor was Norman Kiel; he was replaced by the unconventional Catherine Hughes. Other than Hannah's birthday (3.28.60) and Marty's apartment number (3-K), the program offers no real trivia.

Relatives: Bruce Kirby (Hannah's father, *Leo Miller*), Doris Belack (Marty's mother, *Dorothy Gold*), Tia Carrere (Marty's beautiful foster daughter, *Cey*), Susie Duff (Marty's sister, *Jo Levin*)

Theme: "Anything But Love," by John David Souther

ARCHIE BUNKER'S PLACE

CBS, 9.23.79 to 9.21.83

Principal Cast: Carroll O'Connor (*Archie Bunker*), Danielle Brisebois (*Stephanie Mills*), Denise Miller (*Barbara Lee "Billie" Bunker*), Martin Balsam (*Murray Klein*), Allan Melvin (*Barney Hefner*), Anne Meara (*Veronica Rooney*), Jason Wingreen (*Harry Snowden*)

Trivia: The series is an "All in the Family"

18

spinoff in which Archie Bunker is now a widower and guardian to two beautiful girls—his niece Billie and his ward Stephanie. Still residing at 704 Hauser Street, he now owns Archie Bunker's Place (a.k.a. Archie's Place), a restaurant-bar in Astoria, Queens. (A truck-lettering shop is across the street from the bar.)

Billie, who works as a waitress at the bar, is the daughter of Archie's brother, Fred. She came to live with Archie when Fred was no longer able to care for her. Stephanie, whose birthday is in May, attends Ditmars Junior High School. Archie's friend, Barney Hefner, a regular at the bar, has a dog named Rusty and works as a bridge inspector for the city (New York). Murray Klein, Archie's bar partner, married Marcie Phillips (Cynthia Harris) in the 5.10.81 episode. He left shortly afterward when Archie bought out his share of the bar.

Relatives: Richard McKenzie (Billie's father, *Fred Bunker*), Marty Brill and later Ben Slack (Stephanie's father, *Floyd Mills*), Celeste Holm (Stephanie's grandmother, *Estelle Harris*), Mitzi Hoag (Stephanie's *Cousin Sophie*), Carol Rossen (Murray's ex-wife, *Shelley*), Georgann Johnson (Harry's wife, *Alice Snowden*), Jerry Stiller (Veronica's ex-husband, *Carmine*). Mentioned, but not seen: Stephanie's mother, Marilyn, who was killed in a car crash.

Theme: "Those Were the Days," performed by Ray Conniff

ARNIE

CBS, 9.19.70 to 9.9.72

Federal withholding: $81.26; Social Security: $22.07; State withholding: $4.21; Pension fund: $25.00. These are the weekly deductions from the paycheck of Arnie Nuvo (Herschel Bernardi), an executive—the new head of Product Improvement—for Continental Flange, Inc., a Los Angeles-based conglomerate.

Arnie, a former loading-dock foreman, has been promoted for 12 years of faithful service and now, for the first time in his life, he hopes to become self-sufficient—until additional deductions

(now that he is an executive) make him worse off than before: $10.00 monthly for the secretaries' coffee fund, $25.00 monthly for the executive dining-table fund, $100 yearly for the company charity, Pals of the Poor, and $40.00 weekly for the grocery bill. It is a 26-second walk from Arnie's office to the boardroom, where he attends daily meetings. Arnie earns $20,000 a year and his efforts to adjust to (and cope with) his new lifestyle are the premise of the series.

Number 4650 Liberty Lane is home to Arnie; he lives there with his beautiful wife, Lillian (Sue Ane Langdon), and his children, Andrea (Stephanie Steele) and Richard (Del Russell). Lillian, who purchases ten pounds of peanut butter every Thursday, buys her dresses at Helen's Dress Shop and had a job as a Perfect Figure lingerie model. Andrea, who loves to play the guitar, and Richard both attend Westside High School.

Hamilton Majors Jr. (Roger Bowen) plays Arnie's wealthy boss. His favorite letters are "S-A-V-E." He will shake hands only with his left hand; he babies his right hand—his mallet hand—for polo matches at the Bayshore Polo Club. Charles Nelson Reilly portrays Arnie's neighbor Randy Robinson, who hosts the TV series, "The Giddyap Gourmet." Harry Geller composed the theme song, "Arnie."

ASSIGNMENT: UNDERWATER

Syndicated, 1960

Ex-Marine and professional diver Bill Greer (Bill Williams) and his daughter, Patty (Diane Mountford), operate the charter boat the *Lively Lady* (the radio call letters are WA7257). Albert Glasser composed the theme.

ASSIGNMENT: VIENNA

ABC, 9.28.72 to 6.9.73

Jake Webster (Robert Conrad), a U.S. government undercover agent for the International Central Bureau (I.C.B.), poses as the owner of Jake's Bar and Grill in Vienna. Dave Grusin composed the theme.

THE A-TEAM

NBC, 1.23.83 to 3.8.87

Principal Cast: George Peppard (*John "Hannibal" Smith*), Dirk Benedict (*Templeton "Faceman" Peck*), Mr. T. (*Bosco "B. A." Baracus*), Dwight Schultz (*H. M. "Howling Mad" Murdock*), Melinda Culea (*Amy Amanda Allen*), Marla Heasley (*Tawnia Baker*), Robert Vaughn (*General Hunt Stockwell*)

Trivia: The A-Team: In 1972 in Vietnam, Hannibal Smith, Templeton Peck, B. A. Baracus and H. M. Murdock are convicted of robbing the Bank of Hanoi of 100 million yen four days after the war ended. Although they insist they are innocent—framed by a Colonel Morrison—they are branded the A-Team (military file number 1-HG-422-7) and sentenced to prison. Shortly after, they escape and retreat to the Los Angeles underground, where they become soldiers of fortune and help people who are unable to turn to the police for help.

The government has posted a $20,000 reward for their capture; Colonel Roderick Decker (Lance LeGault) and Colonel Lynch (William Lucking) are the most persistent of the military brass pursuing the A-Team. In last-season episodes the team is captured, tried and convicted—but they are given a chance to redeem themselves by performing missions for General Hunt Stockwell. They are also given a base—a home in Langley, Virginia. The A-Team's code for Stockwell is Empress 6; Stockwell's code for them is Empress 1. The A-Team's mobile phone number is 555-6162, and Stockwell's limousine's license plate is NRB 729.

Colonel John Hannibal Smith: The head of the A-Team, he was commander of the 5th Special Forces Group in Vietnam. Before taking on an assignment, a client must meet with Mr. Lee (Hannibal in disguise), the Chinese owner of Mr. Lee's Laundry Shop on Sixth Street in Los Angeles. (Hannibal finds this deception necessary to evaluate a case and determine that it is not a military trap.) In his spare time, Hannibal is an actor of sorts, playing the Aquamaniac and the Slime Monster in horror movies. Hannibal, who is famous for his expression, "I love it when a plan comes together," has an M-60 gun he calls "Baby." He gets "on the jazz" (a feeling of excitement) during each assignment.

Lieutenant Templeton Peck: Also known as "Face" and "The Faceman," he is a master con-artist and the team's ticket to getting what they need without paying for it. Face, who was orphaned at age five, wandered into and then was raised at the Guardian Angels Orphanage. His favorite TV show is "Dragnet"—where he learned most of his cons. His favorite scam is Miracle Films (slogan: "If it's a good picture, it's a Miracle"), and he had a script called "The Beast of the Yellow Night" ready for "production." (In the pilot, his movie scam was a film called "Boots and Bikinis" for 20th Century-Fox, which was to star Loni Anderson, Bo Derek and Farrah Fawcett). Face's license plate was the only consistent one: IHG 581. His address (a beach house he scams) is 1347 Old Balboa Road. Tim Dunigan played Face in the pilot episode.

Sergeant B. A. Baracus: The toughest and meanest member of the team (the B. A. stands for Bad Attitude), B. A. hates to fly, loves children (he runs a day care center in his spare time) and gold jewelry, and his favorite drink is milk. To rid B. A. of his fear of flying, Hannibal most often spikes his milk, injects him with a tranquilizer or gives him his "beddy-bye drink" (a conk on the head with a two-by-four). B. A.'s nickname (from his mother) is "Scooter," his real first name is Elliott. B. A.'s GMC van (black with red trim) has license plate numbers: 2L8 3000, S96 7238, 2A22029 and 2E14859. B. A. lives in an apartment at the Hotel Regina.

Captain H. M. Murdock: Before the war, Murdock was a pilot for the Thunderbirds, and performed heroic missions in Vietnam. He now pretends (though there is some question about that) to be insane (the H. M. stands for "Howling"

Mad") and he resides in Building 16 of the V. A. Hospital in Los Angeles. While the military suspects H. M. is a member of the A-Team, they can't prove it. Living in the ward provides him with the perfect cover.

Murdock, who shares the same blood type with B. A. (AB negative), has several pets: Billy, the invisible dog; Roger, the hamster; Thermadore, a dead lobster (when reduced to just a claw in a fight, he was called Therm) and a baby crocodile named Wally Gator. Murdock also has a plant he calls "The Little Guy," and some heroes: the Range Rider (from the old TV show) and Captain Bellybuster of the Burger Heaven Food Chain. He also endeavors to make people aware of the plight of golf balls and forms the Golf Ball Liberation Army. In the episode "Say It with Bullets," Murdock thinks he personally was the Golden Age of TV, the star of such shows as "Have Murdock—Will Travel," "Leave It to Murdock," "Candid Murdock," "I Love Murdock," and "Bachelor Murdock." In last-season episodes, Murdock is pronounced sane and released from the hospital; he then resides with the team in Virginia.

Amy Amanda Allen: Called "Triple A" by Hannibal, she is a reporter for the Los Angeles *Courier-Express* and assists the team when a beautiful girl is called for to help in a scam. Amy became part of the team when she hired them to find a missing reporter and became actively involved in the case. Amy's license plate numbers are 1FH 480, 1FHJ 484, and ILBJ 1247.

Tawnia Baker: Tawnia, Amy's friend and another reporter for the *Courier-Express*, becomes part of the team when Amy is transferred overseas. Like Amy, she helps the team when needed. (Before her role as Tawnia, Marla Heasley played Charise, a bikini-clad coed in the episode "Bad Time on the Border.") Tawnia leaves the team to marry Brian Lefcourt (Barry Van Dyke) in the episode "Bend in the River," and remains in the Amazon to help him in his archeological work. Her license plate numbers are 1JFY 515 and 854 022.

Relatives: Della Reese (B. A.'s mother, *Mrs. Baracus*, who lives at 700 Foster Av-

enue in Chicago), Ken Olandt (Hannibal's nephew, *Kid Harmon*), Stuart Whitman (Kid's father, *Jack Harmon*), Toni Hudson (Kid's wife, *Dana Harmon*), Clare Kirkconnell (Face's half-sister, *Ellen Bancroft*)

Theme: "The A-Team," written by Mike Post and Pete Carpenter

Note: In last-season episodes, Eddie Velez joins the team as Frankie Santana, a Hollywood special-effects man, and Judith Ledford plays Carla, General Stockwell's aide.

AUTOMAN
ABC, 12.15.83 to 4.9.84

Walter Nebicher (Desi Arnaz Jr.), head of the Los Angeles Police Department computer division, creates a three-dimensional holographic image called Automan (an automatic man who can do anything) to battle crime. Automan's assistant is Cursor, a glowing hexagon that chases beautiful women and creates anything that Automan requires (including a car that can only make right-angle turns). In the opening theme, the sexy girl Cursor eyes is played by Angela Aames. Cursor also sketches a heart around a poster of Heather Thomas during the opening theme. Since Walter programmed Automan with the sleuthing abilities of everyone from Sherlock Holmes to James Bond, Automan (played by Chuck Wagner) believes Walter's landlady (Gloria LeRoy) is the Bond films' Miss Moneypenny (who has an eye for 007). Heather McNair plays Walter's girlfriend, Officer Roxanne Caldwell; Robert Lansing, their superior, Lieutenant Jack Curtis. Billy Hinsche composed the theme.

THE AVENGERS
ABC, 3.28.66 to 7.1.66
1.20.67 to 9.1.67
1.10.68 to 9.15.69

Principal Cast: Patrick Macnee (*John Steed*), Diana Rigg (*Emma Peel*), Linda Thorson (*Tara King*), Patrick Newell (*Mother*), Ian Hendry (*Dr. David Keel*),

Honor Blackman (*Catherine Gale*), Julie Stevens (*Venus Smith*)

Trivia: The series chronicles the exploits of John Steed, Emma Peel and Tara King as they avenge crimes perpetrated against the British government.

John Steed, a suave, sophisticated ministry agent who exudes old world charm and courtesy, lives at Number 3 Stable Mews in London (originally given as 5 Westminster Mews). Steed first drove a yellow 1926 Vintage Rolls Royce Silver Ghost, then a 1929 Vintage 4.5-litre Bentley in dark green (license plate number YT 3942). When first introduced in 1961, Steed had no first name and was somewhat of a mystery. All that was known was that he had the cover of a dilettante man-about-town. In these early episodes, Steed works with Dr. David Keel and has a dog named Juno.

Catherine Gale, a beautiful blonde with a Ph.D. in anthropology, returns to England to work at the British Museum in 1962, when her husband is killed in Kenya during a Mau Mau raid. Although she is not as professional as Steed, her scientific knowledge and martial arts skills make her and Steed the perfect crime-solving duo when they are teamed by the government.

At this time, Julie Stevens appeared in six episodes as Venus Smith, the nightclub singer who was fascinated by and helped Steed. At this point, Steed had a dog named Freckles. Catherine rode a Triumph motorcycle with license plate 987 CAA.

A slight car accident unites Steed with the totally emancipated Emma Peel, the wealthy widow of a test pilot. She joins Steed (1966–68) for the sheer love of adventure. Emma, whose maiden name is Knight (and whose father ran Knight Industries), drives a 1966 Lotus Elan (license plate number 5JH 4990). Emma, who adores sexy black outfits (called "the Emma Peeler"), lives in London also, but her address was never given.

When Emma's husband, Peter Peel, the test pilot believed killed in a crash, is found alive in 1968, Emma returns to him; Steed is then teamed with Tara King, a shapely brunette who has just completed her agent's training. Tara's address is 9 Primrose Crescent in London. She drives a red Lotus Europa MKI (license plate number NPW 99F).

In early episodes (1961–65), Steed's superior is the mysterious One-Ten (Douglas Muir). Mother, a wheelchair-bound man, was Steed's (and Tara's) superior later in the series (1968–69). The series gimmick is that a woman is never hurt or killed.

Relatives: Joyce Carey (Mother's *Aunt Harriet*), Mary Merrill (Mother's *Aunt Georgina*)

Theme: "The Avengers," written by Laurie Johnson

Spinoff: "The New Avengers" (CBS, 9.15.78 to 3.23.79). Patrick Macnee again portrays John Steed, together with Joanna Lumley as a beautiful agent named Purdy and Gareth Hunt as agent Mike Gambit.

BABY BOOM

NBC, 9.10.88 to 1.4.89
7.13.89 (1 episode)
8.14.89 (1 episode)
9.10.89 (1 episode)

Principal Cast: Kate Jackson (*J. C. Wiatt*), Sam Wanamaker (*Fritz Curtis*), Michelle and Kristina Kennedy (*Elizabeth*)

Trivia: J. C. Wiatt, a management consultant for Sloane-Curtis & Company in New York City, is appointed guardian of a baby named Elizabeth by distant cousin. J. C., the high-powered businesswoman, is nicknamed "the Tiger Lady" at work, and lives in Apartment 15-D (address not given). Elizabeth, nicknamed "Boobie" by J. C., has a stuffed toy kangaroo named Cuppy and four goldfish J. C. named Goldie, Frank, Ernie and Hector.

Relatives: Norman Parker (J. C.'s father, J. C. Wiatt Sr.), Tippi Hedren (*Laura Curtis*, the wife of J. C.'s boss, Fritz Curtis)

Flashbacks: Nikki Feemster (*J. C. as a girl*), Jill Whitlow (*J. C. as a teenager*)

Theme: "Baby Boom," by Steven Tyrell

BACHELOR FATHER

CBS, 9.15.57 to 6.11.58
NBC, 6.18.58 to 9.19.61
ABC, 10.3.61 to 9.25.62

Principal Cast: John Forsythe (*Bentley Gregg*), Noreen Corcoran (*Kelly Gregg*), Sammee Tong (*Peter Tong*), Bernadette Withers (*Ginger*), Jimmy Boyd (*Howard Meechum*), Aaron Kincaid (*Warren Dawson*)

Trivia: When her parents are killed in a car accident, Kelly Gregg, the 13-year-old niece of bachelor attorney Bentley Gregg, comes to live with him and his Chinese houseboy, Peter, at 1163 Rexford Drive in Beverly Hills, California.

Bentley, a private-practice attorney, is a playboy whose life suddenly changes when Kelly arrives. Stories relate his and Peter's efforts to provide love and a home for Kelly.

The suave and sophisticated Bentley Gregg's favorite nightclub is the Coconut Grove, but he finds his dates prefer dancing at the Ambassador Room. Gregg's office (#106) is in the Crescent Building on Crescent Drive in Los Angeles. In last-season episodes, Kelly's boyfriend, Warren Dawson, becomes her Uncle Bentley's law partner. Bentley's license plate number is RXR 553.

Kelly and her friends, Ginger and Howard, attend Beverly Hills High School, where Kelly's favorite subject is math. Their favorite afterschool hangout is Bill's Malt Shop. Kelly becomes the first secretary Bentley has ever kissed when she works for him one afternoon and solves a complicated case.

Ginger lives at 1130 Rexford Drive. The Gregg family dog is named Jasper. Jasper has a "girlfriend" named Stella who is owned by Phyllis Wentworth (played by Elaine Davis).

Peter, who attends night school to improve his knowledge of America, has dinner ready for the Greggs every night at 7:00. He calls Bentley "Mr. Gregg" and Kelly "Niece Kelly." Peter also has many relatives, two of whom appear several times: Grandpa Ling, "a 70-year-old ju-venile delinquent" who believes in the barter system and knows only three words of English—"Hello, Joe" and "Nice," and Cousin Charlie Fong (originally introduced as Charlie Ling), "the beatnik of the family" and a con-artist whose schemes often backfire.

For unexplained reasons (perhaps because of network changes), Ginger has three last names: Farrell (1957–58), with a widowed mother named Louise (Catherine McLeod); Loomis (1958–61) with Whit Bissell and Florence Mac-Michael as her parents, Bert and Amy Loomis; and Mitchell (1961–62), with Evelyn Scott and Del Moore as her parents, Adelaide and Cal Mitchell.

Bentley Gregg has six secretaries: J. D. Thompson (as Vicky in the pilot), Alice Backus (as Vicky in the series), Shirley Mitchell and Jane Nigh (Kitty Devereaux), Sue Ane Langdon (Kitty Marsh), and Sally Mansfield (Connie).

Relatives: Victor Sen Yung (Peter's *Cousin Charlie*), Beal Wong (Peter's *Grandpa Ling*), Cherylene Lee (Peter's niece, *Blossom Lee*), Beulah Quo (Peter's *Aunt Rose*), Kristina Hanson (Ginger's *Cousin Norma*), Joan Vohs (Howard's sister, *Elaine*), David Lewis (Warren's father, *Horace Dawson*), Sheila Bromley (Warren's mother, *Myrtle Dawson*)

Theme: "Bachelor Father," written by Johnny Williams

Note: The original pilot, "New Girl in His Life," aired on "G. E. Theater" on 5.26.57 (the proposed series title at the time was "Uncle Bentley"). In it John Forsythe, Noreen Corcoran and Sammee Tong played the same roles.

B.A.D. CATS

ABC, 1.4.80 to 2.8.80

Principal Cast: Steven Hanks (*Ocee James*), Asher Brauner (*Nick Donovan*), Michelle Pfeiffer (*Samantha Jensen*), LaWanda Page (*Ma*), Vic Morrow (*Captain Eugene Nathan*)

Trivia: Former stock-car racers Ocee James and Nick Donovan are officers with the Burglary Auto Detail, Commercial

Auto Theft division (B.A.D. Cats) of the Los Angeles Police Department. Their assistant, Officer Samantha Jensen, is nicknamed "Sunshine." Their favorite hangout is "Ma's Place," a bar-restaurant owned by Ma. Donovan's license plate is 938 LYN, and Nick and Ocee's car code is Cat-1 (also given as Stray Cat-1). Their captain, Eugene Nathan, has the nickname "Skip," and his license plate number is 264 PPA.

Theme: "B.A.D. Cats," written by Barry DeVorzon

THE BAD NEWS BEARS

CBS, 3.24.79 to 7.26.80

The series chronicles the adventures of the W. Wendall Weever School Bears, an undisciplined Little League baseball team managed by Morris Buttermaker (Jack Warden), a pool cleaner who volunteers for the job rather than spend a year in jail for driving a client's car into a pool. Joyce Bulifant plays Alice Wurlitzer, the mother of the prettiest Bear, Amanda (Tricia Cast); Catherine Hicks plays the principal, Dr. Emily Rappant; and Philip R. Allen appears as Roy Turner, manager of the rival Lions team. Other Bears in this TV adaptation of the feature film are Tanner Boyle (Meeno Peluce), Leslie Ogilvie (Sparky Marcus), Rudi Stein (Billy Jacoby) and Regi Tower (Corey Feldman). The address of the Weever School was given as 1647 Lorraine Court in Los Angeles. David Frank provided the theme music.

BAGDAD CAFÉ

CBS, 3.30.90 to 4.27.90

In the Mojave Desert, in the one-building town of Bagdad, stands the Bagdad Café, a rundown truck stop diner and hotel run by feisty Brenda (Whoopi Goldberg). Jasmine (Jean Stapleton), her friend and helper, is a retired English teacher who left her husband after 25 years of marriage and now resides in Room 102 of the hotel. Also living at the hotel are Brenda's two children, Debbie (Monica Calhoun) and Juney (Scott Lawrence), and Brenda's womanizing ex-husband, Sal (Cleavon Little).

Rooms at the hotel cost $25 a day or $127 a week; Brenda was in labor for 96 hours with Debbie; Jasmine was named after her cousin Mildred—when Mildred was born she was going to be named Jasmine, but she looked like a Mildred. JeVetta Steele sings the title song, "Calling You." The series is based on the feature film of the same title.

THE BAILEYS OF BALBOA

CBS, 9.24.64 to 4.1.65

The series presents the comical bickering between two men: Sam Bailey (Paul Ford), captain of the *Island Princess*, a noisy and decrepit charter boat; and Cecil Wyntoon (John Dehner), his neighbor, commodore of the high-class Balboa Yachting Club in Balboa Beach, California. Judy Carne plays Cecile's daughter, Barbara, and Les Brown Jr., Sam's son, Jim—who add fuel to the fire when they begin dating. Harry Geller composed the theme song.

THE BARBARY COAST

ABC, 9.8.75 to 1.9.76

In New Orleans, riverboat gambler Cash Conover (Doug McClure) accuses the governor's son of cheating at cards. A duel to defend honor ensues and Cash kills his opponent in self-defense. Knowing he would never get a fair trial because it was the governor's son he killed, Cash flees to San Francisco, where he wins the Golden Gate Casino in a card game and begins a new life as a casino owner.

Meanwhile, Jeff Cable (William Shatner), a California police officer, is recruited by the governor of San Francisco to battle the rising tide of crime. Jeff recognizes Cash from a poster as a man wanted for murder in Louisana, but because Cash can be more useful where he is, Jeff recruits Cash to help him. Jeff sets up headquarters in a secret room in the casino and spreads the word that criminals can find refuge at the Golden Gate. Episodes chronicle their adventures as they battle crime on the Barbary Coast during the 1880s.

Jeff, a West Point graduate, uses various disguises to apprehend criminals. Cash knocks three times on wood for luck, and lives by his motto, "Cash Makes No Enemies" (meaning he pays cash for anything he wants; nobody knows for sure whether Cash is Conover's real name or his religion). Jeff's base of operations is a secret room behind the fireplace in Cash's office.

Bobbi Jordan plays Flame, the casino croupier; Richard Kiel plays Moose Moran, the bouncer; and Dave Turner plays Thumbs, the casino's piano player. John Andrew Tartaglia composed the theme. The series was originally titled "Cash and Cable," with Dennis Cole as Cash in the pilot (5.4.75).

BAREFOOT IN THE PARK
ABC, 9.24.70 to 1.14.71

A TV adaptation of the Neil Simon Broadway play about the struggles of Paul Bratter (Scoey Mitchlll), a young lawyer, and his wife, Corie (Tracy Reed). The Bratters live in a fifth-floor walkup at 49 West 10th Street (Apartment 5-B) in New York City, and Paul is a lawyer with the firm of Kendricks, Klein and Klein. Their friend, Honey Robinson (Nipsey Russell), owns Honey's Pool Hall; Thelma Carpenter plays Corie's mother, Mabel Bates. The Charles Fox Singers performed the "Barefoot in the Park" theme.

In the original pilot, which aired as "Love and the Good Deal" on "Love, American Style" (ABC, 11.24.69), Skye Aubrey played Corie Bratter and Philip Clark, Paul Bratter. Jane Wyatt appeared as Corie's mother.

BARETTA
ABC, 1.17.75 to 6.1.78

Unorthodox undercover cop Tony Baretta (Robert Blake) is with the 53rd Precinct of an unidentified eastern city (presumed to be in New Jersey). His badge number is 609 and his car, "The Blue Ghost," has the license plate 532 BEN. He lives in Apartment 2-C of the King Edward Hotel (where his friend, Billy Truman, is the house detective), and has a pet cockatoo named Fred (played by Lala). Tom Ewell plays Billy, and Sammy Davis Jr. sings the theme, "Keep Your Eye on the Sparrow."

BARNABY JONES
CBS, 1.23.73 to 9.4.80

Los Angeles-based private detective Barnaby Jones (Buddy Ebsen) owns Barnaby Jones Investigations (located at 3782 Clinton Avenue), and is also an investigator for the California Meridian Insurance Company. Lee Meriwether is his daughter-in-law and assistant, Betty Jones (she was married to Barnaby's late son, Hal), and Mark Shera plays Barnaby's Chicago cousin, Jedediah (J. R.) Jones, who, while studying to be a lawyer, works as Barnaby's legman. Jerry Goldsmith composed the theme.

THE BARON
ABC, 1.20.66 to 7.14.66

John Mannering (Steve Forrest), an American antique dealer in London who investigates crimes in the art world for British intelligence, is known as the Baron and drives a car with license plate BAR I. His place of business is Mannering Antiques. Sue Lloyd plays his assistant, Cordelia Winfield. Edwin Astley composed the theme.

BATMAN
ABC, 1.12.66 to 3.14.68

Principal Cast: Adam West (*Bruce Wayne/Batman*), Burt Ward (*Dick Grayson/Robin*), Yvonne Craig (*Barbara Gordon/Batgirl*), Neil Hamilton (*Commissioner Gordon*), Stafford Repp (*Chief O'Hara*), Alan Napier (*Alfred Pennyworth*), Madge Blake (*Aunt Harriet Cooper*), William Dozier (*Narrator*)

Trivia: Following the death of his parents, who were killed by a gangster, 10-year-old Bruce Wayne inherits vast wealth and vows to avenge their deaths by devoting his life to battling crime in Gotham City. With the help of Alfred Pennyworth, his ever-faithful butler, Bruce works in near-total isolation to develop his scientific abilities. Fourteen years later, after developing the world's greatest crime lab—the Batcave beneath Wayne Manor—Bruce adopts the disguise of Batman, a mysterious caped crusader designed to strike fear in the hearts of criminals.

Some time later, while attending the circus with a group of orphans, Bruce witnesses a tragic accident: the death of the Graysons, a husband-and-wife high-wire act. When Bruce learns that the Graysons' only child is their teenage son, Dick, he takes on the responsibility of caring for him, eventually becoming his legal guardian. Bruce reveals his secret identity to Dick and teaches him how to perfect his mental and physical skills. Dick, instilled with a desire to battle evil, adopts the disguise of Robin, the Boy Wonder, and the two form the Dynamic Duo. Dick attends Woodrow Roosevelt High School.

When Barbara Gordon, daughter of Police Commissioner Gordon, finishes college she returns home and takes a job in the Gotham City Library. Feeling the need to help her father battle crime, she adopts the disguise of Batgirl—and, though usually operating independently of Batman and Robin, she sometimes works with them and forms the Terrific Trio.

At Wayne Manor, the button to access the Batcave is located in the bust of Shakespeare in Bruce's den. When the button is pressed, a secret entrance is revealed and Bruce and Dick become Batman and Robin as they descend their respective Batpoles (when they ascend, they don their street clothes again). In the Batcave, located 14 miles from Gotham City, are various Batcomputers and the Batmobile (license plate 2F 3567; later, B-1), Batman and Robin's main mode of transportation. The Batmobile is powered by atomic batteries, uses turbines for speed, and has controls such as the Bat Ray Projector, a Bat Homing/Receiving Scope, the Bat Ram, the Bat Parachute (to stop the car at high speeds) and the start-decoy button, which fires rockets if an unauthorized person tries to start the car. Batman also has the Batcopter (I.D. Number N3079; later, N703) and the Batman Dummy Double (which Bruce stores in the Bat Dummy Closet). After an assignment, Alfred serves Bruce and Dick milk and sandwiches in the study. In Bruce's office at the Wayne Foundation Building, Bruce hides a safe behind a painting of the safe that hangs on the wall over it. The safe contains the Wayne family jewels. According to the villain King Tut (a.k.a. William Omaha McElroy), there is a supply of Nilanium, the world's hardest metal (after it is refined), under the Batcave.

Barbara, who lives in mid-town Gotham City in Apartment 8-A (address not given) with her pet bird Charlie, conceals her Batgirl costume in a secret closet behind her bedroom wall (she activates the wall with a hidden button on her vanity table). Her mode of transportation, the Batgirl Cycle, is hidden in a secret freight elevator in the back of her building.

Barbara is also the chairperson of the Gotham City Anti-Littering Committee. Her favorite opera is *The Marriage of Figaro*. Batgirl received the first Gotham City Female Crime Fighter and Fashion Award, "The Battie," for her crusade against crime in her sexy costume. In one episode, Batgirl rides Bruce's horse, Waynebow, in the Bruce Wayne Foundation Handicap.

Gotham City's Police Commissioner Gordon has two means of contacting Batman: the red Bat Phone in his office or the Bat Signal, flashed from the roof of city hall. Alfred can contact Batman via his emergency Bat Buckle signal button.

The series was based on the comic strip by Bob Kane.

The Criminals: Burgess Meredith (*the Penguin*), Cesar Romero (*the Joker*), Frank Gorshin and John Astin (*the Riddler*), Julie Newmar, Lee Meriwether and Eartha Kitt (*Cat Woman*), Ethel Merman (*Lola Lasagne*), Art Carney (*the Archer*), Milton Berle (*Louie the Lilac*), Joan Collins (*the Siren*; her voice is two octaves above high C), Carolyn Jones (*Marsha, Queen of Diamonds*),

Cliff Robertson (*Shame*), Victor Buono (*King Tut*), Roddy McDowall (*the Bookworm*), Zsa Zsa Gabor (*Minerva*), Glynis Johns (*Lady Penelope Peasoup*), Rudy Vallee (*Lord Marmaduke Ffogg*), Roger C. Carmel (*Colonel Gumm*), Tallulah Bankhead (*the Black Widow*), Vincent Price (*Egghead*), Anne Baxter (*Olga*), Ida Lupino (*Dr. Cassandra*), Howard Duff (*Cabala*), Malachi Throne (*Falseface*), Michael Rennie (*the Sandman*), Maurice Evans (*the Puzzler*), Kathleen Crowley (*Sophie Starr*), Liberace (*Chandell*), David Wayne (*the Mad Hatter*), George Sanders, Eli Wallach and Otto Preminger (*Mr. Freeze*), Shelley Winters (*Ma Parker*), Walter Slezak (*Clock King*), Van Johnson (*the Minstrel*) and Barbara Rush (*Nora Clavicle*). Van Williams (as the Green Hornet) and Bruce Lee (as Kato) appear in the episodes "A Piece of the Action" (3.1.67) and "Batman's Satisfaction" (3.2.67).

Themes: "Batman," written by Neil Hefti; "Batgirl," written by Billy May and Wally Mack

---

BEARCATS!

CBS, 9.16.71 to 12.30.71

Hank Brackett (Rod Taylor), a former Army captain, and Johnny Reach (Dennis Cole), orphaned as a child and raised by the Cherakawa-Apache Indians, are freelance troubleshooters who help people in the Southwest in 1914. Hank and Johnny, who drive a white Stutz Bearcat (license plate 4596 NYD), receive a blank check for expenses; they fill in the amount based on what they feel the case is worth. Their friend, Fernando Raoul Estevan (Henry Darrow), runs the one-plane Mexican Air Force. John Andrew Tartaglia composed the theme. The two-hour pilot film, *Powderkeg*, aired on CBS on 4.16.71.

BEAUTY AND THE BEAST

CBS, 9.25.87 to 8.4.90

Principal Cast: Ron Perlman (*Vincent*), Linda Hamilton (*Catherine Chandler*), Roy Dotrice (*Father*), Jo Anderson (*Diana Bennett*), Stephen McHattie (*Gabriel*)

Trivia: In the 1950s, Dr. Jacob Wells, a scientist with the Chitterdon Research Institute, resigns when he is accused of being un-American. He flees to a forgotten subterranean world beneath New York City's subway and becomes "Father," the leader of a group of misfits. Sometime later, Father finds an abandoned infant in front of St. Vincent's Hospital. The misfit infant, whom he names Vincent, grows to become the beast of the series title.

Vincent's world is mysterious and beautiful, untouched by the crime of the big city. Its tunnels lead to all areas of the city, allowing access to the outside world. The most dangerous part of the city for these people is Prince Street on Manhattan's Lower East Side; there are only two tunnels in this area and they are rarely used. The people live as one, looking to Father for leadership and keeping in constant communication with each other by tapping on the main pipes that run throughout the underworld city.

Beauty is Catherine Chandler, a woman who is mistaken by thugs for someone else and brutally beaten and slashed across the face. Her body is dumped on the street and she is left for dead. She is found by Vincent, who takes her to his world. There, she is saved by Father. Before she leaves, Catherine promises Vincent that she will keep his world a secret.

Plastic surgery restores Catherine's scarred face to normal and she takes a job with the D.A.'s office to battle crime. She has the secret help of Vincent, who can sense when she is in danger (and, via the tunnels, comes to her aid). (Although Catherine was left with a large scar on the right side of her chin and neck following the surgery, it is mysteriously "healed" in some scenes, but not in others.)

In the episode "Though Lovers Be Lost" (12.12.89), Catherine, pregnant by Vincent and about to give birth, is kidnapped by Gabriel, the tycoon who heads a criminal empire. Shortly after Catherine gives birth to a boy, Gabriel orders her to be killed by drug overdose. Catherine's death enrages Vincent—who vows to find his son and destroy Gabriel. (When Vincent is united with his son, he names him Jacob.)

While investigating Catherine's death, detective Diana Bennett comes to know and help Vincent in his quest. (In the last episode, Diana confronts Gabriel and shoots him dead at point-blank range.)

Theme: "Beauty and the Beast," by Lee Holdridge

BEST OF THE WEST

ABC, 9.10.81 to 2.26.82

Principal Cast: Joel Higgins (*Sam Best*), Carlene Watkins (*Elvira Best*), Meeno Peluce (*Daniel Best*), Leonard Frey (*Parker Tillman*), Tom Ewell (*Jerome "Doc" Kullens*), Tracey Walter (*Frog Rothchild Jr.*), Valri Bromfield (*Laney Gibbs*), Christopher Lloyd (*the Calico Kid*)

Trivia: During the Civil War, Union Captain Sam Best meets southern belle Elvira Devereaux when his troops begin burning her father's Georgia plantation. Though it seems an unlikely match, Sam, a widower and the father of a young son (Daniel), and Elvira marry shortly afterward. With the dream of beginning a new life out west, the Bests move from their home in Philadelphia to Copper Creek, Montana, and become shopkeepers. Shortly after opening their General Store, Sam becomes marshal when he stands up to a feared gunfighter (the Calico Kid) and is elected to the office by the citizens.

Other citizens: Parker Tillman, the crooked owner of the Square Deal Saloon; Jerome "Doc" Kullens, the intoxicated town doctor; Frog Rothchild Jr., Tillman's right-hand man; and Laney Gibbs, the fur trapper.

Relatives: Andy Griffith (Elvira's father, *Lamont Devereaux*), Eve Brent Ashe (Elvira's mother, *Lily Devereaux*)

Theme: "Best of the West," vocal by Rex Allen

BEST TIMES

NBC, 4.19.85 to 6.2.85

Joanne Braithwaite (Janet Eilber) teaches English at John F. Kennedy High School in Ventura, California. Her daughter, Mia (Beth Ehlers), and Mia's friend, Giselle (Tammy Lauren), work at the Potato Palace in the mall. Giselle drives the "coolest" car on campus—a red 1986 Camero; license plate not shown. Michael Ruff sings the theme, "Best Times."

THE BETTY WHITE SHOW

CBS, 9.12.77 to 1.9.78

The on- and off-the-set life of Joyce Whitman (Betty White), the star of the mythical (assumed to be CBS) TV series "Undercover Woman" (a take-off on NBC's "Police Woman"), directed by her ex-husband, John Elliott (John Hillerman). The network's motto is "Action is what we do; violence is what the other networks do," and the local hangout is the Out-Take Inn. Hugo Muncey (Charles Cyphers) is Joyce's stunt double; Fletcher Huff (Barney Phillips) plays the police chief; and Mitzi Maloney (Georgia Engel) is Joyce's roommate.

Relatives: Florence Halop (Fletcher's wife, *Marian Huff*), Joanna Barnes (John's first ex-wife, *Connie Desmond*), Janis Paige (Mitzi's *Cousin Wilma*) and Elizabeth Kerr (the terror of Joyce and John's life, *Mother Elliott*)

Stan Daniels composed the theme.

THE BEULAH SHOW

CBS, 10.10.50 to 9.22.53

Principal Cast: Ethel Waters (*Beulah*, 1950–51), Hattie McDaniel (*Beulah*, 1951–52), Louise Beavers (*Beulah*, 1952–53), Ginger Jones (*Alice Henderson*, 1950–52), Jane Frazee (*Alice Henderson*, 1952–53), William Post Jr. (*Harry Henderson*, 1950–52), David Bruce (*Harry Henderson*, 1952–53), Clifford Sales (*Donnie Henderson*, 1950–52), Stuffy Singer (*Donnie Henderson*, 1952–53), Butterfly McQueen (*Oriole*, 1950–51), Ruby Dandridge (*Oriole*, 1951–

53), Percy "Bud" Harris (*Bill Jackson*, 1950–52), Dooley Wilson (*Bill Jackson*, 1952), Ernest Whitman (*Bill Jackson*, 1952–53)

Trivia: Beulah, the irrepressible Queen of the Kitchen, is maid to Harry Henderson, a New York attorney; his wife, Alice; and their son, Donnie. Beulah, who is in the market for a husband ("but they don't sell husbands in markets") is a member of the Ladies Auxiliary Sewing Circle. Beulah's boyfriend, Bill Jackson, owns Wm. Jackson's Fix-It Shop, and, when not eating in Beulah's kitchen, he partakes of food at Slippery Joe's Diner. Oriole, Beulah's girlfriend, who knows everything about nothing (but nothing about anything), reads a magazine called *True Tales of Passion and Purity* and has been called "Miss Public Address System of 1952" by Bill for her inability to keep a secret. Donnie, whose birthday is January 16th, has a homemade soap-box racer called the Fire Streak, which he races on the 36th Street hill.

Relatives: Madge Blake (*Alice's mother*), Ruth Robinson (*Harry's mother*)

Theme: "Beulah," by Ted Cain

THE BEVERLY HILLBILLIES

CBS, 9.26.62 to 9.7.71

Principal Cast: Buddy Ebsen (*Jed Clampett*), Irene Ryan (*Daisy "Granny" Moses*), Donna Douglas (*Elly Mae Clampett*), Max Baer (*Jethro Bodine*), Raymond Bailey (*Milburn Drysdale*), Nancy Kulp (*Jane Hathaway*)

Trivia: In the Ozark community of Sibly lives Jed Clampett, a poor mountaineer, his beautiful daughter, Elly Mae, his mother-in-law, Daisy "Granny" Moses, and his nephew, Jethro Bodine. One day, while hunting for food, Jed misses his target and the bullet strikes the ground. Oil spurts from the ground and before long, the O.K. Oil Company purchases the rights.

With their newfound wealth, Jed and his clan pack their belongings on Jed's car (a 1920 Oldsmobile) and move into a 32-room, 14-bathroom mansion at 518 Crestview Drive in Beverly Hills, California.

Milburn Drysdale, president of the Commerce Bank of Beverly Hills, oversees the vast Clampett wealth (mentioned as $35 million in one episode).

Jed, who dresses as he did in the hills, has a bloodhound named Duke and longs for the simple life he once enjoyed. Through investments, he also owns the Mammouth Film Studios in Hollywood.

Elly Mae, who has a fondness for "critters," has a rooster named Earl (who knows one trick — playing dead) and two monkeys named Beth and Skipper.

The not-too-bright Jethro, born on December 4th, was "educated and graduated from the sixth grade." He is the only one who delights in the excitement of the big city and is forever trying to attract the opposite sex "and find me a sweetheart."

Granny, who won the "Miss Good Sport Award" at the Bugtussle Bathing Beauty Contest at Expo '97, still practices her mountain doctoring, but complains that she can't make her lye soap in Beverly Hills (the process pollutes the air), or find needed ingredients (for example, possum innards) in the local stores. Granny, who has an all-around cure for what ails you called Granny's Spring Tonic, has a cousin named Homer Gribble who painted the Burma Shave signs in Bugtussle (a community in Pike County); he also composed the slogans (e.g., "When your beard is stiff and bristly, shave every morning and every night.").

Margaret Drysdale, Milburn's wife, has a pampered poodle named Claude ("married" to a poodle named Fifi). She and Milburn, who was born in South Chicago, have a butler named Ravenswood (Arthur Gould Porter). In Sibly, the outhouse was 50 feet from Jed's cabin; Jethro's teacher was Millicent Schyler Potts (Eleanor Audley). According to *USA Today* (1.5.87), the actual mansion used in the series belonged to Arnold Kirkeby, who bought it shortly after it was built in 1933. It was sold in 1987 to TV executive Jerry Perenchio.

Relatives: Bea Benedaret (Jethro's mother, *Pearl Bodine*), Max Baer (Jethro's sister, *Jethrene Bodine*; voice by Linda Kaye Henning), Roy Clark (Jed's *Cousin Roy*), Harriet MacGibbon (*Margaret Drysdale*), Louis Nye (the Drysdales' son, *Sonny Drysdale*), Charlie Ruggles (Milburn's father-in-law, *Lowell Reddings Farquhar*), Eddy Eccles (Milburn's nephew, *Milby Drysdale*)

Theme: "The Ballad of Jed Clampett," vocal by Jerry Scoggins

Note: In the TV movie *The Return of the Beverly Hillbillies* (CBS, 10.6.81), Jed has moved back to Sibly, Elly Mae has opened Elly's Zoo and Jethro now runs Mammouth Studios in Hollywood.

BEWITCHED

ABC, 9.17.64 to 7.1.72

Principal Cast: Elizabeth Montgomery (*Samantha Stephens*), Dick York and later Dick Sargent (*Darrin Stephens*), Agnes Moorehead (*Endora*), Maurice Evans (*Maurice*), Erin and Diane Murphy (*Tabitha Stephens*), David and Greg Lawrence (*Adam Stephens*), David White (*Larry Tate*), Irene Vernon and Kasey Rogers (*Louise Tate*), Alice Pearce and Sandra Gould (*Gladys Kravitz*), George Tobias (*Abner Kravitz*), Bernard Fox (*Dr. Bombay*)

Trivia: Shortly after a beautiful witch named Samantha (no last name given) and a mortal named Darrin Stephens meet (accidentally, bumping into each other on several occasions), they marry and purchase a home at 1164 Morning Glory Circle in Westport, Connecticut, from the Hopkins Realty Company. Their address is also given as 164 Morning Glory Circle and their telephone number is 555-2134. Trash pickups are on Tuesdays and Fridays.

Darrin, whose license plate reads 4R6 558, works as an account executive for the McMann and Tate Advertising Agency in Manhattan (his office phone number is 555-6059).

Samantha, who can have literally anything she wants by twitching her nose and invoking her powers, has agreed to live by Darrin's rules and not use her witchcraft. However, when Samantha does use her witchcraft and Darrin gets upset, he retreats to Joe's Bar and Grill to drown his sorrows.

This agreement has upset Samantha's mother, Endora, a powerful witch (who is 118 pounds and five feet, six inches tall). Unable to accept her daughter's reasoning—or understand why she married Darrin (whom she most often calls "Durwood"), she delights in casting spells on him (for example, always having to tell the truth, speaking in rhyme, instant dislike). When Darrin first met Endora, he asked "Mrs . . . ?" Endora responded with the reason no last name is given, "You'd never be able to pronounce it."

Samantha's father, Maurice, a distinguished warlock, accepts Darrin (whom he calls "Dobbin") and often sides with Samantha when Endora puts up a fuss. When Samantha has a craving for food, she must have Ring-Tail Pheasant to satisfy herself.

Other Characters: Tabitha and Adam, Samantha and Darrin's children, are also a witch and warlock. When Tabitha was born, January 13, 1966, no credit was listed; that episode also marked the first appearance of Samantha's beautiful "Goddess of Love" cousin, the mischievous Serena (Elizabeth Montgomery, who played the role, originally received no credit; she later used the name Pandora Spocks).

Larry Tate is Darrin's greedy boss. Abner Kravitz and his nosy wife, Gladys, are the Stephens' neighbors. Dr. Bombay, the nurse-chasing warlock, is Samantha's somewhat wacky family physician (whom Darrin calls a "witch doctor").

Relatives: Marion Lorne (Samantha's *Aunt Clara*, who is famous for her doorknob collection), Paul Lynde (Samantha's *Uncle Arthur*, who loves practical jokes), Ysabel MacClosky and Reta Shaw (Samantha's *Aunt Hagatha*), Estelle Winwood (Samantha's *Aunt Enchantra*), Jane Connell (Samantha's *Aunt Hepzibah*), Arte Johnson (Samantha's *Cousin Edgar*), Steve Franken (Samantha's *Cousin Henry*), Robert F. Simon and Roy Roberts (Darrin's father, *Frank Stephens*), Mabel Albertson (Darrin's mother, *Phyllis Stephens*), Louise Glenn (Darrin's *Cousin Helen*), Mitchell Silberman (Larry's son, *John*

Tate), Ricky Powell (Gladys's nephew, *Sidney*), Mary Grace Canfield (Abner's sister, *Harriet*)

Mentioned, but not seen, were Darrin's Aunt Madge, who believes she is a lighthouse; and Gladys's Uncle Harold.

Theme: "Bewitched," by Howard Greenfield and Jack Keller

Spinoffs: "Tabitha." On April 24, 1976, ABC presented the first pilot with Liberty Williams as Tabitha Stephens, now a beautiful 24-year-old witch and an editorial assistant at San Francisco's fashionable *Trend* magazine. Bruce Kimmel played her warlock brother, Adam, and Barbara Cason her editor, Roberta. The second pilot (ABC, May 7, 1977), which sold the series (9.10.77 to 1.14.78), features Lisa Hartman as the beautiful Tabitha, now a production assistant at KXLA-TV in Los Angeles. David Ankrum played her brother Adam, and Karen Morrow her Aunt Minerva.

BEYOND WESTWORLD

CBS, 3.5.80 to 3.19.80

Westworld, the futuristic adult playground, was built by the Delos Corporation. Simon Quaid (James Wainwright) designed the robots, and Delos agents John Moore (Jim McMullan) and Pauline Williams (Connie Sellecca) are assigned to stop Quaid from going "Beyond Westworld" and using his robots for evil. Pre-"Elvira, Mistress of the Dark" Cassandra Peterson plays the robot dancehall girl in the opening theme. George Romanis composed the theme.

BIG SHAMUS, LITTLE SHAMUS

CBS, 9.29.79 to 10.6.79

The title refers to Arnie Sutter (Brian Dennehy), house detective at the Arsonia Hotel in Atlantic City, New Jersey, and his son, Max (Doug McKeon), a budding gumshoe. Kathryn Leigh Scott plays the hotel manager, Stephanie Marsh. Mike Post and Pete Carpenter composed the theme.

THE BIG VALLEY

ABC, 9.25.65 to 5.19.69

Principal Cast: Barbara Stanwyck (*Victoria Barkley*), Richard Long (*Jarrod Barkley*), Peter Breck (*Nick Barkley*), Linda Evans (*Audra Barkley*), Lee Majors (*Heath Barkley*)

Trivia: With a dream of settling in California, young marrieds Tom and Victoria Barkley begin their journey west during the 1830s. After a long, hazardous trek, they settle in Stockton's San Joaquin Valley and establish the 30,000-acre Barkley Cattle Ranch. Over the years the Barkley name becomes one of power—a name to be feared—but one that also stands for right against wrong, a name that the people of the valley look to for wisdom and leadership in troubled times.

Following the death of Tom Barkley in the 1860s (he was killed by railroad officials when they attempted to rob him of his land), Victoria assumes control of the Barkley empire. She is assisted by her grown children: Jarrod, the first-born, a lawyer (with offices in Stockton and San Francisco); Nick, the second-born, the two-fisted ranch foreman; Audra, her beautiful, untamed daughter; and Heath, Tom's bastard son (born of an Indian maiden in the town of Strawberry), who fought for and achieved his birthright—the name Barkley.

Audra, who buys her dresses and material at Ida Nell's Seamstress Shop, also does volunteer work at the Children's Orphanage (which is located next to the Old Mill). Victoria's horse is named Misty Girl. Heath carries a rattlesnake's rattler as a good-luck charm. First season episodes feature Victoria's youngest son, Eugene (Charles Briles), who was shy and sensitive (and dropped, though said to be attending school).

Theme: "The Big Valley Theme," by George Duning

THE BIONIC WOMAN

ABC, 1.14.76 to 5.4.77
NBC, 9.10.77 to 9.2.78

Principal Cast: Lindsay Wagner (*Jaime Sommers*), Richard Anderson (*Oscar Goldman*), Martin E. Brooks (*Dr. Rudy Wells*), Jennifer Darling (*Peggy Callahan*, a.k.a. *Janet Callahan*)

Trivia: A spinoff of "The Six Million Dollar Man," featuring Jaime Sommers, tennis pro and the girlfriend of astronaut Steve Austin (Lee Majors)—the man who became the first cyborg (cybernetic organism) when he crashed in an M3F5 test plane and was given two nuclear-powered legs, an arm and an eye to save his life.

When Jaime is critically injured following a sky-diving accident, Oscar Goldman of the Office of Scientific Intelligence (O.S.I.), arranges a bionic operation to save her life. Jaime's legs, her right arm and her right ear are replaced with synthetic, nuclear-powered mechanisms that produce superhuman abilities.

Jaime's bionic parts (those given):
1. Bionic Audio Sensor, Catalogue Number 6314-KAH. Amplification 1400; .081 Distortion; Class BC.
2. Bionic Neuro Link Forearm (Upper Right Arm Assembly), Catalogue Number 2822/PJI.
3. Neuro Feedback Power Supply: Atomic Type AED-4 (Catalogue Number 2821 AED-4). 1550 Watt Continuous Duty.
4. Bionic Neuro Link Bi-Pedal Assembly, Catalogue Number 914-PAH.
5. Neuro Feedback Terminal Power Supply: Atomic Type AED-9A (4920 Watt Continuous Duty).
6. Overload Follower, 2100 Watt Reserve, Intermittent Duty, Class CC.

Although the cost of Jaime's operation is not revealed (listed as Classified), Steve's was six million dollars. Jaime's is assumed to be higher due to a rejection of her bionic parts by her body at first and the need for a second operation.

In return for her life-saving operation, Jaime agrees to work for the O.S.I. (where her Clearance Authorization Level is 6). Jaime, who relinquishes her career as a tennis pro, becomes a schoolteacher (grade levels seven, eight and nine) at the Ventura Air Force Base in California. She also moves into her foster parents' home (address not given) in Ojai, California (her phone number was given as 311-555-2368, but a camera shot of her phone listed the number as 311-555-7306).

Other Characters: Peggy Callahan, Oscar's secretary and Jaime's friend, who lives at 22 Land Cliff Drive; Dr. Rudy Wells, the O.S.I. surgeon who is responsible for Jaime's bionic upkeep; and Lisa Galloway, Jaime's evil twin (through plastic surgery). Played by Lindsay Wagner, Lisa sought to learn the secret of Jaime's strength and almost died when she stole Dr. Wells' experimental Hydrazene—a taffy-like substance that produces incredible strength, but is fatal when taken in large doses.

Relatives: Martha Scott (Jaime's foster mother, *Helen Elgin*), Ford Rainey (Jaime's foster father, *Jim Elgin*), Peter Lempert (Oscar's brother, *Sam Goldman*)

Theme: "The Bionic Woman," written by Jerry Fielding

Note: Two TV movies reuniting Jaime and Steve appeared on NBC: *The Return of the Six Million Dollar Man and the Bionic Woman* (5.17.87), and *The Bionic Showdown* (4.30.89).

In the first movie an evil organization called Fortress begins stealing advanced weapons, so Oscar Goldman recruits his two former agents (now retired) to help him: Jaime Sommers, who now works for a rehabilitation center, and Steve Austin, who now runs a charter-boat service called Summer Babe. The movie also introduces Steve's estranged son Michael (Tom Schanley) who, after a near-fatal accident testing an airplane, is given a bionic operation to save his life (receiving replacements of both legs, his right arm, ten ribs and his right eye). The movie also served as a pilot for a proposed series to feature Michael's exploits.

The Bionic Showdown teams Steve, Jaime and a young bionic woman named Kate

Mason (Sandra Bullock) to battle a villainous cyborg. Richard Anderson and Martin E. Brooks reprised their original roles in both movies.

B. J. AND THE BEAR

NBC, 2.10.79 to 9.13.80
1.13.81 to 8.1.81

Principal Cast: Greg Evigan (*Billie Joe "B. J." McKay*), Laurette Spang (*Snow White*), Judy Landers (*Jeannie Campbell*), Candi Brough (*Teri Garrison*), Randi Brough (*Geri Garrison*), Barbra Horan (*Samantha Smith*), Linda McCullough (*Callie Everett*), Sherilyn Wolter (*Cindy Grant*), Sheila DeWindt (*Angie Cartwright*), Sam (*Bear*)

Trivia: Former Vietnam chopper pilot B. J. McKay is an independent trucker who will haul anything legal anywhere for $1.50 a mile plus expenses. B. J., who rides with his simian companion, Bear, drives a red Kenworth 18-wheeler truck that is registered in Milwaukee (his home town). The license plates given for the truck are: 806 536, 635 608 and 4T 3665.

B. J., whose favorite truck stop is the Country Comfort Trucker's Stop in Bowlin County, named Bear (a chimp) after Bear Bryant—whom B. J. considers to be the greatest football coach ever—of the University of Alabama. (B. J. befriended Bear while in Vietnam; he was a P.O.W. and Bear would bring him food to help him survive.) B. J.'s CB handle is "the Milwaukee Kid."

In 1981 episodes, B. J. establishes Bear Enterprises (formally Chaffey Enterprises), an independent truckers' company in Hollywood staffed by seven beautiful girls (Jeannie, Teri, Geri, Cindy, Samantha, Callie and Angie), and housed over Phil's Disco. Jeannie has the nickname "Stacks" (for her well-developed chest; measurements not given); Angie, who is also a radio disc jockey, has the air name "the Nightingale"; and twins Teri and Geri work as waitresses in the disco. In 1980 episodes, Snow White, a trucker friend of B. J.'s, heads the all-girl Piston Packin' Mamas trucking outfit in Winslow County. The "Mamas" are:

Tommy (Janet Louise Johnson), Honey (Angela Aames), Leather (Carlene Watkins), Sal (Julie Gregg), Clancy (Spray Russo), Angel (Darlyn Ann Lindley) and Chattanooga (Sonia Manzano).

Out To Get B. J.: Sheriff Elroy P. Lobo (Claude Akins) of Orly County, Georgia, who is after B. J. for breaking up his white slavery ring; Captain John Sebastian Cain (Ed Lauter) of Bishop County; Deputy Beauregard Wiley (Slim Pickens) of Winslow County; J. P. Pierson (M. P. Murphy), the head of the organized High-Ballers Trucking Outfit (opposes independents taking their business); Rutherford T. Grant (Murray Hamilton), the crooked head of SCAT (Special Crime Action Team of the L.A.P.D.); and Jason T. Willard (Jock Mahoney), the head of Trans-Cal Trucking.

Relatives: Deborah Ryan (B. J.'s sister, *Shauna McKay*)

Theme: "B. J. and the Bear," vocal by Greg Evigan

Spinoffs: "The Misadventures of Sheriff Lobo" (NBC, 9.18.79 to 9.2.80) relates the exploits of Sheriff Elroy P. Lobo (Claude Akins), the corrupt sheriff of Orly County, Georgia, his equally dishonest and dim-witted assistant, Deputy Perkins (Mills Watson), and his honest deputy, Birdwell "Birdie" Hawkins (Brian Kerwin).

"Lobo" (NBC, 12.30.80 to 8.25.81), actually a spinoff of a spinoff, continues to relate the misadventures of Lobo, Perkins and Birdie as law enforcement officers in Atlanta, Georgia.

B. L. STRYKER

ABC, 2.13.89 to 5.5.90

Principal Cast: Burt Reynolds (*Buddy Lee "B. L." Stryker*), Ossie Davis (*Oz Jackson*), Dana Kaminsky (*Linda Lennox*), Rita Moreno (*Kimberly Baskin*)

Trivia: The exploits of B. L. Stryker, a former New Orleans police officer (suspended for being out of control) who returns to his hometown of Palm Beach, Florida, to become a private investigator (Stryker Investigations). His friend and assistant is Oz Jackson, a former world-famous boxer; Linda Lennox is his flighty secretary; and Kimberly Baskin is his recently remarried ex-wife.

B. L., who has a parrot named Gilbert, drives a classic Cadillac (license plate not readable), lives on a houseboat called the *No Trump* (docked at 22 Ocean Park Marina—which is the address of Maxie's Marina, later called Oliver's Marina). Linda has a dog named Fred; Oz's license plate reads OZ II; and Kimberly's Rolls Royce license plate is CIT 86R.

Relatives: Abe Vigoda (Kimberly's husband, *Clayton Baskin*), Maureen Stapleton (B. L.'s aunt, *Susan Stryker*), Denise Nicholas (Oz's daughter, *Darlene Carter*)

Theme: "B. L. Stryker," written by Mike Post

BLACK SADDLE

ABC, 1.10.59 to 9.28.60

Clay Culhane (Peter Breck) is an ex-gunfighter turned lawyer in Latigo, New Mexico, in the 1860s. Nora Travers (Anna-Lisa) owns the Marathon Hotel (later called the Travis House Hotel). The "Black Saddle Theme" was written by Jerry Goldsmith, J. Michael Hannigan and Arthur Morton.

BLANSKY'S BEAUTIES

ABC, 2.12.77 to 6.27.77

"The Major Putnam Spectacular—La Plume De La Putnam" is the main glitzy show at the Oasis Hotel in Las Vegas, Nevada. Nancy Blansky (Nancy Walker) is the show's producer. Most people believe her name is "Nanky Blanky" because the show's announcer says Nancy's name so fast, nobody can understand the correct pronunciation. Becoming one of "Blansky's Beauties" is the dream of all budding showgirls and an important start on the road to a dream—to become famous. Joey DeLuca (Eddie Mekka) is Nancy's assistant (his cousin is Carmine Raguso of "Laverne and Shirley"). He and his younger brother, Anthony (Scott Baio), live with Nancy at 64 Crescent Drive.

The Showgirls: Bambi Benton (Caren Kaye) is from Southern California ("I was a showgirl at six hotels and I've been fired six times for having fun; like the time I came down from the ceiling on a trapeze with a seltzer bottle to give the audience a few squirts"). Her mother loved the movie *Bambi* and named her after the main character. Ethel Akalino (Lynda Goodfriend) is from Wichita, Kansas ("They call me Sunshine because I smile a lot"); Arkansas Baits (Rhonda Bates) is from Arkansas ("I don't sing too good, and I don't dance too good, but I sure do a mean hog call—suuuu-weeee!").

Jackie Outlaw (Gerri Reddick) is unmarried and "cool"; Hilary Prentiss (Taaffe O'Connell) is a stunning blonde beauty and got the job because "I'm a close personal friend of Major Putnam, who owns the hotel, and I wanna be a chorus girl"; Sylvia Silver (Antoinette Yuskis) is a street-wise but sweet girl from the Bronx; Bridget Muldoon (Elaine Bolton) is the prim and proper British girl. As the series progresses, three more girls become "Blansky's Beauties": Lovely Carson (Bond Gideon), Gladys "Cochise" Littlefeather (Shirley Kirkes) and Misty "Knight" Karamazov (Jill Owens).

George Pentecost plays Horace "Stubs" Wilmington, the hotel manager; Pat Morita, Arnold Takahashi, the coffee shop owner. Anthony's favorite sandwich is peanut butter and bologna and he has a crush on Bambi; Nancy's dog is named Blackjack. Cyndi Grecco sings the theme, "I Want It All."

THE BOB NEWHART SHOW

CBS, 9.16.72 to 9.2.78

Principal Cast: Bob Newhart (*Bob Hartley*), Suzanne Pleshette (*Emily Hartley*), Bill Daily (*Howard Borden*), Peter Bonerz (*Jerome "Jerry" Robinson*), Marcia Wallace (*Carol Kester*)

Trivia: Dr. Robert "Bob" Hartley, Social Security number 352-22-7439, is a private practice psychologist whose office is located in the Rampo Medical Arts Building in Chicago. Bob, whose birthsign is Virgo, played drums in his high school band and in Korea was with the 193rd Combat Support Orchestra. At this time, Bob was noted for "having the best wrists south of the 38th Parallel." Enthused about becoming a professional drummer, Bob went to New York after his army hitch and auditioned for the Buddy Rich Orchestra. While Bob thought he did great, Buddy Rich had only three words to say to him: "You stink, man." Though discouraged, Bob went on to college and studied to be a psychologist.

Bob's office number changes from episode to episode: sometimes it is 751, other times it is 715; his office phone number is 726-7098. When Bob wants to dress sloppily around the house (Apartment 523 in a building owned by the Skyline Management Corporation), he wears a neatly pressed sweatshirt. When Bob appeared on the TV show "Psychology in Action" with his therapy group, he was called "Dr. Robert Hartman" by the announcer. Bob also took a temporary job with Loggers' Casualty Life Insurance Company; their slogan: "We Gotta Insure These Guys."

Emily Hartley, Bob's wife, originally taught third grade at Gorman Elementary School. Later she is vice principal at Tracy Grammar School. Emily, whose maiden name is Harrison, was born in Seattle, Washington; she and Bob married on April 15, 1970. On their first wedding anniversary, Emily and Bob received a radio from Bob's parents and a car from Emily's.

Howard Mark Borden, Bob and Emily's neighbor, was originally a 747 navigator for an unnamed airline. After nine years on the job, Howard was replaced by a computer and found the same kind of work with EDS (European Delivery Service) Airline. Howard, who is divorced, and the father of a young son (Howard Jr., who was conceived during the great airplane strike of 1963) has a sister (Debbie) and two brothers: Gordon Borden, the game warden, and Norman Borden, the Mormon doorman.

Other regulars: Jerome "Jerry" Merle Robinson, Bob's friend, a children's orthodontist (who washes his hands an average of 46 times per day), and Carol Kester, Bob and Jerry's secretary, who was born in Collinsville, Iowa. She has a tape recording of a barking dog that she switches on when her doorbell rings; the dog is named Lobo and she lives in Apartment 7 (no address given). Carol later marries Larry Bondurant (Will MacKenzie).

Relatives: Pat Finley (Bob's sister, *Ellen Hartley*), Barnard Hughes (Bob's father, *Herb Hartley*), Martha Scott (Bob's mother, *Martha Hartley*), John Randolph (Emily's father, *Cornelius "Junior" Harrison*), Ann Rutherford (Emily's mother, *Aggie Harrison*), Heather Menzies (Howard's sister, *Debbie Borden*), William Redfield (Howard's brother, *Gordon Borden*), Moosie Drier (Howard's son, *Howard Jr.*)

Theme: "Home for Emily," by Lorenzo and Henrietta Music

BONANZA

NBC, 9.12.59 to 1.16.73

Principal Cast: Lorne Greene (*Ben Cartwright*), Pernell Roberts (*Adam Cartwright*), Dan Blocker (*Eric Hoss Cartwright*), Michael Landon (*Joseph Francis "Little Joe" Cartwright*), Victor Sen Yung (*Hop Sing*)

Trivia: One year after Ben Cartwright, a former first mate who runs a ship chandler store in New England, marries his fiancée, Elizabeth Stoddard, a son (whom they name Adam) is born to them. When Elizabeth dies shortly after (of childbirth complications), Ben sells his business and begins journeying west in hopes of settling in California. His journey ends, temporarily, in St. Joseph, Missouri, where, eight years later, Ben marries a Swedish woman named Inger.

With Inger's help, Ben organizes a wagon train and resumes his journey west. During the hazardous trek through Nevada, Inger gives birth to a son they name Eric Hoss. Shortly after, during an Indian attack, Inger is killed. Abandoning his dream forever, Ben settles in Virginia City, Nevada, and establishes the Ponderosa Ranch. (The birth of Ben's third son, ~~Little Joe, is the result of Ben's marrying~~ Marie DeMarne, the widow of a former ranch hand. Marie, like Elizabeth and Inger, is "killed off" when she is thrown from her horse.)

The Ponderosa Ranch (on the outskirts of Virginia City) is a 1,000-square-mile timberland ranch in the Comstock Lode Country. Ranch hands earn $30 a month, a bunk and beans. The Sierra Freight and Stage Lines deliver mail and freight to Virginia City. The town newspaper is the *Enterprise* and the Overland Stage Lines provides passenger service.

Eric's middle name, Hoss, is a Swedish mountain name for a big, friendly man — something Inger knew Eric would be even though she only lived long enough to see him as an infant. Eric's horse is named Chuck; Ben's is Buck; and Little's Joe's horse is named Cochise. In one episode, Michael Landon played Little Joe's evil twin Angus Borden.

Relatives: Mitch Vogel (Ben's adopted son, *Jamie*), Guy Madison (Ben's nephew, *Will Cartwright*), Bruce Yarnell (Ben's cousin, *Muley Jones*)

Flashbacks: Geraldine Brooks (Ben's first wife, *Elizabeth*), Inga Swenson (Ben's second wife, *Inger*), Felicia Farr (Ben's third wife, *Marie*), Johnny Stephens (*Adam as a boy*)

Theme: "Bonanza," written by Jay Livingston and Ray Evans; performed by David Rose

Note: In the syndicated TV movie, *Bonanza: The Next Generation* (3.16.88), John Ireland plays Aaron Cartwright, the late Ben's brother and new head of the Ponderosa Ranch; Barbara Anderson, Annabelle Cartwright, the wife of Little Joe (killed while serving with Teddy Roosevelt's Rough Riders); Michael Landon Jr. is Benji Cartwright, Little Joe's son; and Brian A. Smith is Josh Cartwright, Hoss's illegitimate son.

BOOKER
Fox, 9.24.89 to 8.26.90

A "21 Jump Street" spinoff in which Dennis Booker (Richard Grieco) leaves the Los Angeles Metropolitan's undercover police unit, Jump Street Chapel, to become the head investigator of the Teshima Corporation, a Los Angeles-based, Japanese-owned insurance company located in the Teshima Building. Marcia Strassman plays Alicia Rudd, vice president in charge of corporate acquisitions, and Lori Petty, Booker's assistant, Suzanne Dunne.

Booker's car license plate number is DVP 762; Suzanne's license plate number is PX29190. Steve Inwood appeared as Booker's father, Nicholas, and Linda Darlow as his mother, Joyce. Lori Petty played Suzanne's twin sister, Diane Dunne. Mentioned, but not seen, were Dennis's sister, Taffy, and his Aunt Connie. Billy Idol sings the theme, "Hot in the City."

THE BRADY BUNCH
ABC, 9.26.69 to 8.30.74

Principal Cast: Robert Reed (*Mike Brady*), Florence Henderson (*Carol Brady*), Maureen McCormick (*Marcia Brady*), Eve Plumb (*Jan Brady*), Susan Olsen (*Cindy Brady*), Barry Williams (*Greg Brady*), Christopher Knight (*Peter Brady*), Michael Lookinland (*Bobby Brady*), Ann B. Davis (*Alice Nelson*)

Trivia: Michael Paul Brady, a widower and the father of three sons (Greg, Peter and Bobby), and Carol Ann Tyler Martin, a widow and the mother of three daughters (Marcia, Jan and Cindy), marry and establish housekeeping in a four-bedroom, two-bathroom home at 4222 Clinton Avenue in Los Angeles. Their phone number is 762-0799 (also given as 555-6161), the family dog is named Tiger, and the family car license plates are TEL 635 (sedan) and 746 AEH (station wagon). In the pilot episode, the girls have a pet cat named Fluffy.

Mike, an architect, works for an unnamed company (in one episode, Jim Backus plays his boss, Henry Matthews). As a kid, Mike was known as the checkers champion of Chestnut Street, and in 1969, he was voted "Father of the Year" by the *Daily Chronicle* (because of a letter Marcia sent to the newspaper).

Carol, who attended West Side High School, had the nickname "Twinkles" and wrote an article about her new family for *Tomorrow's Woman* magazine (the article's title was not given).

Marcia, the eldest of the girls, was a member of the Sunflower Girls scout troop. She attended Fillmore Junior High, was editor of its newspaper, the Fillmore *Flier*, and the senior class president. Marcia later attended Westdale High School and was president of her chapter of the Davy Jones Fan Club (when she had a crush on the Monkees band member). Marcia yearned to attend Tower High School but was unable to because her home is in the Westdale school zone. At Westdale, Marcia was a cheerleader for the Bears football team, and she later had an after-school job as a waitress at Hanson's Ice Cream Parlor.

Jan, "pretty, smart and kind," is the middle girl; she attended the same schools as Marcia. Voted the most popular girl in her class at Fillmore Junior High, she worked after school with Marcia at Hanson's Ice Cream Parlor. Her favorite cookies are cinnamon spice. At age 11, when she felt she was unattractive, Jan pretended to have a boyfriend she called George Glass. In another episode, when Jan wanted to be different from her blonde sisters, she wore a brunette wig to cover her own natural blonde hair.

Cindy, the youngest of the Brady girls, attends Clinton Elementary School. Her hero is Joan of Arc, she had a favorite doll named Kitty Carry-All and two pet rabbits named Romeo and Juliet.

Greg, the eldest boy, was a Frontier Scout and attends Westdale High School. He had a pet white mouse named Myron, and attempted to break into the music business as a singer named Johnny Bravo. With his brothers and sisters, he formed the singing group the Brady Six (they recorded the song "Time to Change").

Peter, the middle boy, attended both Clinton Elementary and Fillmore Junior High. His hero is George Washington and he was a member of the Treehouse Club. In one episode, Christopher Knight played Peter's look-alike friend, Arthur Owens.

Bobby, the youngest brother, attends the same school as Cindy. His hero is Jesse James, and he had a pet parakeet he called Bird. In one episode, he tried to make a million dollars by selling Neat and Natural Hair Tonic for two dollars a bottle (but the product turned hair orange).

Alice Nelson, their housekeeper, had been working for Mike for seven years when he and Carol married. Her boyfriend is Sam Franklin (Allan Melvin), owner of Sam's Butcher Shop.

The family appeared together in a TV commercial for a laundry detergent called Safe. In the opening theme, the Bradys are seen in a series of squares arranged like a tic-tac-toe board. In the top sequence, from left to right are Marcia, Carol and Greg. Left to right in the middle sequence are Jan, Alice and Peter. Cindy, Mike and Bobby are in the bottom sequence, left to right.

Relatives: Robbie Rist (Carol's nephew, *Oliver*), J. Pat O'Malley (Carol's father, *Henry Tyler*), Joan Tompkins (*Carol's mother*), Imogene Coca (Mike's *Aunt Jenny*), Robert Reed (Mike's grandfather, *Hank Brady*), Florence Henderson (Carol's grandmother, *Connie Hutchins*), Ann B. Davis (Alice's *Cousin Emma*).

Theme: "The Brady Bunch," vocal by the Peppermint Trolley Company (first season), then the Brady Kids

Spinoffs: "The Brady Kids" (ABC, 9.9.72 to 8.31.74). The animated antics of Marcia (Maureen McCormick), Jan (Eve Plumb), Cindy (Susan Olsen), Greg (Barry Williams), Peter (Christopher Knight) and Bobby (Michael Lookinland). Their pets: Moptop the dog, Marlon the magic bird (both voices by Larry Storch) and

Panda bears Ping and Pong (voices by Jane Webb).

"The Brady Bunch Hour" (ABC, 1.23.77 to 5.24.77). A musical comedy in which the Bradys entertain from their home in Southern California. Geri Reischl replaced Eve Plumb in the role of Jan.

"The Brady Girls Get Married" (NBC, 2.6.81 to 2.20.81). Marcia, now a fashion designer, marries Wally Logan (Jerry Houser), a designer/tester for the Tyler Toy Company; Jan, now a college student (majoring in architecture), marries Philip Covington III (Ron Kuhlman), a college chemistry professor.

Mike is still an architect (company name not given); Carol is a saleswoman for Willowbrook Realty. Greg is now a doctor, Peter has joined the air force and Cindy and Bobby are college students.

Relatives: Jean Byron (Philip's mother, *Claudia Covington*), Ryan McDonald (Philip's father, *Philip Covington II*), Carol Arthur (Wally's mother, *Mrs. Logan*), James Gallery (Wally's father, *Mr. Logan*)

"The Brady Brides" (NBC, 3.6.81 to 4.17.81). Marcia is a fashion designer for Casual Clothes and Jan is an architect (company name not given). Marcia and Wally and Jan and Philip set up housekeeping in the same home to save on expenses. The only other regulars to appear are Carol (Florence Henderson) and Alice (Ann B. Davis).

A Very Brady Christmas (CBS, 12.18.88). A TV movie that reunites most of the original Brady family cast in a story that finds the family returning home for a Christmas reunion. Cindy is now played by Jennifer Runyon; Carol works for Advantage Properties Real Estate; Wally is employed by Prescott Toys.

In the seven years that elapsed between the fourth and fifth spinoffs, the following additions were made to the families: Marcia's daughter, Jessica (Jaclyn Bernstein), Marcia's son, Mickey (J. W. Lee), Greg's wife, Nora (Caryn Richman), Greg's son, Kevin (Zachary Bostrom), and Peter's girlfriend, Valerie Thomas (Carol Huston).

"The Bradys" (CBS, 2.9.90 to 3.9.90).

An hour series that continues to follow events in the lives of the Brady family.

Cast Changes: Leah Ayres plays Marcia; Michael Malby, Marcia's son, Mickey; Valerie Ick, Jan's adopted daughter, Patty; and Jonathan Weiss, Greg's son, Kevin. New to the cast is Martha Quinn as Bobby's wife, Tracy.

Trivia: Mike has retired and is now a city councilman for the fourth district, having won the election with 13,119 votes. Carol is still in real estate (her company name is not given). Marcia and Wally, who were both fired from their jobs, establish their own business—the Party Girls Catering Company. Jan, still an architect, has taken over what is now her father's company (name still not given). Cindy is a radio disc jockey with station KBLA (the phone number of which is 213-555-KBLA) and the host of her own show, "Cindy at Sunrise."

Greg is still a doctor (hospital name not given), and Nora is a nurse. Bobby is now a race car driver, and Peter is his father's assistant. To make the Bradys more contemporary, Marcia was given a drinking problem and Bobby was almost crippled in a racing accident.

BRAND NEW LIFE
NBC, 9.18.89 to 4.15.90

Principal Cast: Barbara Eden (*Barbara McCray*), Jennie Garth (*Ericka Stephanie McCray*), Alison Sweeney (*Christy McCray*), David Thom (*Bart McCray*), Don Murray (*Roger Gibbons*), Shawnee Smith (*Amanda Gibbons*), Byron Thames (*Laird Gibbons*), Eric Foster (*Barlow Gibbons*)

Trivia: Barbara McCray, a divorced mother of three (Ericka, Christy and Bart), and Roger Gibbons, a widower with three children (Amanda, Laird and Barlow) meet in a diner called Order in the Court (located next to the Los Angeles Supreme Court Building)—where Barbara is a waitress and where Roger, a lawyer, has come to eat apparently for the first time. He orders "An Exhibit A with no sausage" from Barbara, and it's love at first sight. They become engaged one month later, marry shortly after that and spend their honeymoon (with the kids) at Lake Hellgramite (where Ericka injures her neck in a water-skiing accident and Laird gets the worst case of poison oak the doctors have ever seen).

Barbara, who is pursuing a career as a court stenographer, attends classes at Pacific Southwest School. Roger, a widower for two years before he met Barbara, is a corporate lawyer (company not named). He attended Yale University (Class of '59), where he was a member of the Pi Gamma Signu Fraternity. The family of eight now resides in Bel Air at 31304 South Birch Street. Amanda and Ericka attend J.F.K. High School; Christy attends the Willow Crest School; and Bart is enrolled in the Hank E. Woodruff School. Christy is a talented violinist who hopes to one day perform in an orchestra; Laird's license plate (sports car) is 2AS0043. It is mentioned that after he quit the Army, Barbara's husband walked out on her and his family. The series was originally titled "Blended Family."

Relatives: Lou Hancock (Barbara's ex-mother-in-law, *Grandma Zora*, who has a dog named Mombo). Mentioned, but not seen, is Roger's late wife, Constance.

Theme: "Brand New Life," vocal by Jill Colucci

BRET MAVERICK
see MAVERICK

BRIDGES TO CROSS
CBS, 4.24.86 to 6.12.86
Tracy Bridges (Suzanne Pleshette) and Peter Cross (Nicholas Surovy) are a divorced couple and the reporter-columnists of "Bridges to Cross," a column for the Washington, D.C.-based *World Week* magazine. José Ferrer plays their editor, Morris Kane, and Eva Gabor, Tracy's society friend, Maria Talbot. Mark Snow composed the theme.

BROADSIDE
see McHALE'S NAVY

BRONK
CBS, 9.21.75 to 7.18.76
Alex "Bronk" Bronkov (Jack Palance), whose badge number is 25, is an undercover police inspector for Mayor Pete Santori (Joseph Mascolo) of Ocean City, California. His daughter, Ellen (Dina Ousley), was crippled in a car accident that killed her mother. Outside the office, Alex is also partners with Harry Mark (Henry Beckman) in the M&B Junkyard.

THE BRONX ZOO
NBC, 3.19.87 to 7.6.87
Joe Danzig (Edward Asner), a tough and dedicated teacher, is assigned principal of Benjamin Harrison High, an unruly New York school nicknamed "the Bronx Zoo." Drama and art teacher Mary Caitlin Callahan (Kathleen Beller) rides a motorcycle to school; she attended Mary Mount School as a child. Gorgeous English teacher Sara Newhouse (Kathryn Harrold) has few, if any, problems with students hitting on her. Janet Carroll appears as Joe's wife, Carol; Randee Heller plays Jeannine, the sister of history teacher Harry Burns (David Wilson). Gary Scott composed the theme.

BROTHERS AND SISTERS
NBC, 1.21.79 to 4.6.79
College hijinks with Gamma Delta Iota sorority members Suzie Cooper (Mary Crosby) and Mary Lee (Amy Johnston), and Checko Sabolick (Chris Lemmon) and Stanley Zipper (Jon Cutler) of the Pi Nu fraternity. William Windom appeared as Larry Krandall, Dean of Larry Krandall College. Mark Snow composed the theme.

THE BUCCANEERS

CBS, 9.22.56 to 9.14.57

"Let's go a roamin', a roamin' across the oceans, oh, let's go a roamin' and join the Buccaneers . . . " Dan Tempest (Robert Shaw) captains the ship *Sultana*, based in the Caribbean Colony of New Providence during the 1720s. The series is also known as "Dan Tempest." Albert Elms composed the theme.

BUCK ROGERS IN THE 25TH CENTURY

NBC, 9.27.79 to 9.13.80
1.15.81 to 8.20.81

Principal Cast: Gil Gerard (*Captain William "Buck" Rogers*), Erin Gray (*Lieutenant Wilma Deering*), Tim O'Connor (*Dr. Elias Huer*), Pamela Hensley (*Princess Ardella*), Henry Silva and Michael Ansara (*Kane*), Felix Silla (*Twiki*), Mel Blanc (*Twiki's voice*), Wilfred Hyde-White (*Dr. Goodfellow*), Jay Garner (*Admiral Ephraim Asimov*; a.k.a. *Isaac Asimov*), Thom Christopher (*Hawk*)

Trivia: While he is testing *Ranger III* for NASA in 1987, a freak accident puts Buck Rogers, its captain, into a state of suspended animation. In the year 2491, Buck awakens to a new world and joins the Earth Federation, a universal defense organization based in America's new capital, New Chicago. Dr. Elias Huer is head of the Earth Federation and Wilma Deering, who was called "Dizzy Dee" as a kid, is a lieutenant with the Third Force of the Earth Directorate. When Buck becomes a member, he is assigned an Ambuquad named Twiki (serial number 2223-T). Twiki houses the highly intelligent computer named Dr. Theopolis (voice by Eric Server). The Capitol Building in New Chicago is the Directorate Building, and the national retirement age has risen to 85.

Beautiful Princess Ardella from the planet Draconia appears in several episodes and seeks to marry Buck. Ardella, who measures 34-24-34, is one of 28 daughters of Emperor Drakos; she commands a two-mile-wide spaceship, the *Draconia*. (As next in line to rule her planet, Ardella must marry the most perfect man she can find. She chooses Buck, but is never able to complete her mission.)

In second-season episodes, the format changes to relate Buck and Wilma's experiences as members of *Searcher*, a spaceship seeking the lost tribes of Earth. Admiral Asimov is the ship's commander; Dr. Goodfellow, the scientific genius; and Hawk, their man-bird ally. While the role of Twiki has been cut back, that of Crichton, the robot who refuses to believe he is manmade, has been added (voice by Jeff Davis).

Theme: "Buck Rogers Theme," by Glen A. Larson

Note: A previous "Buck Rogers in the 25th Century" aired on ABC from 4.15.50 to 1.3.52 with the following cast: Kem Dibbs (1950) and Robert Pastine (1951) as Buck Rogers, Lou Prentis as Wilma Deering and Harry Sothern as Dr. Huer.

Even earlier, in an unaired 1949 pilot, Earl Hammond played Buck Rogers and Eva Marie Saint portrayed Wilma Deering.

BURKE'S LAW

ABC, 9.20.63 to 8.31.65

Millionaire Police Captain Amos Burke (Gene Barry) is with the Metropolitan Division of the Los Angeles Police Department (phone number Madison 6–7399). He is a ladies' man, resides at 109 North Milbourne, and has a chauffeur-driven limo with the license plate JZG063 (sometimes JE8495). His combination houseboy-chauffeur, Henry, is played by Leon Lontoc.

(213) 676–4882 is the phone number of his partner, Tim Tillson (Gary Conway), and Detective Lester Hart (Regis Toomey) also assists him. In the episode "Who Killed the Grand Piano?" Gene Barry also plays Amos's uncle, Patrick Harrigan. Herschel Burke Gilbert composed the "Burke's Law" theme.

In the spinoff series, "Amos Burke, Secret Agent" (ABC, 9.15.65 to 1.12.66), Burke quits the police force to become a U.S. government undercover agent. Carl

Benton Reid plays his superior, "The Man."

CAGNEY AND LACEY

CBS, 3.25.82 to 9.12.83
3.19.84 to 8.25.88

Principal Cast: Tyne Daly (*Detective Mary Beth Lacey*), Meg Foster and Sharon Gless (*Detective Christine "Chris" Cagney*), John Karlen (*Harvey Lacey*), Al Waxman (*Lieutenant Albert Samuels*), Carl Lumbly (*Detective Mark Petrie*), Martin Kove (*Detective Victor Isbecki*)

Trivia: Mary Beth Lacey, Badge #340, and Christine Cagney, Badge #763, are with the 14th Precinct of the New York Police Department. Their mobil code is Car 27. Mary Beth (maiden name is Biskey) lives in Queens with her husband, Harvey, a construction worker, and her children Harvey Jr., Michael and Alice. Chris, who has never married, lives in Manhattan; like her father, she has a drinking problem. Her license plate number is 562 BLA (later, 801 FEM).

In the TV-movie pilot (CBS, 10.8.81), Loretta Swit played Chris Cagney; Robert Hunter, Harvey Lacey; and Jefferson Mapin, Victor Isbecki. Mary Beth's children were played by Evan Routbard (Michael) and Jamie Dick (Harvey Jr.).

Relatives: Tony LaTorre (Mary Beth's son, *Harvey Jr.*), Troy Slaten (Mary Beth's son, *Michael*), Donna and Paige Bardolph (Mary Beth's daughter, *Alice*), Dick O'Neill (Chris's father, *Charlie Cagney*), David Ackroyd (Chris's brother, *Brian Cagney*), Amanda Wyss (Chris's niece, *Bridget Cagney*), Richard Bradford (Mary Beth's father, *Martin Biskey*), Penny Santon (Harvey's mother, *Muriel Lacey*), Barbara Tarbuck (Albert's wife, *Thelma Samuels*), Matthew Barry (Albert's son, *David Samuels*), Suzanne Stone, Jonelle Allen and Vonetta McGee (Mark's wife, *Claudia Petrie*), Alexandria Simmons (Mark's daughter, *Lauren*)

Theme (first season): "Ain't That the Way," vocal by Marie Cain

Theme (series): "Theme from Cagney and Lacey," by Bill Conti

CALL TO GLORY

ABC, 8.13.84 to 2.12.85

The series, originally called "Air Force," tells the story of Colonel Raynor Sarnac (Craig T. Nelson) and the men and women of the U.S. Air Force's 4080th Strategic Reconnaissance Wing. Cindy Pickett plays his wife, Vanessa; Elisabeth Shue, his daughter, Jackie; David Hollander, his son, Wesley; Gabriel Damon, his son, R. H.; and Keenan Wynn, his father, Carl, who lived at 295 Canyon Drive. Episodes were originally set at Loughlin Air Force Base in Texas, but later moved to Edwards Air Force Base in California when Sarnac became commander of the base's test-pilot school. Charles Gross composed the theme.

CAMP RUNAMUCK

NBC, 9.17.65 to 9.2.66

TV's only aired comedy series to be set at summer camp features the slipshod Camp Runamuck for Boys, and the impeccably run Camp Divine for girls. The child-hating Commander Wivenhoe (Arch Johnson) heads Runamuck; Mahala May Gruenecker (Alice Nunn) runs Divine for its owner, Eulalia Divine (Hermione Baddeley). The ultra-sexy Divine counselor, Caprice Yeudleman (Nina Wayne), is about the only asset the program has (it lost all semblance of reality when two talking bears began commenting on camp activities). Pre-"Brady Bunch" Maureen McCormick plays Divine camper Maureen Sullivan. The catchy theme was composed by Frank DeVol, who also played Runamuck counselor Doc Joslyn.

Note: Perhaps due to the success of the Kristy McNichol-Tatum O'Neal film *Little Darlings*, ABC subsequently attempted another series set in a summer camp. However, only an unsold pilot called "Camp Grizzly" (6.30.80) resulted. In it, Carl Ballantine played Uncle Bernie, the owner of a rundown coed summer camp called Uncle Bernie's Camp Grizzly. Like Runamuck, the camp was populated with brats and inept counselors. Hilary Thompson (as Missy) provided female influence; she was the only girl counselor—and the only employee who demonstrated having "brains."

In 1982, NBC produced a pilot (also unaired) called "Little Darlings," based on the previously mentioned movie. Pamela Segall played Angel, a streetwise inner-city girl; Tammy Lauren portrayed Ferris, a rich girl from Beverly Hills. Not surprisingly, the two meet and become friends at camp. Heather McAdam played flirtatious Lisa; Anne Schedeen and Michael MacManus played the camp counselors.

In a more dramatic format, the syndicated "Camp Wilderness" (which aired in 1980) presented the adventures of a group of children at another summer camp. Franci Hogle (Franci) and Stefan Hayes (Stefan) played the counselors. Campers included Ruth Ingersol (Ruth), Nora Lester (Nora) and Matt Bronson (Matt).

CAPTAIN MIDNIGHT

CBS, 9.4.54 to 4.28.56

Principal Cast: Richard Webb (*Jim Albright/Captain Midnight*), Sid Melton (*Ichabod "Icky" Mudd*), Olan Soule (*Aristotle "Tut" Jones*)

Trivia: As the tide of World War II turns and the Allies begin to suffer horrible defeats, a young Allied Army captain named Jim Albright undertakes a hazardous mission in an attempt to obtain vital information. As the deadline nears with Albright's plane nowhere in sight, it seems that his mission has failed. The seconds tick by and the midnight hour approaches before the faint sound of a distant plane finally disrupts the still night. Jim Albright returns with the information, and the grateful colonel in charge of the operation renames him, saying, "He'll always be Captain Midnight."

After the war, Captain Midnight forms the Secret Squadron, an organization designed to battle evil. Ichabod "Icky" Mudd is his mechanic, and Aristotle "Tut" Jones, the Captain's scientific adviser. The Captain's plane is called the *Silver Dart*. Members of the Secret Squadron are assigned and referred to by a number, for example, S.Q. 7, S.Q. 10, and so on.

Ovaltine, the owner and original sponsor of the show (since its debut on radio) refused to sponsor the show in syndication and reserved the right to the original name. Consequently, when the program was first syndicated, the title was changed to "Jet Jackson, Flying Commando," as was Richard Webb's character's name via voice-over dubbing. Richard Webb did the original commercials and viewer members of the Secret Squadron were given codes to unscramble with Secret Squadron Decoder Rings at the end of each episode.

Theme: "Captain Midnight," by Don Ferris

CAPTAIN NICE

NBC, 1.9.67 to 9.4.67

"Look, it's the man who flies around like an eagle . . . Look, it's the nut who walks around in his pajamas. That's no nut, boy, that's Captain Nice . . . "

"Captain Nice" is about police chemist Carter Nash's battle against crime as Captain Nice, the heroic defender of the oppressed in Big Town, U.S.A. To transform himself into the Captain, Carter drinks Super Juice (his own invention) and wears a red, white and blue costume with "Captain Nice" printed on the front. (His powers include super strength, super speed and the ability to fly.) William Daniels plays Carter Nash; Ann Prentiss, his girlfriend, Sergeant Candy Cane; and Alice Ghostley, his overbearing mother, Mrs. Nash. Vic Mizzy composed the theme.

CAPTAIN SCARLET AND THE MYSTERONS

Syndicated, 1967

Principal Cast (Voices): Francis Matthews (*Captain Scarlet*), Donald Gray (*Colonel White*), Paul Maxwell (*Captain Grey*), Ed Bishop (*Captain Blue*), Jeremy Wilkins (*Captain Ochre*), Gary Files (*Captain*

Magenta), Cy Grant (*Lieutenant Green*), Jana Hill (*Symphony Angel*), Sylvia Anderson (*Melody Angel*), Liz Morgan (*Destiny Angel* and *Rhapsody Angel*), Shin-Lian (*Harmony Angel*), Charles Tingwell (*Dr. Fawn*)

Trivia: When Spectrum, an organization based on Cloudbase whose mission is to safeguard the world, begins an exploration of the planet Mars, the Mysterons (the planet's inhabitants) believe they are under attack and, in return, declare a war of revenge on the Earth. Seeking a companion in their cause, the never-seen Mysterons contrive an accident that claims the life of Spectrum agent Captain Scarlet. The Mysterons, who possess the ability to recreate any person or object, then restore the Captain's life in order to put him to work for them. Scarlet, however, fails to join them, instead becoming their indestructible enemy. The series depicts Earth's battle against the Mysterons. The show's characters are marionettes named after the colors of the spectrum.

Members of Spectrum:

Captain Scarlet: Spectrum's number one agent, possessing the ability to defy death. Born in England in the year 2036 to a family of distinguished soldiers, he holds degrees in technology, history and math, and has also been trained in field combat.

Colonel White: Commander-in-Chief of Spectrum. Born in England and highly educated in computer control, navigation and technology, he served with the World Navy and the Universal Secret Service. He and Captain Scarlet love to play war games.

Captain Grey: An American born in Chicago. He is a Navy man and served with the World Aquanaut Security Patrol, where he was in charge of the submarine *Stingray*. His pastime is swimming, and he spends hours developing new styles and strokes.

Captain Blue: Born the eldest son of a wealthy financier in Boston, Massachusetts, he is a brilliant scholar with degrees in economics, technology, computer control, applied math and aero-

dynamics. He applied this knowledge to become a top test pilot with the World Aeronautic Society before becoming an agent for Spectrum.

Captain Ochre: An American, he acquired his pilot's license at age 16 and served with the World Government Police Corps. Before joining Spectrum, he broke up one of the toughest crime syndicates in the U.S.

Captain Magenta: Born in Ireland, but after his parents emigrated to America, he was brought up in a poor New York suburb in an atmosphere of poverty and crime. Encouraged by his mother, he worked hard at school, won a scholarship to Yale and graduated with degrees in physics, electrical engineering and technology. Yearning for a life of high adventure and big money, he turned to crime and became a big-time operator who controlled two-thirds of New York's crime organization. When Spectrum realized that they would need such a man—respected and trusted in the underworld—they offered him the job and he accepted.

Lieutenant Green: Born at Port of Spain in Trinidad, he is Colonel White's right-hand man. Holding degrees in music, telecommunications and technology, he served with the World Aquanaut Security Patrol and with the Submarine Corps. He then became sole commander of communications at the Marineville Control Tower before he joined Spectrum.

Dr. Fawn: Born in Australia, he serves as Spectrum's Supreme Medical Commander. After earning degrees in biology and medicine, he developed robot doctors with the World Medical Organization before joining Spectrum.

Symphony Angel: Born in Cedar Rapids, Iowa, she holds degrees in math and technology; she also served with the Universal Secret Service. Within five years, she revolutionized the spy game, and her methods are copied all over the world. When she began training as a pilot for a special mission, Symphony fell in love with flying and joined Spectrum as a pilot. Her hobby is creating new hairstyles for herself and the other Angels.

Melody Angel: Born on a cotton farm

in Atlanta, Georgia, she was a tomboy as a child and later took up professional motor racing. It was during her stay at a Swiss finishing school that she developed an interest in flying. Expelled for her unruly behavior, she joined the World Army Air Force where she displayed amazing courage and nerves of iron, which led to an approach by Spectrum.

Rhapsody Angel: Born in Chelsea, England to aristocratic parents, she is a London University graduate in law and sociology. As a debutante, she met Lady Penelope (see "Thunderbirds") and joined the F.A.B. (Federal Agents Bureau). She took over the bureau's command when Penelope went over to International Rescue (I.R.). Later Rhapsody became chief security officer for an airline before starting her own airline company. She joined Spectrum when they asked her to become an Angel. Her pastime is playing chess.

Harmony Angel: Born in Tokyo, Japan, she is the daughter of a wealthy flying taxi owner. Having grown up in a world of high speed jets, she became a member of the Tokyo Flying Club. She was educated in Tokyo and London, flew around the world non-stop (breaking all records) and inherited her father's business. It was at this time that she was asked to join Spectrum. Harmony loves sports and spends her spare time teaching the Angels karate and judo.

Destiny Angel: Born in Paris and educated in both France and Rome, she joined the World Army Air Force and was transferred to the Intelligence Corps before heading the women's Flight Squadron. Three years later, she started her own firm of flight contractors. Her intelligence, leadership ability and talent in flying resulted in Spectrum naming her leader of the Angels.

Theme: "Captain Scarlet and the Mysterons," by Barry Gray

CAPTAIN VIDEO AND HIS VIDEO RANGERS

DuMont, 6.27.49 to 8.16.57

"Master of Space! Hero of Science! Captain of the Video Rangers! Operating from his secret mountain headquarters on the planet Earth, Captain Video rallies men of good will everywhere. As he rockets from planet to planet, let us follow the champion of justice, truth and freedom throughout the universe. Stand by for Captain Video and His Video Rangers!"

Captain Video, "The Guardian of the Safety of the World," heads the Video Rangers, an organization that battles evil throughout the universe in the year 2254. His assistant is the Video Ranger, and his rocketships are the *X-9*, the *Galaxy* and the *Galaxy II*.

Richard Coogan played the Captain from 1949 to 1950; Al Hodge portrayed him from 1950 to 1957. Don Hastings plays the Video Ranger and Dave Ballard, Tobor the Robot (Tobor is "robot" spelled backward). Bob Hastings appears as the Video Ranger's brother, Hal. Dr. Pauli (played by Bram Nossen, Hal Conklin and Stephen Elliott) is the Captain's enemy, who is President of the Asteroidal Society and invented the Cloak of Invisibility. Captain Video's superior, Commissioner Bell (Jack Orsen, 1949–50) and Commissioner Carey (Ben Lackland, 1950–55) are based on the 144th floor of the Public Safety Building in Planet City. All prisoners are sent to the moon (now a penal colony). Copter Cabs escort people through space. Captain Video's code to his base is 398.

Note: During the 1949–50 season, when Richard Coogan played Captain Video and the program was broadcast live, scenes from old theatrical films were inserted to allow costume and scene changes. The stars of these old films were called Video Rangers, and the action scenes shown were said to be adventures of other Video Rangers fighting for justice (their code was KRG-L6, and they were said to be seen via Remote Carrier Delayed-Circuit TV screens). On episodes

44

broadcast without commercials, viewers saw a "Video Ranger Message," a public service announcement geared to kids. Fred Scott, who later played Video Ranger Rogers, announced and narrated.

CAR 54, WHERE ARE YOU?

NBC, 9.17.61 to 9.8.63

Principal Cast: Joe E. Ross (*Officer Gunther Toody*), Fred Gwynne (*Officer Francis Muldoon*), Paul Reed (*Captain Martin Block*), Al Lewis (*Officer Leo Schnauser*), Beatrice Pons (*Lucille Toody*), Charlotte Rae (*Sylvia Schnauser*), Nipsey Russell (*Officer Anderson*), Nathaniel Frey (*Officer Sol Abrams*), Hank Garrett (*Officer Ed Nicholson*)

Trivia: New York police officers Gunther Toody and Francis Muldoon are with the 53rd Precinct on Tremont Avenue in the Bronx and ride in patrol car 54. They both belong to the Brotherhood Club, and ever since they were first teamed nine years earlier (on August 16th), it has been clear that only Toody can ride with Muldoon—and vice versa. (Toody talks constantly and his "Oooh, Oooh, Jumpin' Jehosifat" remarks drive other partners batty; Muldoon, who rarely talks, makes other partners uneasy—"It's like riding with a spook.") The 53rd Precinct housekeeper is Mrs. Bortak (not credited), who was paid $1.00 per hour.

Gunther Toody, who has been married fifteen years to Lucille, lives in a five-room, rent-controlled apartment in the Bronx and pays $45 monthly rent. Gunther, whose badge number is 453, was born on August 15th, and is five feet, eight inches tall. Lucille, whose maiden name is Hesselwhite, is a graduate of Hunter College. Toody's parents (never seen) live on East 160th Street, also in the Bronx.

Francis Muldoon, named after his mother's idol, Francis X. Bushman, lives with his mother and his sister, Peggy, at 807 East 175th Street in the Bronx. Francis, whose badge number is 723, was born in July, weighs 183¾ pounds, and is six feet, seven inches tall. He collects stamps and belongs to the Bronx Stamp Club. His father, Patrick Muldoon (not seen) made captain in 1919, when, at age 25, he captured the Baby Face Gordon Gang. Peggy, an aspiring actress, auditioned for a part in a play called *Waiting for Wednesday* (later retitled *Copper's Capers*).

Leo Schnauser, badge number 1062, was born on Friday the 13th and has been on the force for 20 years. He married the former Sylvia Schwarzcock 15 years earlier on August 18th. He has six sisters, yet Leo is considered the pretty one in the family! The suspicious Sylvia believes that every time Leo goes out with the boys he is having a secret affair with Marilyn Monroe.

Relatives: Helen Parker (Muldoon's sister, *Peggy*), Ruth Masters (*Muldoon's mother*), Nancy Donohue (Muldoon's sister, *Cathy*), Paul O'Keefe (Toody's nephew, *Marvin*), George S. Irving (Toody's *Uncle Igor*), Louise Kirtland and Patricia Bright (Martin's wife, *Claire Block*)

Relatives Not Seen: Muldoon's Cousin Kevin, Muldoon's Aunt Martha, Lucille's brother, Julius, Lucille's Aunt Nettie (seen, but not credited), Leo's sister, Felice

Theme: "Car 54, Where Are You?" by John Strauss and Nat Hiken

THE CARA WILLIAMS SHOW

CBS, 9.23.64 to 9.10.65

Principal Cast: Cara Williams (*Cara Wilton*), Frank Aletter (*Frank Bridges*), Paul Reed (*Damon Burkhardt*), Jack Sheldon (*Fletcher Kincaid*)

Trivia: File clerk Cara Wilton and efficiency expert Frank Bridges are secretly married and publicly employed by Fenwick Diversified Industries, Inc. (a.k.a. Fenwick Industries), a Los Angeles company that prohibits employee marriages. Cara, whose license plate number is T1204, lives with Frank in an apartment at 6758 Riverdale Lane (telephone number 736–8876); their neighbor, Fletcher Kincaid, is a jazz musician whose favorite TV shows are "Space Mouse," "Charlie

Chipmunk" and "Mightyman from Mars." Damon Burkhardt, Cara and Frank's no-nonsense boss, is a henpecked pussycat at home with his stern wife, Martha (played by Hermione Baddeley and, later, by Reta Shaw).

The format changed midway through the series to allow married couples to work at the company because Cara approached Mr. Fenwick (Edward Everett Horton) and convinced him that, since Fenwick manufactures baby furniture and accessories, the company should employ members of a group of people who support it with their purchases.

Theme: "Cara's Theme," by Kenyon Hopkins

CASEY JONES

Syndicated, 1957

Principal Cast: Alan Hale Jr. (*Casey Jones*), Mary Lawrence (*Alice Jones*), Bobby Clark (*Casey Jones Jr.*), Eddie Waller (*Red Rock*), Dub Taylor (*Wallie Simms*)

Trivia: "Stop, look, and listen 'cause you're gonna hear a brand new story 'bout a brave engineer . . . Casey Jones, steamin' and a rollin' . . . When you hear the tootin' of the whistle, it's Casey at the throttle of the Cannonball Express." John Luther "Casey" Jones is the engineer of the Cannonball Express, a ten-wheeler 1890s-style steam engine (#382), for the Illinois Central Railroad. (The engine number is also given as #1.) Casey, his wife Alice, and their son Casey Jr., live in the town of Jackson, Tennessee; their dog's name is Cinders. Red Rock is the Cannonball conductor and Wallie Simms, the train's fireman.

CASSIE AND COMPANY

NBC, 1.29.82 to 8.20.82

Originally intended to star Angie Dickinson as a beautiful divorcée struggling to make a new life for herself, the series evolved to relate Angie's exploits as Cassidy "Cassie" Holland, a private detective (owner of Holland Investigations) who uses her expertise as a former police officer and criminologist to solve crimes. Alex Cord played Cassie's ex-husband, Mike Holland (now the District Attorney), and A Martinez portrayed Benny Silva, Cassie's legman and owner of the Silva and Gould Gym. Cassie's license plate number is 1GB 0927. Grover Washington Jr. composed "Cassie's Theme."

THE CAVANAUGHS

CBS, 12.1.86 to 3.9.87
8.8.88 to 10.3.88
6.29.89 to 7.27.89

Principal Cast: Barnard Hughes (*Francis Cavanaugh*), Christine Ebersole (*Katherine "Kit" Cavanaugh*), Peter Michael Goetz (*Charles "Chuck" Cavanaugh*), Mary Tanner (*Mary Margaret Cavanaugh*), John Short (*Father Charles Cavanaugh Jr.*)

Trivia: Francis Cavanaugh, a staunch Irish-Catholic Democrat, owns the Cavanaugh Construction Company in Boston. Widower of Bridget, he is constantly at odds with his brother, James, a Republican he calls "the Weasel." His daughter, Kit, a divorced actress, previously appeared nude in the movie *Wild Women of Malibu*. Mary Margaret, his granddaughter, calls him "Poppi" and attends Our Lady of Perpetual Sorrow High School (as did Kit).

Francis's son (and Mary Margaret's father), Charles, now runs Cavanaugh Construction and is constantly in conflict with his father over how the company should be run. Charles's son, Charles Jr., is a priest (parish name not given). The curse of the Cavanaugh family is that no Cavanaugh lives to see age 72.

Relatives: Art Carney (Francis's brother, *James Cavanaugh*), John Getz (Kit's ex-husband, *Tom Elgin*), James Greene (Francis's *Uncle Shamus*), Scott Curtis and Danny Cooksey (Chuck's son, *John Cavanaugh*), Matt Shakman and Parker Jacobs (Chuck's son, *Kevin Cavanaugh*)

Flashbacks: Matt Shakman (*Francis as a boy* in 1928), Danny Cooksey (*James as a boy* in 1928), Lauren Taylor (*Bridget as a girl* in 1928), Christine Ebersole (*Bridget as a woman*)

Theme: "The Cavanaughs," by Paul Pilger

THE CHAMPIONS

NBC, 5.26.68 to 9.9.68 (10 episodes)
Syndicated, 1968 (20 additional episodes)

Sharron Macready (Alexandra Bastedo), Craig Stirling (Stuart Damon) and Richard Barrett (William Gaunt) are agents for Nemesis, a Geneva, Switzerland-based organization that handles sensitive international assignments. During an assignment to retrieve deadly bacteria specimens from Chinese scientists in Tibet, the plane on which Sharron, Craig and Richard are traveling is hit by gunfire and crashes into the forbidding Himalayas. The lifeless agents are found by a mysterious Old Man (Felix Aylmer) and taken to a lost city inhabited by an unknown race. There, a mysterious light heals the agents and endows them with superhuman powers. Agreeing to keep the secret of the lost world, they vow to use their powers to help mankind. Anthony Nicholls played their sometimes bewildered superior, W. L. Tremayne. Albert Elms composed the theme.

CHARLES IN CHARGE

CBS, 10.30.84 to 7.24.85

Principal Cast: Scott Baio (*Charles*), Julie Cobb (*Jill Pembroke*), James Widdoes (*Stan Pembroke*), April Lerman (*Lila Pembroke*), Jonathan Ward (*Douglas Pembroke*), Michael Pearlman (*Jason Pembroke*), Willie Aames (*Buddy Lembeck*), Jennifer Runyon (*Gwendolyn Pierce*)

Trivia: When Jill and Stan Pembroke, a busy working couple, require help in caring for their three children (Lila, Douglas and Jason), they hire a college student named Charles as their live-in assistant.

The Pembrokes live at 10 Barrington Court in New Brunswick, New Jersey. Charles and his friend Buddy attend Copeland College and their favorite hangout is the Lamplight (a hamburger joint). Their misguided effort to make a million dollars was "Charles Are Us," a franchise to market clones of Charles as live-in-housekeepers. Charles's favorite seafood restaurant is the Grotto and his favorite movie star is Darby Peterson (played by Dawn Merrick). In high school, Charles was in a band called the Charles Tones. He helped Stan's mother, Irene, launch a business called Mama Garabaldi's Pizza. For unknown reasons Charles has no last name; he introduces himself to everyone as Charles. Buddy, whose real name is Buddence, is a Leo and was born in California (Charles was born in Philadelphia). Buddy will only take courses with five or less books to read (any more will cause him to cheat).

Jillian "Jill" Ann Pembroke is the theater critic for the New Jersey *Register*; she is later promoted to art and fashion editor, but turns it down when it means spending too much time away from her family. Her favorite place to eat is Willie Wong's Chinese Palace and when in high school, Jill Gardner (her maiden name) was called "Pixie." Jill's father calls her "Jillybean." Stanley "Stan" Albert Pembroke is one of 49 vice-presidents in an unnamed company.

Lila Beth "is sweet and lovely and dots her *i*'s with little hearts." She first attends Lincoln Elementary School, then Northside High School. Lila reads *Co-ed* magazine and is a member of the Circle of Friendship Club with her friends Enid (Mandy Ingber), Kim (Samantha Smith), Linda (Jade Chin) and Heather (Allison Sturges). Lila is also a member of Stan's company's softball team (not named)—she is so inept that she plays deep, deep roving right field. She calls Buddy "Goon Machine," and longs to wear makeup and high heels.

Jason and Douglas both attend Lincoln Elementary School. Jason is the mischievous one; Douglas, the smart one (the only "F" he ever received was for a book report he did on *TV Guide*, which his teacher didn't consider classic literature). The kids also have a never-seen cat named Putty Cat. (They've had her for three years.)

"When God made Gwendolyn," Buddy says, "He knew He was God." Gwendolyn Pierce, Charles's girlfriend, is a stunning beauty and also attends Copeland College. They broke up midway through the series—and yes, Buddy says, "Charles, you're foolish to let Gwendolyn go." Although Jennifer Runyon's name appears in each show's opening credits, she did not appear in every episode. (See also the following entry.)

Relatives: Dick O'Neill (Jill's father, *Harry Gardner*), Rue McClanahan (Stan's mother, *Irene Pembroke*), Jerry Levine (Stan's nephew, *Elliott*)

Theme: "Charles in Charge," written by Michael Jacobs, Al Burton and David Kurtz

---

CHARLES IN CHARGE

Syndicated, 1.87 to

Principal Cast: Scott Baio (*Charles*), Willie Aames (*Buddy Lembeck*), Sandra Kerns (*Ellen Powell*), Nicole Eggert (*Jamie Powell*), Josie Davis (*Sarah Powell*), Alexander Polinsky (*Adam Powell*), James Callahan (*Walter Powell*), Ellen Travolta (*Lillian*)

Trivia: A revised version of the above show. When Charles returns from a two-week vacation (mountain climbing in Great Gorge), he learns that the Pembrokes have moved to Seattle and sublet their home to the Powell family: Ellen; her children Sarah, Jamie and Adam; and Ellen's father-in-law, Walter. Since Ellen's husband, Robert, is a naval commander stationed in the South Seas, Charles quickly finds employment as their live-in helper.

The Powell address is 10 Barrington Court in New Brunswick, New Jersey. Before Charles, the Powells' live-in helper was Julie Mercer (played by Liz Keifer).

Charles, who still sports no last name, was born in Scranton, Pennsylvania, and majors in education at Copeland College. His mother, Lillian, called him "Doodlebug" when he was a kid and, at age eleven, Charles won a spelling bee on the word "quixotic." In a two-part episode, Charles bumped his head, became Chazz, and married a beautiful bimbo named Tiffany (Denise Miller). Another bump on the head returned him to Charles (the marriage was voided because Chazz used the name Charles Lambergini, which is not his real name). Lillian first owned Sid's Pizza, then the Yesterday Café—both of which were hangouts for Charles and his friends.

Buddy, whose real name is Buddence, attends Copeland College as well (his major is political science although on an aptitude test, the results rated Buddy as a jack-of-no-trades best suited for jury duty). Buddy, who was born in California, had a dog named Kitty and a hand-puppet called Handie as a kid. He now lives in a dorm on campus, where he is banned from performing chemistry assignments and bringing livestock into the room. He also has a pet ant named Arlo who lives in the ant farm in his room. Buddy, who believes he receives mind transmissions from the planet Zargon, also thinks Barbara Mandrell is in love with him (she sent him an autographed picture signed "Love, Barbara"). He once smashed 57 cans of beer against his forehead before passing out ("I could have done more if the cans were empty"). He briefly hosted a radio show called "The Buddy Lembeck Show" on WFNZ but had to give it up when he—and everyone else—realized he was unable to speak over the air. In high school, Buddy was voted the class flake, and he has an "autographed" Mickey Mantle baseball (when he bought the ball, Mickey wasn't around, so Buddy signed it for him). Of all the troublesome puzzles in the world, the one that most bothers Buddy is why the park ranger won't let Yogi Bear have a picnic basket. Kelly Ann Cann played Buddy's often discussed (but seen only twice) girlfriend, Nurse Bennett. If Buddy had three wishes, he'd wish for "X-ray vision, a portable water bed and a date with Connie Chung."

Jamie, the eldest of the Powell children, attends Central High School and yearns to be a model. She starred with her sister, Sarah, in a TV commercial for Banana Cream Shampoo and Hair Lotion. She wears a size five shoe. Jamie, who is becoming a beautiful young woman, is still considered a child by her father, who calls her "Little Scooter." She entered and won the Yesterday Café Beauty Pageant and the Miss New Brunswick Beauty Pageant, sponsored by Jeannie's Boutique. Jamie worked part time as a waitress at Sid's Pizza; in one episode, she joined the Followers of Light, a phoney religious sect.

Middle child Sarah also attends Central High School and longs to be a writer. While Sarah reports for the New Brunswick *Herald*, she also has her first story, "What It Is Like to Be a Teenager," published in *Teen* magazine. Sarah, the sensitive child, has a pet turtle named Ross and a favorite doll named Rebecca. She is a member of the Shakespeare Club at school. If she had three wishes, she'd wish for "world peace, a cleaner environment and an end to world hunger." In the first episode, Sarah mentions that Elizabeth Barrett Browning is her favorite poet; in a later episode, she mentions Emily Dickinson as being her favorite. Sarah, who is taller than Jamie, won the first runner-up title in the Yesterday Café Beauty Pageant.

Adam, the youngest of the Powell children, attends an unnamed grammar school. Walter, who was a Navy career man, belongs to the John Paul Jones Society for retired Navy Men. The mascot of Copeland College is Mr. Hobbs the goat.

In the first episode, Lisa Donovan plays Jill Pembroke, Charles's employer in the first series, in a story that shows her introducing Charles to the Powell family.

Relatives: James O'Sullivan (Ellen's husband, *Robert Powell*), Kay Lenz (Ellen's cousin, *Joan Robinson*), Justin Whalen (Charles's *Cousin Anthony*), John Astin (Charles's *Uncle Joe*, "The Pickle King of Brooklyn"), Mindy Cohn (Buddy's sister, *Bunny Lembeck*), Lewis Arquette (Buddy's father, *Clarence Lembeck*), Ruta Lee (Buddy's gorgeous grandmother, *Gloria*), Dabbs Greer (Walter's Father, *Ben "Buzz" Powell*). Not seen: Buddy's mother, Florence Lembeck.

Theme: "Charles in Charge," by Michael Jacobs, Al Burton and David Kurtz

Note: See also prior title.

CHARLIE AND COMPANY
CBS, 9.18.85 to 1.28.86
Charlie Richmond (Flip Wilson) is an administrative assistant with the Department of Highways in Chicago; Diana, his wife (Gladys Knight), is a schoolteacher at McCormick High School. Charlie's children, Lauren, Charles Jr. and Robert, are played by Fran Robinson, Kristoff St. John and Jaleel White. Della Reese appears as Diana's Aunt Rachel. Gladys Knight sings the theme, "We're Family."

CHARLIE'S ANGELS
ABC, 9.22.76 to 8.19.81
Principal Cast: Kate Jackson (*Sabrina Duncan*), Farrah Fawcett (*Jill Munroe*), Jaclyn Smith (*Kelly Garrett*), Cheryl Ladd (*Kris Munroe*), Shelley Hack (*Tiffany Welles*), Tanya Roberts (*Julie Rogers*), David Doyle (*John Bosley*), John Forsythe (*voice of Charles Townsend*)

Trivia: Private detectives Sabrina Duncan, Jill Munroe and Kelly Garrett are three beautiful ex-Los Angeles Police Department police officers who work for Charles Townsend, the wealthy but never seen (he is only heard through a speaker phone) owner of the Los Angeles-based Townsend Investigations.

Jill's gorgeous sister, Kris Munroe, a San Francisco police officer, becomes an "Angel" when Jill leaves to pursue her race-car career in Europe (where she hopes to become the first woman to win at Le Mans). Boston police officer Tiffany Welles, the stunning daughter of the Lieutenant of Detectives (and a friend of Charlie's), replaces Sabrina when she leaves the agency to marry for a second time and raise a family. When Tiffany leaves the agency to pursue a modeling career in New York, Charlie hires Julie Rogers, a beautiful Los Angeles police officer, to replace her.

Before Kelly and Kris have the opportunity to meet Tiffany, Charlie prepares them to meet the daughter of a friend who graduated with top honors from the police academy. When there is a knock at the office door, a stunning blonde in tight jeans, a clinging T-shirt and an I.Q. about the size of her well-developed chest, enters, shocking the girls—"Tiffany?" The unnamed blonde (Judy Landers) was the agency's linen-service girl; when the real Tiffany appears there is a sigh of relief from Kris and Kelly. (The blonde wore a low-cut v-neck T-shirt that read "Super Star.")

While each of the Angels was desperate to see Charlie and know what he looked like, it was only John Bosley, Charlie's lawyer and representative, whom they actually saw. The agency phone number is 213-555-0267. Although an actual address is not given, the building in which the Townsend Agency is housed has the number 193.

While "Charlie's Angels" is famous for its "jiggle TV" (no bras and "plots that cause the Angels to trot"), the episode of October 20, 1976, "Angels in Chains," is even more famous because of an accidental(?) bit of nudity. While escaping from prison and running through a swamp, Jill (who measures 33½B-23-34) exposed part of her right breast and nipple when she bent over and her mostly unbuttoned blouse opened to reveal more than it should have. Whether this was intentional or not, the episode scored a huge 56 share rating (how did people know in advance?) and a 52 share on the rerun.

Relatives: Michael Bell (Sabrina's ex-husband, *Bill Duncan*)

Theme: "Charlie's Angels," by Jack Elliott and Allyn Ferguson

Note: The episode of April 2, 1980 ("The Male Angel Affair") was a pilot for a proposed but unsold series called "Toni's Boys." Barbara Stanwyck played Antonia "Toni" Blake, who runs a detective agency at 612 Essex Road, and has three male operatives: Bob Sorenson (played by Bob Seagren), Cotton Harper (Stephen Shortridge) and Matt Parrish (Bruce Bauer).

THE CHARMINGS

ABC, 3.20.87 to 4.24.87
8.6.87 to 2.11.88

Principal Cast: Caitlin O'Heaney (*Snow White Charming*, first six episodes), Carol Huston (*Snow White Charming*), Christopher Rich (*Eric Charming*), Judy Parfitt (*Lillian White*), Brandon Call (*Thomas Charming*), Garette Ratliff (*Cory Charming*), Dori Brenner (*Sally Miller*), Paul Eiding (*Don Miller*), Paul Winfield (*Lillian's mirror*)

Trivia: Once upon a time, when the vain Queen Lillian is told by her magic mirror that her stepdaughter, Snow White, is the fairest of all, she casts an evil spell that backfires and puts Snow White, Snow's husband, Eric, and their children, Thomas and Cory, to sleep for 1,000 years. When the series begins, the Charmings have awakened and are attempting to adjust to life in 1987.

The Charmings live at 427 Van Oakland Boulevard in Burbank, California, in a house that resembles a castle. Snow White, whose favorite color is peach, is a fashion designer (company name not mentioned) and Eric, whose horse is named Gendel, is a children's story book writer (his first book was *The Four Billy Goats Gruff*). Lillian, whose maiden name is Lipschitz, suffers from P.M.S. (Post Magic Syndrome) once every 28 years; she has a pet thing (an unknown creature) called Muffin, and a crow named Quo.

Sally and Don Miller, their neighbors, live at 425 Oakland Boulevard. Don owns Don's Carpet Kingdom Store, and he and Eric are members of Don's Carpet Baggers baseball team; his license plate reads CRPT KING. Sally has a dog named Friskie, and Thomas and Cory have a pet lizard named Spike.

Relatives: Jacob Kenner (Sally's son, *Donny*)

Theme: "The Charmings," by Jonathan Wolff

CHEERS

NBC, 9.30.82 to

Principal Cast: Ted Danson (*Sam Malone*), Shelley Long (*Diane Chambers*), Kirstie Alley (*Rebecca Howe*), Rhea Perlman (*Carla Tortelli*), Nicholas Colasanto ("*Coach*" *Ernie Pantusso*), George Wendt (*Norm Peterson*), John Ratzenberger (*Cliff Claven*), Woody Harrelson (*Woody Boyd*), Kelsey Grammer (*Dr. Frasier Crane*)

Trivia: In 1889, a bordello called Mom's was established at 112½ Beacon Street in Boston. In 1895, it became the bar Cheers (beer at that time cost five cents a glass; in 1984, it was a dollar a glass). According to a sign that hangs above the front door, Cheers has a legal capacity of 75 people. The wooden Indian that stands to the right of the front door is named Tecumseh and the restaurant above Cheers is Melville's Fine Sea Food. There is a sign on the wall that reads, "This is a square house. Please report any unfairness to the proprietor." Cheers's competition is Gary's Old Town Tavern.

Sam Malone, the owner, was a relief pitcher for the Boston Red Sox before buying Cheers. His good luck charm is a bottle cap that he found when he was a ball player, and he once did a TV commercial for Fields Beer. He has a moosehead in the bar named Sam and a wood carving of a whale that hangs over his office door. Sam, a ladies' man, sold the bar to a large, unnamed corporation when he became bored with it. He used the money to buy a ketch and sailed around the world. His ketch sank in the Caribbean and he found an uncharted atoll that he named "No Brains Atoll" (for selling the bar). When he found he missed the bar, he returned to learn that the corporation had already replaced him with Rebecca Howe as the bar's new manager. After hearing Sam's pathetic story, she took pity on him and hired him as a bartender.

Diane Chambers, the prim and proper barmaid, is an art student and substitute teacher at Boston University. She is interested in rare first-edition books and has a pet cat named Elizabeth Barrett Browning (after her favorite poet). When Diane enters the 45th Annual Miss Boston Barmaid competition, she wins based on her beauty, perkiness and congeniality. As a kid, Diane was called "Muffin" by her father (because "she is sweet and tasty"); she leaves Cheers after a rocky romance with Sam to pursue a writing career (when her attempt to write a novel failed, she moved to Hollywood to write for TV). Diane used the pen name Jessica Simpson Bordais to help Sam write his memoirs in a book that never materialized. She gets a facial tic when she becomes nervous.

Ernie Pantusso, affectionately called "Coach," was the Boston Red Sox pitching coach and was given the job as bartender by Sam when he retired. His favorite time of the day is 1:37 in the morning (he doesn't know why, he just likes it) and his favorite movie is *Thunder Road* with Robert Mitchum. When he gets angry, he bangs his head on the bar's serving area near the beer dispensers. When Ernie was a coach, he had the nickname "Red" (not because he had red hair, but because he once read a book).

Carla Lozupone Tortelli LeBec is the nasty twice-married waitress who worked in a bar called the Broken Spoke before coming to work for Sam. Carla attended the St. Clete's School for Wayward Girls and her phone number is 555-7834. At age 16, Carla danced on the TV show "The Boston Boppers," and from her wealthy grandfather, Tony Lozupone, she inherited his lucky quarter. Carla, who calls Diane "Fish Face," was called "Muffin" by her brothers (who stuffed her ears with yeast and tried to bake her face). Carla has eight children: five by her first husband, Nick Tortelli, one (Ludlow) by Dr. Bennett Ludlow and two (twins) by her second husband, Eddie LeBec.

Rebecca Howe became the manager of Cheers in 1987 when the corporation that purchased the bar made her its manager. Gorgeous and always fashionably dressed, she is easily exasperated and often wonders why she took the job. She is part of that major (unnamed) corporation and her computer password is

51

"Sweet Baby." When she first took over the bar, Rebecca hung a picture of her favorite actor, Robert Urich, on the wall; "Spenser: For Hire" was her favorite TV show.

Cliff Claven, a bar regular, is a mailman with the South Central Branch and a member of the Knights of the Scimitar Lodge. He originally had the Meadow View Acres route near the airport, is an amateur inventor and has created such things as attack submarines and the "beetabaga" (a cross between a rutabaga and a beet). His worst fear is the day the Sears catalogue comes out (it puts an extra strain on him).

Norm Peterson, a bar regular, was originally an accountant for H. W. Sawyer and Associates, a real estate salesman, and a house painter/decorator with his own company: K&P Painting, Inc. (Originally called AAAA Painting). In high school, Norm was nicknamed "Moonglow," and his favorite eatery is the Hungry Heifer. His never-seen wife is named Vera.

Woodrow "Woody" Boyd, a hopeful actor whose middle name is Tiberius, was born and raised in Hanover, Indiana, and now assists Sam in tending bar. He attended Hanover High School and his rich girlfriend, Kelly Susan Gaines (Jackie Swanson), has over a thousand Barbie dolls in her collection.

Relatives: George Bell (Sam's brother, *Derek Malone*), Glynis Johns (Diane's mother, *Helen Chambers*), Marcia Cross (Rebecca's sister, *Susan Howe*), Allyce Beasley (Coach's daughter, *Lisa Pantusso*), Cady McClain (Coach's niece, *Joyce*), Dick O'Neill (Cliff's father, *Cliff Claven Sr.*), Frances Sternhagen (Cliff's mother, *Esther Claven*), Bebe Neuwirth (Frasier's wife, *Dr. Lilith Sternin*, whom he calls "Peanut Butter Cup," among other endearments), Nancy Marchand (Frasier's mother, *Hester Crane*)

Relatives of Carla: Dan Hedaya (her exhusband, *Nick Tortelli*), Jay Thomas (her husband, *Eddie LeBec*) Rhea Perlman (her sister, *Annette Lozupone*), Mandy Ingber (her daughter-in-law, *Annie Tortelli*), Timothy Williams (her son, *Anthony Tor-*

telli), Jarrett Lennon (her son, *Ludlow*), Jean Kasem (Nick's new wife, *Loretta Tortelli*), Anne DeSalvo (Eddie's other wife, *Gloria LeBec*; he was married to Carla and Gloria at the same time)

Theme: "Where Everybody Knows Your Name," vocal by Gary Portnoy

Note: See also "The Tortellis," the spinoff series

CHICKEN SOUP
ABC, 9.12.89 to 11.7.89

The romance between Jackie Fisher (Jackie Mason), a 52-year-old, single Jewish man, and Maddie Peerce (Lynn Redgrave), a widowed Catholic woman with three children: Molly (Allison Porter), Patty (Kathryn Erbe) and Donny (Johnny Pinto). Jackie, who worked as a pajama salesman for Sleep Soft, Inc., quit his job after 22 years to experience life and love; Maddie, who lives next door to Jackie, is the supervisor of the Henry Street Settlement House in New York City. While exact addresses are not given, Jackie lives in house number 3266 and Maddie in number 3268.

Rita Karin plays Jackie's mother, Bea Fisher, and Brandon Maggart plays Maddie's brother, Mike. Gordon Lust composed the theme song.

CHINA BEACH
ABC, 4.26.88 to

Principal Cast: Dana Delany (*Lieutenant Colleen McMurphy*), Marg Helgenberger (*Karen "K. C." Colosky*), Nan Woods (*Nurse Cherry White*), Chloe Webb (*Laurette Barber*), Megan Gallagher (*Wayloo Marie Holmes*), Jeff Kober (*Evan "Dodger" Winslow*), Robert Picardo (*Dr. Dick Richard*), Concetta Tomei (*Major Lila Garreau*), Ricki Lake (*Holly Robinson*)

Trivia: A gruelling, sometimes difficult to watch perspective of the Vietnam War, as seen through the eyes of Nurse Colleen McMurphy. The title refers to the U.S. Armed Forces R&R facility in Da Nang, Republic of Vietnam. The medical personnel are attached to the 510th Evac Hospital, 63rd Division. The unit has 180 hospital beds and 33 surgical units, but can't handle critical neurological surgery.

Colleen McMurphy: In 1966, Colleen was a nurse who was inspired by J.F.K to believe that she can make a difference. She joined the Army, trained in Houston, and volunteered for service in Vietnam. Colleen, a triage nurse, mentions her bra size to be 34C, has the serial number N91574, and represents the 50,000 women who served in Nam. Her hometown is Lawrence, Kansas. When Colleen first arrived at the base, she was called an "F.N.G." (Fairly New Guy).

K. C.: The only civilian on the base, she is a prostitute who charges $100 an hour for her services. K. C., whose real name is Karen Colosky, has Type O blood and calls herself K.C. after her hometown of Kansas City. As a kid, Karen loved the rain—it made her feel safe (she would snuggle under the bed covers and gain a sense of safety). On China Beach, the rains provide Karen with the only sense of safety and security she can feel amid the devastation that surrounds her. Although K. C.'s real name was mentioned several times in one episode, she says her real name was Charlene in another episode.

Wayloo Marie Holmes: The U.S. Air Force TV reporter who covered the misery of China Beach; she leaves to become a reporter for ABC-TV in New York.

Laurette Barber: The sweet U.S.O. entertainer who becomes an active participant in helping the wounded was an orphan raised at the Lady of Perpetual Hope Orphanage. She left the series when the tour show moved on to another base.

Cherry White: An A.R.C. (American Red Cross) nurse who volunteered for duty in Vietnam. Cherry is killed during an enemy shelling in one of the series' most emotional episodes.

Major Lila Garreau: The hospital commander, whose life is the Army, is nicknamed "Scooter," and most often finds herself pushing herself and her nurses far beyond the call of duty.

Other Characters: Dodger, the seldom talking, tough-on-the-outside, but sensitive-on-the-inside combat soldier; Nurse Holly Pelligrino; Dr. Dick Richard.

In the first "Miss China Beach" contest (9.27.89 in the episode "Skin Deep"), Colleen was "Miss Triage," Lila was "Miss Combat Boots" and Holly was "Miss Kool-Aid Kid."

Relatives: Penny Fuller (Colleen's mother, *Margaret McMurphy*), Donald Moffat (Colleen's father, *Brian McMurphy*), John Laughlin (Colleen's brother, *Brenden McMurphy*), Harold Russell (Colleen's *Uncle Conal*), Kevin McCarthy (Wayloo's father, *Congressman Holmes*), Penelope Windust (Dodger's mother, *Jean Winslow*), Tom Bower (Dodger's father, *Archie Winslow*), Arlene Taylor (Dodger's sister, *Annie Winslow*), Frederic Lehne (Cherry's brother, *Rick White*)

Theme: "Reflections," by the Supremes

CIRCUS BOY

NBC, 9.23.56 to 9.8.57
ABC, 9.19.57 to 9.11.58

Big Tim Champion (Robert Lowery), the owner of the traveling one ring Champion Circus, is also the guardian of Corky (Mickey Braddock), a young boy whose parents, the Flying Falcons, were killed in a tragic high-wire accident. Corky is waterboy to Bimbo, the elephant; Alexander Philip Perkins (Noah Beery Jr.) works as Joey the Clown. (Today Mickey Braddock is known as Mickey Dolenz, of "The Monkees" fame.)

THE CISCO KID

Syndicated, 1950 to 1956

A TV adaptation of the radio series (and O. Henry stories) about the Cisco Kid (Duncan Renaldo), who was the Robin Hood of the Old West, and his partner, Pancho (Leo Carrillo), as they fight injustice. Cisco's horse is named Diablo and Pancho's horse, Loco. Albert Glasser composed the theme.

Note: "The Cisco Kid" was the first TV series to be filmed in color.

COACH

ABC, 2.28.89 to

Events in the life of Hayden Fox (Craig T. Nelson), coach for Minnesota State University's Screaming Eagles football team. His girlfriend, Christine Armstrong (Shelley Fabares), is a sportscaster for KCCY-TV, Channel 6. She and Hayden dine most often at the Touchdown Club. Hayden's assistant, Coach Luther Van Dam (Jerry Van Dyke), has a pet parrot named Sunshine, whom he feeds Acme Bird Seeds. (Luther, now 52, received the parrot from his father when he was 10 years old.)

Hayden's daughter, Kelly (Clare Carey), is a student at the college and marries fellow classmate Stuart Rosebrock (Kris Kamm). Pam Stone plays Hayden's nemesis, Coach Judy Watkins, and Michael "Dauber" Dybinski (Bill Fagerbakke) is the team's star player (and is in love with Judy). Hayden nicknamed Michael "Dauber" after the Dauber Wasp, because Michael's moves on the field remind Hayden of a wasp.

Relatives: Lenore Kasdorf (Hayden's ex-wife, *Beth*), James Staley (Stuart's father, *Wilson Rosebrock*), Charlotte Stewart (Stuart's mother, *Peg Rosebrock*), Nancy Marchand (Judy's mother, *Marlene Watkins*), John McMartin (Judy's father, *Judge R. J. Watkins*). Judy's parents live in her hometown of Atlanta. Marlene has a pampered poodle named Pepper. John Morris composed "The Coach Theme."

CODE RED

ABC, 11.1.81 to 3.28.82

The work of the Los Angeles Fire Department (L.A.F.D.) as depicted through the experiences of Joe Rorchek (Lorne Greene), captain of Battalion #6, Station #1; his son, Ted (Andrew Stevens), a fireman (his code is "Charlie 10"); his younger son, Chris (Sam J. Jones), a fireman who pilots Fire Chopper #5 (I.D. Number: N405A6); and his young adopted son, Danny Blake (Adam Rich), a Junior Fire Explorer.

Martina Deignan portrays Haley Green, the city's first female firefighter; and Julie Adams plays Joe's wife, Ann. Joe's home phone number is 555-2364. Danny's dog is named Sophie. Morton Stevens composed the theme, "Code Red." In the TV movie pilot (9.20.81), Joe is an arson investigator with Task Force 5, Station #49 of the L.A.F.D.

Note: 1954 saw the first series about the L.A.F.D., called "Alarm" with Richard Arlen as the fire captain. In 1974, James Drury played Spike Ryerson, captain of Engine Company #23 on "Firehouse," the second series to depict the exploits of the L.A.F.D.

COLONEL MARCH OF SCOTLAND YARD

Syndicated, 1957

Colonel Perceval Clovis Adelbart March (Boris Karloff) is a British police inspector who heads Department D-3 (the Office of Queens Complaints) of the New Scotland Yard. The intrepid Colonel March, who wears a black patch over his left eye, uses deductive reasoning to solve complex crimes. Philip Green composed the theme.

COLUMBO

NBC, 9.15.71 to 9.1.78
ABC, 2.6.89 to 5.14.90

The underpaid and untidy (rumpled raincoat) Lieutenant Philip Columbo (Peter Falk) is attached to the Central Division of the Los Angeles Police Department. Columbo, whose badge number is 436 and whose car license plate number is 448 DBZ, likes his coffee hot, strong and black—"No decaf for me." His never-seen wife is named Kate (she wears Maidenform brand panties) and his dogs are Fang (on NBC) and Dog (on ABC)—both basset hounds. The character Columbo was first played by Bert Freed on the "Enough Rope" episode of "The Chevy Mystery Show" on July 31, 1960. (See also "Mrs. Columbo.")

COMING OF AGE

CBS, 3.15.88 to 3.29.88
10.24.88 to 11.21.88
6.29.89 to 7.27.89

Principal Cast: Alan Young (*Dr. Ed Pepper*), Glynis Johns (*Trudie Pepper*), Paul Dooley (*Dick Hale*), Phyllis Newman (*Ginny Hale*), Ruta Lee (*Pauline Spencer*)

Trivia: This is the story of two couples who live at the Dunes Retirement Resort in Arizona: Dr. Ed Pepper, a retired chiropractor and his wife, Trudie; and retired airline pilot Dick Hale and his wife, Ginny. Ed and Trudie live in Condo 7-C, Dick and Ginny, in Condo 9-C. Ed is president of the Duffer's Club, the Lapidary Club and the Floating Tanner's Club; and Dick heads the Resident's Association. Trudie and Ginny are members of the Theater Club; because of limited backdrops at the Dunes (owned by the Walnut Corporation), only the plays *Oklahoma* and *Paint Your Wagon* can be staged. The beautiful and seductive neighbor, Pauline, is nicknamed "the Black Widow" for her knack of marrying and losing husbands.

Relatives: Nada Despotovich (Dick's married daughter, *Cindy Krainik*), Jim Doughan (Cindy's husband, *Tom Krainik*), Taylor Fry (Cindy's daughter, *Nancy Krainik*), Jarrett Lennon (Cindy's son, *Scott Krainik*), Van Johnson (Ed's brother, *Red Pepper*)

Theme: "Coming of Age," performed by Doc Severinson and His Orchestra

---

CONVOY

NBC, 9.17.65 to 12.10.65

Commander Dan Talbot (John Gavin) is captain of the World War II *Escort Destroyer DD181*; Captain Ben Foster (John Larch) is head of the freighter *Flagship*—both of which are part of a convoy of 200 heavily-armed American ships assigned to the European theater. Bernard Herrmann composed the theme.

THE CORNER BAR

ABC, 6.21.72 to 8.23.72
8.3.73 to 9.7.73

A pre-"Cheers" series about life at a bar. In 1972, Harry Grant (Gabriel Dell) owns a bar called Grant's Toomb, located at 137 Amsterdam Avenue in New York City. (The spelling of Toomb was left as is after a stagehand, preparing the sign for the show, misspelled Tomb.) Mary Ann (Langhorne Scruggs) and Meyer Shapiro (Shimen Ruskin) are the bar's waiters; Wall Street executive Phil Bracken (Bill Fiore), male fashion designer Peter Panama (Vincent Schiavelli) and cab driver Fred Costello (J. J. Barry) are the bar regulars.

In the 1973 version, the bar name was changed to the Corner Bar and Anne Meara (as Mae) and Eugene Roche (as Frank Flynn) were the new owners; the address remained the same. Mae Questel appeared in one episode as Mae's Aunt Blanche. Norman Paris composed the theme.

THE COSBY SHOW

NBC, 9.20.84 to

Principal Cast: Bill Cosby (*Cliff Huxtable*), Phylicia Rashad (*Clair Huxtable*), Lisa Bonet (*Denise Huxtable*), Sabrina LeBeauf (*Sondra Huxtable*), Malcolm-Jamal Warner (*Theo Huxtable*), Tempestt Bledsoe (*Vanessa Huxtable*), Keshia Knight Pulliam (*Rudy Huxtable*), Geoffrey Owens (*Elvin Thibodeaux*), Joseph C. Phillips (*Lieutenant Martin Kendall*), Raven Symone (*Olivia Kendall*)

Trivia: Ten Stigwood Avenue in Brooklyn, New York, is the residence of the Huxtable family: parents Cliff and Clair, and their children Sondra, Denise, Theo, Vanessa and Rudy.

Cliff, whose real name is Heathcliff, a graduate of Hillman College in Georgia, is an obstetrician and a jazz fan who calls himself "Mr. Jazz." In college (where Cliff met and fell in love with Clair Hanks), Cliff called Clair "Lum Lum" and Clair called Cliff "Baby Cakes." Cliff, whose favorite western movie is *Six Guns for Glory*, starring Colt Kirby, accidentally sat on (and killed) his pet bird, Charlie, when he was a kid. Cliff's office is in his home; he also works at Corinthian Hospital in Brooklyn.

Clair, who is a lawyer with the firm of Greentree, Bradley and Dexter, was also a panelist on the TV show "Retrospective," a program on channel 37 that explores history. When Clair graduated from law school, she and Cliff celebrated by having dinner at Michael & Ennio's Restaurant.

Sondra, the eldest child, attended Princeton University and was the first of the Huxtable kids to marry. She and her husband, Elvin, run a sporting goods business called the Wilderness Store; they are also the parents of twins Winnie and Nelson. Elvin calls Sondra "Muffin" and in 1990, Sondra decided on a career as a lawyer and enrolled in a law school (not named).

Denise, the second-born and most troublesome child, attended Central High School and three semesters at Hillman College (where she received five D's, one C and seven incompletes). With no interest in college, she quit (much to her parents' regret), and returned home to hold jobs at the Wilderness Store and Blue Wave Records (where she made $25 a week as the assistant to the executive assistant). She later went to Africa for one year as a photographer's assistant (written out of the show) and returned one year later (back as a regular) married to a Navy lieutenant (Martin Kendall) and the stepmother of his young daughter, Olivia. In the episode of April 26, 1990, Denise, who has a dream of teaching disabled children, enrolled in the Medgar Evers College of the City University of New York and began taking education courses.

Theo (Theodore Aloysius), the only son, attended Central High School and later N.Y.U. He lives in Manhattan in Apartment 10-B of an unidentified building. In high school, Theo was called "Monster Man Huxtable" as a member of the wrestling team. Vanessa attends Central High School, and is a fan of old movies. Rudy, the youngest, attends grammar school (not named) and has a stuffed teddy bear named Bobo.

Relatives: Earle Hyman (Cliff's father, *Russell Huxtable*), Clarice Taylor (Cliff's mother, *Anna Huxtable*), Joe Williams (Clair's father, *Al Hanks*), Ethel Ayler (Clair's mother, *Ethel Hanks*), Yvette Erwin (Clair's sister, *Sara*), Marcella Lowery (Elvin's mother, *Francine Thibodeaux*), Donovan and Darrian Bryant (Sondra's son, *Nelson*), Jalese and Jenelle Grays (Sondra's daughter, *Winnie*), Nancy Wilson (Martin's mother, *Lorraine Kendall*), Moses Gunn (Martin's father, *Joel Kendall*)

Theme: "The Cosby Show Theme," written by Bill Cosby and Stu Gardner

THE DANNY THOMAS SHOW

see MAKE ROOM FOR DADDY

DARK SHADOWS

ABC, 6.27.66 to 4.2.71

Due to the complexity of this series, which includes a very large cast, information has been limited principally to the first few months of the series—episodes that are not syndicated and have not been seen since their original broadcast. (These concern the Collins family before the arrival of Barnabas Collins.)

Principal Cast: Alexandra Moltke (*Victoria Winters*), Joan Bennett (*Elizabeth Collins Stoddard*), Nancy Barrett (*Carolyn Stoddard*), Louis Edmonds (*Roger Collins*), Kathryn Leigh Scott (*Maggie Evans*), David Henesy (*David Collins*), David Ford (*Sam Evans*), John Karlen (*Willie Loomis*), Mitchell Ryan (*Burke Devlin*), Thayer David (*Matthew Morgan*), Diana Millay (*Laura Collins*), Jonathan Frid (*Barnabas Collins*)

Trivia: "My name is Victoria Winters. My journey is beginning—a journey that I hope will open the doors of life and link my past with my future. A journey that will bring me to a dark place—to the edge of the sea high atop Widow's Hill; and a house called Collinwood. A world I've never known with people I've never met. People who, tonight, are still only shadows in my mind but who will soon fill the days and nights of my tomorrows . . . "

As she rides a train from New York to Maine, Victoria Winters speaks these words in the very first episode of "Dark Shadows." Abandoned as a young girl, Victoria Winters grew up in a foundling home in New York City. Now, for the first time in her life, she feels she will find the answers to her unknown past at Collinwood, where she has been hired by Roger Collins to tutor his troublesome nine-year-old son, David.

Arriving in Collinsport, a small fishing village in Maine, Victoria first meets Burke Devlin, a man with a score to settle, who warns her to turn around and go back to New York. At the Collinsport Inn, Victoria meets Maggie Evans, the waitress, who also warns her of impending danger at Collinwood.

Ignoring their warnings, she arrives at the forbidding Great House on the Collinwood estate. There, she meets Elizabeth Collins Stoddard, the mistress of Collinwood, who has not left the estate in 18 years—not since the mysterious disappearance of her husband, Paul Stoddard; Carolyn Stoddard, Elizabeth's rebellious 18-year-old daughter; Roger Collins, Elizabeth's brother; and Roger's son, David.

While her first meeting with the family appears normal, it is on that first night at Collinwood that the terrifying secrets of the Collins family begin to "fill the days and nights" of Victoria's tomorrows. As she prepares for bed, Victoria is disturbed when she hears the mysterious sound of a woman crying. Investigating, she traces the cries to behind a door on the main floor. Mystified as to why no one else can apparently hear the cries, she turns the knob and finds the door to be locked. The crying stops—but her involvement in the lives of the Collinses has only just begun.

To summarize the series prior to the arrival of Barnabas Collins: With the help of Sam Evans (Maggie's father, a painter), Burke Devlin proves that Roger

framed him for a hit and run murder that sent Burke to prison for five years. The crying woman is Elizabeth, repenting each night for what she thinks was her murder of her husband Paul (Joel Fabiani). As it turns out, Paul and his unscrupulous friend, Jason McGuire (Dennis Patrick), led Elizabeth to believe she had killed him after an argument (she did hit him, but only knocked him unconscious). Convincing Elizabeth that she killed Paul, Jason "buried" him beneath the cellar floor and promised to keep the incident a secret. Elizabeth, repenting, vowed never to leave the estate again.

The return of Roger's wife and David's mother, Laura Collins, forces Victoria into a life-and-death battle to save David from Laura—an immortal phoenix who is reborn from fiery ashes every 100 years.

In another terrifying adventure, Victoria is kidnapped and held captive in the Old House by Matthew Morgan, the estate caretaker, when Victoria learns that he killed Bill Malloy, the head of the local fishing fleet. Victoria is helped—and saved—by the ghost of Josette Collins, a friendly spirit who haunts the Old House. (Josette killed herself over 100 years ago by jumping from Widow's Hill, an ominous cliff overlooking the sea. When Josette appears, her portrait glows and one can smell her perfume, Jasmine, in the air.)

The series, as it is known today, begins when Willie Loomis, the drifter friend of Jason McGuire, arrives in Collinsport. Becoming intrigued by the legend of the Collins jewels, especially those worn by an ancestor named Barnabas Collins in a portrait that hangs in the foyer, Willie formalizes a plan to rob the Collins crypt at Eagle Hill Cemetery. There, he finds the coffin of Barnabas Collins—hidden behind a wall and bound by heavy chains. Upon breaking the chains and opening the coffin, he restores to life Barnabas Collins, a 175-year-old vampire.

After convincing Elizabeth that he is their distant cousin from England, Barnabas is allowed to stay at the Old House on the estate—and thus begin Barnabas's supernatural adventures in the 1960s and the first TV soap opera to feature horror as its theme.

Over the course of 1,000 episodes, many characters and situations developed.

The first continuing storyline involving Barnabas dealt with his attempts to recreate the image of Josette DuPres—his love from the 19th century—through Maggie Evans. When Barnabas first sees Maggie, he is taken aback by her uncanny resemblance to Josette, who died shortly after their marriage over 100 years ago. It is when Maggie is bitten by Barnabas that the rumors of a vampire begin to spread. Later, when Maggie's body is found in Eagle Hill Cemetery and she is thought to be dead, Barnabas finally gains control over her. For the next several months viewers were held in suspense as Barnabas tried (but failed) to accomplish his goal.

Additional characters of note: The evil witch, *Angelique* (Lara Parker); *Julia Hoffman* (Grayson Hall), the doctor who attempts to cure Barnabas of his vampirism; *Joe Haskell* (Joel Crothers), Maggie's boyfriend; *Peter Bradford* (Roger Davis), Victoria's love interest when she is transported to the past; *Adam* (Robert Rodan), the Frankenstein-like man created by Julia; *Reverend Trask* (Jerry Lacy), the man out to destroy Angelique; *Quentin Collins* (David Selby), a family relation from the past; and *Sarah Collins* (Sharon Smyth), the spirit of a nine-year-old girl, who befriends David.

In 1968, Alexandra Moltke left the series. Betsy Durkin and later Carolyn Groves replaced her as Victoria Winters.

Theme: "Dark Shadows," by Robert Cobert

Note: On August 30, 1969, ABC presented the unsold pilot "In the Dead of Night" with "Dark Shadows" producer Dan Curtis at the helm. The story focused on Jonathan Fletcher (Kerwin Matthews), a ghost hunter who attempts to exorcise the spirits from the estate of Angela Marten (Marj Dusay). With a music score almost identical to that of "Dark Shadows" and borrowing "Shadows" regulars Louis Edmonds and Thayer David, it would have

become a prime-time "Dark Shadows," had it sold.

Also in 1969, the syndicated "Dark Shadows" rip-off "Strange Paradise" appeared. It, too, used horror for its stories and followed Jean-Paul Desmond (Colin Fox) as he attempts to restore to life his dead wife, Erica (Tudi Wiggins).

On July 31, 1981, CBS presented still another "Dark Shadows" rip-off called "Castle Rock." In it, Cyndi Girling played Celena McKenna, an Irish girl who becomes the governess of 10-year-old Annabell Stratton (Tangie Beaudin) on a mysterious farm called Castle Rock. Her involvement in the supernatural activities of the Stratton family was the focal point of the unsold pilot.

In 1990, Dan Curtis produced a two-hour pilot film called *Dark Shadows* that revolves around the supernatural existence of the Collins family: Jean Simmons (as Elizabeth Collins Stoddard), Ben Cross (Barnabas Collins), Roy Thinnes (Roger Collins), Joanna Going (Victoria Winters), Barbara Blackburn (Carolyn Stoddard) and Joe Gordon (David Collins).

DAVY CROCKETT

ABC, 12.15.54; 1.26.55; 2.23.55; 11.16.55; 12.14.55

The series relates incidents in the lives of Davy Crockett (Fess Parker) and his friend Georgie Russell (Buddy Ebsen), pioneers of the 1830s. Helen Stanley appears as Davy's wife, Polly, and Eugene Brindle and Ray Whitehead as his sons, Billy and Johnny. Davy's Nemesis, Mike Fink, "King of the River," is played by Jeff York.

Davy's horse is named Sophie, his rifle, Betsy, and his boat, the *Bertha Marie* (Mike's boat is the *Gully Wumper*). The five episodes aired as part of the "Disneyland Frontierland" series.

A new version of "Davy Crockett" appeared on NBC (11.20.88 to 6.18.89) as part of "The Magical World of Disney." Johnny Cash appears in the first episode as the elder Davy Crockett; Tim Dunigan plays Davy 25 years younger for the series and Gary Grubbs, his friend Georgie Russell.

DEAR JOHN

NBC, 10.6.88 to

John Lacey (Judd Hirsch), Kate McCarron (Isabella Hoffman), Mary Beth (Susan Walters), Kirk Morris (Jere Burns), Louise Mercer (Jane Carr) and Ralph (Harry Groener) are members of the One-on-One Club, a singles group for lonely, divorced and separated people. The club holds its meetings on Friday nights at the Rego Park Community Center in New York City and its members frequent Clancy's Bar after each session. John, who is divorced, is a teacher and was nicknamed "Moochie" as a kid. As a child, Kate had a dog named Skipper. Louise lives in Apartment 5G (address not given).

Relatives: Carlene Watkins (John's ex-wife, *Wendy*), Ben Savage (John's son, *Matthew Lacey*), Stephen Elliott (John's father, *Phil Lacey*), Elizabeth Franz (John's Aunt Emma), Wendy Schaal (Kate's sister, *Lisa*), Judd Trichter (Kate's nephew, *Danny*), Pat Crawford Brown (*Kirk's mother*), Jenny Agutter (Louise's sister, *Sarah*), Lila Kaye (Louise's mother, *Audrey Mercer*), Clive Revill (Louise's father, *Nigel Mercer*).

Theme: "Dear John," vocal by Wendy Talbot

THE DEBBIE REYNOLDS SHOW

NBC, 9.16.69 to 9.8.70

Homemaker Debbie Thompson (Debbie Reynolds), who yearns to be a newspaper feature writer, lives at 804 Devon Lane with her husband, Jim (Don Chastain), a sportswriter for the Los Angeles *Sun*. Debbie's married sister, Charlotte (Patricia Smith), and Charlotte's husband, Bob Landers (Tom Bosley), an accountant, live next door at 802 Devon Lane. While Debbie pursues her dream, Jim wants her to remain "a loving and beautiful housewife devoting herself to making her lord and master happy." Debbie

Reynolds sang the theme, "With a Little Love."

DECOY

Syndicated, 1957 to 1958

Patricia "Casey" Jones (Beverly Garland) works as a policewoman with the 16th Precinct of the N.Y.P.D. Casey, whose badge number is 300, earns $75 a week, and appears both as a uniformed officer and an undercover cop. She lives in an apartment at 110 Hope Street, and her phone number is Murray Hill 3-4643. The series is based on actual files and is a tribute to the Bureau of Policewomen of the City of New York. Vladimir Selinsky composed the theme.

DENNIS THE MENACE

CBS, 10.4.59 to 9.22.63

Principal Cast: Herbert Anderson (*Henry Mitchell*), Gloria Henry (*Alice Mitchell*), Jay North (*Dennis Mitchell*), Joseph Kearns (*George Wilson*), Sylvia Field (*Martha Wilson*), Gale Gordon (*John Wilson*), Sara Seeger (*Eloise Wilson*), Billy Booth (*Tommy Anderson*), Jeannie Russell (*Margaret Moore*)

Trivia: The mischievous young Dennis Mitchell and his parents, Henry and Alice, live at 627 Elm Street in the town of Hilldale. Henry is an engineer for Trask Engineering, and Alice, the typical American homemaker, has the maiden name of Perkins.

George Wilson, their neighbor, is married to Martha, and has a dog named Freemont. He is constantly plagued by Dennis's antics. George, whose hobbies include bird watching and coin collecting, is a member of the Lookout Mountain Bird Sanctuary and the National Bird Watchers Society. His brother, John Wilson, is a writer for the *National Journal*.

"That dumb old girl" Margaret, who has a rag doll named Pamela and a baby doll named Gwendolyn, is Dennis's nightmare—the school chum who has a crush on him and just won't leave him alone.

The series was based on the comic strip by Hank Ketchum.

Other Roles: Charles Lane (as Lawrence Finch, the 60-year-old owner of Finch's Drug Store); Mary Wickes (Esther Cathcart, the woman looking for a husband); Will Wright (Mr. Merivale, the owner of the Merivale Florist Shop); and Willard Waterman (Mr. Quigley, the owner of Quigley's Supermarket).

Relatives: Nancy Evans (George's sister, *June Wilson*), Edward Everett Horton (George's uncle, *Ned Matthews*), Elinor Donahue (George's niece, *Georgianna Ballinger*), Kathleen Mulqueen (*Henry's mother*), James Bell (Alice's father, *"Grandpa" Perkins*), Verna Felton (John's *Aunt Emma*). Mentioned but not seen are Henry's older brother Bud, and Henry's distant relative, Phil Tyler, who "owns a farm upstate."

Theme: "Dennis the Menace," written by Irving Friedman

Note: An animated "Dennis the Menace" series appeared via syndication in 1986 with the voices of Brennan Thicke (Dennis), Brian George (Henry), Louise Vallance (Alice), and Phil Hartman (George).

A two-hour TV movie called *Dennis the Menace* (syndicated 9.87) featured Victor DiMattia (Dennis), Jim Jansen (Henry), Patricia Estrin (Alice), William Windom (George) and Patsy Garrett (Martha). The movie also featured Dennis's dog, Ruff (played by O.J.).

DEPARTMENT S
Syndicated, 1971

Jason King (Peter Wyngarde), Annabelle Hurst (Rosemary Nicols) and Stewart Sullivan (Joel Fabiani) are investigators for Department S, a special investigative branch of the International Police Force (Interpol) based in Paris.

Jason is the successful writer of Mark Cain mystery novels (like *Two Plus One Equals Murder*), and drives a car with the license plate BE2083E. He attempts to solve each case as if it were one of the plots in his books; he also acquires story ideas from his cases.

Annabelle, a pretty, scientific-minded young woman, drives a white car with the license plate 874Y3L. She possesses the uncanny ability to spot a phony American $20 bill simply by its color, and can unravel the most complex of codes.

Stewart, the American member of the British team, provides muscle when needed, and drives a car with the license plate YYM 297. Their superior, Sir Curtis Sereste (Dennis Alaba Peters) has a chauffeur-driven limo with the license plate 6939PE.

A not-widely-seen spinoff series, "Jason King," appeared in 1972 with Peter Wyngarde solving crimes on his own as Jason King. Edwin Astley composed the theme.

DESIGNING WOMEN
CBS, 9.29.86 to

Principal Cast: Dixie Carter (*Julia Sugarbaker*), Delta Burke (*Suzanne Sugarbaker*), Annie Potts (*Mary Jo Shively*), Jean Smart (*Charlene Winston*), Meshach Taylor (*Anthony Bouvier*)

Trivia: Sisters Julia and Suzanne Sugarbaker own Sugarbakers, a decorating firm at 1521 Sycamore Street in Atlanta, Georgia. They are assisted by Mary Jo Shively, Charlene Winston and Anthony Bouvier. The company's phone number is given as both 404-555-8600 and 404-555-6787.

In describing Julia and Suzanne, Mary Jo states simply, "Julia got the brains and Suzanne got the boobs"—the sisters are as different as night and day.

Julia, fashion-conscious, well read, outspoken and totally devoted to women's equality, attended Chapel High School, then Southern State University in Georgia. She wears a size-seven shoe and speaks her mind on anything that offends her.

Suzanne, on the other hand, is not as intellectual as Julia. She attended the same schools, exercises with a baton to the tune of "St. Louis Blues," is extremely feminine and flaunts her sexuality (despite Julia's objections). Crowned Miss Georgia of 1975, Suzanne wears a size-six-and-a-half shoe, has a pet pig named

Noel, and a never-seen "maid to end all maids" named Consuela. Like Julia, she is fashion-conscious—but unlike Julia, Suzanne will show cleavage to get what she wants. (Suzanne's ex-husband, Dash Goff, wrote the book *Being Belled*.)

Charlene was born in Little Rock, Arkansas, and worked with the state department there before moving to Atlanta and joining Sugarbakers. She admires Julia and mentions in one episode that Julia is her heroine. She always seems to be in the middle in disputes between Julia and Suzanne; she most frequently sides with Julia. She wears a size-eight shoe. Charlene met and fell in love with Bill Stillfield at the rooftop garden of the Dunwoodie Hotel. At Charlene's wedding in 1989, the song "Ave Maria" was sung, and in a dream in the episode, "The First Day of the Last Decade of the Entire 20th Century," Charlene's "Guardian Movie Star," Dolly Parton, appeared to her to help her through the birth of her daughter, Olivia.

Mary Jo, the youngest of the women, is divorced (as are Julia and Suzanne), the mother of two children, and envious of women with "big bosoms." Being small-chested, she has a fixation about breasts and wishes she were as buxom as Suzanne (she feels a big bust means "power and respect"—not only from men, but from other women). She contemplated implants (she wants to wear a C-cup) but decided against it. Mary Jo, who attended Franklin Elementary School, wears a size-six shoe.

Anthony, the firm's deliveryman, is an ex-con who does volunteer work at the Home for Wayward Boys, and is also always caught in the middle of Julia and Suzanne's bickering. Anthony, whose contracting license is number L3303, has an ultra-sexy but dim-witted girlfriend named Vanessa (Olivia Brown).

Relatives of Julia: Louise Latham (her mother, *Perky Sugarbaker*), George Newburn (her son, *Payne*), Lewis Grizzard (her brother, *Clayton Sugarbaker*), Ginna Carter (her niece, *Camilla*), Mary Dixie Carter (her niece, *Jennifer*)

Relatives of Suzanne: Gerald McRaney (her ex-husband, *Dash Goff*), Alice Ghostley (family friend, *Bernice Clinton*, who lives at the Hillcrest Condominium)

Relatives of Charlene: Douglas Barr (her husband, *Bill Stillfield*), James Ray (her father, *Bud Frazer*), Ronnie Clare Edwards (her mother, *Ione Frazer*), George Wurster (her brother, *Odell Frazer*), Phyllis Cowan (her sister, *Darlene*), Benay Venuta (her mother-in-law, *Eileen Stillfield*)

Relatives of Mary Jo: Priscilla Weems (her daughter, *Claudia*), Brian Lando (her son, *Quentin*), Scott Bakula (her ex-husband, *Ted*), Geoffrey Lewis (her father, *Dr. Davis Jackson*), Eileen Seeley (Ted's new wife, *Tammy*)

Relatives of Anthony: Frances E. Williams (his *Grandma Bouvier*), Marilyn Coleman (his *Aunt Louise*), Gilbert Lewis (his *Uncle Cleavon*)

Theme: "Georgia on My Mind," performed by Doc Severinson

DETECTIVE SCHOOL

ABC, 7.31.79 to 11.24.79

World-famous detective Nick Hannigan (James Gregory) operates the Hannigan Detective School Agency in Los Angeles (located at 1407 Figueroa Street). Student Maggie Ferguson (Melinda Naud) is a model for the LaFlique Lingerie Company; student Teresa Cleary (JoAnn Harris) is a secretary; student Eddie Dawkins (Randolph Mantooth) is a shoe salesman; and Charlene Jenkins (LaWanda Page) is a housewife. Arnold Jackson played Charlene's husband, Walter. Peter Matz composed the theme.

DIAMONDS

CBS, 9.22.87 to 9.13.88

Mike Devitt (Nicholas Campbell) and Christina Towne (Peggy Smithhart) are the divorced owner-operators of a detective agency called Two of Diamonds—Confidential Investigations. Before their divorce, Mike and Christina were the stars of a TV series called "Diamonds" (from which they acquired their knowledge of detecting and decided to put it to good use following cancellation of their series). Domenic Troiano composed the theme, "Two of a Kind."

DIANA

NBC, 9.10.73 to 1.7.74

Principal Cast: Diana Rigg (*Diana Smythe*), David Sheiner (*Norman Brodnik*), Barbara Barrie (*Norma Brodnik*), Richard B. Shull (*Howard Tollbrook*), Robert Moore (*Marshall Tyler*)

Trivia: Diana Smythe is a young divorcée newly arrived in New York City from London who becomes a fashion illustrator for Buckley's Department Store. She resides at her unseen anthropologist brother Roger's apartment (11-B) at 4 Sutton Place in Manhattan, and is the guardian of Roger's Great Dane, Gulliver. (Roger is in Ecuador on assignment.)

Other characters: Norman Brodnik, the store president; Norma, his wife, the head of merchandising; Howard Tollbrook, the copywriter; and Marshall Tyler, the window dresser.

Theme: "Diana," by Jerry Fielding

Note: In the original, unaired pilot version ("The Diana Rigg Show"), produced for NBC in 1973, Diana Rigg played Diana Smythe as a 30-year-old divorcée who comes to New York from London to become the assistant to Mr. Vincent (Philip Proctor), head dress designer at a store called Sue Ellen Frocks. David Sheiner played Rodney Brodnik, the store owner, and Nanette Fabray, his wife, Norma. The 11.12.73 episode ("You Can't Go Back") reunited Diana Rigg and her former "Avengers" star Patrick Macnee.

DICK TRACY

ABC, 9.11.50 to 2.12.51

The city is not identified; the precinct he works for is not named (other than Headquarters); his badge number is not given; his squad car license plate (inserted stock footage) cannot be read; his home address and telephone number are not given. His wife is Tess Trueheart Tracy (Angela Greene); his partner is Sam Catchem (Joe Devlin). He's Dick Tracy (Ralph Byrd), a master police detective who is fair and honest and, when he fires his gun, never wastes a bullet (he always hits what he aims at). He eats hamburgers and hot dogs and drinks coffee between home-cooked meals and has a special two-way wrist radio that allows voice communication between himself and Sam.

Pierre Watkin plays Police Chief "Pat" Patton; John Harmon plays J. Blackstone Springem, the criminal lawyer; and Dick Elliott plays Officer Murphy. The series was based on the comic strip by Chester Gould.

An animated (and syndicated) "Dick Tracy Show" in which Everett Sloan provided the voice of Dick Tracy aired in 1961. Tracy rarely participated in crime solving; he acted more like a dispatcher assigning various cops (e.g., Joe Jitsu, Hemlock Holmes, Speedy Gonzales, Heap O'Calorie) to apprehend the criminals (e.g., Flattop and Bee Bee Eyes, the Brow and Oodles, Stooge Villa and Mumbles, and Prune-Face and Itchy). Other voices were provided by Mel Blanc, Benny Rubin and Paul Frees.

In 1967, William Dozier produced a pilot (never aired) called "Dick Tracy" with the following cast: Ray MacDonnell (Dick Tracy), Davey Davison (Tess Trueheart Tracy), Eve Plumb (Bonny Braids; his adopted daughter), Jay Blood (Junior; his son), Ken Mayer (Chief Patton), Monroe Arnold (Sam Catchem), Liz Shutan (Detective Liz).

In this version, Tracy's address is given as 3904 Orchid Drive, and his phone number is 555–7268. Tracy has a secret lab in his home (located behind a firing-range target figure) and a two-way wrist TV. In the pilot episode, "The Plot to Kill NATO," Mr. Memory (Victor Buono) plans to destroy a NATO peace conference by kidnapping its ambassadors. The Ventures performed the theme, "Dick Tracy."

THE DICK VAN DYKE SHOW

CBS, 10.3.61 to 9.7.66

Principal Cast: Dick Van Dyke (*Rob Petrie*), Mary Tyler Moore (*Laura Petrie*), Larry Matthews (*Ritchie Petrie*), Morey Amsterdam (*Buddy Sorrell*), Rose Marie (*Sally Rogers*), Richard Deacon (*Mel Cooley*), Jerry Paris (*Jerry Helper*), Ann Morgan Guilbert (*Millie Helper*), Carl Reiner (*Alan Brady*)

Trivia: At the Camp Crowder Army base in Joplin, Missouri, a U.S.O. show arrives to entertain the troops. As Sergeant Robert Petrie of Company A (Company E in some flashbacks) begins preparing the stage for the performers, he sees the girl of his dreams—a beautiful brunette named Laura Meeker (also given as Laura Meehan)—a girl he has a difficult time impressing and who soon despises him.

But Rob, "who makes a rotten first impression," is determined to have Laura and arranges to dance with her in one of the show's production numbers. While singing and dancing to the song, "You Wonderful You," Rob, who is wearing combat boots, steps on Laura's foot and breaks her toes.

While all hope for winning Laura seems lost, Rob persists (visiting her at the hospital to give her flowers and recipes) and soon Laura's hatred turns to love. Shortly after, Rob and Laura marry. (Unknown to Rob, Laura is only 17 years old, not 19 as she told him; they are later remarried when Laura confesses.)

Rob and Laura first live in the Camp Crowder housing development, then, following his discharge, move to Ohio where Rob becomes a radio disc jockey at station WOFF (the number-two station in a two-station town; WDDX is number one). It is at this time that Rob has an interview with TV star Alan Brady and secures the job of his head writer in New York City.

Rob's first meeting with his staff, seasoned writers Buddy Sorrell and Sally Rogers, begins on a friendly note—until they learn that the inexperienced Rob

Petrie is to be their boss. Rob is ignored the entire day while Buddy and Sally work on an important sketch for "The Alan Brady Show." Late that day, Rob is approached by producer Mel Cooley and given the sketch—crumbled by Alan. Rob covers for Buddy and Sally (who have since gone home) and rewrites the sketch. The following day, Mel congratulates Rob, Buddy and Sally for handing in a wonderful sketch. When Buddy picks up the sketch and realizes it is not the one he and Sally wrote—but sees his and Sally's name on it—Rob explains what happened and shows Buddy the original sketch. "Yup, that's Alan's crumble," exclaims Buddy, and he and Sally welcome Rob as their head writer.

"The Alan Brady Show," which airs at 8:30 P.M. (network not named) opposite "Yancy Derringer" (which was on CBS), is number 17 in America and number one in Liberia. Alan Brady, who lives in the Temple Towers on East 61st Street in Manhattan, has several business ventures that pay the bills. The Ishomoro Company, which produces motorcycles, pays Rob's salary. Buddy and Sally were originally paid by Tam-O-Shanter, Ltd., which made Martin and Lewis coloring books. When it folds, Alan's mother-in-law's company, Barracuda, Ltd., pays them. The show's band is paid by Alan's wife's company, Brady Lady.

Rob, Laura and their son, Ritchie, live at 148 Bonnie Meadow Road in New Rochelle, New York (their address is also given as 485 Bonnie Meadow Road).

Rob, who bases many of his sketches on Laura's crazy antics, was born in Danville, Ohio, and attended Danville High School. He played Romeo in *Romeo and Juliet* (he tripped over the balcony). His high school sweetheart, Janie Layton (Joan O'Brien) played Juliet. During his hitch in the army, Rob wrote the song "Bumkis" and was nicknamed "Bones." Rob's mentor, Happy Spangler (Jay C. Flippen), who taught Rob how to write comedy, calls him "Stringbean". (Happy now runs a tie store.) Rob, whose middle name is Simpson, has freckles on his back that when connected form a picture of the Liberty Bell. His favorite meals are: beans, franks and kraut (dinner) and cold spaghetti and meatballs (breakfast). Rob, who is allergic to chicken feathers and cats, ran for the position of Ninth District Councilman (he lost 3694 to 3619 to Lincoln Goodheart, played by Wally Cox). Rob's tailor is Vito Schneider.

Laura, who won the title "Bivouac Baby" at Camp Crowder, uses the pen name Samantha Q. Wiggins when she attempts to write a children's book. Her favorite TV soap opera is "Town of Passion," and she hides her old love sonnets from high-school boyfriend Joe Coogan (Michael Forrest) behind some loose bricks behind the furnace in the basement. Laura, whose favorite food is Moo Goo Gai Pan, weighs 112 pounds.

Ritchie, whose favorite TV show is "The Uncle Spunky Show," has the middle name of Rosebud—Robert-Oscar-Sam-Edward-Benjamin-Ulysses-David—one letter for each name various family members wanted for Rob and Laura's newborn baby. Ritchie, who has two pet ducks named Stanley and Oliver, was born after Rob and Laura were trapped in an elevator with Lyle Delp (Don Rickles), the crook with a heart of gold.

Rob and Laura paid $27,990 for their home, which has a huge rock in the basement. (The rock provides Rob with protection from flooding when it rains. He pays his neighbor, Jerry Helper, $37.50 a year to tar his back wall because the rock causes Jerry's basement to flood if the outside is not waterproofed). The Petrie's doorbell rings in the keys of E and G flat minor and there are 208½ roses on the wallpaper in Rob and Laura's bedroom. Rob's most unusual gift to Laura was the grotesque Princess Carlotta Necklace, and the Petrie family heirloom is a cumbersome brooch made in the shape of the United States (jewels mark the birthplace of each member of the family). The Petries' cemetery plots are at Rock Meadows Rest, located on the 15th hole of a golf course.

Buddy and Sally, who perform as the comedy team Gilbert and Solomon at Herbie's Hiawatha Lodge, have past TV experience. Buddy, whose real name is Maurice, worked for "The Billy Barrows Show" and had his own series called "Buddy's Bag." Sally, who attended Herbert Hoover High, was a staff writer on "The Milton Berle Show" before joining Alan's staff.

Buddy, famous for his "baldy" jokes about Mel, is married to a former showgirl named Pickles (her real name is Fiona, but all girls named Fiona in her hometown are nicknamed Pickles). Buddy has a German Shepherd named Larry, and once (after an argument with Pickles) overdosed on Dozy Doodles Sleeping Pills. Pickles, whose favorite ice cream product is Strawberry Sundae-on-a-Stick (from the ice cream truck), was previously married to a forger named Barton Nelson (a.k.a. Floyd B. Bariscale, played by Sheldon Leonard). Buddy, whose favorite drink is tomato juice, plays the cello at every opportunity.

Sally is single and looking desperately for a husband. She has two cats (Mr. Henderson and Mr. Diefenthaler) and a mother-dominated boyfriend named Herman Glimshire (Bill Idelson); in some episodes, he is called Woodrow Glimshire. Sally's (not seen) Aunt Agatha's maxim: "It's better to get a rose from a friend than a can of succotash from an enemy."

Jerry and Millie Helper are Rob and Laura's neighbors. They have an iron jockey on their front lawn and Jerry detests his other neighbor, Gilbert Bester, because his lawn is full of crabgrass. Rob and Jerry, a dentist, bought a boat together called the *Betty Lynn*. Rob wanted to call it *Shangri-La* and Jerry's choice was *The Challenger*. Millie has a pet mynah bird named Herschel and keeps a statue of a bull on the mantel; her father was a clothes presser.

Relatives: Jerry Van Dyke (Rob's brother, *Stacey Petrie*), Carol Veazie and Isabel Randolph (Rob's mother, *Clara Petrie*), Will Wright, Tom Tully and J. Pat O'Malley (Rob's father, *Sam Petrie*), Denver Pyle (Rob's *Uncle George*), Cyril Delevanti (Rob's grandfather, *Edward Petrie*), Dick Van Dyke (Rob's great uncle, *Hezekiah Petrie*), Carl Benton Reid (Laura's father,

Ben Meehan), Geraldine Wall (*Laura's mother*; first name not mentioned), Eddie Firestone (Laura's cousin, *Thomas Edson*), Joan Shawlee (Buddy's wife, *Pickles Sorrell*), Phil Leeds (Buddy's brother, *Blackie Sorrell*), Peter Oliphant and David Fresco (Millie and Jerry's son, *Freddie Helper*), Willard Waterman (Laura's *Uncle Harold*), Herb Vigran (Hezekiah's half-brother, *Alfred Reinbeck*)

Theme: "Theme From the Dick Van Dyke Show," by Earle Hagen

Note: In the original pilot, "Head of the Family" (CBS, 7.19.60), Carl Reiner played Rob Petrie; Barbara Britton, Laura; Gary Morgan, Ritchie; Morty Gunty, Buddy Sorrell; and Sylvia Miles, Sally Rogers. Jack Wakefield portrayed Alan Sturdy, the story's TV star.

DIFF'RENT STROKES

NBC, 11.3.78 to 8.31.85
ABC, 9.27.85 to 3.21.86

Principal Cast: Conrad Bain (*Phillip Drummond*), Dana Plato (*Kimberly Drummond*), Gary Coleman (*Arnold Jackson*), Todd Bridges (*Willis Jackson*), Dixie Carter (*Maggie McKinney*, NBC), Mary Ann Mobley (*Maggie McKinney*, ABC), Danny Cooksey (*Sam McKinney*), Charlotte Rae (*Edna Garrett*), Mary Jo Catlett (*Pearl Gallagher*), Nedra Volz (*Adelaide Brubaker*)

Trivia: Following the death of his housekeeper, Lucy Jackson, New York millionaire Phillip Drummond, a widower and the father of a young daughter, Kimberly, keeps a promise he made to Lucy: to take care of her two boys, Willis and Arnold, if anything should ever happen to her. Having previously lived in Harlem at 259 East 135th Street (Apartment 12), Willis and Arnold suddenly find their lives changed for the better when they move into Phillip's 30th-floor penthouse apartment A (in some episodes Penthouse B) at 679 Park Avenue in Manhattan.

Phillip, who owns Drummond Industries (also given as Trans-Allied, Inc.), attended the Digby Prep School as a boy, and his original last name was Van Drum-

mond. In one episode, Conrad Bain played Phillip's Dutch cousin, Anna. In 1984, Phillip married Maggie McKinney, a divorcée with a young son, Sam; she is host of the TV show "Exercise with Maggie."

Kimberly, Phillip's pretty and perky daughter, first attended the Eastlake Academy in Peekskill, New York, then Garfield High School in Manhattan. Although born into wealth, Kimberly lives on her weekly allowance ($10) and has a job at the Hula Hut, a fast-food hamburger restaurant in Manhattan. Dana Plato also played Kimberly's Dutch cousin, Hans, in one episode. Kimberly became a spokesperson for a cleaner environment when she used the all-natural Mother Brady's Shampoo and her blonde hair turned green (it was explained that Kimberly used rain water, affected by acid, in a copper bowl; when she used the shampoo, there was a chemical reaction and thus the green hair).

Arnold, the younger Jackson brother, attended the following schools: P.S. 89, P.S. 406, Roosevelt Junior High and Edison Junior High. Arnold, whose favorite expression is "What you talkin' about," loves model railroading (he has both "HO" and "O" scale pikes), has a ratty old doll (first season) named Homer, a goldfish named Abraham and a lucky cricket named Lucky. Arnold, whose favorite afterschool hangout is Hamburger Heaven, was the video champ at the arcade game Space Sucker (where he scored one million points); he was also a reporter for his school newspaper at P.S. 89—the *Weekly Woodpecker*.

Willis, the elder Jackson brother, attends Garfield High School and as a kid had a doll named Wendy Wet'ems. Willis, whose favorite expression is "Say what," forms a rock band called the Afro Disiacs; Kimberly and Willis's girlfriend, Charlene (Janet Jackson), are its vocalists.

Relatives: Dody Goodman (Phillip's sister, *Sophia*), Irene Tedrow (Phillip's mother, *Mrs. Drummond*), LaWanda Page (Arnold's cousin, *Muriel Waters*), Hoyt Axton (Maggie's ex-husband, *Wes McKinney*). Mentioned but not seen were Arnold and Willis's mother and father, Lucy and Henry Jackson

Theme: ~~"Diff'rent Strokes,"~~ written by Alan Thicke, Gloria Loring and Al Burton

Spinoff Series: "The Facts of Life" (see separate entry)

DIRTY DANCING

CBS, 10.29.88 to 1.14.89

Frances Kellerman (Melora Hardin) is nicknamed "Baby" and teaches dancing at Kellerman's Mountain Resort, owned by her divorced father, Max (McLean Stevenson). Dance instructor Johnny Castle (Patrick Cassidy) was born John Callahan; Baby's cousin Robin (Mandy Ingber) is nicknamed "Duchess." Allyn Ann McLerie plays Baby's mother, Elizabeth; Gerald S. O'Loughlin, Johnny's father, Tom; and Patricia Allison, Johnny's mother, Margaret. Michel Rubini and Michael Lloyd provided the music for the series, which is based on the feature film and set in 1963.

DIVER DAN

Syndicated, 1960

Principal Cast: Frank Freda (*Diver Dan*), Suzanne Turner (*Miss Minerva*), Allen Swift (*all fish voices*)

Trivia: "He protects and he saves his friends under the sea, that's where you'll find Diver Dan . . . " Fearless ocean explorer Diver Dan and his underwater assistant, Miss Minerva the Mermaid, risk their lives to protect the good creatures of the sea from the Baron, an evil barracuda who is bent on controlling life in the Sargasso Sea.

While Dan and Miss Minerva are the only live characters, the marionette sea creatures are: Trigger Fish (the Baron's dim-witted, cigarette-smoking accomplice), Sawfish Sam, Gabby the Clam, Sea Biscuit the Seahorse, the Glowfish, Finley Haddock, Skipper Kipper, Scout Fish (complete with tomahawk and feather), Goldie the Goldfish, Gill-Espie the Beatnikfish (bongo drums and all) and the Hammer-Head Shark.

The beautiful Miss Minerva, who contacts the fish with the magic Shell-o-Phone, lives in an area called Minerva's Palace (which is opposite the Bottomless Pit, the home of the Glowfish). Baron and Trigger have their hideout in a cave near the treacherous Teetering Rock.

DOBIE GILLIS /THE MANY LOVES OF DOBIE GILLIS

CBS, 9.29.59 to 9.18.63

Principal Cast: Dwayne Hickman (*Dobie Gillis*), Bob Denver (*Maynard G. Krebs*), Frank Faylen (*Herbert T. Gillis*), Florida Friebus (*Winifred "Winnie" Gillis*), Sheila James (*Zelda Gilroy*), Tuesday Weld (*Thalia Menninger*), Steve Franken (*Chatsworth Osborne Jr.*), Herbert Anderson and later William Schallert (*Leander Pomfritt*), Jean Byron (*Imogene Burkhart*), Warren Beatty (*Milton Armitage*)

Trivia: In the mythical Central City, which has a movie theater (the Bijou), two newspapers—the *Daily Record* (seven cents a copy) and the *Daily Courier*, a police chief named Rosenbloom and a justice of the peace, Jethro R. Wiggins (Burt Mustin), live hard-working shopkeeper Herbert T. Gillis, his wife, Winnie, and their son, Dobie.

Herbert, who owns the Gillis Grocery Store at 285 Norwood Street (address also given as Elm Street, 3rd and Elm, and 9th and Main), was once voted "The Citizen Most Likely to Hang onto His Last Dollar." He is a member of the Benevolent Order of the Bison Lodge and always claims he is 46 years old. In one episode, Herbert mentions he met and fell in love with Winnie while dancing the Kangaroo Hop; in another episode, he recalls falling in love with her when they met at a high school beauty contest where Winnie finished 27th out of 29 entrants. They later honeymooned in Tijuana, Mexico. Herbert's favorite expression (when affected by Dobie's antics) is, "I gotta kill that boy, I just gotta." Herbert also frequents the Scarpitta Barber Shop (which is named after the show's producer, Guy Scarpitta).

Dobie and his friend Maynard G. Krebs

attend Central City High School and later S. Peter Pryor Junior College. Their favorite afterschool hangout is Charlie Wong's Ice Cream Parlor and they both serve a hitch in the army in 1961 (in some episodes they are in Company A; in others, Company Q and Company C). In college, Dobie was the second assistant editor of the school newspaper, the *Pryor Crier*. The college radio station was KSPP. While in the service, Dobie gained 14 pounds eating army food.

Dobie is the girl-chasing, all-American teenage boy; unfortunately, he "picks girls with caviar tastes for his peanut-butter wallet." While schoolmate Zelda Gilroy has a never-ending crush on him and has set her sights on marrying him, Dobie has eyes for beautiful girls who seem to cause him only misery. While almost every episode features Dobie falling head-over-heels in love with a girl, he is most famous for his infatuation with the stunning Thalia Menninger, the girl who knows Dobie is dirt poor and the son of a cheap father, but who has high hopes of his making "oodles and oodles of money"—not for her but for her family: "a 60-year-old father with a kidney condition, a mother who isn't getting any younger, a sister who married a loafer and a brother who is becoming a public charge."

Dobie's rival for Thalia is Milton Armitage, the rich, spoiled schoolmate who nicknamed her "Mouse" for her inability to choose between him and Dobie. While Dobie can't afford to buy Thalia even one ounce of her favorite perfume (MMMM, which costs $18 an ounce), she always returns to him with the hope of improving him.

Although the Thalia character was dropped when Tuesday Weld left the series, a new beauty—Linda Sue Faversham (Yvonne Craig)—was brought in to tempt Dobie in 1961.

Like Thalia, Linda Sue seeks only to marry money and has high hopes of turning Dobie into a success so they can marry and support her unemployable family. Linda Sue considers herself blessed with a "stunning body, perfect teeth, beautiful

hair and fabulous face"—her "equipment" as she calls it—for only one purpose: "to marry money and support her dismal relatives."

Following in Linda Sue's footsteps is her gorgeous sister, Amanda Jean (Annette Gorman), who had "the same fabulous face, perfect teeth, beautiful hair and stunning body," and who is being groomed by Linda Sue to marry money. And, following in Dobie's footsteps was his younger, dirt-poor cousin, Duncan Gillis, who fell for Amanda Jean and found, like Dobie, that girls like Linda Sue (and Amanda Jean) are not for "poor slobs like us."

Maynard G. Krebs, Dobie's beatnik friend who loves to play the bongo drums, lives at 1343 South Elm Street and has a stuffed armadillo named Herman. Maynard, a jazz fan, hangs out at Riff Ryan's Music Shop (where he plays records so much he wears out the grooves), and claims that the G in his name stands for Walter. He has a weekly allowance of 35 cents, was turned down 46 times in six years for a driver's license, has three cousins named Flopsy, Mopsy and Cottontail, and the world's largest collection of tin foil.

While the longest word that he can pronounce is delicatessen, Maynard's idea of great Americans includes General MacArthur, Admiral Dewey and Captain Kangaroo. Maynard's favorite activities are watching the old Endicott Building being knocked down and watching workmen paint a new white line down Elm Street. Maynard's favorite movie is *The Monster That Devoured Cleveland* (apparently the only movie that ever plays at the Bijou). Maynard, who dresses in torn T-shirt and jeans or sweat shirt and pants, would always respond "You rang?" when he was called on or his name was mentioned.

Other Characters: Zelda Gilroy: The girl who taught Dobie to play the guitar; she has six sisters (played by Sherry Alberoni, Jeri Lou James, Larraine Gillespie, Judy Hackett, Marlene Willis and Anna Marie Nanassi). Pretty, but not as attractive as the girls Dobie falls for, she is always there for Dobie when he is dumped by his latest heart-throb.

Chatsworth Osborne Jr.: The rich son of Clarissa Osborne, he has type "R" (for royal) blood and is heir to the fabulous Chatsworth fortune: the First Osborne National Bank. He lives in a 47-room Louis XIV home (with broken glass embedded in the wall that surrounds it), belongs to the Downshifters Club, is president of the Silver Spoon Club (for snobs) at S. Peter Pryor Junior College and dreams of getting into Yale University. His favorite expression is "Mice and rats!" and he calls his mother "Mumsey" (she calls him "You Nasty Boy"). He calls Dobie "Dobie Do."

Professor Leander Pomfritt: Teaches English at the high school and later at the college and refers to his students as "young barbarians." He wrote nine novels (then destroyed eight of them) and wishes, at times, he had gone into the aluminum-siding business (also the air-conditioning business in some episodes).

Dr. Imogene Burkhart: Teaches Psychology 1-B and Biology at the high school. In early episodes, Jean Byron appeared as Ruth Adams, the math teacher at Central High. The character of Imogene Burkhart was originally played by Jody Warner—not as a teacher, but a classmate on whom Dobie had a crush.

Relatives: Darryl Hickman (Dobie's brother, *Davey Gillis*), Bobby Diamond (Dobie's cousin, *Duncan Gillis*), Roy Hemphill (Dobie's cousin, *Virgil T. Gillis*), Gordon Jones (Winnie's brother, *Wilfrid*), Jeane Wood (Winnie's sister, *Gladys*), Esther Dale (*Winnie's mother*), Michael J. Pollard (Maynard's cousin, *Jerome Krebs*), Kay Stewart (Maynard's mother, *Alice Krebs*; a.k.a. *Ethel Krebs*), Willis Bouchey (*Maynard's father*), Dabbs Greer (Zelda's father, *Walter Gilroy*), Joan Banks (Zelda's mother, *Edna Gilroy*), Doris Packer (Chatsworth's mother, *Clarissa Osborne*), Lynn Loring (Chatsworth's third cousin, twice removed, *Edwina Kagel*), Iris Mann (Chatsworth's cousin, *Sabrina Osborne*), Barbara Babcock (Chatsworth's cousin, *Pamela Osborne*), Joyce Van Patten (Leander's wife, *Maude Pomfritt*)

Unseen Relatives: Herbert's brother (Duncan's father), Tim; Winnie's sister, Margaret (who lives in Cleveland)

Theme: "Dobie," by Lionel Newman and Max Shulman

Note: In the pilot, "Whatever Happened to Dobie Gillis?" (CBS, 5.10.77), Dobie (Dwayne Hickman) is married to Zelda (Sheila James) and the father of a teenage son, Georgie (Stephen Paul). Maynard (Bob Denver) is an entrepreneur, and Dobie and his father, Herbert (Frank Faylen), have an expanded Gillis Grocery Store.

In the TV movie, *Bring Me the Head of Dobie Gillis*, (CBS, 2.21.88), Dobie and Zelda are still married, the parents of Georgie (Scott Grimes) and owners of the Gillis Market and Pharmacy. Recreating their original roles were Dwayne Hickman, Bob Denver, Sheila James, Steve Franken and William Schallert. Connie Stevens played Thalia Menninger and Tricia Leigh Fisher was Chatsworth Osborne III, Chassie for short.

DOCTOR, DOCTOR

CBS, 6.12.89 to 7.24.89
11.13.89 to 2.26.90

Principal Cast: Matt Frewer (*Dr. Mike Stratford*), Maureen Mueller (*Dr. Deirdre Bennett*), Julius Carry III (*Dr. Abraham Butterfield*), Beau Gravitte (*Dr. Grant Linowitz*), Sarah Abrell (*Pia Bismark*)

Trivia: The antics of the eccentric Dr. Mike Stratford, a general practitioner who uses unusual but effective methods to deal with patients. Mike and his fellow doctors, Deirdre Bennett, Abraham Butterfield and Grant Linowitz, are partners in the Rhode Island-based Northeast Medical Partners. Mike, who has written a medical book called *Panacea: A Medical Love Story*, is also the advice doctor on "Wake Up, Providence," a local morning news show on WNTV-TV hosted by Pia Bismark. Mike is said to have attended Harvard Medical School. Deirdre's maiden name is Murtagh. Abraham's license plate reads BIG DOC.

Relatives: Inga Swenson (Mike's mother, *Connie Stratford*), Dick Matthews (Mike's father, *Harold Stratford*), Tony Carreiro (Mike's brother, *Richard Stratford*), Candy Ann Brown (Abraham's wife, *Gail Butterfield*), Marlon Taylor (Abraham's son, *Justin Butterfield*), Dion Anderson (Deirdre's father, *Bill Murtagh*)

Theme: "Doctor, Doctor," by Artie Butler

DOLPHIN COVE
CBS, 1.21.89 to 3.11.89

Principal Cast: Frank Converse (*Michael Larson*), Karron Graves (*Katie Larson*), Trey Ames (*David Larson*), Virginia Hey (*Allison Mitchell*), Nick Tate (*Baron Trent*), Ernie Dingo (*James "Didge" Desmonde*)

Trivia: On behalf of Baron Trent, the owner of Trent Enterprises in Australia, Michael Larson, a widowed American scientist with two children, Katie and David, moves to Queensland (from Los Angeles) to begin a research project on the study of dolphins.

Katie, who suffered a traumatic shock in a car accident that killed her mother, is unable to speak and attends the all-girl Southberry School; she receives special instruction at home from one of its teachers, Allison Mitchell. Katie's birthdate is given as April 24, 1976. David attends the all-boy St. Crispin's School. Michael's research dolphins are named Slim and Delbert. Michael, who drives a truck with the license plate 471 PZU, is assisted by Didge, a local Aborigine.

Relations: Teresa Wright (Michael's mother-in-law, *Nina Rothman*), Stephen Elliott (Michael's father-in-law, *Jeff Rothman*), Anthony Richards (Allison's son, *Kevin Mitchell*), Richard Moir (Allison's ex-husband, *Scott Mitchell*), Bill Sandy (Didge's grandfather, *Vince*)

Theme: "Dolphin Cove," written by Bill Conti

THE DON RICKLES SHOW
CBS, 1.14.72 to 5.26.72

Don Robinson (Don Rickles), the frustrated account executive for the Manhattan advertising firm of Kingston, Cohen and Vanderpool, lives with his wife, Barbara (Louise Sorel), and their daughter, Janie (Erin Moran), at 43 Oak Lane in Great Neck, Long Island, New York. Earle Hagen composed "The Theme from the Don Rickles Show."

THE DONNA REED SHOW
ABC, 9.24.58 to 9.3.66

Principal Cast: Donna Reed (*Donna Stone*), Carl Betz (*Alex Stone*), Shelley Fabares (*Mary Stone*), Paul Petersen (*Jeff Stone*), Patty Petersen (*Trisha Stone*), Bob Crane (*Dave Kelsey*), Ann McCrea (*Midge Kelsey*), Candy Moore (*Bebe Barnes*), Daryl Richard (*Morton "Smitty" Smith*)

Trivia: Pediatrician Alex Stone, his wife, Donna, and their children, Mary and Jeff, live in the small town of Hilldale. Their phone number is given as Hilldale 43926 and later as Hilldale 7281; no address is given. Amanda Featherspoon Bullock (Sarah Marshall) had lived in the house prior to the Stones. When the series begins, Donna and Alex have been married 15 years, and Mary is 14 years old. Their house, which is in the fifth district, has a carob tree growing on the front lawn.

Through the efforts of his friend, Dr. Matthews (not seen), intern Alex Stone was introduced to Donna Mullinger, a nurse. On the night Alex proposed to Donna (who was wearing a flowered-print dress), they went to an unnamed restaurant where they were seated next to the kitchen and ignored by waiters. To make matters worse, Alex's plans for a romantic evening soured when the check came and he didn't have enough money to pay for the meal. Although a locale was not mentioned, Donna and Alex held their wedding reception in a club where Tony Bennett was performing (he dedicated a song to them). In another episode, Donna mentions that she and Alex were watching *Strange Cargo* (with Joan Crawford) at the Loew's Orpheum theater when Alex proposed.

Donna, who was born in Dennison, Iowa, is the dedicated wife, loving mother and all around problem solver. She is said to have a younger brother, but no name is given. Alex, who works out of an office in his home (next to the kitchen), is mentioned as having a couple of brothers (not named); lamb curry is his favorite meal. When Donna applied for a credit card at Leslie's Department Store, she was denied approval by its computer, C.A.L. (Credit Application Liaison). She applied again under the name Samantha Simian (Samantha was the name of a monkey Trisha was caring for while her friend, Kathy Thompson, was on vacation). Donna got the card, and the credit manager was enraged when he found out that the computer had issued the card to a monkey. All Donna wanted to do was purchase a pair of gloves for $5.20.

Donna once chaired the "Have a Heart, Hilldale" charity campaign, and she and Alex carved their initials in a tree at a summer house called Evans' Heaven, where they vacationed with a group of friends. The home was located on Echo Lane and the initial carving process took 42 minutes. During their honeymoon, Alex heard the song "Melancholy Baby" over and over again and came to hate it; as an early birthday gift, Donna gave Alex a musical apothecary jar that played the song. Alex was stationed at Fort Dix, New Jersey, during World War II. He and Donna read a daily paper called the *Sentinel*.

Mary, the elder child, is three years older than Jeff. She first attended Hilldale High School, then a college (not named) that is four and two-tenths miles from the Stones' home. Mary, who wears a size eight dress, usually frequents the Blue Lantern, a burger and soft drink place. After dances, she and her friends hang out at Kelzey's Malt Shop; her favorite place for dancing is the Round Robin. In one episode, Mary sings the song "Johnny Angel," which became a hit record for Shelley Fabares. In high school, Mary ran against Betsy Cartwright (Melinda Bryon) for the office of class president.

Jeff, who weighed 10½ pounds at birth, has perfect pitch but no other discernible musical talent. As a kid, he put on puppet shows for his friends with a marionette named Bongo. He and his friends once broke into the empty Willoughby House to use it as a place to hold their club meetings. When Donna organized a renovation committee to refurbish it for the kids, the house lost its appeal. Jeff has a pet mouse named Herman, was a member of the Bobcats football team (their uniforms were blue and gold) and attended Hilldale High School. He wanted to be a counselor at Camp Win-A-Pal and his favorite TV western is "Gunbutt" (sponsored by Happy Gum—"the all-purpose chewing gum"). His hangouts are mentioned as Kelzey's and Hotenmeyer's (a hamburger joint); his favorite club for dancing is also the Round Robin. At age 16, Jeff was five feet, eight and one-half inches tall. His girlfriend Bebe, who lives at 1650 Maple Street, dreams of wearing her Aunt Martha's wedding dress at her wedding.

Trisha, a young girl whose parents died two years before her appearance on the show, was being raised by her uncle, Fred Hawley, who had hired a woman to care for her. One day, while the Stones play touch football in a nearby park, Trisha, longing for a family, attaches herself to them. When the Stones and Hawley meet and Fred learned that Trisha is not happy with him, he allows Donna and Alex to adopt her. Trisha's favorite TV show is "Jingo the Clown."

The most expensive restaurant in Hilldale is Pierre's. Code 34592 bars eviction from one's home. The local college custom a couple observes to let each other know they are "serious" was called "Walking the Lion." The couple walks behind a huge lion statue in town and shares a kiss. The City Commissioner is Timothy "Tiger" Trimmitt (Paul Reed).

The Stones' neighbors are Dave and Midge Kelsey. When Bob Crane first appeared, he was called Dave Blevins (his last name changed when he and Midge bought a house in the Stones' neighborhood next door to the Corbetts). Before buying this house, they lived with Midge's parents; they were said to have been married for nine years. During the last season, when Bob Crane left to do "Hogan's Heroes," Midge still appeared but Dave was only mentioned. Midge is an only child, and her mother's name is Helen. The Kelsey's phone number is 538-4192.

Jimmy Hawkins played a series of Jeff's friends: George Haskell in the first season, Jerry Hager (later), Jerry Scott in 1963 and finally, Scotty Simpson.

Relatives: Gladys Hurlbut (Alex's *Aunt Belle*), Rhys Williams (Donna's uncle, *Frederick Jonathan Sutton*), Charles Carlson (Trisha's uncle, *Fred Hawley*), Marlo Thomas (Dave's goddaughter, *Louise Bissell*), John Stephenson (Bebe's father, *Ben Barnes*), Hollis Irving (Bebe's mother, *Harriet Barnes*), Ray Montgomery (*Smitty's father*)

Unseen Relatives: Alex's Aunt Lettie, Alex's Aunt Rhoda, Donna's Uncle Ralph

Theme: "Happy Days," by William Loose and John Seely

THE DORIS DAY SHOW

CBS, 9.24.68 to 9.3.73

Principal Cast: Doris Day (*Doris Martin*), Denver Pyle (*Buck Webb*), Philip Brown (*Billy Martin*), Todd Starke (*Toby Martin*), McLean Stevenson (*Michael Nicholson*), John Dehner (*Cyril Bennett*), Kaye Ballard (*Angie Palucci*), Bernie Kopell (*Louie Palucci*), Billy DeWolfe (*Willard Jarvis*)

Trivia: "One scoop of strawberry, chocolate and vanilla ice cream. On the strawberry goes chocolate topping; on the chocolate goes strawberry topping. But on the vanilla goes pineapple topping. Cover it all with hot marshmallow sauce and whipped cream—and heavy on the whipped cream." Though unnamed and a dieter's nightmare, this is the favorite dessert of Doris Martin, a widow who relinquishes her career as a singer (in San Francisco) to return to her father Buck

Webb's ranch in Mill Valley, California, to raise her children, Billy and Toby.

The following year (1969), Doris secures a job in San Francisco as the executive secretary to Michael Nicholson, the editor of *Today's World*—"The Now Magazine." In 1970, Doris leaves 32 Mill Valley Road and moves to San Francisco where she, her kids and a dog named Lord Nelson move into Apartment 207 over Palucci's Italian Restaurant at 965 North Parkway. Her rent is $140 a month. Cyril Bennett becomes her new boss; Angie and Louie Palucci, her landlords; and Willard Jarvis, her neighbor who feels his life is plagued by the Martin gang.

Doris, who in 1971 becomes a reporter for *Today's World*, has a car with the license plate 225 NOZ; Cyril's license plate is 495 CCF.

Theme: "Que Sera, Sera," vocal by Doris Day (scoring by Bob Mersey; written by Jay Livingston and Ray Evans for the film *The Man Who Knew Too Much*)

DOUBLE TROUBLE

NBC, 4.4.84 to 5.30.84
12.1.84 to 4.20.85

Principal Cast: Jean Sagal (*Allison Foster*), Liz Sagal (*Kate Foster*), Donnelly Rhodes (*Art Foster*), Patricia Richardson (*Beth McConnell*), Barbara Barrie (*Margo Foster*)

Trivia: The story of Allison and Kate Foster, identical twins who are as different as night and day: Allison is quiet and serious; Kate is devil-may-care. The girls originally live in Des Moines, Iowa (address not given). Their widowed father, Art, and his partner, Beth, own Art's Gym, where Allison and Kate work as aerobics instructors in the gym's dance studio.

Later (second date listing), Allison and Kate move to New York to pursue career ambitions: Allison as a fashion designer, and Kate as an actress. They move in with their Aunt Margo, the famous author of the "Bongo the Bear" children's stories, who lives at 49 West 74th Street (later given as 51 West 74th Street). Allison attends the Manhattan Fashion Institute, and

Kate, who most often works as a dancer for the Wacko Wiener Works, attends audition after audition hoping for her big break. Kate, who has brown eyes, is five feet, three inches tall, weighs 95 pounds, and her driver's license expires 10.9.87.

Theme: "Double Trouble," by Ray Colcord

DR. CHRISTIAN

Syndicated, 1956

An adaptation of the radio series about Mark Christian (Macdonald Carey), a young doctor who takes over his retired Uncle Paul's (Jean Hersholt) medical practice in the small town of River's End, Minnesota. While maintaining his private practice, Mark also works for Parkside Hospital. Jan Shepard plays his office nurse, Betty, and Mark's car license plate number is KHE 458. Albert Glasser composed the theme.

DUET

Fox, 4.19.87 to 8.20.89

Principal Cast: Mary Page Keller (*Laura Kelly Coleman*), Matthew Laurance (*Ben Coleman*), Jodi Thelen (*Jane Kelly*), Chris Lemmon (*Richard Phillips*), Alison LaPlaca (*Linda Phillips*), Arlene Sorkin (*Geneva*), Ginger Orsi (*Amanda Phillips*)

Trivia: Events in the lives of two married couples: Laura and Ben Coleman, and Linda and Richard Phillips. Laura, a caterer, runs Laura's Cornucopia with her sister, Jane. Ben, a mystery writer, penned the novel *Death in the Fast Lane* and writes the column "True Stories" for the L.A. *Daily Banner*. Ben, whose fictional detective is Zack Murdock, has a dog named Reuben.

Linda, originally a high-powered executive for an unnamed movie studio, joins Laura's company (now called Cornucopia Caterers) when she is fired. In the last episode, she and Laura secure jobs with the Juan Verde Real Estate Company (see "Open House"). Richard was originally a patio furniture salesman at the House of Patio before becoming a piano player

(his true calling) at Jasper's Bar & Restaurant. Geneva is the Phillips' sexy maid and babysitter for their young daughter, Amanda. Linda's father called her "Cookie Nose" when she was a child.

Relatives: Reid Shelton (Laura's father, *Frank Kelly*), K Callan (Laura's mother, *Rose Kelly*), Jane Persky (Laura's older sister, *Mary Margaret Kelly*), Nick Segal (Laura's brother, *Michael Kelly*), Summer Phoenix and Mary Tanner (Laura's younger sister, *Molly Kelly*), Allan Arbus (Ben's father, *Nate Coleman*), Bette Ford (Ben's mother, *Barbara Coleman*), Pat Harrington Jr. (Linda's father, *George Hartley*), Christopher Templeton (Linda's sister, *Diana Hartley*), Robert Reed (Richard's father, *Jim Phillips*)

Flashbacks: Maia Brewton (*Linda as a girl*)

Theme: "Duet," vocal by Ursula Walker and Tony Franklin

EIGHT IS ENOUGH

ABC, 3.15.77 to 8.29.81

Principal Cast: Dick Van Patten (*Tom Bradford*), Diana Hyland (*Joan Bradford*), Betty Buckley (*Sandra Sue "Abby" Bradford*), Lani O'Grady (*Mary Bradford*), Laurie Walters (*Joanie Bradford*), Kimberly Beck (pilot) and Dianne Kay (*Nancy Bradford*), Connie Needham (*Elizabeth Bradford*), Susan Richardson (*Susan Bradford*), Mark Hamill (pilot) and Grant Goodeve (*David Bradford*), Chris English (pilot) and Willie Aames (*Tommy Bradford*), Adam Rich (*Nicholas Bradford*), Joan Prather (*Janet McCarther*), Brian Patrick Clarke (*Merle "The Pearl" Stockwell*), Michael Thoma (*Dr. Craig Maxwell*)

Trivia: At 1436 Oak Street in Sacramento, California, lives the 10-member Bradford family. Tom, the father, is a columnist for the *Sacramento Register*; Joan, his first wife and the mother of his eight children was married to Tom for 25 years and loved photography. Joan "died" when Diana Hyland lost her life to cancer in 1977.

Abby, Tom's second wife, is a guidance counselor at Memorial High School. She lived at 1412 Compton Place before marrying Tom; her first husband, Frank, died as a P.O.W. in Vietnam.

David, the eldest Bradford child, is a contractor (license number 789 3382). He originally worked for the Mann Construction Company before forming Bradford Construction with his father. David dated and later married Janet McCarther, a lawyer with the firm of Goodman, Saxon and Tweedy. Janet lived at 2475 DeVanna Place and later worked for the firm of Ted O'Hara and Associates.

Mary, the most studious of the Bradford children, is in medical school (not named) struggling to become a doctor. She interns at St. Mary's Hospital where her inspiration, Dr. Craig Maxwell, also practices. Craig, who is a family friend and called Dr. Max, was also said to be associated with Sacramento General and Sacramento Memorial Hospital.

Joanie, named after her mother, has her mother's eyes, smile and sensitivity. She works as a researcher, then as a reporter for KTNS-TV, Channel 8, in Sacramento. While all the Bradford children found it difficult to adjust to Abby at first, it was Joanie who felt most out of place. Before the misunderstanding was cleared up, Joanie believed that because she bore her mother's name and looked like her, Abby resented her.

Nancy, the prettiest of the Bradford girls, attended Sacramento High School, but dropped out of State College when she felt incapable of doing the required work. Before working for the Bates, Callahan and Chester Brokerage House (later called the Fenwick, Hargrove and Elliott Brokerage House), Nancy worked as a model and appeared on the cover of *Epitome* magazine; she was also the "Sunshine Soda Girl" in TV commercials.

Susan, the most sensitive of the Bradford children, attended Sacramento Central High School and, while undecided about her future, attempted to become a police officer (but failed the physical endurance test). Her fondness for children, and a disastrous attempt by Nancy to start a day care center, led Susan to find her true calling in an unnamed day care center. Susan later married Merle Stockwell,

a minor league pitcher for the Cyclones baseball team who later became a pitcher for the New York Mets. In 1981, after an arm injury ended his career, he became a coach at Central High School.

Tommy, the most troublesome of the Bradford children, attends Sacramento High and formed his own band, Tommy and the Actions. Constantly rebelling against parental authority, Tommy longs to quit school and become a rock musician.

Elizabeth, who attends Sacramento High, and Nicholas, who attends the Goodwin-Knight Elementary School, are the youngest of the Bradford children.

The Bradford's telephone number is 555-0263 (later 555-6023); Tom's license plate numbers are 460 EKA (station wagon) and 842 CU1 (sedan). Abby's British M6 car (which she calls Gwendolyn) has license plate number YNH 872; David's van license plate number is HIR 312; Tommy's license plate number is 553 VFZ.

Tommy's hangouts are the Cluck 'n' Chuck (fast-food chicken) and Bennie's Burger Bin. Nicholas, who has two pet hamsters (Ron and Marsha) also won a racehorse named Royal in a contest. (As a kid, Abby had a horse named Blaze.)

Relatives: Janis Paige (Tom's sister, *Vivian "Auntie V" Bradford*), David Wayne (Tom's estranged father, *Matt Bradford*), Dennis Patrick and Robert Rockwell (Abby's father, *Harry Mitchell*), Louise Latham (Abby's mother, *Katherine Mitchell*), Ralph Macchio (Abby's nephew, *Jeremy Andretti*), Sylvia Sidney (Abby's *Aunt Felicity*), Joan Tompkins (Joan's mother, *Gertie Wells*), Robert F. Simon (Joan's father, *Paul Wells*), Richard Herd (Janet's father, *George McCarther*), Fay de Wit and Emmaline Henry (Janet's mother, *Sylvia McCarther*), Sondra West (Merle's sister, *Linda Mae Stockwell*)

Theme: "Eight Is Enough," vocal by Grant Goodeve

Note: The following trivia is culled from the TV movie, *Eight Is Enough: A Family Reunion* (NBC, 10.18.87): Tom is now editor of the Sacramento *Register* and Abby, played by Mary Frann, owns her own restaurant (the Delta Supper Club). Mary, a doctor, is married to Chuck (Jonathan Perpich), and Susan and Merle have a daughter named Sandy (Amy Gibson).

Elizabeth and her husband Mark (Peter Nelson) own a car restoration business; Tommy is a struggling lounge singer. Joanie, having been an actress, married film director Jean Pierre (Paul Rosilli); David, an architect, is divorced from Janet. Nancy is married to Jeb (Christopher McDonald) and is now a sheep rancher; Nicholas is in college.

In a second TV movie, *An Eight Is Enough Wedding* (NBC, 10.5.89), eldest son David marries his second wife, Marilyn "Mike" Fulbright (Nancy Everhard). The role of Abby is played by Sandy Faison.

THE 87TH PRECINCT

NBC, 9.25.61 to 9.10.62

Steve Carella (Robert Lansing), Bert Kling (Ron Harper), Meyer Meyer (Norman Fell) and Roger Havilland (Gregory Walcott) are detectives attached to the 87th Precinct in New York City. Relatives include Gena Rowlands (Steve's wife, Teddy), Ruth Storey (Meyer's wife, Sarah), Andrea Margolis (Meyer's daughter, Norma) and Larry Adare (Meyer's son, Bucky). The telephone number of the precinct is CI6–4098, and Morton Stevens composed "The Theme from 87th Precinct."

EISENHOWER AND LUTZ

CBS, 3.14.88 to 6.20.88

Bud Lutz Jr. (Scott Bakula) graduated from the Las Vegas School of Law and Acupuncture before moving to Palm Springs and opening the law firm of Eisenhower and Lutz near a high-accident intersection. Patricia Richardson is Kay Dunn, Bud's ex-wife, a lawyer with the firm of Griffith, McKendrick and Dunn; Henderson Forsythe is Bud's father, "Big" Bud Lutz; Leo Geter is Dwayne Spitler, the Sushi House delivery boy. There is no Eisenhower; Bud added the name to

make people think he has a Jewish partner. Amanda McBroom sings the theme, "Boys Like You."

ELECTRA WOMAN AND DYNA GIRL

ABC, 9.11.76 to 9.3.77

Principal Cast: Deidre Hall (*Laurie/Electra Woman*), Judy Strangis (*Judy/Dyna Girl*), Norman Alden (*Frank Heflin*)

Trivia: *Newsmaker* magazine reporters Laurie and Judy (no last names given) are secretly the gorgeous Electra Woman and her stunning partner, Dyna Girl, crime fighters whose secret identity is known only to Frank Heflin, the commander of Crime Scope—an ultra modern computer complex designed to battle evil.

Crime Scope's headquarters is called Electra Base. Devices used by Laurie and Judy are:

The Electra Strobe: A wrist-worn strobing device that allows Electra Woman to perform anything at 10,000 times normal speed.

Electra G: A device that adds gravity to Electra Woman and Dyna Girl's bodies when it is activated.

Electra Comp: Laurie and Judy's portable computerized link to Electra Base.

Electra Beams: Via the Electra Comp, Frank can discharge Electra Power in beam form to help Laurie and Judy when needed.

The Villains: Tiffany Bolling (*the Spider Lady*), Peter Mark Richman (*the Pharaoh*), Claudette Nevins (*the Empress of Evil*), Malachi Throne (*Ali Baba*), Jane Elliot (*Cleopatra*), Michael Constantine (*the Sorcerer*)

Theme: "Electra Woman and Dyna Girl," by Jimmie Haskell

THE ELLEN BURSTYN SHOW

ABC, 9.21.86 to 11.15.86
8.8.87 to 9.12.87

Ellen Brewer (Ellen Burstyn) is a writer and college journalism professor at the University of Baltimore. "Bread on the

Waters" was her first published story; her first book was called *The Woman on Top*. Megan Mullally plays her daughter, Molly, and Elaine Stritch plays Ellen's mother, Sidney Brewer. Rita Coolidge sings the theme, "Nothing in the World Like Love."

ELLERY QUEEN

NBC, 9.11.75 to 9.19.76

An atmospheric series (set in 1947) with Jim Hutton as the fictional gentleman detective and writer, Ellery Queen. Ellery, a bachelor, lives with his father, Inspector Richard Queen (David Wayne), at 212-A West 87th Street in Manhattan. (Richard is with the 3rd Division of the N.Y.P.D.'s Center Precinct.) Frank Flannigan (Ken Swofford) is an investigative reporter for the *New York Gazette*; criminologist Simon Brimmer (John Hillerman) hosts a radio program called "The Case Book of Simon Brimmer" (on which he tries to solve crimes before Ellery does). Elmer Bernstein composed the theme.

EMPTY NEST

NBC, 10.8.88 to

Principal Cast: Richard Mulligan (*Dr. Harry Weston*), Kristy McNichol (*Barbara Weston*), Dinah Manoff (*Carol Olivia Weston*), Park Overall (*Laverne Todd*), David Leisure (*Charlie Deitz*)

Trivia: "Empty Nest" is a "Golden Girls" spinoff about Harry Weston, a widowed pediatrician, and his daughters Carol and Barbara. Harry, who graduated from the Bedford Medical School in 1959, has an office on the 10th floor of the Community Medical Center in Miami Beach, Florida. His office is later moved to the second floor when the Greykirk Corporation purchases the building. Harry, whose dog is named Dreyfuss, was the sponsor of a Little League baseball team called the Pediatric Pirates. Harry's home phone number is 555-3630.

Carol, his eldest daughter, is divorced and works at various jobs. It is said that she has had ten jobs and quit the last one because the air conditioning was too cold. Her current job is assistant director of the University of Miami Rare Books Library. Barbara, the middle child, is a police officer with the Miami Police Department (since 1983); she also co-authored with Harry a children's book called *Jumpy Goes to the Hospital*. Barbara is terrible with money, "guys come and go," and she loves police work. Harry's never-seen youngest daughter Emily was first said to be living in New York, and later "attending college up north." Laverne Todd, Harry's receptionist, is from Hickory, Arkansas, and is married to the rarely seen Nick. To get to Hickory, Laverne takes a plane to Little Rock, then Dwayne's Plane to Hickory. To protect her job, she has a secret decoder to unscramble her filing system.

Relatives: Harold Gould (Harry's father, *Dr. Stanfield Weston*, a surgeon at Boston Community Hospital), Cynthia Stevenson (Harry's niece, *Amy*), Christopher McDonald (Laverne's husband, *Nick Todd*). Mentioned but not seen: Harry's daughter, Emily; Harry's late wife, Libby; Harry's Aunt Rosalie (who lives with 20 cats), and Carol's ex-husband, Gary.

Theme: "Life Goes On," vocal by Billy Vera and the Beaters

Note: The original pilot (5.16.87) focused on the lives of Renee (Rita Moreno) and George (Paul Dooley), a middle-aged couple whose children have left home and who now seek a new meaning to life.

THE EQUALIZER

CBS, 9.18.85 to 9.7.89

Principal Cast: Edward Woodward (*Robert McCall*), Robert Lansing (*Control*), Keith Szarabajka (*Mickey Costmeyer*)

Trivia: "Got a Problem? Odds Against You? Call The Equalizer. 212-555-4200." Thus reads the newspaper ad of Robert McCall, a former operative for a government organization called the Agency, who now helps people facing insurmountable odds. Robert, who is divorced (from Kay) and the father of a son (Scott), lives at West 74th Street in New York City; his license plate reads 5809 AUJ. Control is his former superior; Mickey, his legman; and Police Inspector Isadore Smalls (Ron O'Neill) is with the 74th Precinct in Manhattan. Lieutenant Jefferson Burnett (Steven Williams) is with the 83rd Precinct.

Relatives: Sandy Dennis (Robert's ex-wife, *Kay McCall*), William Zabka (Robert's son, *Scott McCall*), Melissa Sue Anderson (Control's goddaughter, *Yvette*)

Flashbacks: Tim Woodward (*Robert's father*)

Theme: "The Equalizer," by Stewart Copeland

THE FACTS OF LIFE

NBC, 8.24.79 to 9.10.88

Principal Cast: Lisa Whelchel (*Blair Warner*), Nancy McKeon (*Jo Polniaszek*), Kim Fields (*Tootie Ramsey*), Mindy Cohn (*Natalie Greene*), Charlotte Rae (*Edna Garrett*), Cloris Leachman (*Beverly Ann Stickle*), MacKenzie Astin (*Andy*), Sherrie Krenn (*Pippa McKenna*), Julie Ann Haddock (*Cindy Webster*), Julie Piekarski (*Sue Anne Weaver*), Felice Schachter (*Nancy Olson*), Molly Ringwald (*Molly Parker*)

Trivia: This is a "Diff'rent Strokes" spin-off that focuses on the lives of four girls (Blair, Jo, Tootie and Natalie) who attend the Eastland School for Girls in Peekskill, New York (the school was originally called the Eastlake School for Girls).

Blair Warner: The most beautiful girl at Eastland, she is very rich (heir to Warner Textile Industries), very conceited and something of a snob. She won the title "Eastland Harvest Queen" three years in a row, and won her first Blue Ribbon award at Eastland for being "Most Naturally Blonde." The New York-bred Blair also won the Small Businesswoman's Association Award for inventing contour top sheets. Following her graduation from Eastland, Blair attended nearby Langley College, where she is a member of the Gamma Gamma Sorority. Blair, who had a horse at Eastland named Chestnut, is studying law. With her stunning good looks, almost perfect figure (she tends to gain "a little") and always fashionable wardrobe, Blair is simply a picture of beauty; when Blair sustained a black eye in an accident, Tootie summed it all up: "It's like defacing a national treasure."

Jo (Jo Ann) Polniaszek: The complete opposite of Blair. Born in the Bronx, and at Eastland on a scholarship, Jo comes from poor parents (her father is in jail and her mother is a waitress) and acts tough. She drives a motorcycle, cares little about fashion or makeup and prefers to dress in jeans (not even designer—a shock to Blair) and sweat shirts (which makes Blair cringe). Like Blair, Jo also attends Langley College. At Langley, Jo was a disc jockey for the college radio station (WLG, FM 90.8) and later worked for the Hudson Valley Community Center. In one episode, Jo started her own business—Mama Rose's Original Bronx Pizza, Inc.

Tootie (Dorothy) Ramsey and Natalie Greene: Tootie, who lived on roller skates for her first year at Eastland, is the youngest of the girls. With ambitions to become an actress, she became the first black girl in the history of Eastland to play Juliet in *Romeo and Juliet*. The darling of the girls, she has two rabbits (Romeo and Juliet) and a cat named Jeffrey. Natalie, whose ambition is to become a journalist, worked as a reporter for the *Peekskill Press*, where her first article was entitled, "An Eighth-Grader Gets Angry." She is the peacemaker in the group, and constantly tries to resolve the differences between Jo and Blair.

Edna Garrett: The school dietician, she became more a mother to the girls and cared for them like her own children. Divorced (from Robert) and the mother of a son (Raymond), she left her housekeeping duties with the Drummonds (of "Diff'rent Strokes") to work at Eastland. When Edna learns that her pension fund has been lost and she can't get a raise, she leaves Eastland and begins her own business—Edna's Edibles, a gourmet food shop at 320 Main Street in Peekskill (the store she took over was called Ara's Deli). Blair, Jo, Tootie and Natalie work here and at the novelty store Over Our Heads (which replaces Edna's Edibles when it burns down). Edna, whose license plate number is 845 DUD, was born in Appleton, Wisconsin.

Following Edna's marriage in 1987, her sister, Beverly Ann Stickle, was brought on to care for the girls (who now live above the store). Beverly Ann, who is divorced, adopts the orphan Andy (who attends South Junior High School) and takes in a foreign exchange student named Pippa McKenna (from Eastland's sister school, Colunga, in Sydney, Australia).

Other Students: Molly, the free-spirit (who had a ham radio with the call letters WGAIO); Nancy, the hopeful model and boy-crazy beauty; the sensitive Sue Anne, a pretty teenager who had a slight weight problem and strove for the model's figure; and Cindy, a cute, teenaged tomboy.

Headmasters at Eastland: Harold J. Crocker (Jack Riley), Mr. Harris (Ken Mars), Stephen Bradley (John Lawlor), and Charles Parker (Roger Perry).

Relatives: Pam Huntington and Marj Dusay (Blair's mother, *Monica Warner*), Nicholas Coster (Blair's father, *Steve Warner*), Geri Jewell (Blair's cousin, *Geri Warner*), Eve Plumb (Blair's sister, *Meg Warner*), Ashleigh Sterling (Blair's sister, *Bailey Warner*), Robert Alda (Edna's ex-husband, *Robert Garrett*), Joel Brooks (Edna's son, *Raymond Garrett*), Mitzi Hoag (Natalie's mother, *Evie Greene*), Chip Fields (Tootie's mother, *Diane Ramsey*), Duane LaPage and Robert Hooks (Tootie's father, *Jason Ramsey*), Kevin Sullivan (Tootie's brother, *Marshall Ramsey*), Peter Porros (Tootie's *Cousin Michael*), Claire Malis (Jo's mother, *Rose Polniaszek*), Alex Rocco (Jo's father, *Charlie Polniaszek*), Sheldon Leonard (Jo's grandfather, *Joseph*) Megan Follows (Jo's cousin, *Terry Largo*), Donnelly Rhodes (Jo's cousin, *Sal Largo*), Rhoda Gemignani (Jo's *Aunt Evelyn*), William Bogert (Molly's father, *Jeff Parker*), Dick Van Patten (Beverly Ann's ex-husband, *Frank Stickle*), Mike Preston (Pippa's father, *Kevin McKenna*), Billie Bird (Andy's *Grandma Polly*)

"The Facts of Life"'s Last Episode, "The Beginning of the End": When Blair learns that Eastland has gone bankrupt and will soon close, she uses the money she has been saving to open her law office and buys the school. She becomes the Headmistress and changes the enrollment policy to include boys. The show was a pilot for the unsold "Lisa Whelchel Show," a series set to star Juliette Lewis and Mayim Bialik as students Terry Rankin and Jennifer Cole.

Tootie leaves to pursue her acting classes at the Royal Academy of Dramatic Arts in London; Natalie moves to New York's Soho district to pursue her writing career; and Jo marries her boyfriend, Rick Bonner (Scott Bryce).

Theme: "The Facts of Life," vocal by Charlotte Rae (first season) and Gloria Loring

Note: Two TV movies appeared: *The Facts of Life Goes to Paris* (NBC, 9.25.82), in which the regulars spend their summer vacation in Paris; and *The Facts of Life Down Under* (NBC, 2.15.87), in which the regulars visit their sister school, Colunga, in Australia.

THE FALL GUY

ABC, 11.4.81 to 5.2.86

Principal Cast: Lee Majors (*Colt Seavers*), Heather Thomas (*Jody Banks*), Douglas Barr (*Howie Munson*)

Trivia: Colt Seavers, a Hollywood stuntman for the Fall Guy Stunt Association, is also a bounty hunter for the Los Angeles Criminal Courts System. His license plate reads FALL GUY and he is assisted by the voluptous Jody Banks (36–24–36), his girl Friday, and his cousin and business manager, Howie Munson.

Throughout the run of the series, Colt worked for three bail bondswomen: Samantha Jack (JoAnn Pflug), nicknamed "Big Jack" and "Soapie" (because her life was like a soap opera); Teri Michaels (Markie Post), also known as Teri Shannon; and Pearl Sperling (Nedra Volz). Colt also worked for a bail bondsman named Edmond Trent (Robert Donner) in 1986.

Complicating Colt's life: Kim Donnelly (Kay Lenz), the beautiful but greedy insurance investigator; Kay Faulkner (Judith Chapman), his old foe and rival bounty hunter; Charlene "Charlie" Heferton (Tricia O'Neill), "the world's most beautiful stuntwoman"; and Cassie Farraday (Dana Hill), "the rowdy little stuntwoman."

Relatives: Jennifer Holmes (Colt's sister, *Tracy Seavers*), Lee Majors II (Colt's son, *Dustin Seavers*)

Flashbacks: Michael Hartung (*Colt as a child*)

Theme: "The Unknown Stuntman," vocal by Lee Majors

FAMILY

ABC, 3.9.76 to 6.25.80

This series chronicles events in the daily lives of the Lawrences, a middle-income family of six: Doug (James Broderick), an attorney; his wife, Kate (Sada Thompson); their divorced daughter, Nancy Maitland (Elayne Heilveil; later Meredith Baxter Birney); their younger daughter, Buddy (Kristy McNichol); their son Willie (Gary Frank); and their adopted daughter Annie (Quinn Cummings).

The Lawrences live at 1230 Holland Street in Pasadena, California, and their phone number is 555-2789. Nancy attends the Matthew Hamblin School of Law; Buddy and Annie attend Quinton High School; Willie works for the mythical TV show "The Dame Game" (a take-off on "The Dating Game"). Buddy's real name is Letitia, Kate's maiden name is Skinner, and the family station wagon's license plate number is 268 CNP.

Relatives include Nancy's ex-husband Jeff (John Rubinstein), Doug's father James (David Wayne and later Henry Fonda) and Nancy's son Timmy (Michael and David Shackelford).

John Rubinstein composed the theme.

FAMILY AFFAIR

CBS, 9.12.66 to 9.9.71

One year after the death of his brother and his sister-in-law in a car accident, Bill Davis (Brian Keith) takes on the responsibility of raising their three orphaned children: Catherine (Kathy Garver), and twins Buffy (Anissa Jones) and Jody (Johnnie Whitaker), who were first sent to live with relatives in Indiana who don't want them.

Bill, a bachelor who is president of the Davis and Gaynor Construction Company in New York, resides at 600 East 62nd Street, Apartment 27A, in Manhattan; his picture appeared on the cover of *World* magazine for completing an impossible job in India. Catherine, whose nickname is "Cissy," is 15 years old and attends Lexy High School; Bill had originally planned to send her to the Briarfield School in Connecticut. Buffy has a doll named Mrs. Beasley, and Jody is a quarterback for the neighborhood Spartans football team (his jersey number is 24).

Bill's gentleman's gentleman, Mr. French (Sebastian Cabot), has the seldom-used first name of Giles, and opens a restaurant called Our Mr. French's. John Williams appeared as Giles's brother, Nigel French, and Nancy Walker played Bill's maid, Emily Turner. Frank DeVol composed the theme.

A FAMILY FOR JOE

NBC, 3.24.90 to 5.6.90

Joe Whitaker (Robert Mitchum), a maverick, homeless man, becomes the adoptive grandfather of Holly (Juliette Lewis), Mary (Jessica Player), Nick (Dick Lascher) and Chris (Ben Savage) Bankston—four orphaned children (their parents were killed in a plane crash)—when they convince him to become their guardian and keep the family together.

Joe was a merchant marine and, as a vagrant, used to get his meals from the St. Anthony's Soup Kitchen. The Bankston's dog is named Leon (he only eats cat food); Nick has a pet snake named Hugo; Mary's stuffed monkeys are named Judy and Jingles.

In the pilot episode (NBC, 2.25.90), Maia Brewton played Holly, Chris Furrh, Nick and Jarrad Paul, Chris.

"A Family for Joe" is actually a reworking of "The MacKenzies of Paradise Cove" (ABC, 3.27.79 to 5.18.79). Clu Gulager played Cuda Weber, a charter boat-service owner who becomes the adoptive uncle of the five orphaned MacKenzie children: Bridget (Lory Walsh), Kevin (Shawn Stevens), Celia (Randi Kiger), Michael (Sean Marshall) and Timothy (Keith Mitchell). The MacKenzies' parents were killed in a sailing accident; Cuda's boat is called the *Viking*.

Charles Fox composed the theme.

FAMILY MATTERS

ABC, 9.22.89 to

Principal Cast: Reginald VelJohnson (*Carl Winslow*), Jo Marie Payton-France (*Harriette Winslow*), Kellie Shanygne Williams (*Laura Winslow*), Darius McCrary (*Edward Winslow*), Jaimee Foxworth (*Judy Winslow*), Telma Hopkins (*Rachel Cochran*), Rosetta LeNoire (*Estelle "Mama" Winslow*), Jaleel White (*Steve Urkel*), Julius and Joseph Wright (*Richie Cochran*)

Trivia: This is a "Perfect Strangers" spin-off about the Winslow family: parents Carl and Harriette, and their children Laura, Edward and Judy.

Carl, who graduated from Kennedy High School in 1969, is a sergeant with the Chicago Police Department (he is also a member of the Strike Force Bowling Team). In high school, Carl was a member of the singing group the Darnells. His favorite restaurant is Chez Josephine. Carl's worst experience as a cop: running out of gas in the middle of a high-speed car chase. Carl is also a traffic reporter for WNTW, Channel 13's afternoon news-cast. Harriette, originally an elevator operator at the Chicago *Chronicle*, is now the paper's security director and has keys to 300 offices.

While schools for the kids are not mentioned, their afterschool hangout is Le-Roy's Hamburger Palace. Rachel Cochran is Harriette's sister, a widow, and the mother of an infant son Richie; she is a freelance writer. Also residing with Carl is his mother, Estelle.

Steve Urkel, the boy who is said to have

eaten a mouse, has a crush on Laura (who wants nothing to do with him); he mentions his favorite snack as being anchovy paste on a dog biscuit. Relatives do not appear, but Rachel's husband (deceased) was named Robert and Carl's father (deceased) was named Sam.

Louis Armstrong sang the original theme, "What a Wonderful World." Jesse Frederick sings the new theme, "As Days Go By."

FAMILY TIES

NBC, 9.22.82 to 5.14.89

Principal Cast: Meredith Baxter Birney (*Elyse Keaton*), Michael Gross (*Steven Keaton*), Michael J. Fox (*Alex P. Keaton*), Justine Bateman (*Mallory Keaton*), Tina Yothers (*Jennifer Keaton*), Brian Bonsall (*Andrew Keaton*), Marc Price (*Skippy Handelman*), Scott Valentine (*Nick Moore*), Tracy Pollan (*Ellen Reed*), Courteney Cox (*Lauren Miller*)

Trivia: Events in the lives of the Keatons, a family of six living in Columbus, Ohio: parents Steven and Elyse, and their children Alex, Mallory, Jennifer and Andrew.

Steven, the manager of public TV station WKS, Channel 3, and Elyse, a free-lance architect, met in college in the late 1960s, were "flower children," attended Woodstock, and married shortly after. They first lived in a commune where their first child, Alex, was born (they had contemplated naming him Moon Muffin). Steven and Elyse then lived in an apartment on Rosewood Avenue in Columbus before moving into their series house (address not given). Elyse, whose maiden name is O'Donnell, later worked for the firm of Norvacks, Jenkins and St. Clair, and the first building she designed was the Cavanaugh Building in Columbus. Elyse's lifelong ambition was to become a folk singer.

Alex, a staunch Republican, always wears a shirt and tie; he worships money. He first attended Harding High School, then the prestigious Leland College, where he majored in economics. He was president of the college's Young

Businessman's Association and president of the Young Entrepreneurs Club. He also had a show on WLEL (Leland University Radio) and held jobs at the Harding Trust Company Bank and the American Mercantile Bank (Melinda Culea played his boss, Rebecca Ryan). In the last episode, Alex accepts a job offer from the Wall Street firm of O'Brien, Mathers and Clark.

Mallory, always fashionably dressed, first attended Harding High School, then Grant College. Mallory finds schoolwork difficult. She is not as smart as Alex or her younger sister Jennifer, but finds solace in her dream of becoming a fashion designer. At Grant, Mallory majors in fashion design and has a gift for being able to tell fabrics apart blindfolded; she deplores polyester. She is a member of the Gamma Delta Gamma Sorority.

Jennifer, the baby of the family before the birth of Andrew, was a member of the Sunshine Girls Club (Patch #27) and first attended the Thomas Dewey Junior High School. She later attends Harding High and while almost as smart as Alex, she also admires Mallory's beauty and taste in clothes. Jennifer later attends Leland College and has an afterschool job as an order-taker at the Chicken Heaven fast-food restaurant.

Other Characters: Andrew, the youngest Keaton (an Alex clone), attends Harper Pre-School; Nick Moore, Mallory's hood-like sculptor boyfriend; Skippy (Irwin) Handelman, Alex's best friend (who is adopted and has a crush on Mallory); Ellen Reed, Alex's first college girlfriend; and Lauren Miller, Alex's other college girlfriend. (Nick had a dog named Skipper and his father, Joe, owns a used car lot called Joe Moore's Motors.)

Relatives: Priscilla Morrill (Elyse's mother, *Kate O'Donnell*), Karen Landry (Elyse's sister, *Michelle*), Stuart Pankin (Michelle's husband, *Marv*), Dana Anderson (Michelle's daughter, *Monica*), Jeffrey B. Cohen (Michelle's son, *Marv Jr.*), Barbara Barrie (Elyse's *Aunt Rosemary*), Tom Hanks (Elyse's brother, *Ned O'Donnell*),

John Randolph (Steven's father, *Jake Keaton*), Norman Parker (Steven's brother, *Robert Keaton*), Tammy Lauren (Robert's daughter, *Marilyn Keaton*), Edith Atwater (Steven's *Aunt Trudy*), Tanya Fenmore (Skippy's sister, *Arlene Handelman*), Lois DeBanzie (Skippy's mother, *Rose Handelman*), Raleigh Bond (Skippy's father, *Harry Handelman*), Dan Hedaya (Nick's father, *Joe Moore*), Kaylan Romero (Nick's nephew, *Rocco*), Ronny Cox (Ellen's father, *Franklin Reed*)

Flashbacks: Chris Hebert (*Alex as a boy*), Kaleena Kiff (*Mallory as a girl*), Adam Carl (*Steven as a boy*), Margaret Marx (*Elyse as a girl*), Maryedith Burrell (*Steven's mother, May, when young*), Anne Seymour (*Steven's mother, May, when old*), Michael Allredge (*Steven's father, Jake, when young*)

Theme: "Without Us," vocal by Mindy Sterling and Dennis Tufano (first 10 episodes only), then by Johnny Williams and Deniece Williams

Note: On September 23, 1985, NBC presented the TV movie *Family Ties Vacation*, in which the Keatons spend the summer vacationing in England.

THE FARMER'S DAUGHTER
ABC, 9.20.63 to 9.2.66

"She's country style but city design, got a smile that's sprinkled with sunshine, look at the Farmer's Daughter, she'll perk up your morale . . . " Katy Holstrom (Inger Stevens), a Swedish farm girl from Minnesota, was originally seeking a government job teaching underprivileged children in Africa before she accepted Congressman Glen Morley's (William Windom) offer to become governess to his two motherless children, Steve (Mickey Sholder) and Danny (Rory O'Brien). Morley's address is given as 307 Marshall Road in Washington, D.C. Cathleen Nesbitt played Glen's mother, Agatha; Walter Sande and Alice Frost appeared as Katy's parents, Lars and Mama Holstrom; and Jeanette Nolan played Glen's Cousin Stella. Barry Mann and Cynthia Weil composed the theme.

THE FATHER DOWLING MYSTERIES

NBC, 1.20.89 to 3.17.89
ABC, 1.4.90 to

Principal Cast: Tom Bosley (*Father Frank Dowling*), Tracy Nelson (*Sister Steve*), Mary Wickes (*Marie Brody*), James Stephens (*Father Phil Prestwick*)

Trivia: Father Frank Dowling, pastor of St. Michael's Church in Chicago, and Sister Steve of St. Michael's Convent, are also amateur detectives who solve crimes.

Father Dowling, a Cubs fan (he wears a Cubs jacket in the opening theme), has been pastor at St. Michael's for nine years. Sister Steve, whose real name is Stephanie Oskowski (she is also called Sister Stephanie), teaches at St. Michael's Grammar School. Her Christian name (taken at Confirmation) is Sivle (Elvis spelled backwards). Marie, the rectory cook, came to work at the church 22 years ago when Father Hunnicker was the pastor. Marie has two sisters who are mentioned but not seen: Mildred (who lives in Cleveland) and Rose (lives in Florida).

The church funds are kept at the First National Bank of Chicago and the parish station wagon's license plate number is R3H 698. In the pilot episode, "Fatal Confession: A Father Dowling Mystery" (NBC, 11.30.87), the church car is a sedan (license plate AA 101) and Frank's nephew, Phil Keegan (Robert Prescott), was a sergeant with the Metro Police Squad. (For the series, Regina Krueger plays Frank's police department contact, Sergeant Clancey.)

Relatives: Tom Bosley (Frank's con-artist twin brother, *Blaine Dowling*), Stephen Dorf (Steve's brother, *Mark Oskowski*)

Theme: "The Father Dowling Theme," by Dick DeBenedictis

FATHER KNOWS BEST

CBS, 10.3.54 to 3.27.55
NBC, 8.31.55 to 9.17.58
CBS, 9.22.58 to 9.17.62

Principal Cast: Robert Young (*Jim Anderson*), Jane Wyatt (*Margaret Anderson*), Elinor Donahue (*Betty Anderson*), Billy Gray (*Bud Anderson*), Lauren Chapin (*Kathy Anderson*)

Trivia: Jim and Margaret Anderson, and their children Betty, Bud and Kathy, live at 607 South Main Street in the town of Springfield. Jim, the manager of the General Insurance Company, married the former Margaret Merrick, and is known for his ability to solve virtually any problem his family may encounter. Each year Jim and Margaret donate $25 to the Children's Home Society. Margaret is a member of the Women's Club of Springfield.

Betty, the eldest child, is nicknamed "Princess" and attends Springfield High School, then Springfield College; her hangout is the Malt Shop. A typical 1950s American girl, Betty is the smartest of the children and the most sensitive. When Betty is unable to solve a problem on her own or tell her parents about it, she retreats to the shore of a babbling brook in Sycamore Grove Park. In this, her "secret thinking place," Betty most often finds a solution to what has been troubling her. In one episode, Betty won *Photo Screen* magazine's "Donna Stewart Twin Contest" and flew to Hollywood to meet the famous movie star (Elinor Donahue in a dual role).

James Anderson Jr., nicknamed "Bud," is the middle child. He also attends Springfield High and later Springfield College (majoring in engineering).

Kathy, the youngest, nicknamed "Kitten," is a member of the Maple Street Tigers baseball team and attends Springfield Grammar School. Bud's nicknames for Kathy are "Shrimp," "Squirt" and "Shrimp Boat."

Relatives: Sylvia Field (Margaret's mother, *Martha Merrick*), Ernest Truex (Margaret's father, *Emmett Merrick*), Lynn Guild (Margaret's cousin, *Louise Decker*), Katherine Warren (Jim's sister, *Neva Anderson*), Parker Fennelly (Jim's *Uncle Everett*)

Theme: "Father Knows Best," by Irving Friedman

Note: On May 15, 1977, NBC aired *The Father Knows Best Reunion*, wherein the family (original cast) reunites to celebrate Jim and Margaret's 35th wedding anniversary. Betty is now a widow and the mother of two daughters: Jenny (Cari Anne Warder) and Ellen (Kyle Richards); Bud is married to Jean (Susan Adams) and is the father of a young son, Robby (Christopher Gardner); Kathy is engaged to Dr. Jason Harper (Hal England). A second TV movie, *Father Knows Best: Home for Christmas*, aired on NBC on December 18, 1977; the cast remained the same.

In the original NBC pilot film, *Keep It in the Family* (which aired May 27, 1954 on "Ford Theater") Robert Young was Tom; Ellen Drew, his wife, Grace; Sally Fraser, their daughter, Peggy; Gordon Gebert, their son, Jeff; and Tina Russell, their daughter, Patty.

FAWLTY TOWERS
Syndicated, 1977

The rude and incompetent Basil Fawlty (John Cleese) and his overbearing wife, Sybil (Prunella Scales), own Fawlty Towers, a 22-room hotel located at 16 Elwood Avenue in the quaint little town of Torquay in Devonshire, England. They purchased the hotel in 1966 and have been struggling for eleven years to attract guests and make ends meet.

Polly Sherman (Connie Booth), the hotel's chambermaid and waitress, is a hopeful artist; Manuel (Andrew Sachs), the Spanish bellboy who has difficulty speaking and understanding English, has a pet hamster he calls Basil; and Terry (Brian Hall) is the hotel's cook.

Other hotel residents are the apparently senile Major Gowen (Ballard Berkeley) and "two old biddies" named Miss Tibbs (Gilly Flower) and Miss Gatsby (Renée Roberts). Dennis Wilson composed the theme. (See also "Amanda's.")

THE FELONY SQUAD
ABC, 9.12.66 to 1.31.69

Detectives Sam Stone (Howard Duff) and Jim Briggs (Dennis Cole) are with the Los Angeles Metropolitan Police Department, Westland Division. Their car's license plate number is W64905 and their car phone code is 6-Nugent-3. Pete Rugolo composed the theme.

FERNWOOD TONIGHT
see AMERICA 2-NIGHT

FITZ AND BONES
NBC, 10.24.81 to 11.14.81

Ryan Fitzpatrick (Dick Smothers) is the "Newsline 3" on-the-air newscaster for KSFB-TV, Channel 3 in San Francisco; Bones Howard (Tom Smothers) is his street cameraman. Diana Muldaur plays Terri Seymour, KSFB's news director, and Roger C. Carmel portrays Lawrence Brody, the rival reporter who works for KTJ-TV, Channel 9. Stu Phillips composed the theme song.

FIVE FINGERS
NBC, 10.3.59 to 1.6.60

Victor Sebastian (David Hedison) is a U.S. government counterintelligence agent who operates in Europe under the code name "Five Fingers." He and his partner, Simone Genet (Luciana Paluzzi), work undercover for the Wembley and Sebastian Theatrical Agency. Charles Napier plays their superior, Wembley. Miss Paluzzi was the first foreign actress (Italian) to be brought to America to make a TV series. David Raksin composed the theme.

FLASH GORDON
Syndicated, 1953

Flash Gordon (Steve Holland), Dale Arden (Irene Champlin) and Dr. Alexis Zarkov (Joseph Nash) are members of the Galactic Bureau of Investigation (G.B.I.), a 22nd-century Earth-based defense organization. Flash's ship, the *Starflash*, was replaced later by the *Starflash II*; its mascot was Casey the parrot. Kurt Heuser composed the theme to this only American series to be filmed in West Berlin.

THE FLINTSTONES

ABC, 9.30.60 to 9.2.66

Principal Cast (Voices): Alan Reed (*Fred Flintstone*), Jean VanderPyl (*Wilma Flintstone* and *Pebbles Flintstone*), Mel Blanc (*Barney Rubble*), Bea Benaderet and Gerry Johnson (*Betty Rubble*), Don Messick (*Dino* and *Bamm Bamm Rubble*)

Trivia: During the summer of 1,000,056 B.C., 16 years before the show is set, Fred Flintstone and his friend, Barney Rubble, worked as bellboys at the Honeyrock Hotel. There they met Wilma Slaghoople and Betty Jean McBricker, two hotel waitresses. It was love at first sight, and soon after, Fred and Wilma and Barney and Betty married.

Fred and Wilma set up housekeeping at 345 Stone Cave Road in the town of Bedrock; Barney and Betty purchased the cavelike home next to them. Fred and Barney, who work as Dino Operators at the Rock Head and Quarry Cove Construction Company (also mentioned as the Slaterock Gravel Company), are members of the Royal Order of Water Buffalos Lodge. As kids, Fred and Barney were boy scouts in the Saber-Toothed Tiger Troop; they are now members of the Bedrock Quarry Baseball Team, and the Flintstone Canaries, an off-key barbershop quartet. Their favorite TV show is "Jay Bondrock" (a take-off on James Bond) and they bowl at Bedrock Bowl.

While Thomas Edisonstone invented the candle, Fred is also an amateur inventor, creating Fred-A-Cal (a diet drink that reduces people, not weight). Fred's favorite food is Bronto Burgers and Pterodactyl Pie is his favorite dessert. Barney's hometown was mentioned as Granite Town, where he lived at 142 Boulder Avenue. Fred's famous catch phrase is "Yabba Dabba Do."

The Flintstones, whose daughter is named Pebbles, also have a six-foot tall, purple (with spots) pet Snarkasaurus named Dino; Barney and Betty, whose adopted son is named Bamm Bamm, have a pet Hoparoo called Hoppy.

Note: "The Flintstones," TV's first adult cartoon, is actually an animated, stone-age version of "The Honeymooners." The Flintstones and Rubbles face problems similar to those of the 1950s' Kramdens and Nortons.

FLYING HIGH

CBS, 9.29.78 to 1.23.79

Pam Bellagio (Kathryn Witt), Lisa Benton (Connie Sellecca) and Marcy Bower (Patricia Klous) are flight attendants for the Los Angeles-based Sun West Airlines. Pam, born in Trenton, New Jersey, is 22 years old; Lisa, 21, was born in Greenwich, Connecticut; and Marcy, age 19, is from Sweetwater, Texas. Carmen Zapata appeared as Pam's mother, Mrs. Bellagio, and Louis Zitto played her father, Tony Bellagio. David Shire composed the theme.

In 1971 (3.19 to 8.16) NBC presented "From a Bird's Eye View," the first series about flight attendants, with Millicent Martin (Millie Grover) and Pat Finley (Maggie Ralston) working for the London-based International Airlines.

THE FLYING NUN

ABC, 9.7.67 to 9.18.70

Elsie Ethrington (Sally Field) is ordained Sister Bertrille when she becomes a nun in order to help the less fortunate. She is assigned to the order of the Sisters of San Tanco and assigned to the convent San Tanco in San Juan, Puerto Rico. There she discovers she has the ability to fly: her coronets (headgear) have sides that resemble wings; Sister Bertrille weighs only 90 pounds and San Juan is affected by trade winds. When she is caught by strong gales, she is lifted off the ground and able to soar (her coronets control her flight).

The Convent San Tanco was built in 1572 on land given to the sisters by King Philip of Spain; their rent is one dollar a year. Playboy Carlos Ramirez (Alejandro Rey) owns a discotheque nearby called Casino Carlos. His niece, Linda Shapiro (Pamelyn Ferdin) is a young girl who wants to be a sister and was nicknamed "the Little Nun." In high school, Elsie was voted "The Most Far-Out of 1965," and in one episode it is mentioned that she played with a rock band called the Gorries (which refers back to the other Sally Field series, "Gidget," in which Gidget was a member of a group by that name). Elsie was also a counselor at Camp Laughing Water during the summer of 1966.

Other characters include: Reverend Mother Plaseato (Madeleine Sherwood), Sister Jacqueline (Marge Redmond), Sister Ana (Linda Dangcil) and Sister Sixto (Shelley Morrison). Elinor Donahue played Elsie's sister, Jennifer; Henry Corden appeared as Carlos's Uncle Antonio; and June Whitley and Laurance Haddon played Linda's mother and father. Rich Little had a recurring role as Brother Paul Bernardi, whom the sisters considered a jinx. Warren Barker composed the theme.

FM

NBC, 8.17.89 to 9.14.89
3.28.90 to 6.28.90

Ted Costas (Robert Hays) is the program director of WGEO, 91.6 FM, a public radio station in Washington, D.C. (the station's slogan is "Radio Free D.C." and its phone number is 555–4367). Ted's daily show is "Long Day's Journey into Lunch" and his hometown is given as St. Louis (his current residence is given only as Apartment B).

Leann Plunkett (Patricia Richardson) is Ted's ex-wife. She attended Georgetown University, and co-hosts a talk show called "Toe to Toe" with Harrison Green (Fred Applegate). Harrison is also the theater critic for the *D.C. Press*.

Daryl (Rainbow Harvest), the beautiful station volunteer, attends Georgetown University, models nude for art classes, worked as a decorative icer in an erotic bakery, and is now a barmaid at the Ta Ta Room. She drinks only hot Dr. Pepper, and the only meats she will eat are yak and warthog. Daryl was conceived at Woodstock and plays strip Pictionary.

Quenton Lamereaux (James Avery)

hosts "The Classical Show," and Don Baumgartner (John Kassir) hosts a satire show called "Capitol Punishment."

Maude Costas (Nicole Huntington), Ted and Leann's daughter, is a freshman at Georgetown University; Gretchen Schreck (DeLane Matthews), Ted's secretary, had the name Gretchen Schmidt in the original (unaired) pilot; Naomi Sayers (Lynn Thigpen), the station manager, was called Naomi Miller in the pilot; and Jack Bannon appeared as Leann's new husband, Jonathan Plunkett.

Ted and Leann's wedding anniversary is on April Fool's Day and the gang's usual hangout is a bar called P.J.'s. Patrick Williams composed the theme.

FORTUNE DANE

ABC, 2.15.86 to 3.22.86

Ex pro-football player Fortune Dane (Carl Weathers) and Kathy Davenport (Daphne Ashbrook) are special investigators for Amanda Harding (Penny Fuller), the mayor of Bay City, California. Kathy is nicknamed "Speed"; Dane's Porsche's license plate number is 2TZ 0587; their favorite eatery is the Ziedecort Restaurant. Adolph Caesar appeared as Fortune's father, Charles Dane. Douglas Fraser composed the theme.

FREE SPIRIT

ABC, 9.22.89 to 1.21.90

Principal Cast: Corinne Bohrer (*Winnie Goodwin*), Franc Luz (*Thomas J. Harper*), Alyson Hannigan (*Jessie Harper*), Paul Scherner (*Robb Harper*), Edon Gross (*Gene Harper*)

Trivia: When Gene Harper, the youngest son of divorced attorney Thomas J. Harper, wishes for someone to take care of him, his sister Jessie and his brother Robb, a pretty but somewhat dizzy witch named Winnie Goodwin materializes. It seems that Gene made his wish at the exact moment that Winnie's turn for public service duty came up. Through Gene's efforts, Thomas hires Winnie as their housekeeper—but her true identity is known only to the Harper children.

Winnie, who appears to be in her twenties, was born in 1665 and mentions Halloween as being her least favorite holiday (it strains her powers). The "cool club" at Jessie's unnamed school is the Debs; Gene is a member of the Pizza House Cubs Little League team. In the original, unaired pilot (taped in May 1989), Christopher Rich played Thomas and Shonda Whipple, Jessie.

Relatives: Josie Davis (Winnie's beautiful younger sister, *Cassandra*), Michael Constantine (*Winnie's father*)

Theme: "She's a Free Spirit," by Steve Dorff and John Betts

FRIDAY THE 13TH: THE SERIES

Syndicated, 10.87 to 9.90

Cousins Micki Foster (Louise Robey) and Ryan Dallion (John D. LeMay), and their friend, Jack Marshak (Chris Wiggins), run an antique store called Curious Goods. The store, originally called Vendredi Antiques, was owned by Micki and Ryan's Uncle Lewis Vendredi (R. G. Armstrong), who made a pact with the devil to sell cursed antiques. Following Lewis's death by demonic forces, Micki and Ryan inherit the store—and a mission: to retrieve the cursed objects that cause or produce death.

Zachary Bennett played Micki's nephew, J. B.; and Michael Constantine appeared as Ryan's estranged father, Ray Dallion. Fred Mollin composed the chilling "Friday the 13th" theme.

F TROOP

ABC, 9.14.65 to 9.7.67

Principal Cast: Forrest Tucker (*Sergeant Morgan O'Rourke*), Larry Storch (*Corporal Randolph Agarn*), Ken Berry (*Captain Wilton Parmenter*), Melody Patterson (*Wrangler Jane*), Frank DeKova (*Chief Wild Eagle*), James Hampton (*Private Hannibal Dobbs*), Bob Steele (*Private Duffy*), Joe Brooks (*Private Vanderbilt*), John Mitchum

(*Private Hoffenmuller*), Don Diamond (*Crazy Cat*)

Trivia: In the closing months of the Civil War, Wilton Parmenter, a private with the Union Quarter Masters Corps who is in charge of officer's laundry, encounters an excess of pollen one day and sneezes, blurting out what sounds like "Charge!"

Troopers on stand-by are prompted into action that foils a Confederate plan and brings victory to the Union. Wilton is promoted to captain, awarded the Medal of Honor, and assigned to the command of F Troop, a misfit cavalry troop stationed at Fort Courage in Kansas.

Fort Courage, named after the much-decorated General Sam Courage (Cliff Arquette), is situated in the midst of the Apache, Cherakowa and Hekawi Indian tribes. Wilton, who is from a military family (with such relatives as General Thor X. Parmenter and Colonel Jupiter Parmenter) replaces "Cannonball" Bill McCormick (Willard Waterman), the former F Troop commander, who had retired.

Wilton, who was born in June, is called "the Scourge of the West" by Indians and believes that he is responsible for keeping the "ferocious" Hekawis in line. Unknown to him, the Hekawis are a friendly tribe and partners with Sergeant Morgan O'Rourke in the illegal O'Rourke Enterprises.

Morgan Sylvester O'Rourke, a 25-year career army officer, and Randolph (no middle name) Agarn, nine years in the service, run O'Rourke Enterprises from the barracks of Fort Courage. The company, which owns the Fort Courage Saloon, deals in souvenirs, whiskey and anything else that will turn a profit. Their goods supplier is Wild Eagle, chief of the Hekawis, a money-hungry Indian who has brought his tribe to a point where they are totally dependent on money and rapidly forgetting the hard life they once lived.

While Morgan, the president of O'Rourke Enterprises, seeks new ways of increasing business (like adding the International Trading Corporation), his vice president, Agarn, is forever seeking ways to make money on his own (e.g., buying his way out of the army to manage a British rock group called the Bedbugs). Like Chief Wild Eagle, who has problems with Crazy Cat, his assistant chief (seeking Wild Eagle's job), O'Rourke must contend with Agarn's endless antics (like getting carried away by the beat of the tom toms at the Hekawi Festival of the Succotash and yelling, "Kill the Paleface!") and his stream of weird relatives (including his Mexican cousin, El Diablo; his Russian cousin, Dimitri Agarnoff; and his French cousin, Lucky Pierre—all played by Larry Storch). O'Rourke and Agarn are also members of the Hekawi Playbrave Club (an 1866 Playboy type of club). O'Rourke is the only trooper who can read smoke signals. Agarn's horse is named Barney.

While Wilton is totally unaware that O'Rourke is pulling the wool over his eyes, he does find problems of another kind—trying to avoid the matrimonial plans of his girlfriend, the beautiful Jane Angelica Thrift. Called Wrangler Jane, and the owner of Wrangler Jane's (the general store, post office and hay/feed store), she fell in love with Wilton at first sight and has set her cap to marry him (although Wilton has no intentions of marrying her or any other girl).

Jane, whose birthday is in November, wears a size-10 dress, has a horse named Pecos, and was the lead singer in the Termites, a rock group formed by O'Rourke and Parmenter. (Jane sang the songs "Lemon Tree" and "Mr. Tambourine Man.")

Other Troopers: Private Hannibal Shirley Dobbs, the company's inept bugler; Private Vanderbilt, the nearly blind lookout; Private Duffy, a survivor of the Alamo who rambles endlessly about his and Davy Crockett's exploits; and Private Hoffenmuller, the German recruit who is unable to speak English.

Relatives: Patty Regan (Wilton's sister, *Daphne Parmenter*), Jeanette Nolan (*Wilton's mother*), Allyn Joslyn (Wilton's uncle, *Colonel Jupiter Parmenter*), Forrest Tucker (Morgan's father, *Morgan O'Rourke Sr.*), George Gobel (Jane's cousin, *Henry Turkel*), Nydia Westman (Hannibal's mother, *Mama Dobbs*), Mike Mazurki (Wild Eagle's cousin, *Geronimo*), Don Rickles (Wild Eagle's son, *Bald Eagle*), Laurie Sibbald (Wild Eagle's daughter, *Silver Dove*), Cathy Lewis (Wild Eagle's sister, *Whispering Dove*), Paul Petersen (Wild Eagle's nephew, *Johnny Eagle Eye*). In one episode, Ken Berry played Parmenter's outlaw double, Kid Vicious.

Theme: "F Troop," by William Lava and Irving Taylor

THE FUGITIVE

ABC, 9.17.63 to 8.29.67

Principal Cast: David Janssen (*Dr. Richard Kimble*), Barry Morse (*Lieutenant Philip Gerard*), Bill Raisch (*Fred Johnson, the one-armed man*), William Conrad (*Narrator*)

Trivia: Richard Kimble was born on March 27, 1927 in Stafford, Indiana, to parents John and Elizabeth. With ambition to become a doctor, he attended Cornell University in New York and interned at the Fairgreen, Indiana, County Hospital. He did his residency at Memorial Hospital in Chicago, specializing in pediatrics and obstetrics. Richard began his practice in Stafford and married Helen Waverly. After the death of their stillborn first child, Helen was unable to have more children and problems arose: Richard wanted to adopt a child, but Helen refused, feeling it would be living with a lie.

On the night of September 19, 1961, after a heated argument over the possibility of adopting a child, Richard storms out of the house. As he drives off, Helen invites her neighbor, Lloyd Chandler (J. D. Cannon) over to talk about adoption. While upstairs, they hear a noise coming from downstairs. Helen, believing it is Richard, goes down to welcome him home. She startles a burglar, who hits her with a lamp base, killing her. As the burglar, a one-armed man named Fred Johnson, looks up the stairs, he sees Chandler cowering in fear, and leaves the house. Chandler, a former war hero who did nothing to help Helen, now fears that if word gets out, he will be ruined. He decides to keep quiet about having been present.

Meanwhile, as Richard contemplates his actions, he decides to return home and apologize. When Richard enters the driveway, his car headlights catch the figure of the one-armed man running from the house. Richard rushes into the house, finds Helen and, we assume, calls the police (no mention is made as to why the police arrive, but they do). Because he cannot prove his alibi, Richard is arrested and charged with murder.

Kimble is booked (number KB7601863), fingerprinted (classification: 19M 9400013) and sent to jail. When he is tried (Case Number 33972) he is unable to prove his innocence and is sentenced to death. Although Richard insists that a mysterious one-armed man killed Helen, a police search fails to uncover any suspects.

While being escorted to the Death House by Indiana Detective Lieutenant Philip Gerard, Kimble escapes when the train on which they are riding derails. Now Kimble is wanted for interstate flight and murder and a reward is offered for information leading to his capture. Kimble, who weighs 175 pounds and is six feet tall, dyes his salt-and-pepper hair black and begins a cross-country search to clear his name—by finding the one-armed man. His mission is jeopardized, however, by Gerard, who has sworn to apprehend his escaped prisoner.

The two-part finale, "The Judgment": When he learns that a one-armed man has been arrested in Los Angeles (for fighting near a bar), Gerard heads for California to set a trap for Kimble. He has the story broadcast over a national wire service, certain that Kimble will see it and follow up. Kimble, working for a trucking company, sees the story and, as Gerard predicted, quits his job and hitches a ride with a fellow trucker to L.A.

Meantime, police stenographer Jean Carlisle (Diane Baker), a woman who once lived in Stafford and knows Richard, calls Donna Taft (Richard's sister) to warn her that Gerard may be setting a trap for Richard. Donna attempts but fails to track down Richard. When Jean learns from Donna that Richard hitched a ride to L.A., she tracks down the driver and learns that Richard got off at the produce market. There, Jean finds Richard and reintroduces herself to him. To escape from the police who are in the area, Richard buys a box of tomatoes, which he uses to hide his face as he walks to Jean's car. Jean drives Richard to the safety of her apartment.

Shortly afterward, Gerard appears on TV with an appeal: he will help Kimble if he gives himself up. With Jean's help, Kimble finds that it is not a trap and that Johnson is actually in jail. However, just as Kimble is about to surrender, Johnson is released on bail. After an unsuccessful attempt to follow Johnson (whom they lose at the zoo), Jean and Richard return to her apartment.

When Gerard discovers that Jean is from Stafford, he goes to her apartment to question her. Although it appears as if Jean has convinced Gerard that she wouldn't recognize Kimble, Gerard becomes suspicious when he sees the box of tomatoes in Jean's car. The police cars leave. A cab pulls up in front of Jean's apartment house. As Kimble prepares to leave, he is apprehended by Gerard when he comes out of the building.

As Gerard and Kimble head back to Stafford, Johnson is also returning to Stafford—to blackmail Chandler. On the train, Kimble talks Gerard into giving him a chance to prove his innocence. At the same time, Jean returns to Stafford to help Richard.

Believing that Donna's husband, Leonard Taft, is Chandler, Johnson calls the Taft house. Donna answers the phone (Leonard is at work). Johnson explains that he saw what her husband did and demands that Leonard meet him at the old riding stables at 10 P.M.

Just then, Chandler stops by and, in casual conversation, Donna tells him about the phone call. Chandler keeps the appointment with Johnson and the two agree to meet again at an abandoned amusement park. Chandler tells his wife what has happened and that he is going to kill Johnson. Gerard and Kimble learn what has happened from Chandler's wife and rush to the amusement park.

At the park, they spot Chandler, and Gerard orders him to drop his rifle. As they approach Chandler, Johnson fires his gun and hits Gerard in the leg. Gerard gives Kimble his gun and Richard takes off in pursuit. On top of a water tower, when Kimble has Johnson pinned against the railing, he hears what he has been longing to hear since 1961 — Johnson's confession to Helen's murder. Another fight ensues and Johnson manages to get Richard's gun. It looks like curtains for Kimble when Gerard appears and kills Johnson with Chandler's rifle.

A relieved Kimble tells Gerard that Johnson confessed — but it is a worthless confession as Richard is the only one who heard it. Just then Chandler steps forward and tells Gerard that Kimble is innocent and that he will testify for him in court.

Outside a courthouse, Richard Kimble stands a free man. Gerard makes the first move, and he and Richard shake hands for the first time. "Tuesday, August 29th, 1967. The day the running stopped." We assume that Richard will marry Jean and resume his medical practice.

Some of the aliases used by Richard Kimble were: Russell Jordan (episode 104), Jim Parker (episode 106), Bill March (episode 107), Steve Dexter (episode 108), Tom Marlowe (episode 109), Gene Tyler (episode 110) and Jerry Sinclair (episode 111). In Canada, where the final episode aired a week later, narrator William Conrad exclaimed: "Tuesday, September 5th, 1967. The day the running stopped."

Relatives: Robert Keith (Richard's father, *Dr. John Kimble*), Jacqueline Scott (Richard's sister, *Donna Taft*), Andrew Prine (Richard's brother, *Ray Kimble*), James B. Sikking and Richard Anderson (Donna's husband, *Leonard Taft*), Barbara Rush (Philip's wife, *Marie Gerard*; name also given as *Ann Gerard* and played by Rachel Ames), Bill Mumy (Donna's son, *David Taft*), Clint Howard and Johnny Jensen (Donna's son, *Billy Taft*)

Flashbacks: Diane Brewster (Richard's wife, *Helen Kimble*)

Theme: "The Fugitive," by Pete Rugolo

FULL HOUSE

ABC, 9.22.87 to

Principal Cast: Bob Saget (*Danny Tanner*), Candace Cameron (*D. J. Tanner*), Jodie Sweetin (*Stephanie Tanner*), John Stamos (*Jesse Cochran*), David Coulier (*Joey Gladstone*), Andrea Barber (*Kimmy Gibler*), Lori Loughlin (*Rebecca Donaldson*), Mary Kate and Ashley Olsen (*Michelle Tanner*)

Trivia: Following the death of his wife, Pamela, in a car accident, Danny Tanner asks his brother-in-law, Jesse Cochran, and Jesse's best friend, Joey Gladstone, to move in with him (at 1882 Gerard Street) and help him raise his three young daughters (D. J., Stephanie and Michelle). The situation seems unlikely to succeed at first, but proves a good one and the six become a family.

Danny, originally a sportscaster for Channel 8's "Newsbeat," was later made co-host (with Rebecca Donaldson) of "Wake Up, San Francisco," an early morning information series. (In college, Danny had a TV show called "College Rap.")

Jesse, who is partners with Joey in J. J. Creative Services (commercial jingle writers), was originally a pest exterminator. At age 13, Jesse was called "Zorba the Geek" by kids, and before moving in with Danny, he was part of a band called Feedback, and known as Dr. Dare (he would take any dare). Jesse, whose musical idol is Elvis Presley, now has a band called Jesse and the Rippers and a pet turtle named Bubba. His favorite expression is "Have mercy" and the band plays at the Smash Club.

Joey, who with Jesse was a member of the Chi Sigma Sigma Fraternity in college (the mascot was a seal) is a stand-up comic hoping to get his big break. Joey, whose favorite expression is "Cut it out," has a red 1963 Rambler he calls Rosie (license plate JJE 805).

D. J. (Donna Jo), the oldest of the Tanner girls, attends Fraser Street Elementary School, then Beaumont Junior High

School. She has a favorite pillow she calls Pillow Person and her own phone (the number of which is 555–8722).

Stephanie Judith, the middle child, attends Fraser Street Elementary School, and has a favorite stuffed bear doll she calls Mr. Bear. She carries a "Jetsons" lunch box to school, has a doll named Emily, and her favorite expression is "How rude!"

Michelle, the baby of the family (and the scene stealer), attends Meadowcrest Pre-School; her favorite expression is "You got it, dude." On her first day in pre-school, Michelle let the class bird, Dave, out of his cage and he flew away. (On his first day in pre-school, Jesse was goldfish monitor and killed the fish when he took it home for the weekend without the bowl.)

Rebecca, Danny's co-host, was born on a farm in Nebraska and had a pet cow named Janice. Kimmy Gibler, D. J.'s best friend, attends the same school as D. J. and, more often than not, gets D. J. into trouble with her antics. The Tanners have a dog named Comet and the family (including Kimmy) appeared on the "We Love Our Children Telethon," hosted by Danny on May 4, 1990.

Relatives: Alice Hirson and Doris Roberts (Danny's mother, *Claire Tanner*), Rhoda Gemignani and Yvonne Wilder (Jesse's mother, *Irene Cochran*), Beverly Sanders (Joey's mother, *Mindy Gladstone*), John Aprea (Jesse's father, *Nick Cochran*)

Flashbacks: Christine Houser (Danny's wife, *Pamela Tanner*), Philip Glasser (*Danny as a boy*), Kristopher Kent Hall (*Joey as a boy*), Adam Harris (*Jesse as a boy*)

Flash Forwards: Melanie Vincz (*adult D. J.*), Julia Montgomery (*adult Stephanie*), Jayne Modean (*adult Michelle*), Rhoda Shear (*adult Kimmy*)

Theme: "Everywhere You Look," vocal by Jesse Frederick

FUNNY FACE / THE SANDY DUNCAN SHOW

CBS, 9.18.71 to 12.11.71
9.17.72 to 12.31.72

"She's the kind of girl you'd slay dragons for, the one you'd bring home to your folks, the family, and let 'em see the kind of girl she is." In the original series, "Funny Face" (1971), Sandy Stockton (Sandy Duncan), newly arrived in Los Angeles from Illinois, enrolls as a student teacher at U.C.L.A. and takes a part-time job with Maggie Prescott (Nita Talbot), owner of the Prescott Advertising Agency; Sandy becomes the "Yummy Peanut Butter Girl" and the spokesperson for "John E. Appleseed Used Cars in the Heart of the San Fernando Valley" (both on TV commercials). When the series returned in 1972 as "The Sandy Duncan Show," Sandy, who lives in Apartment 2A of the Royal Weatherly Hotel (at 130 North Weatherly Boulevard), is both a student teacher at U.C.L.A. and a part-time secretary for Bert Quinn (Tom Bosley), the senior member of the Quinn and Cohen Advertising Agency. Patrick Williams composed the theme.

FURY

NBC, 10.15.55 to 9.3.66

"Fury" presents stories of a boy's growth to manhood as seen through the eyes of Joey (Bobby Diamond), a young orphan who is adopted by Jim Newton (Peter Graves), the owner of the Broken Wheel Ranch on the outskirts of Capitol City. William Fawcett plays Pete, "Jim's top hand, who says he cut his teeth on a branding iron." Nan Leslie plays Jim's sister, Harriet Newton; Maudie Prickett appears as Jim's Aunt Harriet.

Joey's black stallion is named Fury; his friend Packy Lambert (Roger Mobley) has a horse named Lucky; his other friend Pee Wee Jenkins's (Jimmy Baird) horse is named Pokey. The series is also known as "Brave Stallion" (its syndicated title during the 1950s).

GAVILAN

NBC, 10.26.82 to 12.28.82
3.18.83 (1 episode)

Ex-CIA agent Robert Gavilan (Robert Urich) is a consultant/troubleshooter for the DeWitt Institute, a California-based oceanographic research organization. His home telephone number is 555-3224, and his submarine is named Buzz. Jennifer Wallace plays the girl Gavilan meets on the beach in the opening theme. Patrick Macnee portrays Milo Bentley, the exiled Latin American who lives with Gavilan (the role of Milo was originally intended to be played by Fernando Lamas). Steve Dorf composed "Gavilan's Theme."

THE GEORGE BURNS AND GRACIE ALLEN SHOW

CBS, 9.12.50 to 9.22.58

Principal Cast: George Burns, Gracie Allen, Ronnie Burns and Harry Von Zell (*as themselves*), Bea Benaderet (*Blanche Morton*), Larry Keating (*Harry Morton*)

Trivia: The hectic outside show-business life of comedian George Burns and his scatterbrained wife, Gracie Allen, who reside at 312 Maple Street in Beverly Hills, California, with their son, Ronnie. (In New York episodes, George and Gracie lived in Suite 2216 of the St. Moritz Hotel.)

George Burns, a straight man, and comedienne Gracie Allen met while performing in vaudeville in the 1920s. According to Gracie, it was due to the meat shortage that she and George married. (George came over to Gracie's house for dinner one night in 1927. When Gracie's mother had only enough steaks to feed four of the six people waiting for dinner, she told Gracie to elope—and so she and George did.) They were married in Cleveland, and George's friend Jack Benny was the witness. Gracie mentions in another episode that her mother was also at the wedding and cried all the way through the ceremony. Gracie's mother, who does not care for George, was actually crying

because *The Sheik* with Rudolph Valentino was premiering that night and she had to miss it. George and Gracie first lived at the Edison Hotel in New York for three years before buying their home in California.

Gracie, who sews up the buttonholes on George's shirts so no one will know the buttons are missing, wrote her first article, "My Life With George Burns," for *Look* magazine in 1952 (she had to type two copies; she tried using carbon paper, but it is black "and you can't see what you type on it").

According to George, Gracie inherited her writing ability from her Uncle Harvey. He was the first one in the family to write an article ("Famous Forgers and How They Work"), but he didn't get any money for it: "By force of habit he signed someone else's name." Gracie's never-seen Uncle Harvey is a frequent resident of the San Quentin Prison (every time Gracie mentions him, he is in jail). Gracie's never-seen mother, who lives in San Francisco, has the phone number Market 1-0048.

George and Gracie's neighbors, Blanche and Harry Morton, live at 314 Maple Street; they have been neighbors for 12 years. Blanche grew up on Elm Street in Seattle; Harry, a C.P.A., went to Dartmouth and will drink only one alcoholic beverage—blackberry cordial. In 1953 it was mentioned that the Mortons were married for 13 years; a 1952 episode mentions that George and Gracie were married for 25 years.

Before Larry Keating played Harry, John Brown, Bob Sweeney and Fred Clark played the role: at that time, Harry was a real estate salesman with the firm of Casey and Morton. Hal March played Casey. Harry became an accountant during the 1954–55 season.

Harry Von Zell, George's friend and announcer, most frequently finds himself the pawn in George's efforts to resolve situations that arise from Gracie's antics. Many of the episodes in syndication reflect the show's long-time sponsor, Carnation Milk (cans of the product can be seen in kitchen shots).

Relatives: Russell Hicks (Harry's father, *Harry Morton Sr.*), King Donovan (Blanche's brother, *Roger*), Ann Steffins (Blanche's niece, *Linda*)

Theme: "Love Nest," played by Mahlon Merrick

Note: From 10.21.58 to 4.14.59 "The George Burns Show" aired on NBC. When Gracie retired from show business and left the show in 1958, George becomes a theatrical producer. Ronnie Burns, Harry Von Zell, Bea Benedaret and Larry Keating continued their roles from the previous series.

GET SMART

NBC, 9.18.65 to 9.13.69
CBS, 9.26.69 to 9.11.70

Principal Cast: Don Adams (*Maxwell Smart*), Barbara Feldon (*Agent 99*), Edward Platt (*Chief*), Bernie Kopell (*Conrad Siegfried*), Dick Gautier (*Hymie the Robot*), Dave Ketchum (*Agent 13*)

Trivia: Maxwell Smart, Agent 86, and Agent 99 (real name not given), are secret agents for CONTROL, a U.S. government organization located at 123 Main Street in Washington, D.C., whose phone number is 555-3743. Max, a bumbling klutz, uses the cover of Maxwell Smart, a salesman for the Pontiac Greeting Card Company; 99, the female agent with beauty as well as brains, uses various aliases to protect her true identity (even after she and Max marry, Max continues to call her 99 and her mother, "99's mother"). Max, who drives a red sports car with the license plate 6A7 379, uses the password "Bismark" for entry to his booby-trapped apartment, and became famous for the catch phrases "Sorry about that, Chief," "Would you believe . . . " and "I asked you not to tell me that."

A man named Thaddeus is the head of CONTROL; he is usually called "Chief." (He replaced former CONTROL Chief Admiral Harold Harmon Hargrade, played by William Schallert.) The Chief's cover is Howard Clark, Max's boss at the Pontiac Greeting Card Company.

In the opening theme, Max is seen driving up to CONTROL headquarters. He enters the building, walks down a flight of stairs and passes through an electronic door. Max then walks through four iron doorways (which close behind him). He enters a phone booth, dials a number, and is lowered to headquarters.

Conrad Siegfried, the head of the evil organization KAOS, is CONTROL's number one enemy. CONTROL's dog agent is Fang (K-13). CONTROL's anti-bugging device is the seldom-working Cone of Silence; the agency's top "male" agent is the beautiful Charlie Watkins. As played by Angelique Pettyjohn, Charlie is supposedly a man in drag (Max didn't believe it either). (After a short career in TV, Angelique, who appeared on such shows as "Star Trek," "Bracken's World" and "The Felony Squad," turned to X-rated films and appeared in such titles as *Body Talk* and *Titillation*.)

Hymie the Robot is a former KAOS agent reprogrammed for good by CONTROL. Agent 13 is a CONTROL operative who goes undercover wherever he can find a place to hide (for example, in a mailbox, a vending machine or a grandfather clock).

Relatives: Jane Dulo (*99's mother*), Charles Lane (Max's *Uncle Albert*), Maudie Prickett (Max's *Aunt Bertha*)

Theme: "Get Smart," written by Irving Szathmary

Note: On February 26, 1989, ABC aired *Get Smart, Again*, a TV movie reuniting Don Adams and Barbara Feldon as Max and 99. When KAOS threatens to destroy the world with a weather machine, the U.S. Intelligence Agency decides to reactivate CONTROL, which was closed in 1974. Max, now a protocol officer for the State Department, 99, Hymie the Robot and Agent 13 are reunited and ordered to stop Siegfried. Ken Mars played the new head of CONTROL, Commander Drury.

GIDEON OLIVER

ABC, 2.20.89 to 5.22.89

Gideon Oliver (Louis Gossett Jr.) is a crime sleuth and anthropology professor at New York's Columbia University. His address is 3 West 67th Street in Manhattan. His daughter and sometimes assistant, Zina Oliver (Shari Headley), lives at 651 West 117th Street (in an 11th floor apartment). Mike Post composed the theme.

GIDGET

ABC, 9.15.65 to 9.1.66

Principal Cast: Sally Field (*Gidget Lawrence*), Don Porter (*Russell Lawrence*), Betty Conner (*Anne Cooper*), Peter Deuel (*John Cooper*), Lynette Winter (*Larue*), Steven Mines (*Jeff "Moondoggie" Matthews*)

Trivia: "If you're in doubt about angels being real, I can arrange to change any doubts you may feel. Wait until you see my Gidget, you'll want her for your valentine . . . " Fifteen-and-a-half-year-old Frances Lawrence, nicknamed Gidget (a girl who is neither tall nor a midget—a Gidget) by her surfer friends, resides at 803 North Dutton Drive in Santa Monica, California, with her widowed father, Russell, an English professor at U.C.L.A. Gidget, whose phone number is given as both Granite 5–5099 and 477–0599, attends Westside High School. While Gidget surfs at Malibu Beach and usually wears a two-piece bathing suit (not exactly a bikini), her best friend Larue is allergic to the sun and often covers herself with lightweight clothes and large hats.

At school, Gidget is president of the Civics Club, and she wrote the "Helpful Hannah" advice column for the newspaper, the *Westside Jester*. In one episode, Gidget performed with the rock group the Young People (later changed to Gidget and the Gorries). Gidget and her friends see movies at the Spring Street Theater and her slang for goodbye is "Toodles."

Moondoggie (whose real name is Jeff), Gidget's boyfriend, attends Princeton University; Gidget's well-developed friend, Eleanor Chest (Beverly Adams), is called "Treasure Chest" by the boys. Anne is Gidget's married sister and John is Anne's husband, a graduate student pursuing his master's degree in psychology. Larue has a horse named Snowball. The afterschool hangout is Pop's, a hamburger shop.

Relatives: Hazel Court (Jeff's mother, *Laura Matthews*), Hal March (Jeff's father, *Jim Matthews*), Jan Crawford (Larue's cousin, *Roger Haimes*)

Theme: "Gidget," vocal by Johnny Tillotson

Note: See also "The New Gidget." Before "The New Gidget" series, two other pilots were made: "Gidget Grows Up" (ABC, 12.30.69) with Karen Valentine as Gidget, Paul Petersen as Jeff and Bob Cummings as Russ Lawrence, and "Gidget Gets Married" (ABC, 1.4.72) with Monie Ellis as Gidget, Michael Burns as Jeff and Macdonald Carey as Russ Lawrence.

GILLIGAN'S ISLAND

CBS, 9.26.64 to 9.3.67

Principal Cast: Alan Hale Jr. (*the Skipper*), Bob Denver (*Gilligan*), Tina Louise (*Ginger Grant*), Jim Backus (*Thurston Howell III*), Natalie Schaefer (*Lovey Howell*), Dawn Wells (*Mary Ann Summers*), Russell Johnson (*the Professor*)

Trivia: On September 26, 1964, movie star Ginger Grant, millionaire Thurston Howell III and his wife, Lovey, Kansas girl Mary Ann Summers, and Professor Roy Hinkley, charter the boat the *SS Minnow* for a tour of the Hawaiian Islands. The *Minnow* is captained by Jonas Grumby and his first mate, Gilligan. Unknown to the captain and Gilligan, the Coast Guard has supplied them with an inaccurate weather forecast for clear sailing. Shortly after the *Minnow* leaves the Honolulu harbor for its three-hour tour, the skies darken and, at heading 062, the *Minnow* is hit by a fierce storm.

The Skipper's quick thinking saves the lives of his crew and passengers, but Gilligan's bumbling helps to shipwreck the

Minnow on an uncharted island about 300 miles southeast of Hawaii. The island is named Gilligan's Island, perhaps because Gilligan was one of the first to set foot on it. (A *TV Guide* article reported that when the producers were seeking a title for the show, they opened a phone book and the name Gilligan was selected at random.)

The island, once inhabited by a tribe of headhunters called the Kubikai, soon becomes the home of the Shipwrecked Seven when all attempts at rescue fail. Although they are never rescued in the series, the castaways desperately struggle to find a way off the island.

The Skipper, who calls Gilligan his "Little Buddy," is a Navy man in love with the sea. He lost everything when the *Minnow* was beached but has high hopes of buying a new boat and beginning a new business when rescued.

Gilligan (first name never revealed) was born in Pennsylvania, and is both a friend and a burden to the Skipper. Gilligan, whose favorite dessert is coconut, papaya and tuna fish pie, has a pet duck named Gretchen, a lucky rabbit's foot that seems anything but lucky and a solid steel four-leaf clover. He listens to radio station WKMU from Manila, and heard over KDKA (Pittsburgh) that he was a sweepstakes winner with ticket number G131–131 (the announcer was John Reid King and Gilligan had last year's ticket). Gilligan's best friend stateside was Skinny Mulligan; he had a native Matobi girl named Kaloni as a slave for a short while (it was her way of repaying him for saving her life); and his image, carved in wood, graces the top of a Kubikai totem pole—the natives thus believe he is their once noble chief come back to life. In one episode, Bob Denver played Gilligan's double, an enemy agent who believed the castaways possessed secret information.

Thurston Howell III, "The Wolf of Wall Street," and his wife, Lovey (the former Lovey Wentworth), are multi-millionaires who packed a fabulous wardrobe and several hundred thousand dollars in cash for their three-hour tour. Thurston, who is the head of Howell Industries, has a stuffed teddy bear named Teddy (his security blanket), a favorite stock called Amalgamated and a practice polo pony named Bruce. His favorite club is the New York Stock Exchange and his favorite reading matter is the *Social Register*. He is very particular about his bath, which must occur at 8:05 P.M. with water temperature a consistent 79 degrees. He attended SMU (Super Millionaires University) and if given a choice between giving up his money or his wife, he'd give up his wife. He and Lovey are also members of the Newport Country Club. In one episode, Jim Backus plays Mr. Howell's double, a man who was pretending to be Thurston Howell III. In another episode, Thurston includes the castaways in his will. He gave the Skipper 40 acres of land in downtown Denver, Colorado; Gilligan, an oil well; Ginger, a diamond mine; Mary Ann, a plantation; and the Professor, the Transcontinental Railroad. Lovey was once voted "Queen of the Pitted Prune Bowl Parade."

Ginger, a gorgeous movie actress who measures 38–27–35 (in another episode, 36–25–36) broke into show business in a mind-reading act with Merlin the Mind Reader. Ginger, who was voted "Miss Hour Glass" ("They said I had all the sand in the right places"), appeared in the following movies: *San Quentin Blues, Sing a Song of Sing Sing, Belly Dancers from Bali Bali, The Rain Dancers of Rango Rango* and *Mohawk Over the Moon* (the last picture she made before the shipwreck). In one episode, Tina Louise played Ginger's drab double, Eva Grubb.

Mary Ann, who is from Horners Corners, Kansas (also given as Winfield, Kansas), is a pretty clerk who grew up on a farm. In one episode, she, Ginger and Mrs. Howell formed a singing group called the Honeybees as a ploy to get island visitors the Mosquitos to take them to the mainland. (The band the Wellingtons played Mosquitos Bingo, Bango and Bongo; Les Brown Jr. played their leader, Irving).

The Professor, to whom the castaways owe a debt of gratitude for his ingenuity in making life on the island as modern and convenient as possible, discovered five different mutations of ragweed in his first week on the island. His favorite dessert is halibut with kumquat sauce. On the mainland he is a well-known high-school science teacher and scout troop leader.

In first season episodes, Hans Conried played Wrong Way Feldman, a famed World War I flier who flew *The Spirit of the Bronx*, but had (and still has) no sense of direction. Vito Scotti appeared in several episodes as Dr. Boris Balinkoff, a mad scientist from a nearby island.

In the original unaired pilot, Kit Smythe was Ginger, Nancy McCarthy was Mary Ann and John Gabriel was the Professor.

Theme: "The Ballad of Gilligan's Isle," vocal by the Wellingtons

Spinoffs and TV Movies (Same Cast Except Where Noted): "The New Adventures of Gilligan" (ABC, 9.7.74 to 9.4.77). An animated series that continues to relate the castaways' adventures on the island. Jane Webb voiced Ginger; Jane Edwards, Mary Ann.

"Gilligan's Planet" (CBS, 9.18.82 to 9.10.83). Animated. In an attempt to escape from the island, the Professor builds a rocket that maroons the castaways on an unknown planet. Dawn Wells provided the voices of both Ginger and Mary Ann.

Rescue from Gilligan's Island (NBC, 10.14, 10.21.78). TV movie. When a tidal wave hits the island, the castaways lash their huts together and form an odd-looking raft. They are rescued by the Coast Guard and brought to Hawaii. Several months later, they reunite for a cruise on the Skipper's new boat, the *Minnow II*. During the cruise, the ship is caught in a tropical storm and the seven castaways are again shipwrecked on the same island. Judith Baldwin played Ginger.

The Castaways on Gilligan's Island (NBC, 5.3.79). TV movie. After Gilligan finds the remains of two World War II airplanes, the Professor salvages enough parts to make one operable plane. They leave the island and Mr. Howell later turns it into a tropical resort called the Castaways. Judith Baldwin played Ginger.

The Harlem Globetrotters on Gilligan's Island (NBC, 5.15.81). TV movie. The castaways, all partners in the island resort, attempt to stop J. J. Pierson (Martin Landau) from using a mineral found on the island called Supremium to control the world. Constance Forslund played Ginger.

GIMME A BREAK

NBC, 10.29.81 to 5.5.87

Principal Cast: Nell Carter (*Nell Ruth Harper*), Dolph Sweet (*Carl Kanisky*), Kari Michaelsen (*Katie Kanisky*), Lori Hendler (*Julie Kanisky*), Lara Jill Miller (*Samantha Kanisky*), John Hoyt (*Stanley Kanisky*), Joey Lawrence (*Joey Donovan*), Telma Hopkins (*Addie Wilson*), Jonathan Silverman (*Jonathan Maxwell*)

Trivia: During a performance at Mr. Funky's Night Club in Glenlawn, California, singer Nell Harper meets Margaret Kennedy, an old friend who is now married to a policeman (Carl Kanisky) and the mother of three young daughters. Shortly afterward, when Nell refuses to abide by the club owner's wishes and meet him in his room, she is fired. Margaret offers to let Nell stay with her and her family. There, she quickly wins the affections of Katie, Julie and Samantha, Margaret's daughters.

Five weeks later, when Nell is about to leave for a gig in Bakersfield, Margaret tells her a secret that she has kept from the family: she is dying. Margaret then asks Nell to raise her girls (knowing all too well that Carl could never manage alone). After much thought, Nell agrees to do this one last favor for her dearest friend. The series is set some years later (when Carl is the police chief) and follows Nell's efforts to raise three mischievous girls.

The Kaniskys live at 2938 Maple Lane in Glenlawn, California. Their phone number is 555-8162 (later 555-2932) and they have a pet goldfish named Gertrude. Also living with them are Carl's father, "Grandpa" Stanley Kanisky (who came from Poland to America in 1924 via the ship *Karkov*), and Joey Donovan, an orphan Nell adopts.

Katie, the eldest daughter, is also the prettiest. She attended Glenlawn High School and was a member of the Silver Slippers Sorority. Katie was a part of a rock group called the Hot Muffins. She also had her own business, Katie's, a clothing store in the Glenlawn Mall. In 1986, Katie moved to San Francisco to become a buyer for the Chadwick Department Store.

Julie, the middle child, has an I.Q. of 160 and also attends Glenlawn High. She is the only one of the girls to marry (Jonathan) and have a child (Little Nell). In 1986, Julie and Jonathan (who drives a delivery truck for Luigi's Pizza Parlor) move to San Diego to set up housekeeping.

Samantha, the youngest of the girls, is also the closest to Nell. While her grammar school was not mentioned, she attended Glenlawn High and later (1986) Littlefield College in New Jersey. Her imaginary friend as a child was Debbie Jo.

When Samantha leaves for college, Nell, who was born in Alabama and had been taking child-psychology classes at Glenlawn Junior College, decides to move to New York (where she acquires a job as an editor at the McDutton and Leod publishing house).

Nell's friend Addie Wilson is Phi Beta Kappa, and taught at Glenlawn Junior College. Joey was a member of the fourth grade Dodgers baseball team. The stationhouse dog (a German Shepherd) was named Rex.

Relatives: Lili Valenty, Elvia Allman, Elizabeth Kerr and Jane Dulo (Stanley's wife, *Mildred Kanisky*), Ed Schrum (Carl's brother, *Ed Kanisky*), Ben Powers (Nell's ex-husband, *Tony Tremaine*), Lynn Thigpen (Nell's sister, *Loretta Harper*), Hilda Haynes and Rosetta LeNoire (Nell's mother, *Maybelle Harper*), Matthew Lawrence (Joey's brother, *Matthew Donovan*), Fred McCarren and Patrick Collins (Joey's father, *Tim Donovan*)

Flashbacks: Sharon Spelman (Carl's wife, *Margaret Kennedy*), Nicole Roselle (*Katie, age eight*), Keri Houlihan (*Julie, age six*), Jeann Barron (*Samantha, age four*).

Theme: "Gimme a Break," vocal by Nell Carter

THE GIRL FROM U.N.C.L.E.

see THE MAN FROM U.N.C.L.E.

GLORIA

see ARCHIE BUNKER'S PLACE

THE GOLDEN GIRLS

NBC, 9.14.85 to

Principal Cast: Rue McClanahan (*Blanche Devereaux*), Betty White (*Rose Nylund*), Bea Arthur (*Dorothy Zbornak*), Estelle Getty (*Sophia Petrillo*)

Trivia: When the "two old biddies from Minnesota" she had been living with suddenly leave her, Blanche Devereaux, who lives at 6151 Richmond Street in Miami Beach, Florida, places a notice on a supermarket bulletin board for two new roommates. At the supermarket, she meets her first new roommate, Rose Nylund, who was evicted from her apartment when a new landlord took over her building and would not allow her to keep her cat Mr. Peepers. Later that day, Dorothy Zbornak becomes Blanche's second roommate when she answers the ad. A short time later, Dorothy's mother, Sophia Petrillo, who had been living at the Shady Pines Retirement Home, moves in too.

Blanche, whose home is financed by Miami Federal at seven percent interest, was born in Atlanta, Georgia, and is considered the most attractive of the women, all of whom are over 50. She flaunts her sexuality, and is known to have had many affairs. In 1989, she was "The Citrus Festival Queen," and at age 18, she "ran off to Copenhagen with a tortured painter" (a house painter). Her late husband was named George.

Dorothy, the most outspoken of the women, was born in Brooklyn and is now an English teacher. Her mother, Sophia, born in Sicily, has a part-time job at the Pecos Pete Chow Wagon Diner, and has become somewhat senile in her old age (she is over 80). Dorothy has a never-seen uncle named Nunzio who lives with a goat.

Rose, the most naive of the women, was born in the strange little town of St. Olaf, Minnesota (where she attended St. Olaf Grammar and High schools). Rose and her late husband, Charlie, were married at St. Olaf's Shepherd's Church (the St. Olaf wedding march became very famous when Laurel and Hardy used it for their theme song). Rose, who eats raw cookie dough and is known to drink more than one egg nog at Christmastime, does outrageous things like running through the sprinklers without a bathing cap. She wrote the St. Olaf High School fight song ("Onward, St. Olaf"), has a teddy bear named Fernando, and is a volunteer cadet leader for the Sunshine Cadets. She now works as a production assistant at WSF-TV (for "The Enrique Ross Show," a consumer affairs program). Rose also places stickers of dead bugs on her car windshield to discourage other bugs from messing it up. In the episode "The Inheritance," Rose is awarded custody of Baby, a 29-year-old pig from a rich uncle (on her farm in St. Olaf, Rose had a pet pig named Lester who could predict the Academy Award winners by wiggling his tail).

Sophia plays bingo at St. Dominic's Church; she, Dorothy and Rose are Catholic; Blanche is a Baptist. Rose's maiden name is Gierkleckibiken (her husband, Charlie Nylund, owned a tile-grouting business); Dorothy's maiden name is Petrillo; Blanche's is Hollingsworth.

Relatives of Blanche: Sheree North (her sister, *Virginia*), Billy Jacoby (her grandson, *David*), Hallie Todd (her niece, *Lucy*), Murray Hamilton (her father, *"Big Daddy" Hollingsworth*), Shawn Scheeps and Debra Engle (her daughter, *Rebecca*), Monte Markham (her brother, *Clayton Hollingsworth*), Barbara Babcock (her estranged daughter, *Charmayne*), George Grizzard (her brother-in-law, *Jamie Devereaux*)

Relatives of Dorothy: Herb Edelman (her ex-husband, *Stan Zbornak*), Doris Belack (her sister, *Gloria*), Scott Jacoby (her son, *Michael Zbornak*), Marian Mercer (her cousin, *Magda*), Deena Freeman and Lisa Jane Persky (her daughter, *Kate*)

Relatives of Rose: Polly Holliday (her daughter, *Lily*), Christina Belford (her daughter, *Kirsten*), Marilyn Jones (her daughter, *Bridget*), Jeanette Nolan (her mother, *Alma Lindstrom*), Casey Snander (her *Cousin Sven*), Bridgette Andersen (her granddaughter, *Charley*)

Relatives of Sophia: Bill Dana (her brother, *Angelo*), Nancy Walker (her sister, *Angela*)

Flashbacks: Estelle Getty (*young Sophia, 50 years old*), Lyn Greene (*young Dorothy*), Sid Melton (Sophia's husband, *Salvatore Petrillo*), Kyle Hefner (*young Salvatore, in his 30s*), Bea Arthur (*Sophia's mother*), Rue McClanahan (*Blanche's mother*)

Theme: "Thank You for Being a Friend," vocal by Cindy Fee

Note: See also the spinoff series, "Empty Nest."

GOOD TIMES

CBS, 2.8.74 to 8.1.79

Principal Cast: John Amos (*James Evans*), Esther Rolle (*Florida Evans*), Jimmie Walker (*J. J. Evans*), BernNadette Stanis (*Thelma Evans*), Ralph Carter (*Michael Evans*), Ja'net DuBois (*Willona Woods*), Janet Jackson (*Penny Gordon*), Ben Powers (*Keith Anderson*), Johnny Brown (*Nathan Bookman*)

Trivia: Their rent is $104.50 a month and they live in Apartment 17-C of the Cabrini Housing Project at 963 North Gilbert in Chicago (the address is also given as 763 North Gilbert). Their telephone number is 555–8264. They are the Evanses, a poor black family struggling for survival during the bad times of the 1970s.

James, the father, is a totally dedicated husband to Florida and a loving but stern father to his three children (J. J., Thelma and Michael). He takes what work he can get and usually holds down several jobs at a time.

Florida, nicknamed "Pookie Poo" as a child, becomes a schoolbus driver (for the Roadway Bus Company) to support the family when James is killed in a car accident in Mississippi.

J. J. (James Jr.), a ladies' man who considers himself "the Ebony Prince," is a hopeful artist, and later works as an art director for the Dynomite Greeting Card Company. J. J., whose favorite expression is "Dyn-O-Mite," hides his money in "that sock" in his dresser drawer. At age 12, J. J. painted a naked lady eating grits on an elevator wall (he didn't know how to draw clothes then). When he needs money, J. J. borrows it from "Sweet Daddy" (Teddy Wilson), a shyster who charges 25 percent a week interest. In one episode, Dennis Howard played a white version of J. J. in a dream sequence; artist Ernie Barnes produced the pictures J. J. paints. In first season episodes, J. J. was a delivery boy for the Chicken Shack fast food store.

Thelma, the middle child, was born on June 15, 1957, and like J. J. attends an unnamed high school. While J. J. sees Thelma as "a face whose mold could make gorilla cookies" (Thelma sees J. J. as "Beanpole"), Thelma is actually a very attractive girl with aspirations to become an actress. She attends classes at the Community Workshop and marries her boyfriend, Keith Anderson (a former football player who now drives a cab for the Windy City Cab Company).

Michael, the smartest of the children, attends Harding Elementary School, and is dedicated to the Black Movement. While his high school is not named, we know that he was a member of the Junior War Lords Gang for a short time.

Willona, the family friend, worked in a beauty parlor, a department store, and George's Fashion Boutique. She adopted Penny Gordon, a battered child, in later episodes. Nathan Bookman, the overweight building super, is called "Buffalo Butt" by J. J. and Willona, and is a member of "The Jolly Janitors Club." His middle name is Millhouse. Gary Coleman appeared in several episodes as Gary Daniels, the obnoxious kid who lived in the building; Sandra Sharpe played his mother. Willona calls Michael "Gramps."

Relatives: Richard Ward (James's father, *Henry Evans*), Percy Rodrigues (Florida's cousin, *Edgar Edwards*), Calvin Lockhart (Florida's *Cousin Raymond*), Kim Hamilton (Raymond's wife, *Betty*), Carl Lee (Willona's ex-husband, *Ray*), Chip Fields (Penny's natural mother, *Mrs. Gordon*), Marilyn Coleman (Nathan's wife, *Violet Bookman*)

Theme: "Good Times," by Dave Grusin, Alan Bergman and Marilyn Bergman

Note: "Good Times" is a spinoff of "Maude" (see "All in the Family" for more information), in which Florida Evans was the maid to Maude and Walter Findlay (Bea Arthur and Bill Macy).

GRAND

NBC, 1.18.90 to

This series portrays life in the town of Grand, Pennsylvania. Harris Weldon (John Randolph) owns the Grand Piano Works Company (a Weldon Grand takes one year to make); Janice Pasetti (Pamela Reed) lives in a mobile home with her daughter Edda (Sara Rue) and earns a living by cleaning the Weldon Mansion.

Harris's niece, Carol Ann Smithson (Bonnie Hunt) and her husband Tom (Michael McKean) form their own business, the Smithson Group (a realty company) when Tom is fired from the piano company. Tom calls Carol Ann his "Hamster." Norris Weldon (Joel Murray), Harris's indecisive son, took on the personality of comedian Jack E. Leonard (believing it was his goal in life to be a stand-up comic) and had a cable-access TV show called "Let's Not Think with Norris Weldon" on Channel 128.

Wayne Kazmersky (Andrew Lauer) is the local motorcycle cop (Grand Police Department) who has a crush on Janice and is forever trying to impress her. Desmond (John Neville) is Harris's ever-faithful butler.

Janice, who takes three sugars in her

coffee, attended Grand High School (as now does Edda); the bar hangout is called Beethoven's; and Norris has a dog named Fallon.

Relatives: Britt Ekland (Harris's gorgeous ex-wife, *Viveca*), Ed Marinaro (Janice's estranged husband, *Eddie Pasetti*), Jacky Vinson (Tom's son from a former marriage, *Dylan Smithson*), Jane Hoffman (Wayne's mother, *Dot Kazmersky*).

Michael Leeson and Tom Snow composed the theme, "Play It Grand."

GRAND SLAM

CBS, 1.28.90 to 3.14.90

The exploits of Dennis Bakelenekoff (John Schneider) and Pedro Gomez (Paul Rodriquez), bickering bounty hunters who team up to catch bail jumpers. Dennis, who works for the Blue Bird Bail Bonds Company, has a dog named Grace and a van with license plate 92LT07. He was a cop with the San Diego Police Department (fired after a bad shooting), and a professional baseball player for two months. Nicknamed "Hardball" and making $175,000 a year, he was notorious for giving up the only home run hit in the Jack Murphy Stadium.

Pedro, whose car license plate reads VATO UNO, works for Aztec Bail Bonds. In the third episode, Dennis and Pedro decide to cut out the middle man and open their own private detective organization—Hardball and Associates (later called Associate and Associate after they began bickering over the company name). Lupe Ontiveros plays Pedro's Grandma Gomez in two episodes; Larry Gelman plays Dennis's boss at Blue Bird, Irv Schlosser; and Abel Franco plays Al Ramirez, the owner of Aztec Bail Bonds. Joseph Conlan composed the theme.

THE GREATEST AMERICAN HERO

ABC, 3.18.81 to 2.3.83

Principal Cast: William Katt (*Ralph Hinkley*), Robert Culp (*Bill Maxwell*), Connie Sellecca (*Pamela Davidson*), Faye Grant (*Rhonda Harris*), Michael Pare (*Tony Villacona*), Mary Ellen Stuart (*Holly Hathaway*)

Trivia: While on a field trip with his special education students in Palmdale, California, Ralph Hinkley, a teacher at Whitney High School, and Bill Maxwell, an FBI agent with the Los Angeles bureau who is stranded in the area, are chosen by aliens to save the planet Earth from destroying itself.

Ralph is given a special costume (red tights with a black cape and silver belt) that endows him with superhuman powers and an instruction manual on how to use the costume (which Ralph calls "the Suit"). Complications set in when Ralph and Bill lose the instruction book and Ralph has to play being the Greatest American Hero by ear.

Ralph, who married his girlfriend, Pamela Davidson, on January 6, 1983, attended Union High School and his telephone number is 555-4365 (later 555-0463). When Ralph wears the Suit, which Bill calls "the jammies," he acquires a number of super powers, including incredible speed and the abilities to fly, to appear and disappear at will, to deflect bullets and to tune into people's whereabouts via a mental image he gets by touching something that person touched. The *Daily Galaxy* was the first newspaper to publish a picture of Ralph flying.

Bill, who calls the aliens "the little green guys," is a hotheaded FBI agent who snacks on Milkbone dog biscuits; his license plate numbers are 293XUJ and 508 SAT.

Pam, a lawyer with the firm of Carter, Bailey and Smith, is their unwitting assistant in most cases that involve Ralph and the Suit. Pam is later with the firm of Selquist, Allen and Minor, and has a car with the license plate 793 LAF (later 733 LBL).

One of Ralph's students, Rhonda, was a member of the musical group L. A. Freeway. In 1983, when Ralph's identity as a superhero becomes known, and "the little green guys" learn what has happened, they summon Ralph and Bill. Ralph is told to find someone else to wear the suit (he will know when he finds that person). In the meantime, mankind's memory of Ralph is erased. Shortly after, Ralph meets Holly Hathaway—the girl who is to take his place. The would-be spin-off series was to have related Holly's adventures as she attempts to battle crime in the same fumbling manner as Ralph, as "The Greatest American Heroine." ("The Greatest American Heroine" was produced as a 20-minute pilot and is now in "The Greatest American Hero" package as a 60-minute episode; footage from other episodes has been added to stretch it.)

Relatives: Simone Griffeth (Ralph's ex-wife, *Alicia Hinkley*), Brandon Williams (Ralph's son, *Kevin Hinkley*), E. J. Peaker (Rhonda's mother, *Rose Harris*), June Lockhart (Pam's mother, *Alice Davidson*), Norman Alden (Pam's father, *Harry Davidson*)

Theme: "Believe It or Not," vocal by Joey Scarbury

GREEN ACRES

CBS, 9.15.65 to 9.7.71

Principal Cast: Eddie Albert (*Oliver Wendell Douglas*), Eva Gabor (*Lisa Douglas*), Tom Lester (*Eb Dawson*), Pat Buttram (*Eustace Haney*), Frank Cady (*Sam Drucker*), Alvy Moore (*Hank Kimball*), Hank Patterson (*Fred Ziffel*), Fran Ryan and Barbara Pepper (*Doris Ziffel*), Sid Melton (*Alf Monroe*), Mary Grace Canfield (*Ralph Monroe*)

Trivia: With a lifelong dream to become a farmer, New York lawyer Oliver Wendell Douglas purchases, sight unseen, the 160-acre Haney farm in Hooterville, a small farming community. (Prior to buying the farm, Oliver grew crops in his office desk drawer and corn on his Park Avenue patio.)

Over the objections of his glamorous and sophisticated wife, Lisa, the Douglases relinquish their life of luxury and move to a shabby, broken-down nightmare called Green Acres, which is four miles outside of the town of Hooterville.

Despite its appearance, Oliver, who does his farming wearing a suit and tie, is determined to make a go of the farm and become part of "the backbone of the American economy." Oliver, who attended Harvard Law School and was a fighter pilot in World War II, plows in an ancient, run-down Hoyt Clagwell tractor, and lives in a historic Hooterville landmark —the home and birthplace of Rutherford B. Skrug, the founder of "the great state of Hooterville." Oliver, a member of the Hooterville Fire Department Band, has his mind made up to be a farmer and constantly makes his famous farmer's speech: "It is the dream of my life to buy a farm. Move away from the city; plow my own fields; get my hands dirty; sweat and strain to make things grow. To join hands with other farmers, the backbone of the American economy . . . "

Lisa, his Hungarian wife, whom he met during the war, is the only person who hears a fife playing when Oliver gives his patriotic speech. She calls the town "Hootersville" and has a cow named Eleanor and a group of chickens she calls "the girls" (she originally had only one chicken, named Alice). Eleanor gives just the amount of milk Lisa requires (she merely places a glass under Eleanor and says, "One cup, please") and "the girls" give Lisa the exact number of eggs she asks for, too.

Eb Dawson, Oliver's farm hand, has a poster of Hoot Gibson, his hero, on his bedroom wall, and calls Oliver "Dad." Eb has a second job—standing in for Stuffy, Oliver's scarecrow, when he goes to the neighboring town of Pixley for lunch.

Sam Drucker, the owner of the town's General Store, publishes the community's only newspaper, the Hooterville *World Guardian*, and is its postmaster (their zip code is 40516½), as well.

Farmers Fred and Doris Ziffel are the "parents" of Arnold the pig, the most colorful resident of Hooterville. Unable to have children, the Ziffels raised Arnold as their son (his official name is Arnold Ziffel). Arnold is in the third grade, drinks lime soda, has tea with Lisa, predicts the weather with his tail, gets "the shys" in front of beautiful women, plays cricket

99

(he has his own cricket bat), looks forward to watching "The CBS Evening News with Walter Cronkite" and is allowed to paint his own room (he is partial to orange walls).

Mr. Haney, the valley's con artist (who sold Oliver Green Acres) is a member of the Hooterville Chamber of Commerce and chairman of the Bringing Outside Money Into Hooterville Committee. Haney, who works out of his truck—and will sell anything to make a dollar—has a wooden Indian named Irving Two Smokes.

Alf and Ralph Monroe are the inept brother and sister carpenters Oliver hires to repair Green Acres; Hank Kimball is the forgetful state agricultural representative.

Oliver likes his coffee black with sugar; Lisa prefers cream; Eb, cream with no sugar. Oliver's telephone is located at the top of a nearby telephone pole (the phone company ran out of wire); Fred Ziffel has no phone receiver (he uses a hammer to represent one and can only talk to people, not hear them); Hooterville, according to a sign at the train station, has an elevation of 1427 feet.

On May 18, 1990, CBS presented the TV movie, *Return to Green Acres*. After years of frustration, Oliver sells Green Acres back to Mr. Haney and he and Lisa return to their penthouse at 255 Park Avenue in New York City. However, when Oliver learns that the Armstrong Development Company is planning to turn Hooterville into a modern development, he and Lisa return to Hooterville to represent the people. When Oliver wins the case and realizes he still loves Hooterville, he buys back Green Acres.

The original cast recreated their roles with the exception of Fred and Doris Ziffel (who had passed away). Their lovely niece, Daisy Ziffel (Mary Tanner), inherited the farm and Arnold (Frank Welker was credited as "Arnold's Voice"). Mr. Haney, still a con artist, runs a hotel called Haney's House of Hospitality. Sam has a new sign in his store that reads "Credit Cards Not Accepted."

Relatives: Eleanor Audley (Oliver's moth-

er, *Eunice Douglas*), Lilia Skala (*Lisa's mother*)

Flashbacks: Jackie J. Jones (*Oliver as a boy*)

Theme: "Green Acres," by Vic Mizzy (vocal by Eddie Albert and Eva Gabor)

THE GREEN HORNET
ABC, 9.9.66 to 7.14.67

Principal Cast: Van Williams (*Britt Reid/the Green Hornet*), Bruce Lee (*Kato*), Wende Wagner (*Lenore "Casey" Case*), Walter Brooke (*Frank Scanlon*), Lloyd Gough (*Mike Axford*)

Trivia: After publisher Dan Reid (not seen) builds his newspaper, the *Daily Sentinel*, into America's greatest publication, he turns over its management to his playboy son, Britt, hoping the responsibility will mature him. He then hires ex-cop Mike Axford to secretly watch over Britt's activities.

Shortly afterward, when reading about his great-grand-uncle, John Reid ("the Lone Ranger"), Britt decides to follow in his footsteps and protect the rights and lives of decent citizens. Britt adopts the disguise of the Green Hornet (the insect that is most deadly when aroused) and establishes a base in an abandoned building. He reveals his secret identity to only three people: Kato, his Asian houseboy (who also serves as the Green Hornet's assistant), Lenore Case, his secretary, and Frank Scanlon, the District Attorney.

Because they are considered criminals and wanted by the police, the Green Hornet and Kato avenge crimes as semi-fugitives rather than as a law enforcement organization, always disappearing before the police arrive.

Britt, as the Green Hornet, drives the Black Beauty (license plate V 194), a 1966 Chrysler Imperial. Its features include rockets front and rear, knock-out gas in the front, and smoke in the rear for a smoke screen. The District Attorney's phone number is 555–6789.

Theme: "Flight of the Bumble Bee," trumpet solo by Al Hirt

GROWING PAINS

ABC, 9.24.85 to

Principal Cast: Alan Thicke (*Dr. Jason Roland Seaver*), Joanna Kerns (*Maggie Seaver*), Tracey Gold (*Carol Seaver*), Kirk Cameron (*Mike Seaver*), Jeremy Miller (*Ben Seaver*), Julie McCullough (*Julie Costello*), Chelsea Noble (*Kate McDonald*), Josh A. Koenig (*Richard "Boner" Stabone*), Kristen and Kelsey Dohrig (*Chrissy Seaver*)

Trivia: Fifteen Robin Hood Lane in Huntington, Long Island, New York, is the address of the Seaver family: parents Jason and Maggie, and their children, Mike, Carol and Ben.

Jason, a psychologist who works out of an office in his home, was originally associated with Long Island General Hospital. Maggie, originally a reporter with the Long Island *Daily Herald*, later became a TV reporter for Channel 19's "Action News" (where she uses her maiden name, Maggie Malone). Maggie and Jason, who is 13 months younger than Maggie, met at Boston College, where Jason was a member of the Wild Hots, a rock group. In 1989, Maggie won the "Working Mother of the Year Award."

Mike (Michael Aaron), the eldest child, first attended Dewey High School, then the Alf Landon Junior College. Mike, who has acting aspirations, starred in the Dewey High production of *Our Town* and had his first professional acting job on the TV series "New York Heat" as Officer Bukaski—who was killed off. In addition, Mike's name was misspelled in the credits as Michael Weaver. In college, Mike is a member of the Alf Landon Drama Club; he and girlfriend Kate McDonald starred together in the play, *The Passion*. Mike's previous jobs: paper boy for the Long Island *Herald* (200 customers on his route); waiter at World of Burgers; salesman at Stereo Village; car wash attendant; and nightman at the Stop and Shop Convenience Store.

Carol Ann, the middle child, is sensitive, very smart and much prettier than she thinks she is (her confidence improved when she switched from wearing glasses to contact lenses and Mike admitted to her, after years of ugly jokes, that she is very pretty—an admission, however, that is strictly a secret between them). Carol, who attended Dewey High, then Columbia University for a short time, took a job as a computer page breaker at GSM Publishing. As a young girl (age seven), Carol was a member of the Happy Campers scout troop; in 1988, she won the "Dewey High Homecoming Queen" title.

Ben, the second-born son, first attended Wendell Wilke Elementary School, then Dewey High—where he exhibits the potential to become another Mike (in his day, the school's number one problem student). His girlfriend (1989–90) is a very pretty but bossy girl named Laura Lynn (Jodi Peterson).

Julie Costello, a sophomore at Columbia University, is Chrissy Seavers' nanny and Mike's first steady girlfriend. In 1989, when Mike and Julie broke up, Julie apparently quit school and became a waitress at the La Village French restaurant.

Kate McDonald, a student at Alf Landon, became Mike's romantic interest after Julie. Boner is Mike's best friend "and cohort in crime."

FEM 412 is the license plate of the family station wagon; 6PU (later BLA 595) is Mike's license plate. In the original, unaired pilot film, Elizabeth Ward played Carol Seaver.

Relatives: Jane Powell (Jason's mother, *Irma Seaver*), Gordon Jump (Maggie's father, *Ed Malone*), Betty McGuire (Maggie's mother, *Kate Malone*), James Callahan (Jason's *Uncle Bob*), Ruth Silveira (*Boner's mother*), Richard Marion (*Boner's father*)

Flashbacks: Victor DiMattia (*Mike, five years old*), Judith Barsi (*Carol, four years old*)

Flash Forwards: Khrystyne Haje (*Chrissy, age 18*)

Theme: "We've Got Each Other," vocal by B. J. Thomas and Jennifer Warnes (later by B. J. Thomas and Dusty Springfield)

Note: See also "Just the Ten of Us," the spinoff series.

HAPPY DAYS

ABC, 1.15.74 to 7.19.84

Principal Cast: Tom Bosley (*Howard Cunningham*), Marion Ross (*Marion Cunningham*), Ron Howard (*Richie Cunningham*), Erin Moran (*Joanie Cunningham*), Henry Winkler (*Arthur "Fonzie" Fonzarelli*), Anson Williams (*Warren "Potsie" Webber*)

Trivia: A slice of 1950s life seen through the eyes of the Cunninghams, a family of five living in Milwaukee, Wisconsin: parents Howard and Marion, and their children, Richie, Joanie and Chuck.

Howard and Marion apparently married in 1936 (based on first season episodes set in 1956) and set up housekeeping at 618 Bridge Street. Howard, called "Cookie" during his hitch in the Army during World War II, owns the Cunningham Hardware Store and is a member of the Leopard Lodge (Local 462). His favorite color is blue and omelets are his favorite breakfast. Howard, a Republican, drives a black DeSoto (license plate F-3680) and when he has an aggravating day at work, his back goes out.

Marion, a secretary for an unnamed company before she married Howard, has a favorite drinking glass with a picture of Rudolph Valentino on it. She is a member of the Milwaukee Women's Club and her mother ("Mother Kelp") calls Howard "Fatso."

Richie weighs 135 pounds, is five feet, nine inches tall, and has blue eyes and red hair. He had the nickname "Freckles" at age nine, when he attended summer camp and was said to resemble Howdy Doody. He first attended Jefferson High School, then the University of Wisconsin. (In first-season episodes, Richie is a high school junior; the theme of his junior prom was "Teen Angel.")

Blueberry pancakes and fresh-squeezed orange juice is Richie's favorite breakfast (meat loaf is his favorite dinner) and in the family photo album, there is a full page devoted to Richie as a baby attempting to eat his first bowl of oatmeal. In grammar school, Richie received a medal for reading comprehension.

"The Love Bandit," license plate F-7193, is what Richie called his '52 Ford. In high school, Richie was a member of the French Club, his ROTC 3rd Squad leader, and a reporter for the school newspaper, the Jefferson *Bugle*. Richie first aspired to be a lawyer, then a journalist. He was also a disc jockey at radio station WOW (where he earned $25 a week), and he appeared as a contestant on the WZAZ-TV quiz show "Big Money" (his category was baseball). Cheap Work ("any job for money") was the short-lived company Richie formed with friends Potsie and Ralph to make extra spending money.

Arlene (Tannis G. Montgomery), Gloria (Linda Purl) and Lori Beth Allen (Lynda Goodfriend) were Richie's girlfriends. He married Lori Beth and they had a son named Richie Jr. Richie left the series when he joined the Army and was transferred to Greenland.

Richie's older brother, Chuck (see "Relatives"), who appeared to do nothing but bounce a basketball, left the series during the second season (written out)—he was said to be attending college.

Joanie Louise, Richie's sister, is a member of the Junior Chipmunks scout troop and later attends Jefferson High (her grammar school is not named). She has the nicknames "Shortcake" and "Pumpkin" and her first word as a baby was "hardware." Joanie's favorite meal is baked macaroni and apple sauce and when she had a crush on Richie's friend, Potsie, she would play "Secret Love" (Selection H-14) on the Seebring 100 Selecto-Matic Juke Box at Arnold's Drive-In. Her first nighttime date was with Fonzie's nephew, Spike, and she has a pet hamster named Gertrude.

Fonzie, whose full name is Arthur Herbert Fonzarelli (known as "the Fonz"), is the cool high school dropout who once rode with a motorcycle gang called the Falcons. After quitting the Falcons, he worked as a mechanic at Otto's Auto Orphanage (then at Herb's Auto Repairs, and at Bronco's Auto Repairs). In the final season, Fonzie, who returned to Jefferson High to get his diploma, becomes the

Dean of Boys at the rowdy George S. Patton High School. Fonzie was also a member of the Demons gang and his "offices" at Arnold's Drive-In are the "Guys Room" and the four-for-a-quarter photo booth outside.

Fonzie portrayed Hamlet in the local church production of *Hamlet* and played bongo drums in an unnamed band formed by Richie (keyboard), Ralph (sax) and Potsie (vocalist). His favorite restaurant is the North Bay Yacht Club. In one episode it is mentioned that Fonzie's father deserted his family when Fonzie was only three, and that his grandmother called him "Skippy." Fonzie first lived in Apartment 154 (an address is not given) before moving into the room above the garage at the Cunninghams (his rent is $50 a month). Fonzie attended high school for one-and-a-half years before dropping out.

As a boy Warren Webber often made things out of clay, so his mother nicknamed him "Potsie." He is Richie's best friend, weighs 145 pounds, is five feet, ten inches tall, and has blue eyes and black hair. He attended the same schools as Richie and together they shared many misadventures, such as using fake I.D.'s to see Bubbles the Stripper (Barbara Rhoades) at Eddie's Pink Palace; attempting to join the Demons gang to become "cool"; getting drunk at a stag party; and pooling their resources to pay $175 for a car whose best feature was the chrome eagle ornament on the hood. When Potsie visits the Cunninghams, he wears a white shirt with blue stripes. His parents' car license plate number is BFJ 380.

The afterschool hangout is Arnold's Drive-In, a hamburger joint located at 2815 Lake Avenue. It was originally owned by Arnold Takahashi (Pat Morita), then by Al Delvecchio (Al Molinaro). In the first episode, the hangout is called Arthur's Drive-In. The vending machine at Arnold's dispenses a soda called Spring Time Cola and the local haven for making out is Inspiration Point.

During the opening theme, the record seen being played on the juke box has a label that reads "Happy Days. Lyrics by Norman Gimble. Music composed by Charles Fox." While this song is heard in the closing theme (later the opening theme), the song "Rock Around the Clock" by Bill Haley and the Comets is actually heard while the record is played.

In the original pilot, "Love and the Happy Days" (broadcast on "Love, American Style" on 2.25.72), Harold Gould played Howard and Susan Neher was Joanie. Fonzie did not appear and the roles of Richie, Marion and Potsie were played by the same performers as in the series.

Other Characters: *Ralph Malph* (Donny Most), Richie and Potsie's friend; *Charles "Chachi" Arcola* (Scott Baio), Joanie's boyfriend; *Jenny Piccolo* (Cathy Silvers), Joanie's boy-crazy girlfriend; *Ashley Pfister* (Linda Purl), Fonzie's romantic interest for a short time; *Pinky Tuscadero* (Roz Kelly), Fonzie's biker friend; *Leather Tuscadero* (Suzy Quatro), Pinky's sister, a singer (in one episode, Joanie became a Suede, one of Leather's singers in her group, the Suedes); *Roger Phillips* (Ted McGinley), the basketball coach at Jefferson High; and *Danny* (Donny Ponce), the orphan Fonzie adopts (1984).

Relatives: Ric Carrott, Gavan O'Herlihy, and Randolph Roberts (Richie's brother, *Chuck Cunningham*), Jackie Coogan (Richie's *Uncle Harold*), Peggy Rea (Richie's *Aunt Bessie*), Bo Sharron (Richie's son, *Richie Jr.*), Crystal Bernard (Howard's niece, *K. C. Cunningham*), Richard Paul (Howard's brother, *Dick Cunningham*), Pat O'Brien (Howard's *Uncle Joe*), Eddie Fontaine (Fonzie's father, *Vito Fonzarelli*), Danny Butch (Fonzie's nephew, *Spike*), Frances Bay (Fonzie's *Grandma Nussbaum*), Ellen Travolta (Chachi's mother, *Louisa Arcola*), Heather O'Rourke (Ashley's daughter, *Heather Pfister*), Marla Adams (Ashley's mother, *Millicent Pfister*), Craig Stevens (Ashley's father, *George Pfister*), J. J. Barry (Chachi's *Uncle Gonzo*), Alan Oppenheimer and Jack Dodson (Ralph's father, *Mickey Malph*), Al Molinaro (Al's brother, *Father Delvecchio*), Alice Nunn (Al's *Mama Delvecchio*)

Theme: "Happy Days," by Charles Fox and Norman Gimble

Spinoffs: "Laverne and Shirley" and "Mork and Mindy" (see entries), and "Joanie Loves Chachi" (ABC, 3.23.82 to 9.13.83) in which Al Delvecchio and Louisa Arcola (Ellen Travolta), the widowed mother of Chachi, marry and move to Chicago to open their own business (Delvecchio's Family Restaurant at 1632 Palmer Street). Shortly after, Chachi joins a motley music group as a singer and asks Joanie to join him. Joanie receives permission to move to Chicago and the series relates their efforts to make a name for themselves in the music world.

HARDBALL
NBC, 9.21.89 to 6.29.90

Charlie Battles (John Ashton), a veteran cop, and his partner, Joe "Kaz" Kaczierowski (Richard Tyson), a streetwise cop, are with the Metro Division of the Los Angeles Police Department. Charlie, who was with the Fighting 52nd Unit of the U.S. Army in Korea, weighs 205 pounds, eats Oaties Breakfast Cereal, and has a car with the license plate 2LYN 596; his badge number is 6483. Kaz, whose badge number is 696, and who weighs 192 pounds, uses various disguises to apprehend criminals; he was a former Vice Squad detective with the San Diego Police Department. Both are members of the Slammers Baseball Team. Their car code is 1-K-9.

Kaz rides a motorcycle with the license plate 25862L, Charlie's favorite meal to cook is chili, and Kaz listens to radio station KRTW (where his favorite D.J. is the sexy-sounding Jamie Steele, played by Lydia Cornell).

Yvette Nipar played Charlie's daughter, Cindy Battles; Patricia Harty appeared as Kaz's mother, Beverly Kaczierowski; and Eddie Money sings the theme, "Roll It Over."

HARDCASTLE AND McCORMICK
ABC, 9.18.83 to 7.23.86

Judge Milton C. Hardcastle (Brian Keith), who is nicknamed "Hardcase" for his harsh courtroom sentences and outrageous procedures, gives Mark McCormick (Daniel Hugh Kelly), a two-time loser up for his third auto theft offense, a choice: serve time in jail or work with him in bringing to justice the 200 defendants who were tried before the judge, but whose cases were dismissed due to technicalities.

The judge and Mark set up Hardcastle and McCormick, Inc., at 101 Pacific Coast Highway in Malibu Beach, California. Mark, who is nicknamed "Skid," has a car called Coyote.

Relatives: Mary Martin (Milton's *Aunt Zora*), Mildred Natwick (Milton's *Aunt May*), Maylo McCaslin (Milton's niece, *Warren Wingate*; named after Judge Earl Warren), Ken Mars (Milton's brother, *Jerry Hardcastle*) and Steve Lawrence (Mark's father, *Sonny Dae*)

In a flashback sequence, Mike Turley played Milton Hardcastle as a young man. David Morgan sang the first-season theme, "Drive," and Joey Scarbury performed "Back to Back," the subsequent theme.

HARD COPY
CBS, 1.25.87 to 7.3.87

The series is set in the press room of the California Metro Police Department. Blake Calisher (Wendy Crewson) works for the City Wire Service, Paula Hirschon (Kim Miyori) writes for the *Metro Register*, and Andy Omart (Michael Murphy) is a reporter for the *Morning Express*. David Mansfield composed the theme.

HARPER VALLEY
NBC, 1.16.81 to 8.28.81
10.29.81 to 8.14.82

Principal Cast: Barbara Eden (*Stella Johnson*), Jenn Thompson (*Dee Johnson*), George Gobel (*Otis Harper*), Fannie Flagg (*Cassie Bowman*)

Trivia: Stella Johnson and her daughter, Dee, live at 769 Oakwood Street in Harper Valley, Ohio. Stella, a widow, was born Stella Smith; her job during the first season was salesgirl for Angel Glow Cosmetics. Her second-season job was executive assistant to Otis Harper, the intoxicated mayor, whose ancestors founded Harper Valley. Dee attends Harper Valley Junior High School. Stella's friend, Cassie Bowman, is a beautician at the LaModerne Beauty Shop; later, she publishes the Harper Valley *Sentinel*. Cassie's license plate is TNT 456.

Mills Watson plays Stella's mischievous uncle, William Homer "Uncle Buster" Smith, and Anne Francine portrays Flora Simpson Reilly, owner of the Harper Valley Bank, president of the P.T.A., and the woman who despises Stella's beauty and flamboyant style. Flora's limo license plate is NNT 552. Bridget Hanley plays Flora's married daughter, Wanda Taylor; Rod McCary, Wanda's husband, Bobby (the city attorney); and Suzi Dean, Wanda's rich and spoiled daughter, Scarlett.

Christopher Stone appeared as Tom Meechum, the editor of the *Harper Valley Sun*; and Fred Holliday as Doug Peterson, the news reporter for WHV-TV, Channel 29. The Tri-State Bus Line services Harper Valley and neighboring Columbus, Ohio.

Theme: Jeannie C. Riley performed the first-season theme, "Harper Valley, P.T.A."; Carol Chase sang "Harper Valley, U.S.A." during the second season.

Note: The series is based on both the song and movie "Harper Valley, P.T.A."

HART TO HART

ABC, 9.22.79 to 7.3.84

Principal Cast: Robert Wagner (*Jonathan Hart*), Stefanie Powers (*Jennifer Hart*), Lionel Stander (*Max*)

Trivia: Jonathan Hart, the wealthy head of Hart Industries, located at 112 North Las Palmas, Los Angeles, and his wife, Jennifer, live at 3100 Willow Pond Road in Bel Air. Their phone number is 555-1654, and their dog is named Freeway. Max is their man Friday, and their license plate numbers are HART I, HART II, HART III. Jennifer, formerly world-famous journalist Jennifer Edwards, met Jonathan on assignment; now she assists him in helping people in trouble.

Relatives: Ray Milland (Jennifer's father, *Steven Edwards*), Allyn Ann McLerie (Max's ex-wife, *Pearl*)

Theme: "Hart to Hart," by Roger Nichols

HAVE GUN—WILL TRAVEL

CBS, 9.14.57 to 9.21.63

"Have Gun, Will Travel reads the card of a man; a knight without armour in a savage land . . . " Paladin (Richard Boone), a fast gun-for-hire, operates from the Hotel Carlton in San Francisco, and has a calling card that reads "Have Gun—Will Travel. Wire Paladin. San Francisco." He wears a black outfit with a white chess knight—the Paladin—embossed on his black leather holster. The legend of Paladin evolved when an unnamed ex-Army officer lost more money than he could afford to in a poker game with a wealthy land baron (William Conrad). To pay the debt, the officer agreed to kill Smoke, an outlaw who had been plaguing the baron. Upon completing his task, the officer adopts Smoke's disguise—a black outfit and the symbol of the Paladin—and a policy of hiring out his guns and experience to those who are unable to protect themselves.

Kam Tong and Lisa Lu played Hey Boy and Hey Girl, Paladin's servants at the Hotel Carlton, where Mr. McGunnis (Olan Soule) is the manager. Johnny Western sings the theme, "The Ballad of Paladin."

HAWAII FIVE-O

CBS, 9.26.68 to 4.5.80

Steve McGarrett (Jack Lord) is the head of Five-0, a special branch of the Hawaiian Police Department based in the Iolani Palace (the only palace on American soil). Five-0's regular phone number is 732-5577 and its special emergency number is 277-2977.

McGarrett, who drives a car with the license plate 163958, has an account at the National Bank of Oahu. His astrological sign is Capricorn and he has his hair cut every Tuesday. His assistant, Danny Williams (James MacArthur), whom Steve calls "Dan-O," attended the University of Hawaii (majoring in psychology) for one year, then transferred to the University of California, where he majored in police science.

Steve, who was born in San Francisco, is a commander in the Navy Reserve. Danny was said to have been born both in Honolulu and in the Midwest. CBS affiliate KGMB-TV, Channel 9, is seen frequently as the TV station that covers Steve's cases.

Helen Hayes played Danny's Aunt Clara in one episode. "Book 'em, Dan-O" and "Patch me through to McGarrett" became the series' well-known catch phrases. Wo Fat (Khigh Dhiegh) is Steve's nemesis; Tim O'Kelly played Danny in the pilot. Morton Stevens composed the theme.

HE AND SHE

CBS, 9.8.67 to 9.18.68

On their first date in 1962 in the Adirondacks, Richard Hollister (Richard Benjamin) and Paula (Paula Prentiss) parked their car in a "Watch Out For Falling Rocks" zone. As Richard attempted to kiss Paula, a rock (an Upstate New York Greystone) fell and hit him on the head. Paula kept the rock as a memento of their first kiss and they married shortly after.

Richard, a cartoonist and the creator of the comic strip-turned-TV series, "Jetman," and Paula, an employee of the Manhattan Tourist Aid Society, live in an apartment at 365 East 84th Street in Manhattan. Their side window faces the local firehouse. Fireman Harry Zarakardos (Ken Mars) has placed a plank from their window to the firehouse window to provide easy access to both buildings. When Richard becomes upset, he frequents Hammond's Bar. Paula has their clothes cleaned at the Fiore Brothers Cleaners.

Jack Cassidy plays Oscar North, the egotistical star of "Jetman" and Hamilton Camp, Andrew Humble, the apartment-house handyman. (Andrew's first present from his wife 25 years ago was a blue shirt—which he still wears.) Jerry Fielding composed the theme.

HEART BEAT

ABC, 3.23.88 to 4.21.88
1.3.89 to 4.6.89

Joanne Springsteen (Kate Mulgrew), Eve Autry (Laura Johnson), Marilyn McGrath (Gail Strickland) and Cory Banks (Lynn Whitfield) are doctors with the Women's Medical Arts Practice who also work part-time with Dr. Leo Rosetti (Ben Powers) at Bay General Hospital in California.

For unknown reasons, Kate Mulgrew became Dr. Joanne Halloran and Laura Johnson, Dr. Eve Calvert in 1989 episodes. Hallie Todd played Marilyn's daughter, Allison, and Gina Hecht Marilyn's lover, Patty. The lesbian relationship between Marilyn and Patty was a continuing storyline and a first for a prime-time TV series (the soap spoof "Mary Hartman" touched on the subject with Gloria DeHaven's Annie "Tippy-toes" Wylie character).

Other Relatives: Amy Moore Davis (Eve's niece, *Donna Calvert*), Robert Gossett (Cory's husband, *Dixon Banks*), Julie Cobb (Leo's ex-wife, *Beverly Rosetti*), Michael Faustino (Leo's son, *Nicky Rosetti*)

Joanne's dog is named Noah, and Eve's pet mouse is named Maevette. Bill Conti composed the theme.

HEARTLAND

CBS, 3.20.89 to 7.24.89

B. L. McCutcheon (Brian Keith), his married daughter, Cassandra "Casey" Stafford (Kathleen Layman) and Casey's husband, Tom (Richard Gilliland), run the 350-acre McCutcheon Ranch in Pritchard, Nebraska. Kim (Daisy Keith) is Casey and Tom's adopted daughter, a hopeful violinist; and Johnny (Jason Kristopher) and Gus (Devin Ratray) are their biological children. B. L., who had a dog named Chester, then General Patton, and finally Silky, is a cantankerous widower whose favorite recording star is Elmo Tanner, the world's greatest whistler. Kim, Johnny and Gus attend Pritchard High School; Gus has a pet pig named Dolly. Dion sings the theme, "Heartland."

HELL TOWN

NBC, 9.11.85 to 1.1.86

Father Noah Rivers (Robert Blake) is an ex-con turned Catholic parish priest of St. Dominic's Parish and Orphanage in a tough East Los Angeles neighborhood called Hell Town. Father Rivers, who is called "the Guardian Angel of the Streets," is nicknamed Hardstep. Mother Mary Margaret (Natalie Cole), the nun who runs the orphanage, is nicknamed "Maggie Jiggs"; Sister Anastasia (Isabel Grandin) is nicknamed "Sister Angel Cakes"; and Tracy Morgan plays Brandy Wine, hostess at the local bar, Roy Bean's. Sammy Davis Jr. sings the theme, "Hell Town."

HELLO, LARRY

NBC, 1.26.79 to 4.26.81

Larry Alder (McLean Stevenson) hosts "The Larry Alder Show" (originally called "Hello, Larry"), a radio call-in program on KLOW in Portland, Oregon. The phone number of KLOW is 555-3567. The station is owned by TransAllied, Inc. Larry lives with his two daughters, Ruthie (Kim Richards) and Diane (Donna Wilkes; later Krista Errickson) in Apartment 2-B of an unnamed building. Their phone number is 555-4521.

Joanna Gleason plays Morgan Winslow, Larry's attractive producer; Shelley Fabares, his ex-wife, Marian; and Fred Stuthman, his father, Henry. When living in Los Angeles, Ruthie had a dog named Rusty. She longs for her father to buy a house. Will Hunt played Wendell the Drunk, the president of the Larry Alder Fan Club. (In first-season episodes, Larry's last name is Adler.) John LaSalle and Tom Smith composed the theme.

HERBIE, THE LOVE BUG

CBS, 3.17.82 to 4.14.82

Jim Douglas (Dean Jones), a former race-car driver, now runs the Famous Driving School and owns Herbie, the magical Volkswagen (from the Disney series of films). Patricia Harty plays Susan McLane, a widow and Jim's romantic interest; Julie (Claudia Wells), Martin (Nicky Katt) and Robbie (Douglas Emerson) are her children. Larry Linville portrays Rodney Bigelow, Susan's jealous ex-boyfriend; and Natalie Core, Rodney's mother, Mrs. Bigelow, who owns the Valley Savings Bank in California. Herbie's racing car number is 53, and his license plate is OFP857. The telephone number of the Famous Driving School is 555-7636. Dean Jones sings the theme, "Herbie, My Best Friend."

HIGHWAY TO HEAVEN

NBC, 9.19.84 to 8.4.89

Jonathan Smith (Michael Landon), an Angel of God, was born Arthur Morton in 1917, became an attorney and died in 1948. He then became an angel and was given the name Jonathan Smith. Mark Gordon (Victor French), his human assistant on earth, attended Lathrop High School and then was a cop with the Oakland Police Department for 15 years. In high school, Mark was nicknamed "Stick." Jonathan calls God "The Boss."

Dorothy McGuire played Jonathan's earthly wife, Jane Morton, in the episode of 2.10.88; Joan Wells, his married daughter, Mandy; and Richard McGonagle, Mandy's husband, Martin. Bob Hope made a rare dramatic appearance as Symcopop, the Assignment Angel. David Rose composed the theme.

HIS AND HERS

CBS, 3.5.90 to 8.22.90

Dr. Regina "Reggie" Hewitt (Stephanie Faracy) and her husband, Dr. Doug Lambert (Martin Mull), are newlywed marriage counselors who practice together in the same office of an unidentified building. Together they also host a radio call-in program called "Marriage Talk."

Doug, a Capricorn, was born in Muncie, Indiana. His favorite breakfast is banana pancakes and he estimates that he has saved 84 marriages. He collects Civil War cigar bands, even though he considers it a useless hobby.

Reggie, a Taurus, was born in Los Angeles and was voted "the psychologist you'd most like to share a couch with" in grad school. She and Doug honeymooned at Lake Tahoe. Reggie's mentor (not seen) is Dr. Emile Ludwig.

Lisa Picotte plays Mandy, Doug's daughter, and Blake Soper, Noah, Doug's son (both from a previous marriage that ended in divorce). The family cat is named Fluffy.

Randee Heller appeared as Doug's ex-wife, Lynn; Peggy McCay portrayed Reggie's mother, Marian Hewitt; and William Windom and Barbara Barrie played Doug's parents, Bill and Belle Lambert. James Beasley composed the theme, "Love Crazy."

THE HOGAN FAMILY

see VALERIE

THE HONEYMOONERS

CBS, 10.1.55 to 9.22.56

Principal Cast: Jackie Gleason (*Ralph Kramden*), Audrey Meadows (*Alice Kramden*), Art Carney (*Edward L. Norton*), Joyce Randolph (*Trixie Norton*)

Trivia: At the age of 14 he began working as a newspaper delivery boy to help support his family. During the Great Depression, he managed to find work with the WPA. Though his was a laborious job, the young Ralph Kramden was grateful to have work and kept alive a dream to one day be successful.

Some time later, he met and fell in love with a girl named Alice Gibson. It was definitely love at first sight, but three versions are recounted. In an early episode, it is said that Ralph first notices Alice in a diner when she speaks to the waiter, saying, "Hey, Mac, a hot frank and a small orange drink." In a later episode: On a cold, snowy afternoon, while standing in line for a snow shovel, Ralph meets Alice, a WPA employee who is handing them out. In a 1970 episode, Ralph mentions that he first met Alice in a restaurant called Angie's (they had spaghetti and meatballs). On their first date, Ralph took Alice dancing at the Hotel New Yorker.

In 1941, the courtship ended; Ralph and Alice married and moved in with Alice's mother (whom he calls "Blabbermouth"). When Ralph secured a job with the Gotham Bus Company, they rented their first (and only) apartment at 728 Chauncy Street in Bensonhurst, Brooklyn, New York (the address is also given as 358 and 328 Chauncey Street).

It was then, when an upstairs tenant named Edward L. Norton, a sewer worker for the Department of Sanitation, came down to invite his new neighbors to dinner, that the greatest friendship of all time was born—and through numerous trials and tribulations, it endured.

As a kid, Ralph attended P.S. 73 grammar school and had high hopes of playing the coronet in a band (another episode mentions that he used to hang out in pool halls after school). Ralph and Alice's phone number is Bensonhurst 0-7741, and their typical gas bill is 39 cents a month. Ralph's salary was $42.50 a week in early episodes and $60.00 a week in 1955. To supplement Ralph's income, Alice took two part-time jobs: stuffing jelly into doughnuts at Krausmeyer's Bakery (she was later promoted to jelly-doughnut taster) and a secretarial post to a man named Tony Amico. She was chosen "Cleaning Lady of the Month" by Glow Worm Cleanser. Ralph and Alice dine out most often at a restaurant called the Hong Kong Gardens.

Ralph's astrological sign is Taurus and Alice's is Aquarius (her birthday is February 8th). Ralph, who owns two suits (one blue, one black), drives Bus #247 (also given as #2969) along Madison Avenue in Manhattan. Over the course of his 14 years with the Gotham Bus Company (located at 225 River Street in Manhattan), he has been robbed six times. Five times the robbers got nothing; the sixth time they got the bus and $45. (J. J. Marshall is the president of the bus company and was played by Robert Middleton in one episode.)

With reference to Alice, Ralph's favorite expressions are "Pow! One of these days—right in the kisser" (waving his fist at her), "Baby, you're the greatest" and "You're going to the moon, Alice."

Ed, who majored in arithmetic at vocational school, mentions that the L in his name stood for Lilywhite (his mother's maiden name). As a kid he had a dog named Lulu. He has been working in the sewer for 17 years. His astrological sign was given as both Pisces and Capricorn. His favorite TV show is "Captain Video" and his hero was Pierre Francois de la Brioski (whom Ed thought designed the sewers of Paris; in reality, he condemned them). Ed and his wife, Trixie, have the phone number Bensonhurst 6-0098.

Ralph and Norton belong to the Raccoon Lodge (also referred to as the International Order of the Friendly Sons of Raccoons and the International Loyal Order of Friendly Raccoons). The cost of a lodge uniform is $35, and to become a member, an applicant must comply with Section Two of the lodge rules:

1. Applicant must have earned a public school diploma.
2. Applicant must have resided in the U.S. for at least six months.
3. Applicant must pay $1.50 initiation fee.

Ralph and Norton (who is rarely called Ed, even by Trixie) are also members of the Hurricanes Bowling Team (they bowl at the Acme Bowling Alley on Eighth and Montgomery).

With that dream of making it big, Ralph ventures into many money-making schemes that all eventually fail. He is most famous for investing in the uranium mine in Asbury Park, low-calorie pizza and glow-in-the-dark wallpaper (to save on electric bills). His joint failure with Norton was the Handy Kitchen Helper (where Ralph appeared on TV as "the Chef of the Future"). "Kran-Mars Delicious Mystery Appetizer" and the Ralph Kramden Corporation also failed. Together the two wrote a hit song called "Love on a Bus" (dedicated to Alice) that was later made into a movie, and won a radio contest with the song "Friendship." Ralph also appeared on the TV shows "Beat the Clock" and "The $99,000 Answer" (his category was popular songs but he couldn't answer the first question correctly: "Who wrote 'Swanee River'?" He responded Ed Norton).

Relatives: Ethel Owen played Alice's mother, Mrs. Gibson. Ralph's mother appeared in one episode, but credit was not given. Ralph mentioned his father's name as both Ed and Ralph Sr. He also has an Aunt Fanny who once wrote asking for six dollars he supposedly owed her. Alice has a brother named Frank and a sister named Peggy (not credited).

Theme: "You're My Greatest Love," written by Jackie Gleason and Bill Templeton

Note: "The Honeymooners" first appeared in 1951 on DuMont's "Cavalcade of Stars." Pert Kelton played Alice on the Jackie Gleason-hosted episodes of the series. On "The Jackie Gleason Show" (CBS, 9.17.66 to 9.12.70), Sheila MacRae played Alice and Jane Kean, Trixie in "Honeymooners" segments. Additional segments of the original series (and original cast) appeared on "The Jackie Gleason Show" from 9.29.56 to 1.2.61. On "Jackie Gleason and His American Scene Magazine" (CBS, 9.29.62 to 6.4.66) Sue Ane Langdon was Alice and Patricia Wilson was Trixie.

"The Honeymooners" with Jackie Gleason (Ralph), Art Carney (Ed), Sheila MacRae (Alice) and Jane Kean (Trixie) were also a part of Jackie's only two TV specials, both called "The Jackie Gleason Special" (CBS, 12.20.70 and 11.11.73). Four ABC specials also aired: "The Honeymooners' Second Honeymoon" (2.2.76), "The Honeymooners' Christmas" (11.28.77), "The Honeymooners' Valentine Special" (2.13.78) and "The

Honeymooners' Christmas Special" (12.10.78).

Live segments from Jackie's 1950s series have been syndicated as "The Lost Honeymooners" and hour-long episodes produced in 1970 have been syndicated as "The Honeymooners' European Vacation."

Jackie Gleason's favorite episode was "A Matter of Life and Death." "Alice and the Blonde" is Audrey Meadows' favorite episode. Art Carney's is "Chef of the Future." "The Sleepwalker" is Joyce Randolph's favorite.

HONEY WEST

ABC, 9.17.65 to 9.2.66

Honey West (Anne Francis), TV's first female private investigator, owns H. West and Company, a private detective agency she inherited from her father. Her assistant is Sam Bolt (John Ericson), who was her father's original partner. Honey, who holds a black belt in karate and owns the latest in scientific detection equipment, has a secret office in her apartment (behind a wall in the living room) and a mobile base (a TV-repair truck with the license plate 1406 122; later 1ET 974).

Irene Hervey played Honey's aunt, Meg West. Honey's pet ocelot is named Bruce. Joseph Mullendore composed the opening theme ("Wild Honey") and the closing theme ("Sweet Honey"). The pilot, "Who Killed the Jackpot?" aired on "Burke's Law" (4.21.65).

HONG KONG

ABC, 9.21.60 to 9.27.61

Glenn Evans (Rod Taylor), a foreign correspondent for *World-Wide News*, lives at 24 Peak Road in Hong Kong. His phone number is 004–79 and his license plate number is AB 1651. Jack Kruschen portrays Tully, the owner of Tully's Bar; Mai Tai Sing plays Ching Mei, a waitress at the Golden Dragon Café. Lionel Newman composed the theme.

HOOPERMAN

ABC, 9.23.87 to 9.6.89

Harry Hooperman (John Ritter) is an inspector with the Central Division of the San Francisco Police Department and the landlord of a run-down apartment building at 633 Columbus Avenue (also given as Columbus Street). Harry is also the owner of a nasty dog named Bijoux (played by Britches), and he enjoys playing the saxophone at a nightclub on Tuesday nights. He has a poster on his wall titled, "Valentino: A Sainted Devil." When on call, Harry's car code is 5-George-35.

During the first season, Harry's building manager, Susan Smith, was played by Debra Farentino (who was called Deborah Mullowney in the pilot). Barbara Bosson is Harry's superior, Captain Celeste Stern, and Sydney Walsh is Officer Maureen "Mo" DeMott. Barbara Rush appeared as Susan's mother, Mrs. Smith; Dan Lauria as Celeste's husband, Lou (from whom she is separated). Mike Post composed the theme.

HOUSTON KNIGHTS

CBS, 3.11.87 to 6.7.88

Joey LaFiamma (Michael Pare) and LeVon Lundy (Michael Beck) are sergeants with the Major Crimes Unit of the Houston Police Department. Their lieutenant, Joanne Beaumont, is played by Robyn Douglass. Joey and LeVon's car code is 9214 and their favorite hangout is the Alamo Bar. In the pilot episode, Leigh Taylor Young played their superior, Lieutenant Sherina McLaren. Madlyn Rhue appeared semi-regularly as Annie, the wheelchairbound cop. Dennis McCarthy composed the theme.

HOW TO MARRY A MILLIONAIRE

Syndicated, 1958 to 1960

Principal Cast: Barbara Eden (*Loco Jones*), Merry Anders (*Michele "Mike" McCall*),

Lori Nelson (*Greta Hanson*), Lisa Gaye (*Gwen Kirby*)

Trivia: "On my honor I promise to do my best to help one of us marry a millionaire. So help us Fort Knox." This is the pledge taken by Loco Jones, Mike McCall and Greta Hanson, three beautiful girls who seek to do just that.

The girls meet sharing an apartment on Amsterdam Avenue in New York City. Each found they had the same goal—to marry money—but individually they were dating losers in that category. Figuring it takes money to attract money, the girls pool their resources and rent Penthouse G (on the 22nd floor) of the Tower Apartment House on Park Avenue in Manhattan (their phone number is Plaza 3–5099). Their rent is due on the tenth of each month; they have a perfect record—they haven't paid it on time yet. With their front established, the girls struggle to find men with money and help each other marry the man of her dreams.

At the beginning of the second season (fall 1959), Greta left the series (she was said to have married a man who owns a gas station and moved to California; she simply fell in love and money no longer mattered. Mike caught the bridal bouquet). Needing a third girl to share the rent, Loco and Mike advertise in the *Journal News* for a new roommate. Gwen Kirby answers the ad and becomes the new girl on their team.

"The neckline is a little too low, the hem is too short, the waist is too tight, the back is too low—she looks beautiful!" That is how Mike and Greta describe Loco in a dress. Loco (her given name), was born in North Platt, Nebraska, on February 25th (Loco wouldn't reveal the year). She is a fashion model with the Travis Modeling Agency, later with the Talbot Agency, and she has her photos taken at Marachi's Photography Studio. She reads *Fashion Preview* magazine and was voted "Queen of the Madison Square Garden Rodeo" (1958). She is a bit naive when it comes to world affairs but is a whiz at useless information (for example, she has encyclopedic-class knowledge of the comic strips, which she keeps current by read-ing *Super Comics* magazine). Loco, who is somewhat vain, needs to wear glasses, but won't when she has to (she fears a man will see her and fail to be impressed if she is wearing eyeglasses). She faints standing up with her eyes open, and has been called "a fabulous blonde with an hourglass figure."

"She borrows our nylons and gets runs in them; she doesn't make her bed; she hogs the bathroom to soak in a bubble bath"—using Loco's bubble bath. She is Greta, hostess on a TV game show called "Go For Broke" (a take-off on "The $64,000 Question"), which airs at nine P.M. (station not given). Greta reads *Who's Who in America* (her research source) and has a Marilyn Monroe quality that she uses to lure men.

Mike, the schemer of the group, reads "Dunn and Bradstreet" (her research matter) and works as an analyst on Wall Street. Gwen, who is from Illinois, works for *Manhattan* magazine ("Our Business Is Publicity"). She is almost a clone of Greta—a Marilyn Monroe figure, a borrower (Loco and Mike's nylons) and a bathroom-hogger (loves to take bubble baths using Loco's bubble bath).

The girls shop at Burke's Department Store; they eat at Nate's Deli; they take turns making dinner (when it's Loco's turn, she buys it at Savo's Drugstore); and they each seek men with two qualifications: "Have money, will marry." In one episode, Loco appears on "Go For Broke" as an expert on comic strip characters (but she lost everything she had won up to $2,000 because she wouldn't wear her glasses on TV and couldn't identify the picture of a comic strip character).

Joseph Kearns as Augustus P. Tobey, and Dabbs Greer as Mr. Blandish, play the apartment-house managers. Jimmy Cross plays Jessie, the elevator operator. The series is based on the feature film of the same title.

Theme: "How to Marry a Millionaire," by Leon Klatzkin

Note: Lori Nelson (as Greta), Doe Avedon (as Mike) and Charlotte Austin (as Loco) appeared in the original unaired pilot for the series, which was produced in early 1957.

HUNTER

NBC, 9.18.84 to

Detective Sergeants Rick Hunter (Fred Dryer) and Dee Dee McCall (Stepfanie Kramer) are with Division 122 of the Los Angeles Police Department (also called the Central Division and the Parker Center Police Station). Dee Dee is nicknamed "the Brass Cupcake"; she resides at 8534 Mezdon Drive; Rick is the son of a mobster who turned into an honest but tough cop. His license plate number is 1ADT 849. Their snitch, Sporty James (Garrett Morris), runs Sporty James Enterprises. In flashback sequences, Franc Luz played Dee Dee's late husband, Sergeant Steve McCall (killed in the line of duty). In the episode, "Street Wise" (5.7.90), Dee Dee leaves the force to marry an old boyfriend, Alex (Robert Connor Newman). She is replaced by Darlanne Fluegel as Officer Joann Molenski (badge #1836). Mike Post and Pete Carpenter composed the theme.

I DREAM OF JEANNIE

NBC, 9.18.65 to 9.8.70

Principal Cast: Barbara Eden (*Jeannie*), Larry Hagman (*Tony Nelson*), Bill Daily (*Roger Healey*), Hayden Rorke (*Dr. Alfred Bellows*), Emmaline Henry (*Amanda Bellows*), Vinton Hayworth (*General Winfield Schaefer*), Barton MacLane (*General Martin Peterson*)

Trivia: In Baghdad over 2,000 years ago, a young girl refused the marriage proposal of the Blue Djin, the most powerful of all genies. In punishment, she was turned into a genie, placed in a bottle and sentenced to a life of loneliness on a deserted island.

During the test flight of a NASA rocket in 1965, a third stage misfires and the craft crash-lands on a deserted island in the South Pacific. As its pilot, astronaut Tony Nelson, looks for items to make an S.O.S. signal, he finds a strange looking green bottle and opens it. A pink smoke

emerges that materializes into a beautiful girl dressed as a harem dancer – a genie. "Thou may ask anything of thy slave, Master," she informs him. With her hands crossed over her chest and a blink of her eyes, she produces a rescue helicopter for him. Although Tony sets the girl, whom he calls Jeannie, free, he finds that he cannot get rid of her and finally allows her to remain with him – provided she will refrain from her powers and grant him no special treasures. A reluctant Jeannie agrees and Tony finds his life turned upside down when he attempts to keep Jeannie's presence a secret.

Jeannie, who was born April 1, 64 B.C., when the planet Neptune was in Scorpio, weighs 109 pounds (later mentioned as 127 pounds). Her mischievous sister, Jeannie II, has been married 47 times and would like to make Tony number 48. In 1969, when Jeannie and Tony marry, Jeannie becomes a member of the National Wives Association at NASA. Although it was said in later episodes that a genie cannot be photographed, she did photograph in earlier ones. Gin Gin is Jeannie's genie dog (who hates uniforms – and therefore wreaks havoc at NASA – because the palace guards used to mistreat her). Pip Chicks is the name of Jeannie's homemade candy, which brings out people's hidden fantasies.

Tony, who lives at 1020 Palm Drive in Cocoa Beach, Florida, is first a captain, then a major, as is his playboy friend, Roger Healey – the only other person who knows that Jeannie is a genie. Tony's address was also given as 1137 Oak Grove Street and as 811 Pine Street. Tony, who was born in Fowler's Corners, was called "Bunky" Nelson in his youth and his girlfriend in high school was Bonnie Crenshaw (Damian Brodie). Tony, whose birthday is July 15th, weighs 181¼ pounds (Roger weighs 175 pounds). In one episode, Tony, Roger and fellow astronaut Captain Larkin (Richard Mulligan) fly an Apollo 15 mission. In another, Jeannie writes a book – *How to Be a Fantastic Mother* (published by Woodhouse Publishers in New York) and used Tony's name as her nom de plume.

Dr. Alfred Bellows, the base's psychiatrist, has two goals in life after he meets Tony: to prove to someone else that something strange really is going on, and to figure out what it is. (Dr. Bellows usually just happens to be the only one around when Jeannie has used her powers.) Alfred's wife is Amanda and the base's commanders are General Martin Peterson and General Winfield Schaefer (who has a dog named Jupiter).

Relatives: Barbara Eden (Jeannie's sister, *Jeannie II*), Barbara Eden (*Jeannie's mother*), Henry Corden (*Jeannie's father*), Jackie Coogan (Jeannie's *Great-Uncle Sule of Bensengi*), Ronald Long (Jeannie's *Uncle Asmir*), Arthur Mallet (Jeannie's *Uncle Vasmir*), Hal Taggart (*Tony's father*), Spring Byington and June Jocelyn (*Tony's mother*), Gabriel Dell (Tony's *Cousin Arvid*), Michael Barbera (Amanda's nephew, *Melvin*), Bob Hastings (Amanda's cousin, *Homer Banks*), Butch Patrick (Alfred's nephew, *Richard*), Janice Hanson (Winfield's niece, *Patricia*), Hilary Thompson (Winfield's daughter, *Susie*), Kimberly Beck (Martin's granddaughter, *Gina*)

Theme: "I Dream of Jeannie," by Hugo Montenegro, Buddy Kaye and Richard Weiss

Note: Julie McWhirter provided the voice for Jeannie in an animated version of the series called "Jeannie" (CBS, 9.8.73 to 8.30.75) and Barbara Eden reprised her character in the NBC TV movie *I Dream of Jeannie: 15 Years Later* (10.20.85). Wayne Rogers played Tony Nelson (now a colonel), and he and Jeannie were the parents of a teenager named T. J. Nelson (MacKenzie Astin).

I LOVE LUCY

CBS, 10.15.51 to 6.24.57

Principal Cast: Lucille Ball (*Lucy Ricardo*), Desi Arnaz (*Ricky Ricardo*), Vivian Vance (*Ethel Mertz*), William Frawley (*Fred Mertz*)

Trivia: In 1941, Marian Strong (not seen), a friend of Lucille Esmerelda McGillicuddy, arranged a blind date for her with

Ricky Ricardo Alberto Fernando Acha (a.k.a. Ricky Alberto Ricardo IV), a Cuban drummer. Although an unlikely couple, Lucy and Ricky fall in love, marry and rent an apartment at 623 East 68th Street in Manhattan, a converted brownstone owned by Fred and Ethel Mertz (the building is in Ethel's name). Their later apartment is 3-B, and their rent is $125 a month. Mrs. Benson, played by Norma Varden, was the prior tenant. The Ricardos' phone number is Murray Hill 5–9975; the Mertzes is Circle 2–0799. In California-based episodes, the Ricardos and Mertzes stay at the Beverly Palms Hotel (Ricky goes to Hollywood to make the movie *Don Juan*, which premiered at Radio City Music Hall on February 29th). In European-based episodes, the group books passage on the ocean liner *SS Constitution*. In Connecticut-based episodes, Lucy and Ricky purchase a house in Westport and Fred and Ethel become their boarders. In one very popular episode, Lucy makes a TV commercial for a vitamin product called Vitameatavegamin.

Ricky, who is a bandleader at the Tropicana Club (later, the Ricky Ricardo Babalu Club), was born in Cuba. His favorite meal is roast pig. He and Fred, a former vaudeville performer who was born in Steubenville, Ohio, are members of the Recreation Club. Ricky and Lucy were once the hosts of a TV show called "Breakfast with Ricky and Lucy" (sponsored by Phipps Drug Store).

Lucy, who was born in Jamestown, New York (and attended Jamestown High School), married Ricky when she was 22 years old. Ethel Louise Mertz was born Ethel Potter in Albuquerque, New Mexico (she is called "Little Ethel" by her unseen Aunt Martha and Uncle Elmo). She met "cheapskate" Fred while they were both performing in vaudeville.

Ricky's most annoying habit according to Lucy is tapping; Lucy's to Ricky, making noise stirring her coffee (hitting the spoon against the cup). Fred's most annoying habit to Ethel is jingling his keys; Ethel's to Fred, "chewing like a cow."

In the original pilot (produced in 1951 and aired March 30, 1990), Ricky and

Lucy are already married and live in a seventh floor apartment in Manhattan (Fred and Ethel are not a part of the program). Despite published reports to the contrary, Desi Arnaz played Ricky Ricardo (not Larry Lopez), a bandleader; and Lucille Ball, his wife, Lucy Ricardo (not Lucy Lopez). The pilot has most of the elements of the actual series, including Lucy's desperate desire to break into show business.

Lucie Arnaz, host for the pilot's presentation, mentioned that her mother, Lucille Ball, was six months pregnant with her at the time she and Desi made the pilot; printed sources mention that Lucy was five months pregnant. In the pilot, Lucy poses as a clown at an audition Ricky is doing for sponsors of a proposed TV show.

Relatives: James John Gauzer, Richard Lee Simmons, the Mayer Twins and Richard Keith (Lucy and Ricky's son, *Little Ricky Ricardo*), Catherine Card (Lucy's mother, *Mrs. McGillicuddy*)

Theme: "I Love Lucy," by Eliot Daniel

I MARRIED DORA

ABC, 9.28.87 to 1.8.88

Principal Cast: Daniel Hugh Kelly (*Peter Farrell*), Elizabeth Pena (*Dora Calderon*), Juliette Lewis (*Kate Farrell*), Jason Horst (*Will Farrell*)

Trivia: "We have a marriage license, but we never use it," says Dora Calderon, a pretty young woman from El Salvador, who is married to Peter Farrell, a widower with two children, Kate and Will. Following the death of his wife, Janet, in a car accident, Peter hired Dora to care for his children. When Dora faces deportation because her visa has expired, Peter marries her to keep her in the country and with his family.

Peter, an architect with the firm Hughes, Whitney and Lennox, lives at 46 LaPaloma Drive in Los Angeles (telephone number 555–3636). In high school (not named), Peter was the star football player; he holds the record for making the most touchdowns in a single season.

Dora, who calls Peter "Mr. Peter," is ac-

tually in love with him (as he is with her) but each refuses to admit it. (Dora's jealous streak is evident, though, when Peter is with other women.) While Dora seems the perfect wife for Peter and mother for his children, she respects their marriage of convenience and functions only as his live-in housekeeper. Her pride and joy—and Peter's nightmare—is her kitchen junk drawer where she stores—and can find—"all the stuff you don't know what to do with, but you don't want to throw away, because one day you are going to need that thing that you don't know what to do with right now."

Kate, Peter's 13-year-old daughter, is somewhat dim-witted, and plays miniature golf with Peter at Putter World. As a child, she was a member of a Brownie troop; now she plays saxophone in her high-school band. While Kate is growing into a beautiful young woman, Peter continues to see her as a little girl with posters of Strawberry Shortcake on her bedroom walls (later replaced by Bon Jovi). Kate is also a member of her unnamed high school's cheerleading squad (for the Badgers football team)—she possesses the three required P's: positive, pretty and perky. When Kate, who wears a perfume called Sensual, and her friend Lorie (Mandy Ingber) "dress hot" (in short skirts and tight blouses) and "feel sexy," they go to the local mall (not named) "to drive shoe salesmen crazy."

Will, the smarter of the two Farrell children, attends an also unnamed school (presumably a junior high). Buck, Peter's brother, works for Big Ball Wrecking Company.

Relatives: Peggy McCay (Peter's mother, *Lucille Farrell*), Alley Mills (Peter's sister-in-law, *Janine Desmond*), Frederick Coffin (Peter's brother, *Buck Farrell*), Evelyn Guerrero (Dora's sister, *Marisol*), James Victor (*Dora's father*), Lupe Ontiveros (*Dora's mother*)

Flashbacks: Wendel Meldrum (Peter's wife, *Janet Farrell*)

Theme: "I Married Dora," by Glenn Jordan

I'M A BIG GIRL NOW

ABC, 10.31.80 to 8.7.81

The recently divorced Diana Cassidy (Diana Canova) was originally employed by the Kramer Research and Testing Company, a think tank in Washington, D.C.; later she becomes a columnist for a newspaper called the *Arlington Dispatch*. Edie McKendrick (Sheree North), her employer at Kramer (in episodes 1–17) was later (in episodes 18–20) her editor at the paper. Danny Thomas played Diana's father, Benjamin Douglas, a dentist just divorced after 34 years of marriage, who lives with Diana and her young daughter, Rebecca (Rori King) at 1700 Hope Street in Washington. Diana Canova performed the theme "I'm a Big Girl Now."

IN THE HEAT OF THE NIGHT

NBC, 3.6.88 to

The series centers around the relationship between Bill Gillespie (Carroll O'Connor), the white police chief of the Sparta, Mississippi, police department, and Virgil Tibbs (Howard Rollins), his Philadelphia-bred black chief of detectives. Bill's girlfriend, JoAnn St. John (Lois Nettleton), is a cashier at the Magnolia Café. Ten years earlier, she was a $100-a-night call girl known as Kelly Kaye. Bill, whose police car license plate number is M7246, has a hunting dog named Roscoe. Althea Tibbs (Ann Marie Johnson), Virgil's beautiful wife, is a teacher at Sparta Community High School (a.k.a. Sparta High), and her maiden name is Peterson. Officer Parker Williams (David Hart) has three cats, named Fuzz Face, Old Man and Wrencher. Other officers in the department are Bubba Skinner (Alan Autry) and Wilson Sweet (Geoffrey Thorne).

In 1988, when Carroll O'Connor suffered a heart attack, Joe Don Baker was brought in for four episodes as Tom Dugan, the former police chief (Bill was said to be away at a police convention).

Relatives: Traci Wolfe (Althea's niece, *Nicole Sands*), J. A. Preston (Althea's father, *Calvin Peterson*) and Mitchell Anderson (Bubba's nephew, *Bobby Skinner*).

Bill Champlin sings the theme, "In the Heat of the Night." The series is based on the feature film of the same title.

THE INCREDIBLE HULK

CBS, 3.10.78 to 5.19.82

During an experiment to discover how some people tap hidden resources for strength under stress, Dr. David Banner (Bill Bixby) is exposed to an extreme dose of gamma radiation. The overdose causes a chemical change in his DNA such that whenever he feels angered or enraged, the mild-mannered Banner is transformed into the Hulk (Lou Ferrigno), a green creature of incredible strength. When David relaxes, the metamorphosis reverses and he returns to his normal self.

Complications set in when Jack McGee (Jack Colvin), a reporter for the *National Register*, becomes intrigued by reports of a giant creature and begins to investigate. He tracks the Hulk to a laboratory where David and his assistant, Elena Marks (Susan Sullivan), are experimenting with ways to reverse the process. David and Jack are speaking outside the lab when an explosion inside the lab knocks them to the ground. David rushes inside while a dazed McGee watches. Deperate to save Elena, David becomes the Hulk. McGee sees the Hulk carrying Elena's body out of the lab and assumes David has died in the fire and the Hulk has killed Elena.

Now believed dead, David wanders across the country in search of a way to reverse the process. His search is hindered, however, by McGee, who has vowed to bring the creature to justice.

David's hometown is given as Treverton, Colorado; the cover price of the *National Register* is 50 cents an issue, and Chicago is its home base. Ric Drasin plays the Demi-Hulk (shown during the transformation from Hulk to human); Diana Muldaur appears as David's sister, Dr. Helen Banner; and John Marley as David's father, D. W. Banner. In flashback sequences, Reed Diamond plays young David; Julianne Tutak, young Helen; and Claire Malis, David's mother, Elizabeth Banner. Joe Harnell composed the theme, "The Incredible Hulk" (closing piano solo).

The pilot film aired on 11.4.77. Two TV movies were later produced: *The Incredible Hulk Returns* (NBC, 5.22.88) and *The Death of the Incredible Hulk* (NBC, 2.18.90).

ISIS

CBS, 9.6.75 to 9.2.78

Andrea Thomas (JoAnna Cameron), a science teacher at Larkspur High School in California, becomes Isis, a champion of truth and justice, through the powers of a magic amulet she found while on a scientific expedition in Egypt. The amulet, given to the Queen of ancient Egypt by the Royal Sorcerer, is endowed with the powers of Isis (the Goddess of Fertility) and bestows upon any woman who possesses it the ability to soar, power over animals, and control over the elements of earth, sea and sky. When Andrea holds the amulet and speaks the words "O Mighty Isis," she becomes Isis (the clouds darken, the symbol of Isis is seen, and Andrea is magically transformed into the goddess). She wears a white, miniskirted Egyptian-like costume and a tiara that allows her to see beyond her normal vision. Her hair also increases in length—from Andrea's mid-back length to hip length for Isis. Little effort is made to hide JoAnna Cameron's beauty as Andrea. Conservative dress, glasses and a pony tail are the "disguises" Andrea uses to conceal her secret identity.

Andrea, who lives at 21306 Baker Place (Apartment 4A) in the town of Larkspur, drives a red sedan (later yellow after it is stolen and repainted) with license plate 69 CBE; her phone number is 555-3638. Andrea's teaching assistant (first season) is Cindy Lee (Joanna Pang), and later, Renee Carroll (Ronalda Douglas). Rick Mason (Brian Cutler), Andrea's friend, a teacher, has a boat called the *Star Tracker*.

Andrea has a pet crow named Tut, and when she needs help, she calls on the services of Captain Marvel (John Davey) from the series "Shazam!" (CBS, 9.4.74

to 9.3.77). To perform any feat, Isis must recite special rhymes related to the task at hand; the rhyme most often heard is "O zephyr winds which blow on high, lift me now so I may fly." Yvette Blais and Jeff Michael composed the theme. The series is also known as "The Secrets of Isis."

IT TAKES TWO

ABC, 10.14.82 to 4.28.83

The series chronicles events in the lives of the Quinn family: mother Molly (Patty Duke), an assistant District Attorney; Sam (Richard Crenna), her husband and chief of surgery at Rush-Thornton Medical Center; and their children Lisa (Helen Hunt) and Andy (Anthony Edwards).

The Quinns, whose phone number is 555-6060, live in Apartment 1110 (address not given). Although Sam and Molly have a joint checking account (with blue checks), Molly also has her own personal checking account (with pink checks). Molly and Sam's favorite restaurant is Chez Paolo's, and Sam's fondest memory of their first date together is the pink sweater Molly wore "that wouldn't quit." Lisa, whose high school is not named, works as a waitress at the Pizza Palace and previously did volunteer work for the No Nukes organization. Her favorite hangout is Brandy's Café. Billie Bird plays Molly's senile mother, Mama (Anna). Crystal Gayle and Paul Williams sing the theme, "Where Love Spends the Night."

IT'S A LIVING

ABC, 10.30.80 to 1.29.81
10.24.81 to 1.9.82
2.12.82 to 2.26.82
6.4.82 to 9.10.82
Syndicated, 9.85 to 3.89

Principal Cast: Susan Sullivan (*Lois Adams*), Barrie Youngfellow (*Jan Hoffmeyer*), Ann Jillian (*Cassie Cranston*), Gail Edwards (*Dot Higgins*), Wendy Schaal (*Vickie Allen*), Marian Mercer (*Nancy Beebee*), Louise Lasser (*Maggie McBirney*), Crystal Bernard (*Amy Tompkins*), Sheryl Lee Ralph (*Ginger St. James*), Paul Kreppel

(*Sonny Mann*), Richard Kline (*Richard Grey*), Richard Stahl (*Howard Miller*)

Trivia: Here we share events in the lives of a group of waitresses who work at Above the Top, a posh, 30th-floor Los Angeles restaurant featuring "Sky High Dining." (Above the Top is owned by Pacific Continental Properties.) Lois, Maggie, Jan, Cassie, Dot, Vickie, Amy and Ginger are the waitresses; Nancy, the hostess; Sonny, the lounge singer; and Howard, the chef.

Lois Adams, the most stylish and sophisticated of the waitresses, is married (to the never-seen Bill) and struggling to raise two children (Amy and Joey).

Maggie McBirney, a widow, lives at 1417 Brooke Avenue; her late husband, Joseph, was a salesman for Kitchen Help Dishwashers.

Katie Lou "Cassie" Cranston, the sexiest and most beautiful of the group, was born in Kansas and now lives in a condo at the Sun Palace. She seems like a man-crazy sexpot looking to marry money, but on her night off, Cassie reads to senior citizens at the Willow Glen Rest Home.

Jan Hoffmeyer, divorced and the mother of a young daughter (Ellen), is the only waitress to marry on the show (Richard Grey on 11.24.85). Jan, whose maiden name is Frankel, attended Templar High School (class of '66); she now takes classes at North L.A. Law School. She was born in Los Angeles, has a cat named Ralph, and was arrested in the 1960s during a college demonstration for mooning a cop.

Dorothy "Dot" Higgins, who was born in Detroit, majored in theater at Baxter College. Dot, the hopeful actress, appeared in the plays *Bye Bye Birdie* (as Kim) and *The Garden of Countess Natasha* (as Natasha), and made her TV debut in a commercial for Autumn Years Dog Food. Her character appeared as "Betty Spaghetti, the waitress" in the comic strip "Billy Bonkers." Dot has several pets: Mr. Puss, the cat; Pardon, the dog; and Mouse, the mouse. Her mother (not seen) has a dog named Scrappy.

Vickie Allen, born in Pocatello, Idaho, is best friends with Dot and the most sensitive of the women. She has a pet parakeet named Squeaky.

Amy Tompkins was born in Snyder, Texas, and now lives at the Carrie Nation Hotel for Women in Los Angeles. She has fish named Oscar and Cletus and is a member of the A.G.O.A. (American Gun Owners Association). Amy owns a .357 Magnum with a six-inch barrel and hides it in her Jammy Bunny (a pink cloth pajama holder).

Ginger St. James, who was born in Buffalo, New York, is the only black waitress employed by Above the Top. In high school she was called "booby soxer" for stuffing her bra with socks. Nancy Beebee, the snobbish hostess, was a ballerina for 15 years, then a waitress at Above the Top before acquiring her current position; she was born in South Philadelphia.

Sonny Mann, the restaurant's one-man entertainment center, was born in Reno, Nevada. Aspiring to become a big name singer, his first gig was at a club called Vinnie's Romper Room. Howard Miller, the chef, was born in Trenton, New Jersey. He has a dog named Bluto and two fish named Ike and Mamie.

Relatives: Tricia Cast (Lois's daughter, *Amy Adams*), Keith Mitchell (Lois's son, *Joey Adams*), Sandy Simpson (Maggie's brother, *Bobby*), Lili Haydn and Virginia Keehne (Jan's daughter, *Ellen Hoffmeyer*), Dennis Dugan (Jan's ex-husband, *Lloyd Hoffmeyer*), Georgann Johnson (Jan's mother, *Phyllis Frankel*), Richard McKenzie (Jan's father, *Will Frankel*), Richard Schaal (Vickie's father, *Emmett Allen*), K Callan (Dot's mother, *Harriet Higgins*), Eydie Byrde (*Ginger's grandmother*), Kelly Britt (Nancy's *Cousin Grace*), Linda G. Miller (Nancy's sister, *Gloria*), Arlen Dean Snyder (*Amy's father*), Nita Talbot (*Sonny's mother*), Donnelly Rhodes (Sonny's brother, *Buddy Mann*), Paul Kreppel (Sonny's father, *Irv Manischewitz*), Sue Ball (Howard's daughter, *Lori Miller*), Kathleen Freeman (Howard's mother, *Mae Miller*), Mary Betten (Richard's mother, *Beth Grey*), Maura Soden (Richard's ex-wife, *Cindy*), Andre Gower (Richard's son, *Charlie Grey*)

Theme: "It's a Living," vocal by Leslie Bricusse

Note: Episodes produced under the title "Making a Living" (1981–82) are syndicated under the title "It's a Living."

IT'S ALWAYS JAN

CBS, 9.10.55 to 6.30.56

Jan Stewart (Janis Paige), a widow and the mother of 10-year-old daughter Josie (Jeri Lou James), is a nightclub entertainer who sings regularly at Tony's Cellar, a small supper club in New York City. Jan shares an apartment at 46 East 50th Street in Manhattan with her friends Valerie Malone (Merry Anders), a shapely blonde model, and Patricia Murphy (Patricia Bright), a secretary with a heart of gold.

Jan, who dreams of starring on Broadway and singing at the prestigious Sky Room of the Sherry-Waldorf Hotel, is represented by the Harry Cooper Agency, a one-man operation headed by Harry Cooper (Sid Melton). Earle Hagen and Herbert Spencer composed the theme, "It's Always Jan."

JACK AND MIKE

ABC, 9.16.86 to 5.28.87

The series relates incidents in the lives of newspaper columnist Jackie Shea (Shelley Hack) and her husband, Mike Brennan (Tom Mason), a restaurateur. Jackie writes a column called "Our Kind of Town" for the *Chicago Mirror*; Mike owns a restaurant, the 1935 Café. Carol Potter plays Mike's sister, Kathleen; Beatrice Straight and James Green appear as Mike's mother and father, Mary and John Brennan. Johnny Mandel composed the theme, "Jack and Mike." The series was originally called "Our Kind of Town."

JACKSON AND JILL

Syndicated, 1949

This is a domestic comedy about young marrieds Jackson (Todd Karns) and Jill Jones (Helen Chapman), who live at 167 Oak Street, Apartment 1-A, in Manhattan. Their telephone number is Main 6421, and Jackson's shortwave-radio call letters are W10GEC. Jackson's shortwave "radio buddy" is Gladys Harvey (Jan Kayne), whom Jill calls "the glamour gal of the airwaves"; her call letters are W10GAL.

Each episode opens with Jill jotting an entry in her diary. The audience hears her via voice-over narration and the episode itself explains the entry. The show closes with Jill completing her diary entry. The arranger of the show's theme, a parody of the song "Home, Sweet Home," is not credited.

JAKE AND THE FATMAN

CBS, 9.26.87 to 9.7.88
3.15.89 to

J. L. McCabe (William Conrad) is first the District Attorney of an unnamed Southern California city (1987–88), then the prosecuting attorney for the Honolulu Police Department. He is assisted in both cities by Jake Stiles (Joe Penny), his stylish investigator. Besides the nickname "Fatman," J. L. (for Jason Lockinvar) is also called "Buster"; as a kid Jake was called "Butchie." J. L.'s dog is named Max; Jake's phone number (California) is 555–4796; their favorite bar is Dixie's (Dixie, the owner, is played by Anne Francis). Jake's childhood TV hero, Tom Cody (star of the series "Sky Hawk"), is played in one episode by Ernest Borgnine.

Tom Isbell plays J. L.'s son, Danny McCabe; Cassandra Byram, Jake's sister, Angela Styles; and Rhoda Gemignani appears as Jake's mother, Carla Styles. Dick DeBenedictis composed the theme.

THE JEFFERSONS

CBS, 1.17.75 to 7.23.85

Principal Cast: Sherman Hemsley (*George Jefferson*), Isabel Sanford (*Louise Jefferson*), Mike Evans and Damon Evans (*Lionel Jefferson*), Franklin Cover (*Tom Willis*), Roxie Roker (*Helen Willis*), Berlinda Tolbert (*Jenny Willis*), Paul Benedict (*Harry Bentley*), Marla Gibbs (*Florence Johnston*)

Trivia: "The Jeffersons" is an "All in the Family" spinoff in which Archie Bunker's neighbors, George, Louise and Lionel Jefferson, have moved to Manhattan to begin new lives. George, comically wealthy and snobbish, owns the successful Jefferson Cleaners (with stores in Manhattan, Harlem, the Bronx, Brooklyn and Queens). He and Louise, his long-suffering wife, have been married 25 years—and the reason the marriage lasts, according to George, is that he puts up with all her faults.

Prior to moving to their luxurious New York apartment (12-D), George and Louise lived in Harlem, then on Hauser Street in Queens (where George opened his first dry cleaning shop). Before marrying George, Louise lived on 13th Street and Amsterdam Avenue. Louise, whom George calls "Weezie" and "Weez," has Type O blood; her maiden name is Mills. George, who was born in Georgia, served on a Navy aircraft carrier. (In another episode George mentions he was in the Navy, but did service in the galley). George's competition is Feldway Cleaners.

Tom and Helen Willis, their upstairs neighbors (14th floor), are TV's first interracial couple. Tom (who is white), is an editor for the Pelham Publishing Company. He has been married to Helen (who is black) for 23 years. They have a beautiful daughter, Jenny, who is engaged to George and Louise's son, Lionel. Lionel, who had the street name "Diver" when they lived in Harlem, calls Jenny his "Honey Babes." Helen's maiden name is Douglas.

Harry Bentley, George's across-the-hall neighbor (Apartment 12-E), was born in England, attended Oxford University and now works as an interpreter at the U.N.

Relatives: Zara Cully (George's mother, *Olivia Jefferson*), Leonard Jackson (Louise's father, *Howard Mills*), Josephine Premice (Louise's sister, *Maxine Mills*), Lillian Randolph (Olivia's sister, *Emma*), Ebonie Smith (Jenny and Lionel's daughter, *Jessica*), Leon Ames (Tom's father, *Henry Willis*), Victor Kilian (Tom's *Uncle Bertram*), Fred Pinkard (Helen's father, *"Grandpa" Douglas*)

Theme: "Movin' On Up," by Jeff Barry and Ja'net DuBois

Spinoff Series: "Checking In" (CBS, 4.9.81 to 4.30.81). A four-episode series in which George's maid, Florence Johnston, takes a leave of absence to work as executive housekeeper at the St. Frederick Hotel in Manhattan. Larry Linville co-starred as Lyle Block, the hotel manager.

JEFF'S COLLIE

CBS, 9.12.54 to 12.1.57

The adventures shared by young Jeff Miller (Tommy Rettig) and his collie, Lassie. Jan Clayton plays his widowed mother, Ellen, and George Cleveland, Ellen's father-in-law, George Miller ("Gramps"). The Miller's address is Route 4, Calverton, where they own a small farm outside of Capitol City. Ellen's husband, John (not seen), was apparently killed by a gun (in a 1956 episode Gramps remarks "I put my gun away ten years ago when we heard about your father"). The license plate on Gramps's truck is 98 81304.

Jeff's friend, Sylvester "Porky" Brockway (Donald Keeler), has a "pedigreed basset hound" named Pokey. Jeff and Porky's signal to let each other know where they are is to yell, "Eee-Yock-Eee."

Florence Lake plays the rarely seen, but often needed, telephone operator, Jenny. Paul Maxey plays Porky's father Matt (who is also overweight); Porky's mother, Beatrice, is not seen. Frank Ferguson plays the kindly vet, Dr. Peter Wilson, before Arthur Space appears in the role of Dr. Frank Weaver. The series was originally titled "Lassie" and Raoul Krashaar composed the theme.

In the spinoff series, "Timmy and Lassie" (CBS, 9.8.57 to 8.30.64), Ruth and Paul Martin buy the Miller farm on December 1, 1957, when Ellen can no longer run it alone after Gramps's death. The Martins adopt Timmy (Jon Provost), the orphan Lassie found several months earlier who had been living with them. When Jeff finds he cannot take Lassie to Capitol City with him, he leaves her with Timmy. Cloris Leachman and Jon Shepodd first played Ruth and Paul (subsequently replaced by June Lockhart and Hugh Riley). George Chandler plays Paul's brother, Petrie Martin; Todd Farrell, Timmy's friend, Boomer Bates; Andy Clyde, Timmy's elderly friend, Cully Wilson. Boomer's dog is named Mike; Cully's dog is named Silky (a.k.a. Sam).

Other Versions: "Lassie" (CBS, 9.64 to 9.68). Ranger Corey Stuart (Robert Bray) inherits Lassie when the Martins move to Australia.

"Lassie" (CBS, 6.68 to 9.71). Lassie becomes a wanderer, helping people and animals in trouble.

"Lassie" (Syndicated, 9.72 to 9.73). Lassie's adventures on the California ranch of Keith Holden (Larry Pennell) and his children, Ron and Mike (Skip Burton and Joshua Albee).

"Lassie's Rescue Rangers" (ABC, 9.8.73 to 8.30.75). An animated series in which Lassie becomes the leader of the Rescue Force.

"Lassie: The New Beginning" (9.17, 9.24.78). An ABC pilot in which Lassie finds a home with Samantha and Chip Stratton (Sally Boyden, Shane Sinutko), niece and nephew of Stuart Stratton (John Reilly), the editor of the *Lake Pines Journal* in California.

Note: See also "The New Lassie."

JENNIFER SLEPT HERE

NBC, 10.21.83 to 12.16.83

Principal Cast: Ann Jillian (*Jennifer Farrell*), John P. Navin Jr. (*Joey Elliott*), Georgia Engel (*Susan Elliott*), Mya Akerling (*Marilyn Elliott*)

Trivia: "I just saw the most beautiful ghost in the world . . . and she lived here, she loved here, laughed here and cried here; she slept here and never really left here. Jennifer slept here." Her mother wanted her to become a beautician, but Jennifer Farrell, a young starry-eyed girl, had a dream to become a movie star. At 17, Jennifer left home and journeyed to Hollywood. She made her first appearance on TV as a banana in the audience of "Let's Make a Deal," and, several months later, in 1966, when Jennifer was 18 years old, hungry and flat broke, she posed nude for a calendar. Although the calendar was never seen (because she bought up all the copies), jobs came her way, and soon she became one of America's most glamorous and beloved stars.

Jennifer's untimely death in 1978 saddened the world. In 1983, New York lawyer George Elliott; his wife, Susan; and their children, Joey and Marilyn, move into Jennifer's fabulous Beverly Hills mansion at 32 Rexford Drive. (While it is not made clear, the mansion was apparently seized by the state for nonpayment of taxes. It is also apparent that the Elliotts are not wealthy and we assume they bought the mansion on condition they pay off Jennifer's debts; George complains in several episodes about Jennifer's debts.)

Shortly after, while settling into his room, Joey is startled to see a ghost of Jennifer Farrell—who appears and speaks only to him. While Joey struggles to live the life of a normal teenager, he finds it almost impossible when Jennifer decides to guide his life. Joey attends Beverly Hills High School and calls Jennifer "Farrell." No school for Marilyn is mentioned, nor is a company name for George.

When she was six years old, Jennifer was a tomboy and made a neighborhood kid eat dirt—literally. She attended but dropped out of Lanford High School in Illinois, and her first paying job was as a waitress in a grease pit called Danny's Diner.

Relatives: Debbie Reynolds (Jennifer's mother, *Alice Farrell*, also a ghost)

Theme: "Jennifer Slept Here," vocal by Joey Scarbury

JESSICA NOVAK

CBS, 11.5.81 to 12.3.81

The series depicts the news-gathering assignments of Jessica Novak (Helen Shaver), an on-the-air reporter for "Closeup News" on KLA-TV, Channel 6 in Los Angeles. Jessica resides at 318 Briarwood Avenue and her telephone number is 555–6676. Her car license plate reads 327 WED.

Phil Bonelli (Andrew Rubin) is her field cameraman and Ricky Duran (Eric Kilpatrick) is her field sound man. "The Theme from Jessica Novak" was composed by Fred Karlin.

THE JETSONS
ABC, 9.23.62 to 9.8.63

"The Jetsons" portrays life in the 21st century as experienced by the Jetsons, an animated TV family of the future.

George (voice by George O'Hanlon), the father, is employed by Cosmo G. Spacely (voice by Mel Blanc), the owner of Spacely Space Sprockets. He is also in the Army Reserve (U.S. Space Guards Division at Camp Nebula). His favorite movie star is Gina Lolajupiter and he watches the TV shows "Dr. Ken Stacey" (a take-off on "Ben Casey") and "The Stuntley-Hinkley Report" (a parody of "The Huntley-Brinkley Report").

Jane (voice by Penny Singleton) is George's wife. She is 33 years old, wears a size-eight dress and measures 36–26–36. She buys her dresses in Satellite City and has her hair done at the Constellation Beauty Salon. Jane entered the "Miss Solar System Beauty Pageant" and was crowned "Miss Western Hemisphere." She and George live at the Sky Pad Apartments and their favorite song is "Saturn Doll" by Count Spacey and his orchestra (which they danced to while dating).

Judy (voice by Janet Waldo), their daughter, is 15 years old and attends Orbit High School. She measures 32–22–32, has a jalopy with the license plate 738, and a talking diary she calls Di Di (voice by Selma Diamond).

Elroy (voice by Daws Butler) is their eight-year-old son. He attends the Little Dipper School. He has a pet dog named Astro (voice by Don Messick) and is a member of the Little Dipper League (a baseball team). His favorite TV show is "Spies in Space."

Rosie (voice by Jean VanderPyl), the Jetsons' robot, is a model XB-500 service robot they acquired from "U-Rent-A-

Maid." Henry Orbit (voice by Howard Morris) is the apartment-house janitor. Mr. Spacely and his wife, Stella, reside at 175 Snerdville Drive. Spacely's competition is Cogswell Cogs, a company owned by Mr. Cogswell (voice by Daws Butler). Spacely Space Sprockets produces three million sprockets a day.

JOANIE LOVES CHACHI
see HAPPY DAYS

JUST THE TEN OF US
ABC, 4.26.88 to 7.27.90

Principal Cast: Bill Kirchenbauer (*Graham Lubbock*), Deborah Harmon (*Elizabeth Lubbock*), Heather Langenkamp (*Marie Lubbock*), Jamie Luner (*Cindy Lubbock*), Brooke Theiss (*Wendy Lubbock*), Jo Ann Willette (*Constance "Connie" Lubbock*), Heidi Zeigler (*Sherry Lubbock*), Matt Shakman (*J. R. Lubbock*), Frank Bonner (*Father Robert Hargis*)

Trivia: "Just the Ten of Us" is a "Growing Pains" spinoff in which Dewey High School Coach Graham Lubbock, his wife, Elizabeth, and their eight children have left Long Island to begin new lives in California.

Graham, whose license plate reads YO COACH, is the athletic coach at St. Augustine's, a Catholic high school for boys in Eureka, California. He is the manager of the Hippos football team and his home phone number is 555–3273 (address not given). The family dog is named Hooter, and their milk cow is named Diane.

Graham and Elizabeth (a deeply religious Catholic) met at a Catholic Youth Organization (C.Y.O.) mixer and fell in love at first sight. They married in 1970 and 18 years later their family includes Marie, Cindy, Wendy, Connie, Sherry, J. R. and twins Harvey and Michelle. Marie, Cindy, Wendy and Connie formed the sexy singing group the Lubbock Babes and perform at Danny's Pizza Parlor; Cindy and Wendy use the terms "Hi-ee" and "Bye-ee" for hello and goodbye. Graham, who is overweight and constantly nagged by Elizabeth to go on a diet, has a favorite bedtime snack of Ovaltine and Ho-Ho's. Elizabeth does volunteer work at the Food Bank and, for a while, Graham held down a second job as a counter boy at the Burger Barn.

Marie, the eldest child (18), is attractive, boy-shy and very religious (hoping to become a nun). Marie hides her obvious beauty behind glasses and loosely fitting clothes; she mentioned she wears a size-five dress and (proudly) a 34C bra. Her first job was cooking and serving food at the Eureka Mission. In one episode, Marie starts her career as a nun by taking a two-week seminar at St. Bartholemew's convent.

Wendy, 17, the most beautiful of the Lubbock girls, is boy-crazy and appears totally self-absorbed (although she'll secretly help one of her sisters in a crisis). Wendy wears a size-five dress, a 34B bra, a size seven-and-a-half shoe, the the lipstick shades Midnight Passion and Dawn At His Place. Although she acts like a bimbo—her ploy to attract the opposite sex—she is deeply hurt when called one. She went out to the mall to look for her first job, got sidetracked shopping, and forgot all about the job search. In a dream sequence, Wendy is the star of a comedy series called "Wendy and the Butler" (her father plays the butler).

Cindy, 16, the beautiful but not-too-bright Lubbock Babe, is as boy-crazy as Wendy—but also constantly in a dither about everything else. Cindy, who wears a size-eight dress and a 36C bra, has a slight weight problem and is a member of the Diet Control Clinic. She had her own radio show (over KHPO—the voice of St. Augie's) called "What's Happening, St. Augie's?" and her first job was as a receptionist at the Eureka Fitness Center. Cindy's middle name is Anne, but for years she thought it was Diane.

Connie, 15, the pretty, intellectual and most sensitive of the girls, wears a size-five dress and a 34A bra. While not as boy-shy as Marie, she is quite intimidated by Wendy and Cindy, very sensitive about being flat-chested and sure she will never attract "hunks" as Cindy and Wendy do. Connie, who hopes to become a jour-

nalist, is a writer for the school newspaper, St. Augie's *Herald-Gazette*, and her first job was sweeping animal entrails at the MacGregor Slaughter House.

Sherry, the youngest of the girls before Michelle's birth, is a pre-teen (age 11). The most intelligent Lubbock, she strives for excellent grades in school (although she should be in grammar school, she is seen attending St. Augie's; an exception to the all-boy rule was made to allow the Lubbock girls to attend). Sherry is constantly amazed by the antics of her sisters and has trouble believing Cindy and Wendy are related to her. In later episodes, Sherry wants to be like Wendy "and live on the wild side" (she smokes cigarettes and brags about wearing a training bra in the episode of 4.27.90 to get attention).

J. R. (Graham Lubbock Jr.) is the elder male child; he attends St. Augie's. He loves peanut butter, horror movies and playing practical jokes on his sisters. There is no information to offer on the infants Harvey and Michelle, other than that only Harvey is credited (Jason Korstjens).

Father Robert Hargis is the priest in charge of St. Augie's and Sid Haig plays Janitor Bob, the strange ex-con custodian at the school.

Relatives: Manfred Melcher (Father Hargis's nephew, *Damien*)

Flashbacks: Taylor Fry (*young Marie*), Robyn Say Bookford (*young Wendy*), Hartley Haverty (*young Cindy*)

Theme: "Doin' It the Best I Can," vocal by Bill Medley

KAREN
ABC, 1.30.75 to 6.19.75

Karen Angelo (Karen Valentine) lives at 1460 Cambridge Street in Jamestown, and is a staff worker for Open America, a Capitol Hill citizens lobby in Washington, D.C. Denver Pyle played Dale W. Bush, the founder of Open America, in the pilot; Charles Lane portrays Dale in the series. Benny Golson composed the theme.

KAREN'S SONG

Fox, 7.18.87 to 9.12.87

Karen Matthews (Patty Duke) is a 40-year-old Dexter Publishing executive who falls in love with Steve Foreman (Louis Smith), a 28-year-old caterer for the firm A Tasteful Affair. Teri Hatcher plays Karen's daughter, Laura; and Granville Van Dusen, Karen's ex-husband, Zach. When CBS had the project, Suzanne Pleshette was cast in the role of Karen. Douglas Timm composed the theme.

KATE AND ALLIE

CBS, 3.19.84 to 9.12.88

Principal Cast: Susan Saint James (*Kate McArdle*), Jane Curtin (*Allie Lowell*), Allison Smith (*Jennie Lowell*), Ari Meyers (*Emma McArdle*), Frederick Koehler (*Chip Lowell*), Sam Freed (*Bob Barsky*)

Trivia: Kate (Katherine Elizabeth Ann McArdle) and Allie (Allison Julie Charlotte Adams Lowell) are divorced friends who share a Greenwich Village apartment (address not given) in New York City. (Kate and Allie met as kids at the orthodonist's; "Braces make lasting friends," claims Allie.) Kate's daughter, Emma, and Allie's children, Jennie and Chip, also live with them. Before Emma's birth, Kate and her ex-husband, Max, had contemplated calling her Angela (if a girl) or Che (if a boy). Allie and her ex-husband, Charles, were planning to call their first-born child Tiffany (if a girl) or Brooks (if a boy).

Kate, who originally works for the Sloane Travel Agency, has an account at the Holland Savings and Loan Bank (#375-70-60-572). She took cooking lessons from Julia Peterson (Lindsay Wagner) in Brooklyn Heights and always gives Allie purses as gifts.

Allie, who loves to cook and looked after the kids while Kate worked, had several part-time jobs (e.g., salesgirl in a bookstore, cashier at the box office of the 9th Street Cinema) and attended night school at Washington Square College. She also did volunteer work at Channel G, a Manhattan cable station run by a woman named Eddie Gordon (Andrea Martin). Allie always gives Kate sweaters as gifts. In 1986, Kate and Allie form their own company, Kate and Allie Caterers, working from their apartment.

In the 12.11.88 episode, Allie married former football player Bob Barsky, a sportscaster for WNTD-TV, Channel 10, in Washington D.C. (He commutes between N.Y. and D.C. and does the 11 O'Clock Sports Update.) Allie and Chip move to a new apartment (21-C) on West 55th Street; Kate remains for a short time at their old apartment and later moves in with Allie.

Jennie, Allie's daughter, wears a size-five dress, and had an after-school waitressing job at Le Bon Croissant, a French diner. While her high school is not named, she attended Columbia University and lived in the dorm (Room 512) in 1987.

Emma, Kate's daughter, who also wore a size-five dress, attended the same unnamed high school as Jennie and moved to California in 1987 to attend UCLA.

Chip, Allie's son, attends an unnamed grammar school and has two cats named Iggie and Tristan. He had a Sunday morning job delivering bagels to the neighbors; he also opened a pet cemetery in the back yard. Chip considers Alan Thicke to be America's greatest actor.

In "The Monkey's Paw" episode, Kate inherits a supposedly magic monkey's paw that can grant a secret desire. Kate wished to win the lottery; Allie asked that the national debt be reduced; Emma wanted a new stereo; Jennie wished for breasts (she had a boyish figure at the time); Chip wanted a pony. When he was eight years old, Bob's nickname was "Mickey Pants" (when he was playing ball, a mouse ran up the little left-fielder's pants. The only thing he could do to rid himself of the rodent was to drop his pants in front of everyone).

Relatives: John Herd (Kate's ex-husband, *Max McArdle*) Paul Hecht (Allie's ex-husband, *Dr. Charles Lowell*), Marian Selder (Kate's mother, *Marian*), Wendie Malick (Charles's second wife, *Claire*

Lowell), Rosemary Murphy and Scotty Bloch (Allie's mother, *Joan Adams*), Robert Cornthwaite (Allie's father, *Dr. Ed Adams*), Elizabeth Parrish (Bob's mother, *Eileen Barsky*)

Flash Forwards: Brad Davidson (*adult Chip*)

Theme: "Along Comes a Friend," vocal by John Leffler

KATE LOVES A MYSTERY/MRS. COLUMBO
NBC, 2.26.79 to 3.24.79
10.18.79 to 12.6.79

Principal Cast: Kate Mulgrew (*Kate Columbo/Kate Callahan*), Lili Haydn (*Jenny Columbo/Jenny Callahan*), Henry Jones (*Josh Alden*), Don Stroud (*Sergeant Mike Varrick*)

Trivia: Kate Columbo, the previously unseen wife of TV's famed Lieutenant Philip Columbo, is (in "Mrs. Columbo") a newspaper journalist for the *Weekly Advertiser* in San Fernando, California. Her daughter Jenny attends Valley Elementary School and her pet basset hound is named White Fang. Kate's telephone number is 555–9867, and her license plate reads 044 APD.

In "Kate Loves a Mystery" (second date listing), Kate is divorced from Phil and uses her maiden name, Kate Callahan. She now works for the *Valley Advocate* in the San Fernando Valley and her license plate number is 304 MGD. Her daughter Jenny attends Valley Elementary School and her dog is White Fang. Her friend, Sergeant Mike Varrick, is with the Valley Municipal Police Department, and Josh Alden is the newspaper publisher (both versions).

Theme: "Theme from Kate Loves a Mystery," written by John Cacavas

KAY O'BRIEN
CBS, 9.25.86 to 11.13.86

Kay O'Brien (Patricia Kalember) is a second-year surgical resident at Manhattan General Hospital in New York City. Her nickname is "Kay-O" and she wears a size-six surgical glove. Her parents' home phone number is given as 513–555–8911. The series, originally titled "Kay O'Brien, Surgeon," was first set in Bellevue Hospital (in the unaired pilot version). Lane Smith plays Kay's superior, Dr. Robert Moffitt, and Priscilla Lopez, her friend, Nurse Rosa Villanueva.

Relatives: John McMartin (Kay's father, *Jack O'Brien*), Scotty Bloch (Kay's mother, *Lucille O'Brien*), Walter Boone (Rosa's husband, *Lee Villanueva*), Lisa Jakub (Rosa's daughter, *Allison Villanueva*), Stuart Stone (Rosa's son, *Danny Villanueva*). Mark Snow composed the theme.

KAZ
CBS, 9.10.78 to 4.18.79

Martin "Kaz" Kazinski (Ron Leibman), an attorney with the firm of Bennett, Reinhart and Calcourt, studied for the bar while serving a six-year prison term for auto theft. Patrick O'Neal plays his employer, Samuel Bennett; Gloria LeRoy plays Mary Parnell, the owner of the Starting Gate Night Club (over which Kaz lives); and Linda Carlson plays Kate McKenna, the court reporter for the Los Angeles *Herald*. Fred Karlin composed "The Theme from Kaz."

KNIGHT AND DAYE
NBC, 7.8.89 to 8.14.89

Hank Knight (Jack Warden) and Everett Daye (Mason Adams) host "Knight and Daye," a morning radio show on KLOP in San Diego. Hank and Everett originally hosted "Knight and Daye" on radio station WLMM in New York City during the 1940s. KLOP, 580 on the AM dial, and the number 16 station in a 17-station market, is managed by Janet Glick (Julia Campbell), a pretty, easily upset young woman who attended San Diego State College. The womanizing Hank's claim to fame is his book, *Mr. Fabulous: My 50 Years as the King of Show Business*.

Hope Lange plays Everett's wife, Gloria; Lela Ivey, their married daughter, Ellie Estabar; and Joe Lala, Ellie's husband,

Cito Estabar, a taxi cab driver. Emily Schulman, Shiri Appleby and Brittany Thornton portray Ellie's children, Chris, Amy and Laurie. David Michael Frank composed "The Knight and Daye Theme."

KNIGHT RIDER

NBC, 9.26.82 to 8.8.86

Principal Cast: David Hasselhoff (*Michael Knight*), Edward Mulhare (*Devon Miles*), Patricia McPherson (*Bonnie Barstow;* first and third seasons), Rebecca Holden (*April Curtis;* second season), William Daniels (*voice of KITT*)

Trivia: When Michael Long, an undercover cop, is shot and left for dead, he is saved by Wilton Knight (Richard Basehart), a dying billionaire who provides lifesaving surgery, a new face, a new identity—and a mission: to apprehend criminals who think they are above the law.

Michael, who works for Knight Industries and the Foundation for Law and Government in California (of which Devon Miles is the head), is given an indestructible black TransAm car called KITT (Knight Industries Two Thousand). KITT, whose license plate reads KNIGHT, and whose serial number is Alpha Delta 227529, is made of a molecular bonded shell. The car is able to talk and think via its elaborate and sophisticated circuitry. Bonnie Barstow (and in one season, April Curtis) is KITT's mechanic and provides the delicate maintenance it requires. Bonnie, a computer whiz and electronics expert, invented S.I.D. (Satellite Infiltration Drone), a bugging device that can go places where KITT cannot.

KITT's prototype is KARR (Knight Automated Roving Robot), an evil car voiced by Peter Cullen; KITT's enemy is Goliath, an indestructible truck owned by Wilton's evil son, Garthe. As Michael Long, Michael was with the 11th Precinct of the Los Angeles Police Department and lived at 1834 Shore Road; his badge number was 8043.

Relatives: Kate McGeehan (Wilton's daughter, *Jennifer Knight*), David Hassel-

hoff (Wilton's son, *Garthe Knight*), Lynne Marta (April's sister, *Laura Phillips*)

Theme: "Knight Rider," by Glen A. Larson and Michael Sloan

LADY BLUE

ABC, 9.26.85 to 1.25.86

Detective Katy Mahoney (Jamie Rose), a female Dirty Harry (ABC's "Dirty Harriet") is with the Violent Crimes Division, 39th Street Station of the Chicago Metro Police Department. Katy's badge number is 28668 (668 in the pilot) and her license plate number is 4DJ 56. Nan Woods plays Willow, the niece of Lieutenant Terry McNichols (Danny Aiello); and Diane Dorsey appears as Rose, the wife of Detective Gino Gianelli (Ron Dean). Arnetia Walker sings the theme, "Lady Blue." The two-hour TV movie pilot aired on ABC on 4.15.85.

LAND OF THE LOST

NBC, 9.7.74 to 9.3.77

While exploring the Colorado River on a raft, forest ranger Rick Marshall (Spencer Milligan), his daughter Holly (Kathy Coleman) and son Will (Wesley Eure) are caught in a time vortex and transported to a closed universe called the Land of the Lost. In this prehistoric-like world, they establish a home in a cave they call High Bluff and discover that two other races inhabit the land—the simple, monkey-like Palcus, and the lizard-like Sleestak. Through Enik (Walker Edmiston), a Sleestak who fell through a time doorway and is now in his future, the Marshalls learn that their world is controlled by a series of pyramid-like triangles called Pylons. Each Pylon holds a series of colored crystals; escape can only be made by finding the right series of crystals to open a time doorway. However, the crystals control the delicate balance of life, and so it is extremely dangerous to disturb them.

It is also learned that, although Enik is friendly, the other Sleestak (who hunt with bow and arrow) are not; they pose a constant threat to the Marshalls' survival. Enik's mission is to find the doorway, return to his time, and prevent his people from becoming savages.

Ron Harper joined the cast in 1976 as Rick's brother, Jack. (While experimenting with the crystals, Rick finds the time doorway, but he is swept away before he can get to Holly and Will. Since this world is a closed universe, for each being that leaves, one must take his or her place to maintain the harmony. As Rick is freed, Jack becomes his replacement.)

Dinosaurs co-exist with the inhabitants of the Land of the Lost and Holly befriends a baby brontosaurus she calls Dopey. Grumpy, a Tyrannosaurus Rex, and Big Alice (Dopey's mother) are the creatures that most often plague the Marshalls. Philip Paley plays the Palcu boy Chaka, and Sharon Baird, the Palcu girl Sa. Linda Laurie and Michael Lloyd composed the theme.

LASSIE

see JEFF'S COLLIE and THE NEW LASSIE

THE LAST PRECINCT

NBC, 4.11.86 to 5.30.86

Rob Wright (Adam West) is captain of Precinct 56, nicknamed the Last Precinct and manned by a group of misfit officers, including Randi Brooks as beautiful, sexy Mel Brubaker—who was once a man; Pete Willcox as the King, who believes he is Elvis Presley; Ernie Hudson as Sergeant Tremayne Lane (nicknamed "Night Train"); and Vijay Armitraj as Officer Alphabet, whose real name is Shivamanbhai Pouncawilla. Nicollette Sheridan plays Stacy, the waitress at Honeybunns, the fast-food hangout; Kenneth Mars appears as Mel's bewildered father, Phil, who can't believe his son is now his daughter. Mike Post and Pete Carpenter composed "The Last Precinct Theme."

LAVERNE AND SHIRLEY

ABC, 1.27.76 to 5.10.83

Principal Cast: Penny Marshall (*Laverne DeFazio*), Cindy Williams (*Shirley Feeney*), David L. Lander (*Squiggy Squigman*), Michael McKean (*Lenny Kosnoski*), Eddie Mekka (*Carmine Raguso*), Phil Foster (*Frank DeFazio*), Betty Garrett (*Edna Babbish*), Leslie Easterbrook (*Rhonda Lee*)

Trivia: "Laverne and Shirley" is a "Happy Days" spinoff about two friends, Laverne DeFazio and Shirley Feeney, who live in Milwaukee, Wisconsin, during the 1960s. They originally live at 730 Knapp Street, Apartment A, in Milwaukee (their Milwaukee address is also given as 730 Hampton Street); later at 113½ Laurel Vista Drive in Los Angeles.

In Milwaukee, the girls worked in the bottle-capping division of the Shotz Brewery; in California (Burbank), Laverne and Shirley work in the wrapping department of Bardwell's Department Store. (In the final season, after Shirley marries her fiancé, Dr. Walter Meeney, Laverne finds work at the Ajax Aerospace Company.)

Laverne and Shirley, who shop at Slotnick's Supermarket in Milwaukee, attended Fillmore High School and served a hitch in the Army. They did their basic training at Camp McClellan and Shirley wrote of their experiences under the name S. Wilhelmina Feeney. They played hookers in the Army training film, *This Can Happen to You.*

Laverne, an Italian Catholic, suffers from a fear of small places, loves milk and Pepsi (her favorite drink), Scooter Pies (favorite snack) and her favorite sandwich is peanut butter and sauerkraut on raisin bread. She wears a large capital *L* on all her clothes.

Shirley, an Irish Protestant, is famous for the Shirley Feeney scarf dance, has a stuffed cat doll named Boo Boo Kitty, and uses the Feeney family traditional term, "Hi-Yoooo" (for hello) and "Bye-Yoooo" (for good-bye).

Lenny Kosnoski and Andrew "Squiggy" Squigman are friends of Laverne and Shirley and work as beer truck drivers for the Shotz Brewery. In later episodes, they are co-owners of the Squignoski Talent Agency of Burbank, and ice cream vendors with a truck called Squignoski's Ice Cream. As talent agents, they write a movie called *Blood Orgy of the Amazon* and search for young starlets to appear in it. Their favorite food is Bosco (which they put on everything).

Lenny, whose home away from home is the gutter, likes horror movies and sports; his only toy as a kid was sauerkraut. He also had a pet turtle, but it killed itself trying to scratch Lenny's name off its back.

Squiggy, whose prized possession is his moth collection, is "blessed" with the Squigman birthmark (a big red blotch shaped like Abraham Lincoln) and has two favorite things: old sandwiches and toenail clippings.

In one episode, Lenny inherited his late Uncle Lazlo's restaurant. He and Squiggy reopened the place (naming it Dead Lazlo's Place) and hired Laverne and Shirley. Shirley worked as Betty the waitress, while Laverne did the cooking.

Frank DeFazio, Laverne's father, first owns the Pizza Bowl (a pizzeria and bowling alley); then, after he and Edna Babbish marry and move to Burbank, Cowboy Bill's Western Grub (a fast-food chain). Frank's nickname for Laverne is "Muffin."

Carmine Raguso, Shirley's boyfriend (who calls her "Angel Face"), is nicknamed "the Big Ragu," and works as a singing messenger.

Rhonda Lee, Laverne and Shirley's beautiful Hollywood actress neighbor in Burbank, mentions that she starred in the stage play *Bono Mania*, the life of Sonny and Cher.

Relatives: Ed Begley Jr. (Shirley's brother, *Bobby Feeney*), Wynn Irwin (Squiggy's father, *Helmut Squigman*), David L. Lander (Squiggy's sister, *Squendelyn Squigman*), Linda Gillin (Edna's daughter, *Amy*)

Theme: "Making Our Dreams Come True," vocal by Cyndi Grecco

LAWMAN

ABC, 10.5.58 to 10.9.62

"The Lawman came with the sun; there was a job to be done; so they sent for the badge and the gun of the Lawman . . . " Dan Troop (John Russell) is Marshal of Laramie, Wyoming, during the 1870s. Peter Brown plays his deputy, Johnny McKay; and Peggie Castle, Lilly Merrill, the owner of the Birdcage Saloon. Bek Nelson plays Drew Lemp, the owner of the Blue Bonnet Café; Barbara Lang, Julie Tate, the editor of the town newspaper, the *Laramie Weekly*. "The Lawman Theme" was composed by Mack David and Jerry Livingston.

LEARNING THE ROPES

Syndicated, 10.88 to 10.89

Robert Randall (Lyle Alzado) is a single father (separated from his wife, Anne), vice principal and history teacher at Ridgedale Valley Preparatory School and a wrestler who moonlights as "the Masked Maniac."

Nicole Stoffman and Yannick Bisson play his teenaged children, Ellen and Mark. They attend Ridgedale, hang out at the Burger Palace, and Ellen, the younger of the two, thinks she looks like Madonna when she wears makeup.

Fellow wrestlers call Robert "the Professor." Anne, who is never seen, is in England studying to become a lawyer. Jacqueline Mason plays Beth, Ellen's boy-crazy girlfriend; Sheryl Wilson, Carol Dickson, the French teacher. Dr. Death and Gary Sabaugh perform the wrestling scenes for the Masked Maniac.

In the unaired pilot, it was said that Anne ran off and left the family and that Robert and Carol were romantically involved (not so in the series). David Roberts sings the theme, "Learning the Ropes."

LEAVE IT TO BEAVER

CBS, 10.11.57 to 9.26.58
ABC, 10.3.58 to 9.12.62

Principal Cast: Hugh Beaumont (*Ward Cleaver*), Barbara Billingsley (*June Cleaver*), Tony Dow (*Wally Cleaver*), Jerry Mathers (*Beaver Cleaver*), Ken Osmond (*Eddie Haskell*), Frank Bank (*Lumpy Rutherford*), Rusty Stevens (*Larry Mondello*), Richard Deacon (*Fred Rutherford*), Cheryl Holdridge (*Julie Foster*), Jeri Weil (*Judy Hessler*), Stephen Talbot (*Gilbert Bates*)

Trivia: Ward and June Cleaver and their children, Wally and Beaver, live first at 211 Pine Street in the town of Mayfield (their address is also given as 211 Maple Drive and 211 Pine Avenue). Their second home is at 211 Lakewood Avenue; their phone number is KL5–4763. Ward is a businessman (his exact profession is never revealed) and grew up on Shannon Avenue in Shaker Heights. June, his wife, loves to wear jewelry; her maiden name is Bronson.

Wallace ("Wally") their first-born son, attended the Grant Avenue Grammar School and later Mayfield High. He is a good student, a talented athlete, and plans to attend college.

Theodore, their second child, is named after June's Aunt Martha's brother. Theodore acquired the name "Beaver" from Wally. Wally couldn't pronounce Theodore and said "Tweder." Ward and June thought "Beaver" sounded better. Beaver, who attends the Grant Avenue School, wears a green baseball cap, hates "mushy stuff," likes to mess around with "junk" and would rather smell a skunk than see a girl. His favorite "fishin' hole" is Miller's Pond.

In the first season Beaver is seven years old and Wally is in the eighth grade. Madison is mentioned as the neighboring town to Mayfield. June's Aunt Martha, who sends umbrellas as gifts on Christmas, first appears when June's unseen sister, Peggy, has a baby and Martha comes to stay with them.

Eddie Haskell, Wally's wisecracking friend (who is extremely polite to adults,

but mean to everybody else), attends the same schools as Wally and lives at 175 Grant Avenue. He calls Beaver "Squirt," and Woody Woodpecker is his favorite cartoon character and TV show.

Ward's license plate number is WJG 865; Wally's friend Lumpy's license plate reads PZR 342. Lumpy's real name is Clarence. Gus (Burt Mustin), the old fire chief Beaver visits, is with Fire Station Number 5.

Ward's boss, Fred Rutherford, originally talked about having three children: a girl, Violet (Wendy Winkelman), and two boys who were offered football scholarships. Later he had only two children: Violet (Veronica Cartwright) and Clarence. Three actresses played Fred's wife, Gwen: Helen Parrish, Majel Barrett and Margaret Stewart.

Beaver's friend Gilbert Bates was first introduced as Gilbert Harrison and was later called Gilbert Gates. Beaver's friend Larry Mondello (Rusty Stevens) was originally billed as Robert Stevens. Julie Foster is Wally's girlfriend; Judy Hessler is the girl who annoys Beaver and his friends at school (she was replaced by Karen Sue Trent as Penny in last-season episodes).

Relatives: Edgar Buchanan (Ward's *Uncle Billy*), Madge Kennedy (June's *Aunt Martha*), Carl Swenson and George O. Petrie (Eddie's father, *George Haskell*), Ann Doran and Ann Barton (Eddie's mother, *Agnes Haskell*), Ross Elliott and Bill Baldwin (*Julie's father*), Madge Blake (*Larry's mother*), Carleton G. Young and Alan Ray (Gilbert's father, *John Bates*), Claudia Bryar (*Gilbert's mother*)

Theme: "The Toy Parade," by Michael Johnson and Melvyn Lenard

Note: See also "The New Leave It to Beaver." In the pilot, "It's a Small World" (syndicated in 1957 on "Studio '57"), Casey Adams played Ward and Paul Sullivan, Wally.

LEG WORK

CBS, 10.3.87 to 11.7.87

Claire McCarron (Margaret Colin), a beautiful private detective who operates

McCarron Investigations in New York City, charges $500 a day plus expenses. She lives at 365 East 65th Street and drives a silver Porsche with the license plate DEX 627 (her mobile phone number is 555-4365). She has a dog named Clyde and inherited a collection of rare Lionel "O-Gauge" electric trains from her father. When a case bothers her and she has to think, Claire makes oatmeal raisin cookies—one of two foods she can prepare; the other is coq au vin. The title, which refers to all the walking Claire must do because her car is always in need of repair, also refers to Claire's shapely legs—which she prominently displays by wearing miniskirts.

Fred McCarron (Patrick James Clarke) is Claire's brother, a lieutenant with the Office of Public Relations at One Police Plaza; and Willie Pipal (Frances McDormand) is Claire's friend, the Assistant District Attorney. Michael Omartian composed the theme, "Leg Work." The series' alternative title was "Eye Shadow" (Ms. Colin had the choice of using either title. While she preferred neither, she chose "Leg Work.").

The original series concept began as a pilot called "Adams Apple" (CBS, 8.23.86) in which Sydney Walsh played Toni Adams, a private detective working out of Manhattan. (The title refers to Toni, who works the Big Apple—a jazz term musicians once used to describe New York.) Carolyn Seymour plays Tricia Hammond, the District Attorney; and Cherry Jones, Janice Eaton, Toni's contact at the D.A.'s office. Toni has a dog named Mary Jo. Both "Leg Work" and "Adams Apple" were produced by Frank Abatemarco.

In "Leg Work," Claire is a former Assistant D.A. who quit her job to become her own boss. This refers to the series "Foley Square," in which Margaret Colin played Alex Harrigan, an Assistant D.A. working out of the Criminal Courts Building at Foley Square in Manhattan. It is apparent that aspects of "Foley Square" (CBS, 12.11.85 to 4.8.86) and "Adams Apple" were later combined to create "Leg Work."

LIFE GOES ON

ABC, 9.12.89 to

Principal Cast: Patti LuPone (*Libby Thatcher*), Bill Smitrovich (*Drew Thatcher*), Monique Lanier (*Paige Thatcher*), Kellie Martin (*Becca Thatcher*), Chris Burke (*Corky Thatcher*), Michele Matheson (*Rona Lieberman*), Tanya Fenmore (*Maxie*)

Trivia: "Life Goes On" chronicles events in the lives of Drew and Libby Thatcher, a working-class couple with three children (Paige, Becca and Corky).

Drew and Libby: On their first date, Drew Thatcher, a divorced construction worker with a young daughter (Paige), and Libby Giordano, a singer and dancer, saw the movies *Curse of the Stone Hand* and *Curse of the Swamp Creature* at the Glen Brook Drive-In (in Drew's old Plymouth). Drew and Libby later married. Drew acquired work with the Quentico Construction Company, and Libby gave up her career to raise their family: Paige and their children together, Rebecca and Charles (Corky). In the episode of 3.25.90 ("Pig-O-My Heart"), Drew quits his job and Libby, who had taken a job at the Berkson and Berkson Advertising Agency, resigns to help Drew run the new family business, the Glen Brook Grill (a diner).

Paige, whose natural mother is Katherine Henning, is the eldest child, nicknamed "Button." She loves to paint, has two rabbits (named Sammy and Matilda), and works as a receptionist at the Matthews Animal Hospital.

Rebecca, who is nicknamed "Becca," is 15 years old, weighs 85 pounds and attends Marshall High School. She is a bright student and a talented ballerina and writer who worries that her figure will never develop (during the opening theme, Becca looks sideways into a mirror, and referring to her small bust, remarks, "Come on, where are you guys already?"). Having a friend like the beautiful but conceited Rona Lieberman frustrates Becca and her other friend, Maxie, and makes them want the attention Rona gets.

With the sponsorship of the Salcedo Bagel Company, Rebecca entered the Tri-State Teenage Miss Pageant. She was crowned Third Runner-Up and received a $5,000 scholarship. Rona, who was sponsored by the Glen Brook Savings Bank, was First Runner-Up and won a $10,000 scholarship. Rona, who has been entering beauty contests since she was a kid, loves country and western music. Rebecca, a reporter for the school newspaper, the *Marshall Monitor*, also wrote a story ("Kriminal Kominsky") for the *Underground Marshall*, the school's alternative newspaper. Rebecca, like her mother, took ballet lessons from Lillian Doubcha (Viveca Lindfors), a world famous prima ballerina.

Corky, also called "the Cork," has Down's syndrome and attended the Fowler Institution before entering Marshall High School. Though older than other freshmen, Corky has become "one of the guys," proving that despite having a handicap, he can do what other kids do—from playing the drums to running for class president to helping out at the family diner.

The family dog is named Arnold ("the semi-wonder dog"); Drew's license plate number is JNE 734; the automatic coffeemaker in the opening credits activates at 6:55 A.M.; Drew and Libby's alarm clock rings at 7:00 A.M.; and Libby buys mostly generic (No Frills) products from the supermarket.

Relatives: Penny Santon (Libby's mother, *Teresa Giordano*), Al Ruscio (Libby's father, *Sal Giordano*), Gina Hecht (Libby's *Cousin Angela*), Pat Hingle (Drew's father, *Jack Thatcher*), Rick Rosenthal (Drew's brother, *Richard Thatcher*), Claire Berger (Drew's *Cousin Frances*), Lisa Banes (Paige's mother, *Katherine Henning*), Jennifer Warren (Rona's mother, *Mrs. Lieberman*)

Flashbacks: Jenna Pangburn (*Paige as a girl*)

Theme: "Ob-La-Di, Ob-La-Da," by John Lennon and Paul McCartney

LIVING DOLLS
ABC, 9.26.89 to 12.30.89

Charlie Briscoe (Leah Remini), Caroline Welden (Deborah Tucker), Emily Franklin (Halle Berry) and Martha Lambert (Alison Elliott) are four teenage models who live at 68th Street and Madison Avenue, New York City, in the home of Trish Carlin (Michael Learned), a former model turned agent. Charlie, whose hometown is Brooklyn, first appeared on "Who's the Boss?" ("Life's a Ditch" episode) as Sam's (Alyssa Milano) friend. Martha, whose nickname is "Pooch," is from Idaho; Trish has a houseplant she calls Amadeus.

Relatives: Marion Ross (Trish's sister, *Marion*), David Moscow (Trish's son, *Rick Carlin*), Edward Winter (Trish's ex-husband, *Todd Carlin*), Wilson Smith (*Martha's father*)

In the original, unaired pilot, the cast was: Michael Learned (Trish Curtis), Leah Remini (Charlie), Melissa Willis (Caroline), Vivica Fox (Emily), Alison Elliott (Martha) and Jonathan Ward (Rick). The "Living Dolls" theme was written by John Beasley and John Vester.

MacGRUDER AND LOUD
ABC, 1.20.85 to 9.3.85

Malcolm MacGruder (John Getz) and Jenny Loud (Kathryn Harrold) are patrol car officers with a police department (L.S.P.D.) in an unnamed California city. Malcolm, whose badge number is 459, and Jenny, whose badge number is 449, are secretly married (department regulations forbid married cops to work together). They ride in a car with license plate 275816. Their car code is 8-Z-11. Jenny's badge was also given as 458 and Malcolm's badge was also given as 445. Paul Chihara composed the theme.

MacGYVER
ABC, 9.29.85 to

Principal Cast: Richard Dean Anderson (*MacGyver*), Dana Elcar (*Peter Thornton*),

Elyssa Davalos (*Nikki Carpenter*), Bruce McGill (*Jack Dalton*)

Trivia: He's opposed to firearms and relies heavily on his imagination and duct tape. He's MacGyver, a survival expert and scientific genius who tackles seemingly impossible missions for the U.S. government. MacGyver originally worked for the Company and later the Phoenix Foundation. His boss is Peter Thornton. MacGyver, who was born in Mission City, drives a jeep with license plate IRQ 104.

MacGyver's friend and occasional assistant, Nikki Carpenter, lives at 2723 Foster Lane, has the phone number 555-3082, and was born on March 5, 1959. Jack Dalton, MacGyver's always-in-trouble friend, is a pilot who runs the Dalton Air Service.

Although MacGyver has no official first name, he was called "Stace MacGyver" in an early ABC press release. His grandfather calls him "Bud"; and in the episode "The Lost Amadeus" (3.19.90), guest star Tamsin Kelsey twice tried to learn MacGyver's first name. When she finally got a look at his driver's license, she commented "Oh, that's why you don't use a first name." The license was not shown to the audience.

Relatives: John Anderson (MacGyver's grandfather, *Harry Jackson*), Michele B. Chan (MacGyver's foster daughter, *Sue Ling*), Penelope Windust (Pete's ex-wife, *Connie Thornton*), Scott Coffey (Pete's son, *Michael Thornton*)

Flashbacks: Sean Wohland and Shawn Donahue (*MacGyver as a boy*), Phil Redrow and Martin Milner (MacGyver's father, *James MacGyver*), Sheila Moore (MacGyver's mother, *Ellen MacGyver*), Jan Jorden (*Harry's wife*)

Theme: "MacGyver," written by Randy Edelman

McHALE'S NAVY

ABC, 9.11.62 to 8.30.66

Principal Cast: Ernest Borgnine (*Lieutenant Quinton McHale*), Joe Flynn (*Captain Wallace B. Binghamton*), Tim Conway (*Ensign Charles Parker*), Bob Hastings (*Lieutenant Elroy Carpenter*)

McHale's Crew: Carl Ballantine (*Lester Gruber*), Billy Sands (*Harrison "Tinker" Bell*), John Wright (*Willy Moss*), Gavin MacLeod (*Happy Haines*), Edson Stroll (*Virgil Edwards*), Gary Vinson (*Quarter-Master Christopher*), Yoshio Toda (*Fuji Kobiaji*)

Trivia: This series portrays the conflict between Quinton McHale, the commander of a PT boat in the South Pacific during World War II, and Wallace B. Binghamton, the commanding officer, who is plagued by McHale and his crew of pirates.

Prior to the war, McHale, who was born in Michigan, was the captain of a tramp steamer in the South Pacific; he was commissioned by Admiral Reynolds as a lieutenant. Binghamton, born in New York, was head of the Long Island Yacht Club before the war and is somewhat inadequate as captain. McHale now commands Squadron 19 and PT Boat 73. He is based on the island of Taratupa and resides with his crew on the far side of the island, which is called McHale's Island. McHale's crew calls Binghamton "Old Lead Bottom." Elroy Carpenter, Wallace's assistant, commands PT Boat 16. McHale's unreported Prisoner of War is Fuji, a Japanese soldier who went over the hill and now serves as McHale's cook. Last-season episodes are set in Voltafiore, Italy, when McHale, his crew and Binghamton are all transferred to the European theater of war.

Theme: "McHale's Navy," by Axel Stordahl

Spinoff Series: "Broadside" (ABC, 9.20.64 to 9.5.65). Kathleen Nolan (Lieutenant Ann Morgan), Lois Roberts (Molly McGuire), Joan Staley (Roberta Love), and Sheila James (Selma Kowalski) are WAVES assigned to the motor pool on the South Pacific island of Ranakai during World War II. Edward Andrews plays Roger S. Adrian, the commanding officer, who would like to rid his island of the women and return it to the tropical paradise he knew before they arrived.

THE MacKENZIES OF PARADISE COVE

see A FAMILY FOR JOE

MADAME'S PLACE

Syndicated, 9.82 to 9.83

Principal Cast: Wayland Flowers (*voice of Madame*), Judy Landers (*Sara Joy Pitts*), Johnny Haymer (*Walter "Pinky" Pinkerton*), Susan Tolsky (*Bernadette "Bernie" Van Gilder*), Corey Feldman (*Buzzy St. James*), Barbara Cason (*Lynn LaVecque*)

Trivia: The puppet Madame, who hosts "Madame's Place," a late-night TV talk show, from her Hollywood mansion, was the star of such movies as *A Woman Named Hey You* (with Clint Eastwood) and *Trampoline Honeymoon*. Madame was also set to star in *Ride the Wild Surf* with Tab Hunter but lost the role to Barbara Eden (who had a better figure and looked stunning in a bikini). In an attempt to win back the role, Madame accused Barbara of painting stretch marks on her bikini.

Madame, who has an antique Rolls Royce (license plate MADAME), enjoys reading the *Enquiring Star*, is a member of the Fetish-of-the-Month Club, and uses Me Tarzan—You Jane Body Rub (which she orders from the House of Pleasure catalogue). She orders her groceries from Tony's Market and was married six times; her third husband was a fan who sent her a picture of himself playing polo in the nude. Like many stars, Madame has her harrowing moments: she is kidnapped by Egbert Tegley, a famous criminal known as "Sweet Tooth" Tegley, who holds her hostage at an Atlantic City saltwater taffy stand. Pinkerton, her butler, breaks down the door and rescues her. Madame is also the target of a crazed fan (played by Archie Hahn) who believes she is the most beautiful woman in the world (he also believes that when the moon is full he turns into a parakeet).

Sara Joy Pitts, Madame's ultra-sexy niece, who measures 37–24–36, is described by Madame as "a sexpot who doesn't realize she is a sexpot." Sara Joy, who wears very low-cut and off-the-shoulder blouses, as well as short-shorts, calls Madame "Auntie Madame." Her favorite TV show is a soap opera called "The Young and the Stupid" (which she watches with the sound off because hearing it makes her cry even more).

Other Characters: Bernadette Van Gilder, called "Bernie" by Madame, is her man-shy, mousy secretary; Buzzy St. James is the kid next door; and Lynn LeVecque is Madame's competition, the host of "Naked All-Star Bowling." Hector Elias plays Rollin Espinoza, the leader of the Madame's Place All-Divorced Orchestra; John Moschitta appeared as Larry Lunch, Madame's super-fast-talking agent (and a constant source of aggravation to her). While a network is not mentioned, R. Ray Randall (voice by Chandler Garrison) is the stern head of the network (he is never seen). Don Sparks plays Eric Honest (a.k.a. Mr. Honest), Madame's most frequent and most exasperating guest; and E. J. Peaker and John Reilly play Buzzy's parents, Carla and Max St. James.

Theme: "Here at Madame's Place," vocal by Denise DeCaro

MAGNUM, P.I.

CBS, 12.11.80 to 9.12.88

Principal Cast: Tom Selleck (*Thomas Magnum*), John Hillerman (*Jonathan Higgins*), Larry Manetti (*Rick Orville Wright*), Roger E. Mosley (*Theodore "T. C." Calvin*), Kathleen Lloyd (*Carol Baldwin*)

Trivia: Thomas Sullivan Magnum is an ex-Naval Intelligence Officer turned private detective who operates out of Hawaii and lives on the estate of pulp writer Robin Masters in return for providing security. Magnum, who served with the VM02 in Da Nang during the Vietnam War, was born in the town of Tidewater, Virginia. His first paying job was delivering newspapers for the *Daily Sentinel* (he earned $12 a week plus one penny for each paper he sold). Magnum, who is writing a book called *How to Be a World-Class Private Investigator*, drives a car with license plate 56E 478; his phone number is 555-2131. He charges $200 a day plus expenses for detective work and one of his hangouts is the King Kamehameha Club.

Jonathan Quayle Higgins is the estate's majordomo. He served with M.I. 6 (Military Intelligence) during World War II and has a ham radio with call letters NR6 DBZ. His hobbies are building model bridges and painting; he has two guard dogs named Apollo and Zeus. He also writes his memories of the war in a diary he calls "Crisis at Suez."

Tom's friend Rick runs a bar called Rick's Place, and his friend T. C., a former Golden Gloves Boxer, owns the Island Hoppers Helicopter Service. Carol Baldwin is Tom's friend, the Assistant District Attorney. Robin Masters, who is seen from the back only (Bruce Atkinson) is voiced by Orson Welles; Robin's Ferraris have the license plates ROBIN I and ROBIN II and his favorite charity is the Home for Wayward Boys. Tom (number 14), Rick (number 17) and T. C. (number 32) are members of Robin's softball team, the Paddlers. Robin's first published story was "The Last Days of Babylon."

Relatives: Gwen Verdon (Tom's mother, *Katherine Peterson*), David Huddleston (Tom's stepfather, *Frank Peterson*), Robert Selleck Sr. (*Tom's grandfather*), Julie Cobb (Tom's *Cousin Karyn*), Brendon Call (Tom's *Cousin Billy*), Barbara Rush (Tom's aunt, *Phoebe Sullivan*), Sally Ponting (Higgins' niece, *Jilly Mack*), John Hillerman (Higgins' half-brother, *Father Paddy MacGuinness*), John Hillerman (Higgins' half-brother, *Don Luis Monqueo*), Alice Cadogan (Rick's sister, *Wendy*), Fay Hauser (T. C.'s ex-wife, *Tina*), Shavar Ross (T. C.'s son, *Bryant*), Celeste Holm (Carol's mother, *Abigail*), Linda Grovernor (Carol's niece, *Becky Damon*), Matt Clark (Carol's uncle, *Jack Damon*), Tate Donovan (Robin's nephew, *R. J. Masters*)

Flashbacks: R. J. Williams (*Tom as a boy*), Susan Blanchard (*Tom's mother*), Robert Pine (*Tom's father*), Marta DuBois (Tom's wife, *Michelle*), Robert Mederros III (*Higgins as a boy*)

Theme: "Magnum, P.I.," by Mike Post and Pete Carpenter

MAJOR DAD

CBS, 9.17.89 to

Principal Cast: Gerald McRaney (*Major John D. "Mac" MacGillis*), Shanna Reed (*Polly Cooper*), Marisa Ryan (*Elizabeth Cooper*), Chelsea Hertford (*Casey Cooper*), Nicole Dubuc (*Robin Cooper*), Whitney Kershaw (*Merilee Gunderson*)

Trivia: This is the story of a tough Marine (John) who marries a pretty widow (Polly) with three children (Elizabeth, Casey and Robin) and the misadventures that occur when they set up housekeeping in Oceanside, California.

John, who was a history major at Vanderbilt College, joined the Marines in 1967 and is currently stationed at Camp Singleton (in another episode, John mentions that he has only been in the Marines for 20 years, beginning in 1969). John, who did his basic training on Paris Island, is assigned to building number 52419 on the base and his favorite eatery is Zaff's Hamburgers. In the 5.21.90 episode John retires to become vice president of Product Relations for Teletech Defense. He returns to the Marines when a typo on his retirement papers—dated May 19, 1909 instead of 1990—invalidates his resignation.

Polly, a newspaper reporter for the *Oceanside Chronicle*, is a Democrat and a member of the Officers' Wives Club (where once a year she has to participate in Jayne Wayne Day—when wives of officers become Marines for a day). Her eldest daughter, Elizabeth, attends Keefer High School, and her youngest, Casey, is enrolled in the Martin Elementary School. Robin, who also attends Martin Elementary, is on the school's basketball team, the Condors. Casey has a stuffed animal doll called Whoobie, and the family's pet bird is named Lemon. The Major objects to three things while living with four females: a bedroom with pink walls, having to shower with a Strawberry Shortcake shower curtain and hair clogging the sinks.

Merilee is John's secretary and Matt Mulhern and Marlon Archery are Marines Lieutenant Eugene Holowachuk and Sergeant James.

Theme: "Major Dad," by Roger Steinman

MAKE ROOM FOR DADDY

ABC, 9.29.53 to 7.17.57
CBS, 10.7.57 to 9.14.64

Principal Cast: Danny Thomas (*Danny Williams*), Jean Hagen (*Margaret Williams*), Marjorie Lord (*Kathy Williams*), Sherry Jackson and Penny Parker (*Terry Williams*), Rusty Hamer (*Rusty Williams*), Angela Cartwright (*Linda Williams*), Louise Beavers and Amanda Randolph (*Louise*), Sid Melton (*Charlie Halper*)

Trivia: The series depicts events in the life of Danny Williams, a nightclub entertainer at the Copa Club in New York City, who has little time to spend with his family: his wife, Margaret (1953–57), and later Kathy (1957–64), and their children, Terry, Rusty and Linda.

Danny, who was born in Toledo, Ohio, attended Ursuline Academy (a school run by the nuns of the Ursuline Order). He dropped out after one year to go to work. (In another episode, Danny mentions he was born in Deerfield, Michigan, and raised in Toledo. His school was said to be Woodward High, which later awarded him an honorary diploma.)

Margaret Summers, Danny's first wife, was born in Baraboo, Wisconsin, and met Danny when she was 17 years old (she was a part-time waitress and piano player; Danny, a 24-year-old comedian). In another episode, it is mentioned that Danny has known Margaret since she was a young girl. As a child, Margaret was cared for by Mom and Pop Finch (Kathryn Card, Will Wright) while her mother and father were on the road in vaudeville. Danny and Margaret married in 1941 and honeymooned in the Catskills. She and Danny have two children, Terry and Rusty.

After Margaret's death, Danny meets Kathleen "Kathy" Daly (a.k.a. Kathy O'Hara), a widowed nurse with a young daughter named Patty (Lelani Sorenson; when the series moved to CBS, Patty became Linda). They married in 1957 and spent their honeymoon in Las Vegas (they stayed in Room 509 of the Sands Hotel). Kathy was born in Peoria, Illinois.

Terry (Teresa), Danny's eldest child, attended West Side High School, then an unnamed college where she was a member of the Alpha Beta Chi sorority. She left the series in 1960 when she married Pat Hannegan (Pat Harrington Jr.).

Rusty (Russell), Danny's son, was born on February 15, 1947. He first attended P.S. 54, then Claremont Junior High, and finally West Side High School. Rusty is a member of Scout Troop 44. In a 1956 episode, Rusty, who has a fascination with Elvis Presley and TV's "Wyatt Earp," called himself Elvis Earp, ran away from home and began a career as an orphan at Miss Martin's Children's Home. He thought the best parts of school were recess, lunch and holidays, and he had his first crush on a girl named Sylvia Watkins (Pamela Beaird). His "hatred" turned to "love" publicly when Rusty, the school's champion speller, misspelled the word symmetrical with only one "m" in a spelling bee (to let Sylvia win).

Linda, Kathy's daughter, attends P.S. 54, believes in Santa Claus and the Tooth Fairy, and has an "imaginary friend," who nobody believes exists, called Mr. Jumbo (he is ten feet tall and wears a red coat. He did actually exist—as the doorman at the Drake Hotel).

Other Characters: Louise, Danny's maid; Charlie Halper, Danny's boss, the owner of the Copa Club; Danny's Uncle Tonoose, the head of the family. Tonoose is nicknamed "Hashush-al-Kabaar" (Lebanese for "The Man Who Made a Monkey Out of a Camel") and loves goat cheese and grape leaves. He claims the family ancestors include King Achmed the Unwashed. Prior to his role as Uncle Tonoose (from spring 1956 on), Hans Conried played Margaret's Cousin Carl, who drank a lot and travelled with jugs of wine.

Gina Minelli (Annette Funicello) is the Italian exchange student who came to stay with the Williams family. She attends West Side High School and tutors the school's star football players, Buck Weaver and Bronco Lewis (Mr. Inside and Mr. Outside on the team). Her favorite singer is Frankie Laine and she had a dream become a reality when Danny arranged for Frankie to sing at Gina's bedside when she was stricken with the measles and couldn't attend his performance at the school.

The Williamses first lived at the Parkside Apartments (Apartment 1204); later at 505 East 56th Street, Apartment 542 (also given as Apartment 781) in Manhattan; their phone number is Plaza 3–1098 (later Plaza 3–0198). The Williams' family dog is named Laddie. Danny calls Kathy "Clancey."

Harvey Lembeck (as Chip Collins), Jesse White (Jesse Leeds) and Horace McMahon and Sheldon Leonard (Phil Arnold) played Danny's agents over the years. In several episodes, Steven Gerary played the Williams' family physician, Dr. Berhagen (which is Jean Hagen's real last name).

Relatives: Hans Conried (Danny's *Uncle Tonoose*), Tony Bennett (Danny's *Cousin Steven*), Nana Bryant (Margaret's mother, *Julie Summers*), William Demarest (Kathy's father, *Mr. Daly*), Louise Lorimer (Margaret's *Aunt Faye*), Pat Carroll (Charlie's wife, *Bunny Halper*). Mentioned, but not seen: Margaret's father, Harry, and Danny's Aunt Effie and Uncle Jim.

Theme: "Danny Boy," by Herbert Spencer and Earle Hagen

Spinoffs: The lives of the Williams family were updated in the special "The Danny Thomas TV Family Reunion" (NBC, 2.14.65) with Danny, Marjorie, Rusty and Linda. Two years later, on "The Danny Thomas Hour," the cast reunited for "Make More Room for Daddy" (NBC, 11.6.67) in a story that found Rusty in the Army and preparing to marry Susan McAdams (Jana Taylor).

In 1969 (9.14), CBS aired the one-hour

pilot "Make Room for Granddaddy." In the ensuing series (ABC, 9.23.70 to 9.2.71), Rusty and Susan are struggling newlyweds, Linda is attending a boarding school in Connecticut, and Terry (Sherry Jackson) is married to Bill Johnson (not seen), a serviceman stationed in Japan. Terry is the mother of six-year-old Michael (Michael Hughes); as Terry leaves to join Bill, Michael is left with Dany and Kathy—hence the title.

MAMA'S FAMILY
NBC, 1.22.83 to 9.15.84
Syndicated, 9.86

Principal Cast: Vicki Lawrence (*Thelma "Mama" Harper*), Ken Berry (*Vinton Harper*), Dorothy Lyman (*Naomi Harper*), Karin Argoud (*Sonia Harper*), Eric Brown (*Buzz Harper*), Allan Kayser (*Bubba Higgins*), Beverly Archer (*Iola Bolen*)

Trivia: Events in the lives of the Harpers, a not-so-typical family who live in Raytown, U.S.A. Thelma Harper, the cantankerous head of the family, is called "Mama" and was married to a man named Carl (deceased) who called her "Snooky Ookems." Mama, who wears a perfume called Obsession and cleans her oven with Easy-Off, is a member of the Raytown Community Church League. She can extract truth from people with her gift—the Look (a stare that forces people to be honest) and she marketed Mother Harper's Miracle Tonic to make money (a supposed cold remedy that contained Mama's secret ingredient—pure vanillla extract. With its 35% alcohol content, the tonic made users forget why they even took the tonic in the first place).

Vinton, Mama's son, is married to the former Naomi Oates and works as a locksmith for Kwick Keys, a company that is owned by the Bernice Corporation. Naomi, the sexiest woman in Raytown, is a checker at Food Circus and is called "Skeeter" by Vinton. Vinton's favorite breakfast cereal is Dino Puffs (not for the high fiber count, but for the surprise dinosaur that comes in each box).

Bubba Higgins is Mama's grandson; he

attends Raytown Junior College. Iola Bolen, Mama's friend and neighbor, is a member of the Peppermint Playhouse Theater Company. When Mama found a girlie magazine under Bubba's bed, she formed M.O.P. (Mothers Opposing Pornography). In the original NBC series, Vint was a widower and the father of two teenaged children, Sonia and Buzz (who were written out of the syndicated version). The series is based on skits originally performed on "The Carol Burnett Show."

Relatives: Carol Burnett (Mama's daughter, *Eunice Higgins*), Harvey Korman (Eunice's husband, *Ed Higgins*), Betty White (Mama's sister, *Ellen Jackson*), Vicki Lawrence (Mama's *Cousin Lydia*), Dorothy Van (Mama's sister, *Effie*), Imogene Coca (Mama's *Aunt Gert*), Rue McClanahan (Mama's sister, *Fran Crawley*), Jerry Reed (Naomi's ex-husband, *Leonard*)

Flashbacks: Vicki Lawrence (*Thelma as a young woman*), Tanya Fenmore and Heather Kerr (*Eunice as a girl*), Amy O'Neill (*Ellen as a girl*), David Friedman (*Vinton as a boy*), Nikki Cox (*Iola as a girl*)

Theme: "Bless My Happy Home," written by Peter Matz

A MAN CALLED SLOANE

NBC, 9.22.79 to 12.22.79

This series stars Robert Conrad as Thomas Remington Sloane III, a Priority One Agent for UNIT, a secret U.S. government counter-espionage team. Ji-Tu Cumbuka plays his assistant, Torgue; Dan O'Herlihy plays Mr. Director, the head of UNIT. The front for UNIT is a Los Angeles toy store called the Toy Boutique. The brains behind UNIT is Effie, an EFI series 3000 Computer. Michele Carey provides the off-screen, sexy voice for Effie. The enemy of UNIT is KARTEL—an organization bent on destroying the world. Patrick Williams composed the theme, "A Man Called Sloane."

In the original pilot, "Death Ray 2000," Robert Logan played Thomas R. Sloane, Dan O'Herlihy played Mr. Director, and Ji-Tu Cumbuka played Torgue, who was a villain here. Penelope Windust played Emma Blessing, Sloane's assistant at his business, Sloane & Sons, in Carmel, California. In the NBC pilot broadcast on 3.5.81 (filmed in 1979), UNIT is located in Kentucky, where Mr. Director poses as a rural farmer. John Elizalde composed the original theme.

THE MAN FROM U.N.C.L.E.

NBC, 9.22.64 to 1.15.68

Principal Cast: Robert Vaughn (*Napoleon Solo*), David McCallum (*Ilya Kuryakin*), Leo G. Carroll (*Alexander Waverly*)

Trivia: Located at East 46th Street (between 2nd and 3rd Avenues) in New York City is the Del Floria Tailor Shop—the front for U.N.C.L.E. (United Network Command for Law and Enforcement), a U.S. Government organization that battles the evils of THRUSH (Technical Hierarchy for the Removal of Undesirables and the Subjugation of Humanity), an international organization bent on world domination. Alexander Waverly (Badge #1), is the head of U.N.C.L.E. and Napoleon Solo (Badge #11) and Ilya Kuryakin (Badge #2) are its top operatives. Napoleon and Ilya both use a modified P-38 gun. The eight sections of U.N.C.L.E. are:
1. Policy and Operations
2. Operations and Enforcement
3. Enforcement and Intelligence
4. Intelligence and Communications
5. Communications and Security
6. Security and Personnel
7. Propaganda and Finance
8. Camouflage and Deception

On 4.5.83, NBC presented the TV movie *The Return of the Man from U.N.C.L.E.: The 15 Years Later Affair*. After 15 years of inactive service, U.N.C.L.E. head Sir John Raleigh (Patrick Macnee) recruits former agents Napoleon Solo and Ilya Kuryakin to keep THRUSH from detonating a nuclear bomb called the H-957. (Napoleon has gone into the computer business, and Ilya owns a high-fashion boutique called Vanya's.)

Spinoff Series: In "The Girl from U.N.C.L.E." (NBC, 9.13.66 to 9.5.67), Leo

G. Carroll reprised his role as Alexander Waverly, and Stefanie Powers and Noel Harrison were U.N.C.L.E. agents April Dancer and Mark Slate. In "The Moonglow Affair" episode of "The Man from U.N.C.L.E." (the 2.25.66 pilot for "The Girl from U.N.C.L.E."), Mary Ann Mobley and Norman Fell were agents April Dancer and Mark Slate.

Theme: "The Man from U.N.C.L.E.," by Lalo Schifrin

MANCUSO, FBI

NBC, 10.13.89 to 5.18.90

"Mancuso, FBI" presents the exploits of Nick Mancuso (Robert Loggia), a no-nonsense FBI agent with the Metro Bureau Field Office in Washington D.C. Nick's favorite hangout is Gertie's Bar, and his license plate number reads 8E9 356. Nick grew up on the Lower East Side of New York and his wife, Mary Louise (not seen), died in 1964.

Other characters: Randi Brazen, a.k.a. Randi Brooks (*Jean St. John*, Nick's secretary), Lindsay Frost (*Agent Kristen Carter*, who resides at 1136 Arlington Place, Apartment #7), Charles Siebert (*Dr. Paul Summers*), Fredric Lehne (Nick's superior, *Ed McMasters*)

Relatives: Janet Carroll (Nick's married sister, *Lorraine Kovacs*), Michael Bell (Lorraine's husband, *Andy Kovacs*), Leigh Hughes (Nick's niece, *Lee Ann Kovacs*), Georgann Johnson (Kristen's mother, *Mrs. Carter*), Drew Pillsbury (Jean's ex-husband, *Matt*; a gambler), Jason Lively (Paul's son, *Justin Summers*)

In the opening theme, the clock reads 6:20. Susan Hamilton and Doug Katsaros composed "The Mancuso Theme."

THE MANY LOVES OF DOBIE GILLIS

see DOBIE GILLIS

MARBLEHEAD MANOR

Syndicated, 9.87 to 9.88

"It's a grand life. It's an I've-got-the-world-in-my-hand life. It's an almost-more-than-you-can-stand life. Strike up the band, it's a grand life." Hilary Stonehill (Linda Thorson) and her husband Randolph (Bob Fraser) are eccentric millionaires who live in Marblehead Manor at 14 Sunflower Lane (city not named). Randolph is the owner of a company, Stonehill, Inc. Hilary, whose fabulous figure still turns men's heads (she's over 40), has a dog named Albert (named after their faithful butler, Albert Dudley, played by Paxton Whitehead. Albert is a third-generation butler to a third generation of Stonehills).

Dyana Ortelli is Lupe, the sexy cook and maid (her son, Elvis, played by Humberto Ortiz, weighed 11 pounds, five ounces at birth). Carol Bruce played Randolph's mother, Margaret Stonehill, and Natalie Core appeared as Randolph's Aunt Charlotte. The theme, "It's a Grand Life," was composed by Dan Foliart and Howard Pearl.

MARGIE

ABC, 10.12.61 to 8.31.62

"Margie" chronicles the comic adventures of Margie Clayton (Cynthia Pepper), a pretty teenage girl living in the small town of Madison during the 1920s. Dave Willock and Wesley Marie Tackitt play her parents, Harvey and Nora Clayton, and Johnny Bangert plays her brother, Cornell.

Margie attends Madison High School with her friends Maybelle Jackson (Penny Parker) and Heywood Botts (Tommy Ivo). Margie's phone number is Central 4734 (her address is not given) and the afterschool hangout is Crawford's Ice Cream Parlor.

Margie, as editor of the school newspaper, the *Madison Bugle*, wrote the gossip column "Through the Keyhole." In one episode, "Margie Flies the Coop" (1.4.62), Margie and Maybelle leave home and rent their own apartment at 211 Clark Street. Harvey, who is a loan officer at the Great Eastern Savings Bank, and Nora also attended Madison High School.

Relatives: Hollis Irving (Margie's *Aunt Phoebe*), Maxine Stuart (*Maybelle's mother*), Herb Ellis (*Maybelle's father*)

Lionel Newman composed the theme adaptation of the song "Margie."

MARRIED . . . WITH CHILDREN

Fox, 4.5.87 to

Principal Cast: Ed O'Neill (*Al Bundy*), Katey Sagal (*Peggy Bundy*), Christina Applegate (*Kelly Bundy*), David Faustino (*Bud Bundy*), David Garrison (*Steve Rhodes*), Amanda Bearse (*Marcy Rhodes*)

Trivia: Their phone number is 555–2878, their address is 9674 Jeopardy Lane and they live in Chicago. Husband Al has a pathetic life; his wife, Peggy, doesn't cook or clean and is always in a romantic mood (much to Al's regret); their daughter, Kelly, is blonde, beautiful and dense; and their son, Bud, is a girl-crazy teenager who can't get a date. They rarely speak to each other; Al can't remember his kids' names. They are the Bundys, TV's first raunchy American family. For Thanksgiving, they have "the Bundy turkey" (a pizza) and on Labor Day, the Bundy Barbecue and Bundy Burgers (last year's grease and last year's ashes for this year's burgers). The dreaded Bundy event is the family vacation and the Bundy philosophy is, "If you're gonna lose, lose big." The Bundy credo is, "When one Bundy is embarrassed, the rest of us feel good about ourselves." The Bundy family dog is Buck (who is played in costume in one episode by Derek McGrath), and they store their "junk" at Chico's Storage Bin.

Al works as a salesman for Gary's Shoes and Accessories for the Beautiful Woman in an unnamed mall. Al attended James K. Polk High School (where he was voted the most valuable football player of 1966) and figures his life was "ruined" when he met a fellow student named Peggy Wanker at a hamburger joint called Johnny B. Goods (where Al holds the record for eating ten bags of fries at one sitting). She was a sex kitten, Al was a guy. He let his hormones do his thinking and he has been sorry ever since. Al's pride and joy is his prized collection of *Playboy* magazines—which his father started him on when he was 12 years old (he took Al into the garage, where behind the tool box were the magazines and the beginning of the Bundy legacy). Al's brainstorm to make money is a telephone shoe repair service called Dr. Shoe (555-SHOE; as could be expected, no one called and Al lost $50,000). Al has nightmares about feet and was a judge in the Ugly Feet Contest of 1990.

Peggy, whose job is to be a housewife—and to spend all the money Al makes—holds the record at Jim's Bowlarama for bowling a perfect 300 game. While they have a kitchen, including a stove (which Peggy is not sure how to operate), Peggy never shops for food, cooks or cleans. Finding food is the family's number one priority; while Al's favorite food is turkey, he has become content with eating Tang sandwiches. Peggy, a 36C cup, wears the Perfect Figure model 327 bra. She has a stuffed parrot she calls Winky. On their wedding anniversary, Peggy gives Al a tie (he gives her shoes).

Kelly, who usually dresses in tight pants (or tight miniskirts) and low-cut blouses, is, as Peggy calls her, "a hussy. She became a hussy when she learned how to cut her diapers up the side." Kelly attends James K. Polk High School (though not for an education; just as a place to pick up messages, supply the family with pens and pencils and get a hot meal). Kelly's birthday: "I was born in February. I'm an Aquarium." Her hair color: unknown; she has been bleaching it for so long she forgot (although she started with almost white hair, her natural blonde color is more apparent in later episodes). Kelly, whose sexy dress makes her very popular with the boys, calls herself "the Beatles of the 1980s."

Kelly's career is being beautiful. She knows she is an extremely beautiful girl—and she knows that no other girl can measure up to her—that is, until Al hits on the idea to make $500 a month by hosting a foreign exchange student. A French bombshell named Yvette (Milla Jovovich) became the only threat Kelly has ever experienced. (The Bundys "lost" Yvette, whom Kelly called "Why-Vette," when Yvette followed Kelly's example and cut classes. She failed all her subjects, including French, and was withdrawn from the program.)

Kelly's first paying job was as the "Action News" TV Weather Bunny Girl on Channel 83. What started out as an intern project for school became a $1,000 a week job when management realized that Kelly's stunning good looks were boosting ratings. Despite the fact that Kelly didn't know where "East" Dakota was, she was given a raise to $250,000 a year. She lost the job when she attempted to read off a teleprompter and couldn't. Kelly's favorite meal is veal; Al calls her "Pumpkin." For her final assignment in home economics class, she was asked to make Jello. After hours of wondering how to make it (and how to boil water), she managed to cook it, box and all, and got an A-minus. Kelly played the Rock Slut in the Gutter Cats music video.

Bud, who also attends Polk High, is called "Toad Boy" by Kelly, and has the "hots" for their next door neighbor, Marcy Rhodes. In the opening theme, Bud is seen reading a copy of the girlie magazine *Boudoir*, and calls his cowboy pajamas his "love clothes."

On the first sunny day in May, the Bundy's neighbors, Steve and Marcy Rhodes, go to the beach to shake hands with Mr. Sunshine. Steve, whose middle name is Bartholomew, is a bank loan officer (bank not named) who lost his job for lending Al $50,000 to start Dr. Shoe. He then became a cage cleaner at Slither's Pet Emporium and finally a ranger at Yosemite National Park (at which time he left the series). Steve was a member of a band called the Tuxedos in high school and calls Marcy "Angel Cups." Marcy, whose love name for Steve is "Sugar Tush,"

works as a loan officer at the Leading Bank of Chicago. As a kid, Marcy had a dog named Chester; Al calls her "Chicken Legs."

Relatives: Ed O'Neill (*Al's father*), James Haake (Peggy's *Cousin Otto*), King Kong Bundy (Peggy's *Cousin Irwin*), Milly, Elena and Eadie DelRubio (Peggy's cousins, *Milly, Elena* and *Eadie*). In one episode, they unloaded Peggy's grossly overweight mother (not seen) from the back of a flatbed truck. Al then accidentally saw her nude in the bathtub and went temporarily blind from the shocking sight.

Theme: "Love and Marriage," vocal by Frank Sinatra

MARY

CBS, 12.11.85 to 4.8.86

Mary Brennan (Mary Tyler Moore) was originally a writer for a fashion magazine called *Women's Digest*. When the magazine folded, she took a job as the Consumer Helpline columnist for the newspaper the *Chicago Eagle* (originally called the *Chicago Post*). Ed LaSalle (John Astin), the theater critic, writes the column "Stepping Out with Ed LaSalle," and Josephine "Jo" Tucker (Katey Sagal) pens the column "The Mainline Reporter." The fast-food service used by the staff is Mr. Yummy.

Dennis Patrick and Doris Belack play Jo's parents, Charlie and Norma Tucker. Dan Foliart and Howard Pearl composed the theme, "Mary."

MARY HARTMAN, MARY HARTMAN

Syndicated, 1.6.76 to 7.3.77

Principal Cast: Louise Lasser (*Mary Hartman*), Greg Mullavey (*Tom Hartman*), Claudia Lamb (*Heather Hartman*), Debralee Scott (*Cathy Schumway*), Philip Bruns (*George Schumway*), Dody Goodman (*Martha Schumway*; and *the voice calling "Mary Hartman" in the opening theme*), Mary Kay Place (*Loretta Haggers*), Graham Jarvis (*Charlie Haggers*), Victor Kilian (*Raymond Larkin*), Bruce Solomon (*Sergeant Dennis Foley*)

Trivia: The town is Fernwood, Ohio, a peaceful little community until the famous mass murderer of Fernwood claimed the lives of the Lombardi family, their two goats and eight chickens—all of whom lived on Mary June Street.

Just a short distance from Mary June Street is Bratner Avenue, in the Woodland Heights section of town. At 343 Bratner live Mary Hartman, a housewife who constantly worries about the waxy yellow buildup on her kitchen floor, her husband, Tom, an auto plant assembly line worker, and their daughter, Heather (who witnessed the killings and was kidnapped by the mass murderer, Davy Jessup, played by Will Selzer).

Mary, who is 31 years old (born 4.8.45) and Tom, who is 35 (born 10.4.41) met when they both attended Fernwood High School (Tom and Mary have been married 14 years when the series begins; Mary married Tom when she was 17).

While Tom often cheats on Mary (who often suspects he is unfaithful), Mary has only one extramarital affair—with Fernwood Police Department's Sergeant Dennis Foley. Mary, whose middle name is Penny and whose maiden name is Schumway, was once held hostage by a killer in the Chinese Laundry at 414½ Miller Road.

Mary's parents, George and Martha Schumway, her sister, Cathy, and her grandfather, Raymond Larkin, live at 4309 Bratner Avenue. George works with Tom at the Fernwood Auto Plant and has been married to Martha for 36 years. Grandpa Larkin, now 83, was born in Macon, Georgia, and has been arrested for being the Fernwood Flasher. He is somewhat senile and is always asking, "Where's the peanut butter?" Cathy, who is ten years younger than Mary, is a pretty, man-crazy free spirit.

Mary's next door neighbors are Charlie and Loretta Haggers, who live at 345 Bratner Avenue. Loretta, age 22, is sweet and trusting, a country girl who is hoping to make it big as a recording artist. Charlie, her husband and manager, is 43 years old and works at the auto plant. Loretta, who calls Charlie "Baby Boy" (also the title of

her hit record) has two fish, named Conway and Twitty, and performs in Fernwood at the Capri Lounge.

Theme: "Mary Hartman," by Earle Hagen

Note: With the exception of Louise Lasser (whose character Mary ran off with Sergeant Foley), the series continued under the title "Forever Fernwood" (syndicated, 1977–78).

THE MARY TYLER MOORE SHOW

CBS, 9.19.70 to 9.3.77

Principal Cast: Mary Tyler Moore (*Mary Richards*), Valerie Harper (*Rhoda Morganstern*), Ed Asner (*Lou Grant*), Gavin MacLeod (*Murray Slaughter*), Ted Knight (*Ted Baxter*), Cloris Leachman (*Phyllis Lindstrom*), Lisa Gerritsen (*Bess Lindstrom*), Georgia Engel (*Georgette Franklin*), Betty White (*Sue Anne Nivens*), John Amos (*Gordie Howard*)

Trivia: Following a breakup with her boyfriend, Bill (Angus Duncan), Mary Richards leaves New York and heads for Minneapolis to begin a new life. There she takes Apartment D at 119 North Weatherly in a building owned by her friend, Phyllis Lindstrom. Shortly afterward, she secures a job as the assistant producer of the WJM-TV, Channel 12 "Six O'Clock News" program.

Mary, a Presbyterian, originally applied for a job as a secretary at WJM. The job had been filled, but Lou Grant, the news show producer, hired her as the associate producer instead. Mary has spunk (which Lou hates), "a nice caboose" (which Lou likes) and the job pays $10 a week less than the secretarial job (which is acceptable to both). Mary mentioned that she types 65 words a minute. In an early episode, Mary mentions her mother's name as Marge (see Relatives).

His favorite hangout is the Happy Hour Bar, his bar bill comes to the station on the 15th of every month and he has a bottle of booze in the bottom drawer of his desk. He is Lou Grant, the exasperated producer of the "Six O'Clock News." A distinguished newsman himself, he is the only one who realizes that his show will never become a ratings winner. Lou's favorite actor is John Wayne; in the pilot he mentions he is married (he later breaks up with his wife, Edie).

Ted Baxter, the station's incompetent newscaster, earns $31,000 a year, has trouble pronouncing words (e.g., Arkansas is "Are Kansas") and has a fake newspaper headline in his office that reads, "Ted Baxter Wins 3 Emmys." He longs for an anchor job in New York with his hero, Walter Cronkite. Ted takes six sugars in his coffee and pays a high school senior five dollars a year to do his taxes. *Snow White* is his favorite Disney movie and when he had a non-exclusive contract, he did TV commercials (of all the ads he did—for a tomato slicer, a women's product and a dog food product—only one product was given a name: Ma and Pa's Country Sausage, where Ted was Farmer Ted, the spokesman). His favorite place to eat is Antonio's, he hates to part with money and he calls the station's control room "the Technical Place." He marries Georgette Franklin, a window-dresser at Hempell's Department Store.

Mary's upstairs neighbor is Rhoda Morganstern, a New Yorker who moved to Minneapolis when she couldn't find a job or an apartment in Manhattan. Although she and Mary did not hit it off at first (she wanted Mary's apartment), they became the best of friends. Rhoda is a window-dresser at Hempell's Department Store and mentioned that in high school (in the Bronx) she was a member of the Sharkettes gang. Rhoda, who is Jewish, has a goldfish named Goldfish and once got a $40 ticket at the Minneapolis Zoo for feeding yogurt to the buffaloes.

Murray Slaughter, the newswriter on the show, calls Ted's cue cards "idiot cards," and has been married to his wife Marie since 1955; their home phone number is 555-3727. Sue Ann Nivens, the host of WJM's "Happy Homemaker Show," has "the hots" for Lou (but Lou is not too keen on Sue Ann). Phyllis Lindstrom is the owner of the apartment house in the series, but was only a tenant in the pilot. She has a never-seen husband named

Lars (a dermatologist) and a daughter named Bess. According to Phyllis, "wearing makeup and putting on her mother's wigs" is what Bess does best. Bess calls Mary "Aunt Mary."

The clocks seen in the newsroom (behind Mary and Murray's desks) do not operate (the hands do not move). The most tragic event to hit WJM was the death of its star performer, Chuckles the Clown (whose real name was only given as George). Chuckles was the Grand Marshal of a parade and dressed as Peter Peanut. He was crushed to death when an elephant tried to shell him. Chuckles was played at various times by Mark Gordon and Richard Schaal.

Relatives: Nanette Fabray (Mary's mother, *Dotty Richards*), Bill Quinn (Mary's father, *Dr. Walter Reed Richards*), Eileen Heckart (Mary's aunt, *Flo Meredith*, a foreign correspondent), Joyce Bulifant (Murray's wife, *Marie Slaughter*), Sherry Hursey (Murray's daughter, *Bonnie Slaughter*), Tammi Bula (Murray's daughter, *Ellen Slaughter*), Helen Hunt (Murray's daughter, *Laurie Slaughter*), Lew Ayres (Murray's father, *Doug Slaughter*), Priscilla Morrill (Lou's wife, *Edie Grant*), Nora Heflin (Lou's daughter, *Janie Grant*), Nancy Walker (Rhoda's mother, *Ida Morganstern*), Harold Gould (Rhoda's father, *Martin Morganstern*), Liberty Williams (Rhoda's sister, *Debbie Morganstern*), Brett Somers (Rhoda's *Aunt Rose*), Robbie Rist (Ted's adopted son, *David Baxter*), Liam Dunn (Ted's father, *Robert Baxter*), Jack Cassidy (Ted's brother, *Hal Baxter*), Pat Priest (Sue Ann's sister, *Lila*, who hosts a cooking show in Augusta, Georgia), Robert Morse (Phyllis's gay brother, *Ben*)

Unseen Relatives: Sara and Ruthie (Lou's other daughters), and Amy, Abby, Eric and Matthew (Lou's grandchildren). Lawrence Pressman played Bill Phelps, Sara's husband.

Theme: "Love Is All Around," vocal by Sonny Curtis

Spinoffs: "Rhoda" (see entry) and "Phyllis" (CBS, 9.8.75 to 8.30.77), in which Phyllis and Bess move to San Francisco (4482 Bayview Drive) to live with Lars's parents and begin new lives after Lars's death. Phyllis is first a photographer's assistant to Julie Erskine (Barbara Colby, Liz Torres) at Erskine's Commercial Photography Studio, then administrative assistant to Dan Valenti (Carmine Caridi) of the San Francisco Board of Administration.

M*A*S*H

CBS, 9.17.72 to 9.19.83

Principal Cast: Alan Alda (*Captain Benjamin Franklin "Hawkeye" Pierce*), Wayne Rogers (*Captain John McIntire*), Loretta Swit (*Major Margaret Houlihan*), McLean Stevenson (*Lieutenant Colonel Henry Blake*), Mike Farrell (*Captain B. J. Hunnicutt*), Henry Morgan (*Colonel Sherman Potter*), Larry Linville (*Major Frank Burns*), Gary Burghoff (*Corporal Walter "Radar" O'Reilly*), David Ogden Stiers (*Major Charles Winchester III*), George Morgan and William Christopher (*Father Francis Mulcahy*), Jamie Farr (*Corporal Maxwell Klinger*)

Trivia: "M*A*S*H" is a bittersweet look at the Korean War as seen through the eyes of a group of doctors and nurses assigned to the 4077th M*A*S*H (Mobile Army Surgical Hospital) unit.

Colonels Henry Blake and Sherman Potter are the unit's commanding officers, successively. Henry, born in Bloomington, Illinois, was first in charge. He loved fishing and ordered adult films for his officers from the Tabasco Film Company in Havana, Cuba. He was killed in a helicopter crash on the day he was to return home. Potter, who was born in Riverbend, Missouri, replaced him. He loves horses (has one named Sophie), has made the Army his career, and his wife calls him "Puddin' Head."

Captains Benjamin Franklin Pierce, John McIntire and later B. J. Hunnicutt are dedicated doctors who are opposed to the war and constantly defy authority—as their way of fighting back at the system. Pierce, who is nicknamed "Hawkeye," was born in Crabapple Cove, Maine, and has the serial number 19095607. He has a still in his tent (which he calls "the Well-

spring of Life"), earns $413.50 a month, and reads the magazine *The Joys of Nudity*. McIntire, his first tentmate, is nicknamed "Trapper John" and shares Hawkeye's love of playing practical jokes. His favorite magazines are *Field and Stream* and *Popular Mechanics*. When McIntire leaves, B. J. Hunnicutt replaces him. B. J. (name never revealed) was born in Mill Valley, California, and found it difficult adjusting to the combat conditions of a M*A*S*H unit.

Major Margaret Houlihan, nicknamed "Hot Lips," is head of the unit's nurses and earns $400 a month. For reasons nobody understands, she is attracted to Frank Burns, a wimpy major who is married and fears his wife will somehow find out he is having an affair. Frank, who is nicknamed "Ferret Face," uses the brokerage house of Sanders, Landers and Flynn in New York City. When Frank left in 1977, Margaret married Major Donald Penobscott (Beeson Carroll).

Harvard-educated Major Charles Emerson Winchester III replaced Frank, and resides in the same tent with Hawkeye and B. J. Charles, whose favorite composer is Gustav Mahler, has the newspaper the *Boston Globe* sent to him by his sister, Anoria. Maxwell Klinger, who was born in Toledo, Ohio, was first a corporal then a sergeant and is the unit's resident loon. Totally against the war and desperate to get out, he dresses as a woman (even has a better wardrobe than Margaret) and pretends to be insane to qualify for a Section-eight discharge.

Corporal Walter Eugene O'Reilly, serial number 3911880, was born in Iowa and is nicknamed "Radar" (for his ability to perceive what others think). The company clerk and animal lover, he has a number of pets: Mannie, Moe, Jack, Babette and Margo (guinea pigs), Fluffy and Bingo (rabbits) and Daisy, the mouse. Francis Mulcahy, the company chaplain, raises money for the St. Theresa Orphanage. The signpost on the grounds has arrows pointing to Coney Island, San Francisco, Tokyo and Burbank.

Relatives: Robert Alda (Hawkeye's father, *Daniel Pierce*), Andrew Duggan

(Margaret's father, *Colonel Alvin Houli-han*), Gary Burghoff (*Radar's mother*; seen in home movies), Dennis Dugan (Sherman's son-in-law, *Bobby*).

Unseen Relatives: Henry's wife, Lorraine; Henry's daughter, Molly; Henry's Grandma Mavis; B. J.'s wife, Peggy, and daughter Erin; Sherman's wife, Mildred; Sherman's grandson, Cory; Frank's wife, Louise; Father Mulcahy's sister, Sister Maria Angelica; Trapper's daughter, Becky

Theme: "Suicide Is Painless," by Johnny Mandel

Note: In the spinoff series, "AfterMash" (CBS, 9.16.83 to 10.30.84), Sherman Potter becomes chief of staff of the General Pershing V.A. Hospital in Missouri.

MATT HOUSTON

ABC, 9.26.82 to 3.29.85

Matlock "Matt" Houston (Lee Horsley) is a millionaire oil baron, cattle rancher and playboy who helps people who are in deep trouble. Matt owns Houston, Inc. (located at 200 West Temple Street, Los Angeles 90012; later given as 100 Century Plaza South), the Houston Ranch in Texas and Houston Investigations in Los Angeles (the telephone number is 213-555-3141). His Rolls Royce license plate reads COWBOY I; his other car, Excaliber, has license plate number 21 VE 124; his computer is named Baby; and his helicopter identification is N1090Z.

C. J. Parsons (Pamela Hensley) is Matt's beautiful lawyer cohort; Roy Houston (Buddy Ebsen) is Matt's uncle (and assistant in last season episodes); Vince Novelli (John Aprea) is a lieutenant with the S.C.P.D. (Southern California Police Department); Vince's mother, Rosa (Penny Santon), owns the Mama Novelli Restaurant; Michael Hoyt (Lincoln Kilpatrick) is a lieutenant with the L.A.P.D.; and Murray Chase (George Wyner) is Matt's harried business manager. Matt purchased his ranch from movie star Ramona Landers (Janet Leigh).

Relatives: Lloyd Bridges (Matt's natural father, *Virgil Wade*), David Wayne (Matt's adoptive father, *Bill Houston*), Michael Goodwin (Matt's *Cousin Will*), Christina Hart (Hoyt's daughter, *Kathy Hoyt*), John Moschitta Jr. (Murray's brother, *Myron Chase*).

Dominic Frontiere composed the theme.

MAUDE

see ALL IN THE FAMILY

MAVERICK

ABC, 9.22.57 to 7.8.62

Principal Cast: James Garner (*Bret Maverick*), Jack Kelly (*Bart Maverick*), Roger Moore (*Beau Maverick*), Robert Colbert (*Brent Maverick*)

Trivia: "Who is the tall, dark stranger there, Maverick is the name; ridin' the trail to who knows where, luck is his companion, gamblin' is his game." They're cowards at heart, but more often than not, they find themselves helping people in trouble. They're unconventional, self-centered, untrustworthy and possess a genius for conning the con man. They're brothers Bret and Bart Maverick—gentlemen gamblers who roam the Old West in search of rich prey.

Although they served with the Confederacy during the Civil War, they became Union soldiers when they were captured and figured it would be better to help the enemy than to spend time in a Union prison camp. As "Galvanized Yankees" (as Bart calls it), they were assigned to keep the Indians under control out west. At this same time, another Maverick, Cousin Beau, became a family disgrace when he was honored as a war hero. Beauregard Maverick (James Garner), the head of the family, instilled his sons with his cowardice and con-artist genius. When Pappy, as he is called, learned that Beau did something to bring honor to the Maverick name, he branded him "the white sheep of the family" and banished him to England. (Actually, Beau had been captured. While he was playing poker with a Union general, the

Confederates attacked the camp. Just as the general lost a game and exclaimed "I give up," Confederate troops entered the tent. A typical Maverick—in the wrong place at the wrong time—Beau was credited with a capture.) To make up for this family disgrace, Beau spent five years tarnishing his "good" name and was actually brought back (1960–61) to replace James Garner (who left the series in 1960). The following year, and until 1962, another brother, the previously unmentioned Brent, appeared when Roger Moore left at the end of the 1961 season.

Although Beauregard "Pappy" Maverick appeared only once (in the episode "Pappy," 9.13.59), his proverbs became an established part of the series. One of the Mavericks would exclaim, "As my Pappy would say," followed by the saying (e.g., "No use crying over spilled milk; it could have been whiskey").

Besides the Indians, the outlaws and the sheriff, another threat to Bret and Bart was Samantha "Sam" Crawford (Diane Brewster), a beautiful con artist who was just as cunning and clever as the Mavericks. A Northern girl at heart, Sam faked a Southern accent and used, besides her genius at the con, her feminine wiles to acquire easy money.

Richard Long (as Gentleman Jack Darby) and Efrem Zimbalist Jr. (as Dandy Jim Buckley) had recurring roles as gamblers who also sought easy money and easy prey. David Buttolph and Paul Francis Webster composed the theme.

Spinoffs: On September 3, 1978, CBS aired *The New Maverick*, a TV movie pilot (for "Young Maverick") that reunited Bret (James Garner), Bart (Jack Kelly) and Beau (Roger Moore) Maverick in a story that introduced the newest Maverick—Ben (Charles Frank), Beau's young and inexperienced son who is eager to become a professional gambler like his father.

Ben's exploits as a gambler continued in the series "Young Maverick" (CBS, 11.28.79 to 1.16.80). Susan Blanchard appears as his lady friend, Nell McGarrahan, and John Dehner plays Marshal Edge Troy.

Although "Young Maverick" failed to last more than 13 episodes, NBC brought back James Garner as Bret Maverick in the series "Bret Maverick" (12.1.81 to 8.24.82). Said to be "20 years older and 40 years wiser," Bret finally decides to end his life of wandering and settles down in the town of Sweetwater, Arizona (where he runs the Red Ox Saloon and the Lazy Ace Ranch—both of which he won in a poker game). Other regulars are Mary Lou Springer (Darleen Carr), a photographer for the town newspaper, the *Territorian*; Kate Hanrahan (Marj Dusay), the owner of the Klondike Room Gambling Hall; and Philo Sandine (Arnold Margolin), the con man called Standing Bear by the Comanche Indians. Priscilla Morrill appears as Mary Lou's mother, Estelle, and Ed Bruce sang the theme, "Maverick Didn't Come Here to Lose."

MAX HEADROOM
ABC, 3.31.87 to 5.7.87
8.14.87 to 10.16.87

Max Headroom is the computer generated alter-ego of Edison Carter (Matt Frewer), a newscaster for Network 23, a futuristic TV network. The series, which is set "20 minutes into the future," depicts TV as a medium that cannot be turned off. Ratings are all that count and the viewing audience is called the Blank Generation. Edison, who hosts "The Edison Carter Show," is assisted by Theora Jones (Amanda Pays), the computer genius based in the network's control room. Edison's friend Blank Reg (Morgan Sheppard) operates Big Time Television Network with the sexy Dominique (Concetta Tomei). Charles Rocket plays Ned Grossberg, the head of Network 66—Network 23's main competition; Peter Cohi appeared as Theora's brother, Sean.

MAX MONROE: LOOSE CANNON
CBS, 1.5.90 to 1.26.90
4.5.90 to 4.19.90

Unorthodox detective Max Monroe (Shadoe Stevens) and his partner, Charlie

Ivers (Bruce A. Young), are with Precinct 157 of the Los Angeles Police Department (their car code is 3-Henry-118). Max, who plays chess at the Westside Chess Club, has the police code name Charlie Blue Dog and drives a car with the license plate PEK 560 (also given as IYXQ 753). Yello performs the theme, "Tied Up."

MEET MR. McNUTLEY
see THE RAY MILLAND SHOW

MIDNIGHT CALLER
NBC, 10.25.88 to

While pursuing a felon, police inspector Jack Killian (Gary Cole) accidentally kills his partner. Although exonerated, Jack quits the force. Seeking a host for a late night radio call-in show, radio station owner Devon King (Wendy Kilbourne) hires Jack to help people who are worried about street crime. Stories relate Jack's exploits as he strives to solve crimes that result from listeners' calls.

Jack hosts "Midnight Caller" (12 midnight to three A.M.) on KCJM (98.3 on the FM dial) in San Francisco (located at 9009 Howard Street on the 38th floor). Jack, who calls himself "the Nighthawk," lives at 928 Fargo Street and drives a car with the license plate 2HN 267. His favorite hangout is a bar called Carmen's.

Devon, whose Mercedes license plate is 2RA 0834, lives at 3546 North Weatherly and her phone number is 555–6023. Deacon Bridges (Mykel T. Williamson) is a reporter for the San Francisco *Dispatch* and Carl Zymak (Arthur Taxier) is a lieutenant with the San Francisco Police Department.

Relatives: Bonnie Bartlett (Devon's mother, *Hilary King*), Richard Bradford (Devon's father, *Mel King*), Peter Boyle (Jack's father, *J. J. Killian*), Scott Valentine (Jack's brother, *Frankie Killian*). Thomas Drayden played Devon's father, Mel, as a young man in a flashback. Brad Fiedel composed the theme.

THE MISADVENTURES OF SHERIFF LOBO
see B. J. AND THE BEAR

THE MONKEES
NBC, 9.12.66 to 8.19.68

Davy Jones, Mike Nesmith, Peter Tork and Micky Dolenz are the Monkees, an out-of-work rock group looking for any job anywhere. They live together in an apartment at 1438 North Beachwood Street in Los Angeles and have a car with license plate NPH 623. They use the incompetent Urgent Answering Service and were selected "Typical Young Men of the Year" by *Sheik* magazine.

Davy, born in England, is the most sensible of the group (although he often gets carried away by the antics of the others). Mike, born in Texas, was an Eagle Scout as a kid and now collects fortune cookies to feed to a dog they don't have (but Mike thinks they have). Peter, the most passive of the group, cries at card tricks, gets the hiccups when he auditions for a big producer, has hay fever and is prone to sea sickness. Micky, who was born in Burbank, was called "Goo Goo Eyes" by his mother as a kid. Micky Dolenz played Micky's vicious killer double, Baby Face Morales, "the Most Wanted Man in America," in one episode.

In the opening theme, when the Monkees are credited, Peter's name is seen four times: once for his own credit and once for each of the other three Monkees. On their living room wall they have a sign that says "Money is the root of all evil." (Micky Dolenz was originally known as Mickey Braddock and starred in the series "Circus Boy.") Jacqueline DeWit plays Mike's Aunt Kate and Ben Wright appears as Davy's grandfather. The Monkees sing the theme.

In 1987, Marty Ross, Dino Kovacs, Larry Saltis and Jared Chandler were "The New Monkees," an expensive, syndicated flop that failed to capture the "insanity" of the original series. Added to the cast were Gordon Oas-Heim as Manfred, the butler; Liz Godfrey as the voice of Helen, the computer; and Bess Motta as Rita the waitress.

MORK AND MINDY

ABC, 9.14.78 to 8.5.82

Principal Cast: Robin Williams (*Mork*), Pam Dawber (*Mindy McConnell*), Conrad Janis (*Fred McConnell*), Tom Poston (*Frank Bickley*), Jonathan Winters (*Mearth*), Jay Thomas (*Remo DaVinci*), Gina Hecht (*Jeanie DaVinci*), Robert Donner (*Exidor*), Shelley Fabares (*Cathy McConnell*), Ralph James (*voice of Orson*)

Trivia: An egg-shaped spaceship from the planet Ork lands on Earth in Boulder, Colorado. While driving home from school, Mindy McConnell meets and befriends the alien named Mork and takes him to her home (at 1619 Pine Street). There, she learns that Mork's job is to be an Earth Observer and compile information (his Scorpio Reports) to relate to Orson, his never-seen but apparently overweight superior on Ork, via mind transference. Mork's (and Mindy's) adventures are depicted as Mork seeks to learn about life on Earth.

Ork is a planet about 200 million miles from Earth and has three moons. All Orkan spaceships resemble eggs as Orkans evolved from the chicken. When war breaks out on Ork, patriotic Orkans hide. There are 83 ways to apologize; two were related: to beat yourself with a canary, and to make your left arm longer than the right. The enemies of Orkans are the Necotons (in one episode Raquel Welch played Captain Nevana of the Necoton Black Army, who sought Mork; they considered Mindy a pretty pet and kept her in a huge bird cage).

Mork was born in a test tube (there are no parents on Ork) and comes with a guarantee that covers ankle blowouts and rusted skin; he attended Ork Prep School. On Earth, Mork works as a counselor at the Pine Tree Day Care Center. Mork travels through time via red sequined time traveling shoes (size eight) and has a pet Orkan Nauger Chump named Bee-

bo (he also has a pet caterpillar named Bob). On Ork, Mork was first a dinner diver in a lobster tank, then an explorer who charted 16 galaxies. On Earth, Mork celebrates National Backwards Day (an Orkan holiday).

Mindy, the first girl to play Little League baseball in Boulder, attended Boulder High School (her locker combination was 33–17–3), then the University of Colorado, where she majored in journalism. She first worked in her father's store (McConnell's Music Store), then as a newscaster at KTNS-TV, Channel 31, and finally as the host of "Wake Up, Boulder." Her Jeep license plate number is ML2 9JH; on Earth, Mindy is the first human to eat Fleck, an Orkan food that brings out strange behavioral qualities; on Ork, Mindy is known as "the Soft-Lapped One."

When Mork and Mindy marry (10.5.81), they honeymoon on Ork and Mindy wins the fourth place title in a pet show (Orkans consider Earthlings to be pets). Shortly after they are married, Mork becomes pregnant and lays an egg. The egg hatches and Mork and Mindy become the parents of Mearth (Orkan children are born old and become young with time). The name Mearth is a combination of Mork, Mindy and Earth. Mearth has a teddy bear he calls Teddy. Mork, Mindy and Mearth wear pink pajamas (with dark pink vertical stripes) that read "Mine" (Mork's), "Hers" (Mindy's) and "Ours" (Mearth's). Mearth attends Ork Prep School one day a month via the Orkan schoolbus—the 828 Transport Beam.

Fred McConnell, Mindy's father, was originally the owner of McConnell's Music Store and later, the conductor of the Boulder City Orchestra. Cathy is Fred's new wife and Mindy's young stepmother (Mindy's natural mother, Beth, had died); she plays flute in the orchestra.

Exidor, the local loon (and Mork's friend), has an invisible dog named Brutus (a Doberman) and an invisible aide named Pepe. He wrote an autobiographical book called *Lauren Bacall: By Myself* ("If it worked for her . . . ") and had a business called Exidor T-Shirts that failed.

Frank Bickley, Mindy's downstairs neighbor, is a greeting-card writer and has a dog named Bickey. Remo and Jeanie DaVinci are a brother and sister who own DaVinci's Restaurant (later called the New York Delicatessen). Mork's greeting is "Na-nu Na-nu."

Relatives: Elizabeth Kerr (Mindy's grandmother, *Cora Hudson*), Jim Staahl (Mindy's cousin, *Nelson Flavor*), Jonathan Winters (Mindy's uncle, *Dave McConnell*), Beverly Sanders (Mindy's aunt, *Caroline McConnell*)

Flashbacks: Missy Francis (*Mindy as a girl*)

Theme: "Mork and Mindy," by Perry Botkin Jr.

Note: A cartoon version of "Mork and Mindy" (ABC, 9.25.82 to 9.3.83) related Mork and Mindy's adventures as students at Mt. Mount High School.

MR. BELVEDERE

ABC, 3.15.85 to 12.30.89
7.1.90 to 7.8.90

Principal Cast: Christopher Hewett (*Lynn Belvedere*), Bob Uecker (*George Owens*), Ilene Graff (*Marsha Owens*), Tracy Wells (*Heather Owens*), Rob Stone (*Kevin Owens*), Brice Beckham (*Wesley Owens*), Michele Matheson (*Angela Jostakovic*)

Trivia: Residing near Pittsburgh at 200 Spring Valley Road in the town of Beaver Falls, Pennsylvania, are George and Marsha Owens and their children Kevin, Heather and Wesley, a chaotic family of five who are presided over by Lynn Aloysius Belvedere, a high-tone English butler.

Mr. Belvedere, who appeared on the cover of *World Focus* magazine, possesses medals for climbing Mount Everest and for winning the Pillsbury Bake-Off. He has worked for English royalty, served in World War II and writes a book based on his experiences with the Owens family called *An American Journal: The Suburban Years*. Mr. Belvedere's favorite junk foods are Ding Dongs and Scooter Pies and his favorite store is Donut World.

In the last episode, Lynn marries Louise Gilbert (Rosemary Forsyth), an animal behaviorist he met at a laundromat. Mr. Belvedere then leaves the Owens family to join Louise in Africa where she is assigned the task of taking a gorilla census. In the final moments of the episode, Lynn remarks that he left his weekly journals (diaries) at the Owens home, indicating that he may, one day, return for them.

George, who attended Cleveland High School, originally hosts "Sports Page," a radio program on WBK-AM (its phone number: 555-2222). Later, he is the sports anchor of WBN-TV, Channel 8's "Metro News" and writer of the "Sports Beat" column for the Pittsburgh *Bulletin*. George calls Mr. Belvedere "Big Guy" and his favorite food is pork rinds and Spam dip.

Marsha, originally a law student, passed the bar in 1987 and joined the firm of Dawson, Metcalfe and Bach. The following year, she became an attorney for the Legal Hut. Marsha also worked as a waitress at the Beaver Falls Diner and has a never-seen Porsche she calls "Wolfgang."

Kevin, their eldest child, attends Van Buren High School. He worked part-time at Mr. Cluck's Fried Chicken and as a salesman for Phil's Friendly Motors.

Heather, the middle child, attends Van Buren High School, is called "Kitten" by George, and has a "kooky" girlfriend named Angela (who calls Mr. Belvedere everything but Mr. Belvedere: "Mr. Belly Bottom," "Mr. Bumper Cars," "Mr. Bell Bottoms").

Wesley, the youngest and most mischievous of the Owens children, attended Conklin Elementary School, Allegheny Junior High and finally Beaver Falls Junior High. He has a dog named Spot and a snake named Captain Nemo. Wesley is a member of the Colts Little League Team (coached by George), the Junior Pioneers (Group 12) and his favorite sandwich is tuna fish with marshmallow spread. Wesley, who is called "the Wesman" by George, made a home movie about Mr. Belvedere called "The Housekeeper from Hell." He also delights in playing practical jokes on his never-seen but always complaining neighbors, the Hufnagels.

Relatives: David Rappaport (Lynn's cousin, *Galen Belvedere*)

~~**Flashbacks:** Trevor Thiegen (*young Lynn*)~~

Theme: "Theme from Mr. Belvedere," vocal by Leon Redbone

MR. ED

Syndicated, 1960 to 1961
CBS, 10.1.61 to 9.4.66

Principal Cast: Alan Young (*Wilbur Post*), Connie Hines (*Carol Post*), Alan "Rocky" Lane (*voice of Mr. Ed*), Larry Keating (*Roger Addison*), Edna Skinner (*Kay Addison*), Leon Ames (*Gordon Kirkwood*), Florence MacMichael (*Winnie Kirkwood*)

Trivia: Shortly after Wilbur Post and his wife, Carol, purchase a home at 17230 Valley Spring Lane, Los Angeles, Wilbur discovers an unusual resident in the barn—a talking horse named Mr. Ed (left by the previous owners). Because Wilbur is the only human Mr. Ed likes well enough to talk to, he will talk only to him (and thus Wilbur's misadventures as the owner of a talking horse).

"It's been a long time since I was a pony," were the first words Mr. Ed, "the playboy horse of Los Angeles," spoke to Wilbur. Mr. Ed, who weighed 96 pounds at birth, was an incubator baby, and his birth sign is Taurus. Mr. Ed's favorite word is *filly* (he considers it the prettiest word in the English language) and he inherited the family curse—a fear of heights (begun when his grandfather fell off a cliff while chasing a filly). Mr. Ed, who was seven years old when the series began, loves carrots and wrote the hit song "Pretty Little Filly."

Wilbur, an independent architect, operates from the barn (Mr. Ed's home) and was originally slated to be a lawyer (as depicted in sales pitches for the show). Wilbur's office phone number is Poplar 9-1769, and his home address was also given as 17340 Valley Boulevard, 17290 Valley Spring Lane, and 1720 Valley Road in Los Angeles. Wilbur, whose birth sign is also Taurus, is a member of the Lawndale Men's Club and drives a Studebaker with license plate FIM 921.

Carol, a former dancer, measures 36–22–36, and had a job as a dance instructor at Miss Irene's in Hollywood. Her maiden name is Higgins (also given as Carlyle), and she and Wilbur are newlyweds in the first episode, just settling into their first home (which was sold to them by Mr. Reeves of Golden Acres Real Estate).

Roger and Kay Addison are the Posts' neighbors (replaced later by Gordon and Winnie Kirkwood). Kay and Roger have been married 19 years; their phone number is DLO-2599 and Roger was a member of the Sigma Nu Delta fraternity in college.

Relatives: Eleanor Audley (Wilbur's *Aunt Martha*), Barry Kelly (Carol's father, *Mr. Carlyle*), Jack Albertson (Kay's brother, *Paul Fenton*). Mentioned but not seen was Kay's niece, Peggy.

Theme: "Mr. Ed," by Jay Livingston and Ray Evans

Note: In the unaired pilot version, "The Wonderful World of Wilbur Pope," Scott McKay played Wilbur Pope, Mr. Ed's owner, and Sandra White, his wife, Carlotta Pope. Allan "Rocky" Lane was the voice of Mr. Ed, and Peggy Converse and Ray Walker were their neighbors, Florence and John Reese.

MR. TERRIFIC

CBS, 1.9.67 to 8.28.67

As originally produced in 1966 (but unaired by CBS), Stanley Beemish (Alan Young) was a shoe store clerk who is recruited by the Chief of the Office of Special Assignments (Edward Andrews) to test a new pill—a pill that transforms him into Mr. Terrific, a daring but trouble-prone crime fighter. Sheila Wells played Stanley's girlfriend, Gloria Dickinson, and Jesse White, his employer, Mr. Finney.

In the actual series, Stanley Beemish (Stephen Strimpell) is a partner with Hal Waters (Dick Gautier) in Hal and Stanley's Service Station. Stanley was secretly chosen by Barton J. Reed (John McGiver) of the Bureau of Special Projects to test a government scientist's new discovery—a Power Pill. The pill transforms Stanley into the amazing crime fighter, Mr. Terrific, but Stanley must now lead a double life: ordinary citizen as well as the government's secret weapon against crime.

Stanley's Mr. Terrific costume is a jacket with wing-like sleeves (which he flaps in order to fly), a pair of goggles and a scarf—all of which he stores in a locker at the gas station. When Mr. Terrific is needed, Reed sounds the Purple Alert. Before each assignment, Reed gives Stanley a box with three pills (one base pill that lasts one hour and gives Stanley the strength of 1,000 men and two booster pills that last ten minutes each). Three pills is the maximum Stanley can take in one day. The pills are specially candy-coated so Stanley will take them; before Stanley was found, the pill was thought to make the strongest of men quite ill—it previously worked only on one lab monkey.

Hal and Stanley's Gas Station is located at Northeastern and Wyoming Streets in Washington, D.C.; the telephone number of the bureau is National 8–0397. Hal introduces himself to women as "Hi, I'm Hal, gas station attendant, snappy dresser and lady-killer." Ellen Corby appeared as Hal's meddling mother, Mrs. Waters, and Ned Glass played Dr. Reynolds, the creator of the Power Pill. In the actual series, the role of a girlfriend for Stanley was not incorporated. Gerald Fried composed the theme.

MRS. COLUMBO

see KATE LOVES A MYSTERY

THE MUNSTERS

CBS, 9.24.64 to 9.8.66

Principal Cast: Fred Gwynne (*Herman Munster*), Yvonne DeCarlo (*Lily Munster*), Al Lewis (*Grandpa*), Beverley Owen and Pat Priest (*Marilyn Munster*), Butch Patrick (*Eddie Munster*)

Trivia: Thirteen-thirteen Mockingbird Lane in the town of Mockingbird Heights is the address of the Munsters, a family who resemble movie monsters of the 1930s, but who believe they are normal and the rest of the world is strange.

Dr. Frankenstein's boy, Herman, age 150, works first as a grave digger, then as box boy for the Gateman, Goodbury and Graves Funeral Parlor. He was at the Heidelberg School of Medicine—in several jars—for six years. His body temperature is 62.8 degrees; his pulse, 15; blood pressure, minus three; and his heartbeat, none. He is seven feet, three inches tall and weighs three spins on the bathroom scale. Herman's favorite fairy tale is "Goldilocks and the Three Bears" (he can't wait for it to be made into a movie with Doris Day) and his ham radio call letters are W6XRL4. Herman writes poetry for *Mortician's Monthly* magazine; his first poem was "Going Out to Pasture." In the episode "Follow That Munster," Herman became a private detective for the Kempner Detective Agency and called himself Agent 702. His hot rod license plate number is HAJ 302.

Lily, Herman's wife, is a vampire whose maiden name is Dracula. She is 304 years old and married Herman in 1865. Her favorite charity is Bundles for Transylvania; their favorite food is Bat Milk Yogurt.

Count Vladimir Dracula, called Grandpa, is Lily's father, a 378-year-old vampire and mad scientist. His hometown is Transylvania and he has been married 167 times. Grandpa's favorite TV show is "My Three Sons" and his pet bat is Igor ("a mouse with wings who joined the Transylvanian Air Force"). His newly transistorized divining rod picks up reruns of "My Little Margie."

Marilyn, their normal-looking (to the viewer) niece, is the black sheep of the family and attends State University. Edward Wolfgang, their son, is a werewolf and attends Mockingbird Heights Elementary School. He has a werewolf doll named Woof Woof and a pet snake named Elmer (who lives under the garbage pail in the backyard). Eddie's mechanical brother (created by Grandpa) was Boris the Robot (Rory Stevens).

The family pets are Spot, a fire-breathing dragon Grandpa found while digging in the backyard (he eats Doggie's Din Din brand of pet food and lives under the living room staircase); Kitty Kat, a cat who roars like a lion; and an unnamed raven who says "Never more." John Carradine appeared in several episodes as Herman's employer, Mr. Gateman.

In the original, unaired color pilot (the series is in black and white) titled "My Fair Munster," Fred Gwynne played Herman; Joan Marshall his wife, Phoebe; Al Lewis, Grandpa; Beverley Owen, Marilyn; and Happy Derman, Eddie.

Relatives: Fred Gwynne (Herman's twin brother, *Charlie Munster*; and Herman's prototype, *Johan*), Richard Hale (Lily's *Uncle Gilbert*, the Creature from the Black Lagoon), Irwin Charone (Lily's brother, *Lester Dracula*)

Theme: "At the Munsters," by Jack Marshall

Note: In the 1966 theatrical film, *Munster, Go Home*, Debbie Watson played Marilyn. In the TV movie, *The Munsters' Revenge*, Jo McDonnell was Marilyn and K. C. Martel was Eddie. (Fred Gwynne, Yvonne DeCarlo and Al Lewis recreated their roles in both films.) See also "The Munsters Today."

THE MUNSTERS TODAY

Syndicated, 10.8.88 to

Principal Cast: John Schuck (*Herman Munster*), Lee Meriwether (*Lily Munster*), Howard Morton (*Grandpa*), Hilary Van Dyke (*Marilyn Munster*), Jason Marsden (*Eddie Munster*)

Trivia: This show is an update of "The Munsters." In 1966, Grandpa conducted an experiment that backfired and placed the Munster family in a state of suspended animation. Twenty-two years later, the family (parents Herman and Lily, their son Eddie, niece Marilyn and Lily's father, Grandpa), awakens to a new world—the 1980s. (Unlike the previous series, the Munsters are now more readily accepted by society and not as abnormal as they were previously portrayed. Information about the family differs, too, although they still live at 1313 Mockingbird Lane.)

Herman, now six feet, eight inches tall, was "born" in Dr. Frankenstein's lab in Transylvania over 300 years ago. He was made from many parts, including the nose of Gregory Fabrock, who was the village idiot, and the right arm of Igor Johnson, a pickpocket. His eyes are brown, blue and undetermined; his teeth squeak when he gets thirsty; and his neck bolts (for the electricity that originally supplied life) itch when he gets an idea. He still works for the funeral parlor of Gateman, Goodbury and Graves as a grave digger (Stanley Ralph Ross plays his boss, Mr. Goodbury). In the 4.2.90 episode, Herman opened his own funeral parlor, the House of Herman (in a former donut shop called the Donut Hole), but it folded and Herman went back to work at his old job. The telephone number of Gateman, Goodbury and Graves is 1-FOREVER.

Lily, who is 324 years old, married Herman 299 years ago in 1689. She won the beauty pageant title "Miss Transylvania of 1655" and she gave birth to Eddie within 24 hours of becoming pregnant (a custom in her family).

Grandpa, also known as Count Vladimir Dracula, was married to a woman named Katja (who left him when she got tired of ironing capes and mopping dungeons). They first met at the Joan of Arc roast and the first home they purchased became the Bates Motel (they sold it to "a nice young fellow and his mother"). Grandpa was a member of the Sigma Alpha Aorta fraternity in college and a member in good standing of the A.V.A. (American Vampire Association). His favorite food is leeches and cream; his pet bat is Igor; his rat is Stanley; Leonard is the skeleton he befriended in his college days at Transylvania U. who now lives in the dungeon. He also has a computer named Sam. Grandpa mentioned that he once had a business in Transylvania sharpening fangs and paid his workers 2000 slotskies (about eight cents) an hour.

Marilyn, blonde and beautiful, is still

the black sheep of the family and attends Mockingbird Heights University. Eddie, their son, attends Mockingbird Heights High School and has changed with the times (he dresses and acts like other kids).

The Munsters also own Munster Moor, a swamp at 13 13th Avenue, and their insurance company is Grave Diggers Mutual—"The Good Hands People." Spot, the fire-breathing dragon, still lives under the stairs. In one episode, Daniel Wilson played Herman as a kid and Whitby Hertford was Grandpa as a kid.

Relatives: Jo DeWinter (Lily's mother, *Katja*), Jerry Houser (Lily's *Cousin Wolfgang*), Peter Isacksen (Herman's *Cousin Gill*), Peter Schuck (Herman's brother, *Frank Munster*), Foster Brooks (Herman's *Cousin Igor*), Angelina Fiordellisi (Lily's *Cousin Bella*), Christopher Fielder (Lily's *Cousin Damien*)

Theme: An updated version of "At the Munsters," by Wintermoon Music

---

MURPHY BROWN

CBS, 11.14.88 to

Principal Cast: Candice Bergen (*Murphy Brown*), Faith Ford (*Corky Sherwood*), Joe Regalbuto (*Frank Fontana*), Charles Kimbrough (*Jim Dial*), Grant Shaud (*Myles Silverberg*), Robert Pastorelli (*Elden Berneke*), Pat Corley (*Phil*)

Trivia: Murphy Brown is a beautiful, hard-hitting investigative reporter for "FYI" ("For Your Information"), a CBS-TV, Washington, D.C.-based news magazine series. She auditioned for "FYI" on August 16, 1977 (she was a foreign correspondent at the time) and beat out Linda Ellerbee for the role. Murphy, who was born in May of 1948, won the Robert F. Kennedy Jr. Award for Journalism for her piece "No Place to Call Home" (Robert Kennedy is her hero). She has many awards, including an Emmy and eight Humboldt Awards (for news stories). Murphy's father, Bill, publishes the *Chicago Voice* newspaper. She was lampooned in the D.C. daily comic strips for a while as "Mouthy Brown." Murphy once appeared on the cover of the *National Enquirer* with the headline "Murphy Brown Having Bigfoot's Baby." She has also appeared on the covers of such magazines as *Time, TV Guide, Newsweek, Esquire* and *Harper's Bazaar*; her show was lampooned in *MAD* magazine. She has a reputation for getting even with anyone who crosses her, is easily exasperated, and has a tendency to yell a lot—watch out when she doesn't get her way. She and fellow reporter Jim Dial are members of the previously all-male Dunfries Club for Newsmen. Elden Berneke is Murphy's 24-hour-a-day, seven-days-a-week housepainter. He is struggling to paint what appears to be a rather large house—but has difficulty matching colors with Murphy's moods. (He buys his paints and supplies at Ed's Paints.)

Corky Sherwood, "FYI"'s pretty, perky and cute reporter, was born on a Louisiana farm and won the Miss America title at the age of 19. She won the 1989 Humboldt News Award for her story "A Woman's Touch at West Point" (breaking Murphy's eight-year winning streak). She has a cat named Mr. Puffy and is the cheerleader for the "FYI" football team, the Bulletins.

Jim Dial, who wears expensive Italian suits, has been with CBS news for 25 years. In 1956 he was the only news correspondent to get an interview with John F. Kennedy when he lost the presidential nomination. If Hubert Humphrey had won the presidency in 1968, he planned to make Jim Dial his press secretary.

Frank Fontana, an investigative reporter for "FYI," was originally a reporter for the *New York Times* before joining the program in 1977. He is afraid to sleep with his closet door open as a result of watching the movie *Poltergeist*; his favorite movie is *The Maltese Falcon*.

Myles Silverberg is the young executive producer of "FYI"; he has a car with license plate 400 928 (also given as 452 689J). Phil is the owner of the local hangout, Phil's Bar (established in 1919).

The episode of 1.29.90 featured an "FYI for Kids" with children patterned after the adults of "FYI": Mayim Bialik as Natalie Moore (a mini-Murphy), Laura Mooney as Tracy Knight (mini-Corky), Mark-Paul Gosselaar as Wes Jordan (mini-Jim) and Troy Slaten as Hank Caldwell (mini-Frank).

When the network decided to do a sit-com based on "FYI," Murphy Brown became the model for "Kelly Green," a series starring Julia St. Martin (Morgan Fairchild) as Kelly Green.

The show's gimmick is to push Murphy even beyond her usual level of exasperation by assigning her a different (and rather strange) secretary in almost every episode.

Relatives: Darren McGavin (Murphy's father, *Bill Brown*), Colleen Dewhurst (Murphy's mother, *Avery Brown*), Susan Wheeler (Murphy's younger-than-she-is stepmother, *Karen*; married to Bill), Robin Thomas (Murphy's ex-husband, *Jake Lowenstein*; they were married for five days), Alice Hirson (Corky's mother, *Bootsie Sherwood*), Courtney Gebhart (Corky's sister, *Cookie*), Sarah Abrell (Corky's sister, *Kiki*), Bryan Clark (Corky's father, *Edward Sherwood*) Janet Carroll (Jim's wife, *Doris Dial*), Dena Dietrich (Phil's wife, *Phyllis*), Jon Tenney (Myles's brother, *Josh Silverberg*)

Flashbacks: Jason Marsden (*Myles as a boy*), Eva Charney (*Myles's mother*)

Theme: "Murphy's Theme" (usually heard only during the closing credits), by Steve Dorff

---

MY FAVORITE MARTIAN

CBS, 9.29.63 to 9.4.66

Principal Cast: Ray Walston (*Uncle Martin O'Hara*), Bill Bixby (*Tim O'Hara*), Pamela Britton (*Lorelei Brown*), Alan Hewitt (*Detective Bill Brennan*)

Trivia: While en route to his job at the Los Angeles *Sun*, newspaper reporter Tim O'Hara witnesses the crash landing of a UFO. He investigates and befriends its pilot, Exagitious 12½, a professor of anthropology from Mars whose specialty is the primitive planet Earth.

Tim takes the stranded Martian to his home at 21 Elm Street—a home owned by Lorelei Brown, a slightly dizzy widow. To protect his true identity, the Martian adopts the alias of Uncle Martin, a relative who has come to live with his nephew, Tim (Martin's silver spaceship is hidden in Lorelei's garage). While Martin seeks a way to repair his craft (the metals he needs are still unknown on Earth), he struggles to adjust to a more primitive world and keep his true identity a secret. His task is complicated by Bill Brennan, a detective with the 12th Precinct of the Los Angeles Police Department, who is suspicious of both Tim and Martin.

On Earth, Martin needs an accurate barometer so he can monitor storms. Thunderstorms are a Martian's worst fear on Earth because if struck by lightning and not properly grounded by his antennae, he gets "Popsy," a condition that causes him to uncontrollably appear and disappear. Martin is prone to short circuits, has the ability to project his dreams, read minds, speak to and understand animals, levitate (with his right index finger) and appear and disappear at will (by raising the antennae at the back of his head).

When Bill, the human bloodhound who is called "Bulldog Brennan," is around, Martin's antennae quiver; Mrs. Brown is famous for her fudge brownies. On page 64 of *The Martian Compendium of Home Remedies or What to Do Until the Zigoblat Comes*, there is a recipe for a love potion called the Irresistible Spray (A Formula A-673–5-K^2). The potion brings instant love to anyone who uses it. On Earth, an aspirin dissolves its effects. (*Zigoblat* is Martian for doctor.)

Relatives: Paul Smith (Tim's *Cousin Harvey*), Sean McClory (Tim's grand uncle, *Shamus O'Hara*), Madge Blake (Martin's *mother*), Wayne Stam (Martin's nephew, *Andrometer*)

Relatives of Lorelei: Ina Victor (her daughter, *Annabel Brown*), Ann Marshall (her daughter, *Angela Brown*), Marlo Thomas (her niece, *Pamela*), Bernie Kopell (her nephew, *George*), Bill Idelson (her brother, *Leroy Wanamaker*), Gavin MacLeod (her brother, *Alvin Wanamaker*), Yvonne White (her sister, *Dulcie*), Don

Keefer (Dulcie's husband, *Henry*), Rory Stevens (Dulcie's son, *Stanley*)

Flashbacks: Allan Melvin (Tim's uncle, *Clarence O'Hara*), Sue Taylor (Tim's grandmother, *Martha O'Hara*), Bruce Glover (Tim's grandfather, *Ralph O'Hara*)

Theme: "My Favorite Martian," by George Greeley

Note: The animated spinoff series, "My Favorite Martians," appeared on CBS from 9.8.73 to 8.30.75. Uncle Martin (voice of Jonathan Harris) crash lands on Earth with his nephew Andy (Edward Morris). He is befriended by Tim O'Hara (Lane Scheimer) and his niece, Katy (Jane Webb). Jane Webb also did the voice of Lorelei Brown and Lane Scheimer did the voice for Bill Brennan (now a security officer).

MY FRIEND IRMA

CBS, 1.8.52 to 6.26.54

Principal Cast: Marie Wilson (*Irma Peterson*), Cathy Lewis (*Jane Stacy*), Mary Shipp (*Kay Foster*), Sid Tomack (*Al*), Hal March (*Joe Vance*), Brooks West (*Richard Rhinelander III*), Gerald Mohr (*Brad Jackson*), Donald MacBride (*Milton J. Clyde*), Sig Arno (*Professor Kropotkin*), Gloria Gordon (*Mrs. O'Reilly*)

Trivia: The series presents the experiences of Irma Peterson, Jane Stacy (1952–53) and Kay Foster (1953–54), working girls who share an apartment (3B) at Mrs. O'Reilly's Boarding House at 185 West 73rd Street in Manhattan.

Irma Peterson: "Mother Nature gave some girls brains, intelligence and cleverness. But with Irma, Mother Nature slipped her a mickey"—this is Jane's description of Irma, a beautiful and shapely "dumb blonde" who has a knack for bouncing back and forth across the thin line that separates genius from insanity.

Irma, a secretary to Milton J. Clyde at the Clyde Real Estate Company in Manhattan, is sweet, kind and trusting and will do anything to help someone she believes is in trouble. Most often, however, her good intentions backfire. Then

tears fill her eyes, she sobs, "Oh, Jane . . . ," and it is Jane who has to help Irma out of the mess she has created.

Irma's original boyfriend (1952–53) was Al, an averse-to-work con artist after easy money who called Irma his "Chicken" (Jane called Al a live wire and believes "it is just a matter of time before they hook him up and put a chair under him"). Irma's next boyfriend (1953–54) is Joe Vance, a much more respectable character who works for the Spic and Span Cleaners. When CBS dropped the series, there were plans to continue the program in syndication as "My Wife Irma," which was to depict Irma and Joe's adventures as newlyweds. The project, according to *Variety*, never materialized.

Jane Stacy: With a dream to marry a rich man, Jane leaves her home in Connecticut and heads for New York to seek her prey. While looking for an apartment, she bumps into and is knocked to the ground by a "dizzy dame" named Irma Peterson. In the process of helping Jane to her feet, Irma manages to tear Jane's dress ("Ooops. Look what we did . . . They're wearing split skirts in New York this year," remarks Irma. "Yeah," responds Jane, "but not all the way up to the neck!"). When Irma learns that Jane is having a difficult time finding an apartment, she offers to let Jane share her apartment—"a one-room furnished basement Irma called home."

Jane, a pretty girl with two feet planted firmly on the ground, befriends a secretary at the Richard Rhinelander Investment Company. When the girl leaves to get married, Jane becomes the personal secretary to the wealthy Richard Rhinelander III, her dream man. Jane secretly loves Richard and desperately tries to impress him, despite the fact that she lives with Irma, who is well below his social status.

Kay Foster: In the fall of 1953, when Jane is transferred to Panama, Irma places an ad in the New York *Globe* for someone else to share her apartment. Kay Foster, a bright and beautiful reporter for the *Globe*, answers the ad and becomes the new recipient of Irma's scatter-brained antics.

"Even in the morning," says Kay, "when other girls feel they look their worst, Irma is a picture of beauty. She is so sweet and kind that you just want to mother her and protect her from all harm. Some people say Irma is as sharp as a tack—after it has been hit with a hammer. But you know, after a while, you begin to feel like someone is hitting you with a hammer when you live with and love my friend, Irma." Kay's boyfriend, Brad Jackson, is a fellow reporter on the New York *Globe*.

Their neighbor, Professor Kropotkin, plays violin at the Paradise Burlesque (later the Gypsy Tea Room). To avoid the inconvenience of always having to do her nails, Marie Wilson wears gloves in virtually every episode.

Relatives: Richard Eyer (Irma's nephew, *Bobby Peterson*), Margaret DuMont (*Richard's mother*). Mentioned but not seen was Joe's Cousin Ruthie.

Theme: "My Friend Irma," by Lud Gluskin

MY LIVING DOLL

CBS, 9.27.64 to 9.8.65

Principal Cast: Julie Newmar (*Rhoda Miller*), Bob Cummings (*Dr. Bob McDonald*), Doris Dowling (*Irene Adams*), Jack Mullavey (*Dr. Peter Robinson*), Henry Beckman (*Dr. Carl Miller*)

Trivia: "My Living Doll" is Rhoda, a beautiful female robot created by Dr. Carl Miller for a U.S. space project designed to send robots into outer space. His creation, AF 709, is made of low-modulus polyethelene plastics, miniature computers "and assorted components."

Rhoda, "the ultimate in feminine composition," stands five feet, ten inches tall, and measures 37–26–36. On her back are four small birth-marks—each of which acts as an emergency control button. Her main "Off" switch is located in her elbow, and her eyes provide a source of power obtained from light (covering her eyes causes a system relaxation). Her microscopic sen-

sors keep her body temperature at a constant 98.6 degrees, making her immune to cold. Her memory bank contains 50 million items of information and her computer brain can compute any piece of programmed information in one second. Still an experimental model, Rhoda is influenced by outside elements that can throw her entire system out of balance. (*Alice in Wonderland* confuses her circuits and causes vertigo because Lewis Carroll used precise mathematical patterns in his writing. When Rhoda hears these patterns, it sets up a conflict with her already established patterns—thus confusion in her circuits. To correct the problem, she has to be re-programmed.) Carl calls his "Living Doll" (the original series title) "It," "709" or "the Robot"—and sees her as just that, not a beautiful woman.

Carl assigns her to Dr. Bob McDonald, a psychologist at the Cory Psychiatric Clinic, to mold her character. She poses as Rhoda Miller, Carl's niece. At the office she is Bob's secretary (who types 240 words a minute with no mistakes and no coffee breaks) and at home, where Bob lives with his sister, Irene Adams, Rhoda is a patient who requires special attention and is living with them until she can function on her own.

Bob is a ladies' man and his favorite supper club is the Galaxy Club in Los Angeles. He is also the chairman of the fundraising committee for the Cory Clinic, which was founded in 1937 and has 55 beds. Peter Robinson is Bob's neighbor who, like everyone else, is unaware that Rhoda is robot and has fallen in love with her.

Theme: "My Living Doll," by George Greeley

MY SECRET IDENTITY

Syndicated, 10.9.88 to

Principal Cast: Jerry O'Connell (*Andrew Clements*), Derek McGrath (*Dr. Benjamin Jeffcoat*), Wanda Cannon (*Stephanie Clements*), Marsha Moreau (*Erin Clements*)

Trivia: When 14-year-old Andrew Clements wanders into the lab of his neighbor, Dr. Benjamin Jeffcoat, he is hit by blue gamma rays from an experimental machine. The rays endow Andrew with extraordinary powers he uses to foil evil as Ultraman.

Andrew, who attends Briarwood High School, lives with his mother, Stephanie, and sister, Erin, at 43 Meadow Drive (also given as 51 Meadow Drive) in the town of Briarwood, Canada. Andrew, whose after-school hangout is Jerry's Burger Barn, based his alter-ego on his favorite comic book character, Ultraman (Andrew, however, wears no special costume. His powers consist of the ability to fly, speed and an immunity to harm).

Stephanie, a freelance real estate agent, drives a car with license plate 483 ENX, and does volunteer work at the York Community Center. Erin attends Briarwood Elementary School.

Dr. Jeffcoat, the fifth smartest man in the world, lives at 45 Meadow Drive and writes scientific articles for the *Quantum Quarterley* magazine. He has a boat called the *Kahuna* and a car with the license plate 592 BAJ. His answering-machine tone is 440 cycles and when working (outside of his lab at home) he carries an Albert Einstein lunch box.

Andrew and his friends roller skate at the Rocket Roller Skating Rink. Mrs. Shellenbock (Elizabeth Leslie), Dr. Jeffcoat's nosy neighbor, lives at 47 Meadow Drive and is an Elvis Presley fanatic who has a dog named Elvis. In her youth, she was a member of the Bruise Brothers roller skating team.

Relatives: Susannah Hoffman (Dr. Jeffcoat's niece, *Rebecca*; attends Claridge High School for Girls)

Flashbacks: Jaymie Blanchard (*Andrew as a boy*), Wanda Cannon (*Stephanie as a teenager*), Marc Marcut (*Benjamin as a boy*), Derek McGrath (*Benjamin's father*)

Theme: "My Secret Identity," by Fred Mollin

MY SISTER SAM

CBS, 10.6.86 to 4.13.88

Principal Cast: Pam Dawber (*Samantha "Sam" Russell*), Rebecca Schaeffer (*Patti Russell*), Jenny O'Hara (*Dixie Randazzo*), Joel Brooks (*J. D.*), David Naughton (*Jack Kincaid*)

Trivia: Twenty-nine-year-old Samantha Russell owns the Russell Scouts Photography Studio in San Francisco, California. She runs the business from her apartment (5-C) and her phone number is 555–6687. Sam, who was a straight A student in high school (with the exception of a C-minus in Spanish), had her biggest disappointment in life when *Epicure* magazine rejected her "Table Settings" photo for its cover; her dream is to make the cover of a national magazine before she is 30. Sam alphabetizes her fruit juices in the refrigerator and arranges the shoes in her closet so all the toes point north. At Sam's Homecoming Dance at Bennett High School, the theme was "Undersea Adventure" and featured the group Sharky and the Fins.

Patti Russell, Sam's 16-year-old sister, had been living with her Aunt Elsie and Uncle Bob in Oregon since her parents were killed in a car crash several years earlier. She wanted to be with Sam and moved out. Her cab fare from San Francisco International Airport to Sam's apartment was eight dollars and her fellow passenger was Sunflower Wong Chow (not seen). Patti is a sophomore at Millard Fillmore High School and her goal is to quit school to become a rock star. In one episode, Patti's teacher, Mrs. Friedman, assigned her a five-pound bag of flour to care for as if it were a real baby; she named it Dweezil. She and Sam also attempted to make money by selling hand-decorated sweatshirts (the Serendipity Boutique ordered 150, returned most of them, and Sam and Patti barely broke even).

Jack Kincaid is Sam's neighbor (Apartment 5-D) and a photojournalist who got his first cover story in *Newsweek* magazine when he was 22. He drives a 1955 Buick convertible (not seen), and whenever he gets depressed, he looks into the mirror and sings "Happy Talk" (from *South Pacific*) to himself. Dixie Randazzo, Sam's assistant, is married and the mother of six children (five of whom are not seen). She was a member of the Ink Skulls Club in high school and has a tattoo on her behind that says "I Love Dwayne." J. D., Sam's agent, attended the University of Bridgeport and has a never-seen wife named Lorraine.

There are three flights of stairs to climb before one reaches Sam's apartment. Each flight is made up of 26 steps.

Relatives: Nan Martin (Sam's *Aunt Elsie*), Patrick Breen (Jack's nephew, *Scotty Kincaid*), Stuart Fratkin (Dixie's son, *Mickey Randazzo*)

Theme: "Room Enough for Two," vocal by Kim Carnes

MY TWO DADS

NBC, 9.20.87 to 6.18.90

Principal Cast: Greg Evigan (*Joey Harris*), Paul Reiser (*Michael Taylor*), Staci Keanan (*Nicole Bradford*), Florence Stanley (*Judge Margaret Wilbur*), Amy Hathaway (*Shelby Haskell*), Dick Butkus (*Ed Klawicki*), Vonni Ribisi (*Cory Kupkus*)

Trivia: At the reading of the will of Marcie Bradford, two of her former lovers, Joey Harris and Michael Taylor, are appointed co-guardians of Marcie's 12-year-old daughter, Nicole, when it cannot be determined which of the two is the actual biological father.

Joey, Michael and Nicole live in Apartment 4-B at 627 North Brewster Street in New York City in a building owned by the judge who appointed them Nicole's guardians, Margaret Wilbur (who lives in Apartment 3-B).

Joey is a Greenwich Village artist (1987–88), art director for *Financial Update* magazine (1988), artist again (1989) and finally art teacher at NYU (New York University) in 1990. He also wrote the children's book, *Mr. Biggles* (about a leprechaun).

Michael is first a financial advisor for the Taft-Kelcher Agency (1987–89), then marketing manager for *Financial Update* magazine. As kids, Joey and Michael both attended Camp White Fish.

Nicole, who has a teddy bear named Mr. Beebels, attends an unnamed junior high school, then Kennedy High. With the introduction of her girlfriend, Shelby, the series focuses on Nicole's growth into young adulthood—and the worries faced by her two dads when she "discovers" boys and dating.

Ed, a former football player, owns Klawicki's, a diner located on the ground floor of the judge's building. In the third season, Margaret takes over the diner under the name the Judge's Court Café.

Prior to becoming a judge, Margaret was a lawyer and partner with her husband, Louis Fraser, in the law firm of Fraser and Wilbur in 1960.

Relatives: Kenneth Kimmons (Joey's father, *Lou Harris*), Polly Bergen (Michael's mother, *Evelyn Taylor*), Lisa Sutton (Michael's sister, *Lisa Taylor*), Jan Murray (Michael's *Uncle Raymond*), Robert Mandan (Margaret's ex-husband, *Louis Fraser*), Wendy Schaal (Margaret's niece, *Christine*), Kim Ulrich (Ed's sister, *Patty Ann*)

Flashbacks: Emma Samms (Nicole's mother, *Marcie Bradford*)

Theme: "You Can Count on Me," vocal by Greg Evigan

NANCY

NBC, 9.17.70 to 1.7.71

"Nancy's a love song about to be sung, laughter in April when lovers are young . . . Nancy's an angel and angels are few; so everything I've ever dared to dream has come true." She's pretty, she speaks English, French, German, Italian and Spanish; she's Nancy Smith (Renne Jarrett), the daughter of the President of the United States. He's Adam Hudson (John Fink), a small-town (Center City, Iowa) veterinarian with a kind nature. They meet when he is called to tend Nancy's sick horse, Lady, fall in love and later marry. They set up housekeeping on the former Swenson farm in Center City, and struggle to adjust to a life that is more public than private.

For a wedding ring, Adam first planned on a $2100 two-carat diamond blue whitestone on a platinum setting. When he couldn't afford that (a client didn't pay his promised bill of $900), he settled on a $1200 one-carat emerald-cut diamond in a platinum setting. When a second client failed to pay his $500 bill, Adam purchased a $700 half-carat round-cut diamond in a gold setting—which Nancy loved.

Celeste Holm plays Abby Townsend, Nancy's guardian; Robert F. Simon, Everett Hudson, Adam's uncle; and Eddie Applegate, Willie Wilson, the reporter for the Center City *Daily Clarion*. Sid Ramin composed the theme.

NANNY AND THE PROFESSOR

ABC, 1.21.70 to 12.27.71

"Soft and sweet, wise and wonderful, ooh our mystical, magical Nanny . . . Is there really magic in the things she does or is love the only magic thing that Nanny brings?" Phoebe Figalilly (Juliet Mills), who is neither a witch nor a magician, but possesses the ability to spread love and joy, is the magical housekeeper of widower Harold Everett (Richard Long), a math professor at Clinton College in Los Angeles. Hal (David Doremus), Prudence (Kim Richards) and Bentley (Trent Lehman) are his children. Elsa Lanchester appeared as Phoebe's mystical Aunt Henrietta. The Everetts, who reside at 10327 Oak Street, have a dog named Waldo, a rooster called Sebastian, guinea pigs named Mike and Mertyl and two baby goats: Jerome and Geraldine. Bentley's nickname is "Butch" and Phoebe prefers to be called "Nanny." Nilsson sings the theme.

THE NEW ADVENTURES OF BEANS BAXTER

Fox, 7.18.87 to 4.2.88

Principal Cast: Jonathan Ward (*Benjamin "Beans" Baxter*), Elinor Donahue (*Susan Baxter*), Scott Bremner (*Scooter Baxter*), Karen Mistal (*Cake Lase*), John Vernon (*Number One*), Kurtwood Smith (*Mr. Sue*), Shawn Weatherly (*Svetlana*)

Trivia: Seventeen-year-old Benjamin "Beans" Baxter is a student at Georgetown High School and a spy courier for the Network, a top secret government organization headed by Number One. He lives at 1341 Maple Street in Washington, D.C., with his mother, Susan, and his brother, Scooter; their phone number is 555–6060. Although he has a girlfriend named Cake Lase, Beans sees no one but Svetlana, a gorgeous Soviet defector, when he learns that he is going to be working with her. Scooter, a pint-sized Albert Einstein, has a guinea pig named Alvin. The enemy of the Network is U.G.L.I. (Underground Government Liberation Intergroup) which is headed by Mr. Sue. Beans originally lived in the town of Witches Creek and attended Witches Creek High School.

Relatives: Rick Lenz (Beans's father, *Benjamin Baxter Sr.*), Sarah Sawatsky (Cake's sister, *Cupcake Lase*), Lorraine Foreman (Number One's wife, *Mrs. Number One*), Shawn Clements (Number One's son, *Little One*)

Theme: "The New Adventures of Beans Baxter," written by Joseph Birtelli

THE NEW AVENGERS

see THE AVENGERS

THE NEW GIDGET

Syndicated, 9.86 to 9.88

Principal Cast: Caryn Richman (*Frances "Gidget" Griffin*), Dean Butler (*Jeff "Moondoggie" Griffin*), Sydney Penny (*Danni Collins*), William Schallert (*Russ Lawrence*), Lili Haydn (*Gail Baker*), Jill Jacobson (*Larue Powell*)

Trivia: An update of the "Gidget" series (see entry) that continues to depict events in the life of the pretty surfer girl, now married (to Moondoggie) and the guardian of her niece, Danni (her sister Anne's daughter).

Frances "Gidget" Griffin owns the Gidget Travel Agency in Los Angeles; her VW Rabbit's license plate is GIDG TVL; and in one episode, she made a home video called "Gidget's Guide to Surfing." Her biggest thrill as a kid was appearing on "Romper Room" and being called a "Perky Do-Bee" by the host, Miss Connie. Jeff, still called "Moondoggie" by Gidget, was originally a construction worker for Bedford Construction; he now works as a city planner.

Danni and her girlfriend, Gail, attend Westside High School (as did Gidget) and listen to radio station K-GOLD. Like Gidget, Danni's favorite hangout is Malibu Beach; Gidget and Danni eat Ghost Busters cereal for breakfast.

Russ Lawrence, Gidget's father, is now retired and helps her out at Gidget Travel (as does her long-time friend, Larue). Don Stroud appeared in the recurring role of the Great Kahuna, the world's best (and legendary) surfer (played only once in the original 1965 series by Martin Milner).

In the original pilot, "Gidget's Summer Reunion" (syndicated 6.85), Allison Barron was Gidget's niece, Kim; William Schallert was Gidget's father, Russ Hoover; and Anne Lockhart played Gidget's friend, Larue Powell.

Relatives: J. Michael Flynn (Danni's father, *John Collins*), R. J. Williams (Jeff's nephew, *Dennis*). Danni's mother, Anne, is not seen.

Flashbacks: Shiri Appleby (*Gidget as a young girl*), Bridget Hoffman (*Gidget's mother*)

Theme: "One in a Million," by Jeff Vilinsky, Craig Snyder and Marek Norman

THE NEW LASSIE

Syndicated, 9.24.89 to

A revised version of "Lassie." The story for the new version actually begins 25 years ago when young Timmy Martin (Jon Provost) is taken away from his foster parents, Paul and Ruth Martin. Shortly after, Timmy begins using his middle name, Steve, and is adopted by the McCulloch family.

Many years later (1986), Steve's brother, Chris (Christopher Stone), rescues a collie puppy from a car wreck. Chris and his wife, Dee (Dee Wallace Stone), nurse the puppy back to health. In 1989, Steve, Chris, Dee, and Dee and Chris's children, Megan (Wendy Cox) and Will (Will Nipper), move to the small town of Glen Ridge, California, where Chris opens his own business (McCulloch Construction). Stories follow Lassie's adventures with the McCulloch family.

The McCullochs live on Latimor Road; Chris's car's license plate is 999 358 (later 938 IYN); Megan's stuffed rabbit toy is named Gabby; and the McCulloch cat (apparently a stray who shows up for meals) is named Sam. When budding photographer Megan's photos of thieves robbing an Indian burial ground were shown on Channel 9's "News Beat," she received a T-shirt with "News 9" on it. Steve is a member of the Glen Ridge Hang Gliders Society. Megan and Will attend Glen Ridge Elementary School (where Megan is a cheerleader for the Gophers football team).

June Lockhart appeared in the episode "Roots" as Ruth Martin-Chadwick, Timmy's first adoptive mother, now remarried and the owner of the puppy Steve found in 1986 (she allows the McCullochs to keep Lassie when she sees her with Will and remembers how her son Timmy and his dog Lassie loved each other). Les Baxter provides the whistling for the "Lassie" theme, composed by Al Burton and Timothy Thompson.

THE NEW LEAVE IT TO BEAVER

TBS, 9.86 to 9.89

Principal Cast: Barbara Billingsley (*June Cleaver*), Tony Dow (*Wally Cleaver*), Jerry Mathers (*Beaver Cleaver*), Ken Osmond (*Eddie Haskell*), Janice Kent (*Mary Ellen Cleaver*), Kaleena Kiff (*Kelly Cleaver*), John Snee (*Oliver Cleaver*), Kipp Marcus (*Kip Cleaver*), Ellen Maxted (*Gert Haskell*), Eric Osmond (*Freddie Haskell*), Christian Osmond (*Bomber Haskell*), Frank Bank (*Lumpy Rutherford*), Keri Houlihan (*J. J. Rutherford*)

Trivia: This is an update of "Leave It to Beaver": June, who still lives at 211 Pine Street, is now a widow and a member of the Mayfield City Council.

Wallace, her eldest child, is an attorney and lives at 213 Pine Street. He is married to Mary Ellen and they have a daughter named Kelly. Mary Ellen was Wally's high school sweetheart (played in the original series by Pamela Beaird); Kelly attends the Grant Avenue School and is a member of the Junior Chipmunks. She is also part of the Mayfield Youth Soccer Team and her favorite after-school hangout is the Soda Shop.

Theodore, still called "Beaver," is June's youngest son and the divorced father of two boys, Kip and Ollie. He lives with June, and he and his friend Clarence own the Cleaver and Rutherford Company (exactly what they do is not revealed). Clarence (Lumpy) is now married and the father of a daughter (J. J.); Beaver is divorced from Kimberly (Joanna Gleason). Kip attends Mayfield High School and Oliver, the Grant Avenue School. Ollie has a pet dove named Wilma, hangs out with Kelly and his favorite place to hide is in the clothes hamper. Kip's first job was attendant at Vince's Full Service Gas Station.

Eddie Haskell, now married (to Gert) and the father of two boys (Freddie and Bomber), is the same wise-cracking character he was in the 1960s; he now owns Eddie Haskell Construction Company, still watches "Woody Woodpecker" cartoons on TV, and his favorite breakfast is beer and pop tarts (his favorite dessert is chocolate pudding). Gert's maiden name is Bronson; Freddie (who takes after Eddie) attends Mayfield High, and Bomber is enrolled at the Vicksburg Military School.

The population of Mayfield is 18,240; June's license plate reads NO. 1 MOM; Beaver's license plate is 6102; Lumpy's Mercedes' license plate is 203056.

Theme: "The Toy Parade" (new adaptation by Cabo Frio)

NEWHART

CBS, 10.25.82 to 9.8.90

Principal Cast: Bob Newhart (*Dick Loudon*), Mary Frann (*Joanna Loudon*), Jennifer Holms (*Leslie Vander Kellen*), Julia Duffy (*Stephanie Vander Kellen*), Tom Poston (*George Utley*), Peter Scolari (*Michael Harris*), William Sanderson (*Larry*), Tony Papenfuss (*Darryl One*), John Volstedt (*Darryl Two*)

Trivia: Twenty-eight Westbrook Road (off Route 22) in River City, Vermont, is the location of the 200-year-old Stratford Inn, which is now owned by Dick Loudon, a history buff and "How-To" book author, and his wife, Joanna.

Dick, who attended Cunningham Elementary School, is also the host of the TV show, "Vermont Today" on WPIV-TV, Channel 8. In college, Dick was a drummer with a band (the Jazz Tones) and had the nickname "Slats" Loudon. As a child, Dick had a pet goldfish named Ethel Merman and attended Camp Cowapoka. During "Golden Tomahawk Days" at camp, rubber tomahawks with golden handles were awarded. Dick's favorite sport is diving. He has written such books as *Installation and Care of Your Low Maintenance Lawn Sprinkler, How to Make Your Dream Bathroom,* and *Pillow Talk* (on how to make pillows). His first novel was *Murder at the Stratley* (a take-off on the Stratford Inn). Dick's shoe size is 8½DDD, and in the episode of 11.20.89, a British nobleman bestowed upon Dick the title Lord Richard of Stumpworth on Thames when he couldn't pay his $800 hotel bill. Dick's most devastating act was accidentally burning down the French restaurant Maison Hubert (he carelessly tossed a cigarette in the trash basket in the men's room).

Joanna, who was born in Gainesville, Ohio, met Dick when they worked at an ad agency in New York City. Their first date was at a Memorial Day picnic (to commemorate the event, each Memorial

Day weekend they go picnicking and enjoy their traditional food—blue cheese). Joanna, whose maiden name is McKenna, loves to wear sweaters, but on their anniversary, Dick loves to give her yellow scarfs. Joanna, a real estate broker, hosts a TV show called "Your House Is My House" (later called "Hot Houses"— not because of the homes for sale but because "Joanna is one hot babe") on WPIV. Joanna also holds the town record for renting out the video "60 Days to a Tighter Tummy."

George Utley, Dick's handyman, is a member of the Beaver Lodge (the annual Beaver Bash is on the Memorial Day weekend and the featured meal is a spaghetti-and-tomato sauce sit-down dinner). George, who has a favorite hammer named "Old Blue," invented a board game called "Handyman: The Feel Good Game." He does his birdwatching at Johnny Kaye Lake, and as a kid his favorite radio program was "The Goldbergs"; his favorite TV shows now are "Barnaby Jones" and "It's Always Moisha" (a mythical series starring Don Rickles). George's 40-year hidden secret: When a teen, he wanted to join a gang called the Vermont Hooligans. He had to find a car, turn the radio up very loud and run away. George found a DeSoto—but accidentally released the brake, and the car rolled into a swamp. When George is upset, he rents the movie *It's a Mad, Mad, Mad, Mad World*. He keeps a lucky penny in his shoe or sock.

Stephanie Vander Kellen, Dick's maid, is the daughter of a wealthy family (who live in Newport) and replaced her sister (also referred to as her cousin), Leslie, who was the original maid. Leslie left to complete her education at Oxford; Stephanie took the job to experience real life. She is spoiled, moody and looks down on people of lower social status. Stephanie buys her designer clothes at Peck's Department Store and she had a show on WPIV called "Seein' Double" (wherein she played teenage twins Judy and Jody Bumpter. Dick Loudon played her father, Henry Bumpter, and the show

was produced, written and directed by Stephanie's boyfriend, Michael Harris).

Michael was an executive at WPIV (he produced Dick's show), then a salesman at Circus of Shoes after he was fired for insulting the boss's daughter. He was then a produce clerk at Menke's Market, a mime, and finally a resident of the Ridge Valley Psychiatric Hospital. Michael is totally devoted to Stephanie, calls her "Cupcake," "Gumdrop" and "Muffin" and constantly showers her with gifts. He has a special area in his apartment (9-B) devoted to photographs of Stephanie which he calls "Cupcake Corner." In order to give Stephanie even more gifts, Michael created "Cupcake Day," which comes between Valentine's Day and Easter. As a kid, Michael was the singing assistant to Captain Cookie on the TV show "Captain Cookie's Clubhouse." He and Stephanie once sought professional relationship counseling under the assumed names of Chuck and Dawn. In 1989, they had a baby girl they named Baby Stephanie (played at age five by Candy Hutson).

"Hello. My Name is Larry. This is my brother, Darryl, and this is my other brother, Darryl." Their gas bill is paid by Johnny Carson; they own a diner called the Minuteman Café; they love to eat foods you didn't know were foods; and they seem to live in a world of their own. Larry, the only one of the brothers who talks, attended Mount Pilard Technical School; Darryl I attended Oxford University; Darryl II attended Cambridge University under a rowing scholarship and majored in royalty.

The flying squirrel is the town's bird; the flounder is the town fish; and the key to the city won't open anything, but it will start Willie Frye's tractor. Town ordinance Article Three, Paragraph Two dictates: During "Colonial Days" all residents must dress in colonial garb.

The final episode ("The Last Newhart," 5.21.90): Mr. Takadachi (Gebbe Watanabe) offers each resident of the town one million dollars for their property with a plan to build the 5000-room Takadachi Hotel and golf course. All but Dick and

Joanna sell. Michael and Stephanie, with plans to build "Stefi Land," move to Switzerland; George, who once bought some land when he was drunk to build "Utley Land" (an amusement park for handymen) sells it; and Larry and the Darryls move to Chicago to live with an uncle.

Five years later, the Stratford Inn is on the 14th fairway; it has a Japanese motif, a Japanese handyman (Sunatra, played by Sab Shimono), a Japanese "Stephanie" (Sedaka, played by Shuko Akune) and Joanna has "turned Oriental" and dresses like a geisha. It is also the location for a reunion of the old gang. All have remained the same except for Larry, Darryl and Darryl, who are now married: Larry to Rhonda (Christie Mellor), Darryl I to Sada (Lisa Kudrow) and Darryl II to Zora (Nada Despotovich). This is also the first time the Darryls speak—to yell "Quiet" to their arguing wives ("They never spoke before," Larry says, "because nothing ever pissed them off before").

When the reunion begins to get unruly, Dick decides to leave. He is standing in the doorway when he is hit in the head with a golf ball. As he passes out, the screen goes black. A figure is seen in a bed. As he stretches over to turn on the light, we see that it is not Dick Loudon but Dr. Bob Hartley (from "The Bob Newhart Show"). His wife Emily (Suzanne Pleshette) asks what is wrong and Bob proceeds to tell her about this horrible nightmare wherein he was an innkeeper and married to a beautiful blonde; about an heiress for a maid; about three strange brothers . . .

Apparently, the eight years of "Newhart" were but the one night's dream of Dr. Bob Hartley.

Relatives: Bob Elliott (Dick's father, *Bill Loudon*), Peggy McCay (Joanna's mother, *Florence McKenna*), Nancy Walker (Joanna's *Aunt Louise*), Richard Roat and Jose Ferrer (Stephanie's father, *Arthur Vander Kellen*), Priscilla Morrill (Stephanie's mother, *Mary Vander Kellen*), Ann Morgan Guilbert (George's *Aunt Bess*), Derek McGrath (George's cousin, *Eugene Wiley*), Ruth Manning (Michael's mother, *Lily Cassiano*), Henry Gibson (Michael's father, *Ted Harris*)

Flashbacks: Jason Marin (*George as a boy*), Tom Poston (*George's father*)

Theme: "The Newhart Theme," by Henry Mancini

THE ODD COUPLE
ABC, 9.24.70 to 7.4.75

Principal Cast: Tony Randall (*Felix Unger*), Jack Klugman (*Oscar Madison*), Al Molinaro (*Officer Murray Grechner*), Penny Marshall (*Myrna Turner*), Elinor Donahue (*Miriam Welby*), Joan Hotchkis (*Nancy Cunningham*)

Trivia: Felix Unger, an excessively neat perfectionist, and Oscar Madison, an irresponsible slob, are divorced, mismatched roommates who live together at 1049 Park Avenue (at 74th Street and Central Park West) in Apartment 1102. Together they wrote the song "Happy and Peppy and Bursting with Love" for singer Jaye P. Morgan; their favorite place to eat is Nino's Italian Restaurant.

Felix, who suffers from sinus attacks, was born in Chicago, moved to Oklahoma and grew up on a farm in Glenview, New York (another episode mentions his home town as Toledo, Ohio). He is a member of the Radio Actor's Guild (as a kid he appeared on "Let's Pretend") and in college he had his own radio show called "Felix" (1290 on the AM dial). When in the Army, Felix was stationed in England during World War II and starred in the Army training film *How to Take a Shower*; he originated the line, "Men, don't let this happen to you." While working as a photographer for *Playboy* magazine (where he met his ex-wife, Gloria, a candidate for Playmate of the Month) he used the name Spencer Benedict. He is now a free-lance photographer ("Portraits a Specialty"). Felix has a parrot named Albert and is a member of a band called the Sophisticates. He won the Dink Award for directing a commercial for the Fataway Diet Company. Before moving in with Oscar, Felix and Gloria lived in New Rochelle, New York.

Their first child, Edna, was born at Mid-City Memorial Hospital in Manhattan (from which Felix is now banned due to the fuss he put up when Edna was born). His son, Leonard, has a pet frog named Max. Felix's boyhood friend was Orville Kruger ("the boy with the odd-shaped head") and his first girlfriend was Big Bertha. He is also the founder of the Lexington Avenue Opera Club.

Oscar, a sportswriter for the New York *Herald*, was born at Our Lady of Angels Hospital in Philadelphia (in another episode, Oscar was born in Chicago—where he and Felix met briefly as kids). As a kid, Oscar attended the Langley Tippy-Toe Tap Dancing School and was enrolled in James K. Polk High School. Oscar, whose vice is gambling, wears a size 11-D shoe and his favorite dressing for food is ketchup (lasagna and French fries is his favorite dinner and Boston cream pie, his favorite dessert). Oscar's first job in New York was copywriter for *Playboy* magazine; he had a radio show called "The Oscar Madison Sports Talk Show" (later changed to "Oscar Madison's Greatest Moments in Sports"). His favorite song is "Reckless." The series is based on the play by Neil Simon.

Other Characters: Murray Grechner is a cop with the New York Police Department; Myrna Turner is Oscar's secretary (born in the Bronx, disorganized, sloppy and lazy—the best secretary Oscar ever had); Miriam Welby is Felix's romantic interest; and Dr. Nancy Cunningham is Oscar's lady love.

Relatives: Janis Hansen (Felix's ex-wife, *Gloria*), Pamelyn Ferdin and Doney Oatman (Felix's daughter, *Edna Unger*), Leif Garrett and Willie Aames (Felix's son, *Leonard Unger*), William Redfield (Felix's brother, *Floyd Unger*). Tony Randall (Felix's great uncle, *Albert Unger*, who lives at Sunshine City), Madge Kennedy (*Felix's grandmother*), Brett Somers (Oscar's ex-wife, *Blanche*), Hilary Thompson (Oscar's niece, *Martha*), Elvia Allman and Fran Ryan (*Oscar's mother*), Jane Dulo and Alice Ghostley (Murray's wife, *Mimi Grechner*)

Flashbacks: Adam Klugman (*Oscar as a boy*), Johnny Scott Lee and Sean Manning (*Felix as a boy*), Tony Randall (Felix's father, *Morris Unger*, an optometrist), Jack Klugman (Oscar's father, *Blinky Madison*, a bookie and restaurant owner), Tony Randall (*Felix's grandfather*)

Theme: "The Odd Couple," by Neal Hefti

Note: In "The New Odd Couple" (ABC, 10.29.82 to 6.9.83), Ron Glass played Felix Unger and Demond Wilson, Oscar Madison in a black version of the series (which used mostly old "Odd Couple" scripts).

ONCE A HERO
ABC, 9.19.87 to 10.3.87

Comic book hero Captain Justice is the alias of Brad Steele (Jeff Corey) who battles evil in Pleasantville. His girlfriend is Rachel Kirk (Dianne Kay), his aide is Lobsterman (Trevor Henley) and his enemy is Max Mayhem (Harris Laskawy).

When Captain Justice, who is also known as the Crimson Crusader, begins to fade, he realizes that people are beginning to lose interest in him. He crosses the Forbidden Zone and passes from the Comic Book World to the real world in an effort to make people remember him. To help the Captain, who has lost his powers, the rulers of the Comic Book World send Gumshoe (Robert Forster), a 1940s style private eye, to protect and assist him. The series ends before Captain Justice can accomplish his goal.

Abner Bevis (Milo O'Shea) is the creator of Captain Justice (published by Pizazz Comics); Emma Greely (Caitlin Clarke) is a reporter for the Los Angeles *Gazette*; Dana Short is Rachel's sister, Tippy Kirk; Adam West is T. J. North, the actor who plays Captain Justice on TV; and Richard Lynch appeared as Victor Lazarus, the Captain's nemesis who followed him through the Forbidden Zone. Jim Turner played Captain Justice in the unaired pilot version of the series. Dennis Dreith composed the theme song.

ONE DAY AT A TIME

CBS, 12.6.75 to 9.2.84

Principal Cast: Bonnie Franklin (*Ann Romano*), Valerie Bertinelli (*Barbara Cooper*), Mackenzie Phillips (*Julie Cooper*), Pat Harrington Jr. (*Dwayne F. Schneider*), Mary Louise Weller (*Ginny Wroblinki*), Michael Lembeck (*Max Horvath*), Shelley Fabares (*Francine Webster*), Boyd Gaines (*Mark Royer*), Richard Masur (*David Kane*), John Putch (*Bob Morton*), Ron Rifkin (*Nick Handris*), Howard Hesseman (*Sam Royer*)

Trivia: At 1344 Hartford Drive, Apartment 402 in Indianapolis, Indiana, live Ann Romano, a liberated, 34-year-old divorcée (who has resumed her maiden name) and her two daughters, Barbara and Julie (who carry their father's last name). Their phone number is 555–4142.

Ann was born in Logansport, Indiana, and attended Logansport High School. She was originally an account executive at the Connors and Davenport Advertising Agency, then co-owner (with Nick Handris) of the Romano and Handris Ad Agency (later changed to Handris and Associates) and finally half-owner of the Romano and Webster Ad Agency (with Francine Webster). Her biggest account at Connors and Davenport was Rutledge Toys; her first account after leaving was Startime Ice Cream. Ann's first-season boyfriend was David Kane, her divorce lawyer (with the firm of McInerney, Wollman, Kollman and Schwartz). She later married architect Sam Royer and moved to 322 Bedford Street, Apartment 422; Ann's favorite ice cream flavor is Almond Mocha.

Julie, Ann's eldest and most troublesome daughter, attended Jefferson High School. She wears a size 32B bra, has a stuffed bear doll called TuTu Bear, and her favorite snacks are pickles and bananas, and celery and ice cream. Julie, who did not attend college, was a receptionist for a veterinarian, a freelance fashion designer and a counselor at the Free Clinic. She and Ann have bank accounts at the First Security Bank (Julie's account number is 1–222–1220–877–02453). Julie

married Max Horvath, a flight attendant for PMA Airlines; he was later a waiter at Barney's Tavern and hoping to make it big as a writer. Julie and Max had a daughter named Annie, and Julie attended the Berkum Management Institute in Ohio for training as manager of a donut shop. Max calls Ann (his mother-in-law) "Shortie."

Barbara, Ann's youngest daughter, began the series as a tomboy and evolved into a beautiful young woman. She attended Jefferson High School and later City College (but dropped out) and held the following jobs: cook at Quickie Burger, salesclerk at Olympia Sporting Goods (owned by Erickson Enterprises) and travel agent at the Gonagin Travel Agency. Her favorite snack is a huge banana split, and Rocky Road is her favorite flavor of ice cream.

At school both Julie and Barbara were envious of Trish the Dish, a well-built girl (never seen) who is the dream of all the boys. While Julie went only so far as to pad her bra with Kleenex to attract boys, Barbara took it one step further and pretended to be on the pill.

Barbara's greatest disappointment occured shortly after her marriage to Mark Royer (a dentist). Having always dreamed of raising a family, Barbara learned that she cannot bear children (an inability to conceive that even surgery could not cure). On a more playful note, Barbara ate a caterpillar as a kid when Julie told her it was a fuzzy Tootsie Roll.

Dwayne Schneider, the building super, lives in the basement (Apartment 1) and is a member of I.B.M. (Indianapolis Building Maintenance). Dwayne's first job was at age two months as a model in diaper ads. Dwayne, who was born in Secaucus, New Jersey, attended Irvington High School. He married in 1957 but the marriage lasted only one week. (His wife got up one morning, hot-wired his truck and just took off. However, in the pilot episode, Dwayne is married; in some episodes it is mentioned that Dwayne was married for five days and got a divorce.) Dwayne, whose C.B. handle is "Super Stud," is a member of the Secret Order of Beavers Lodge, North Central Chapter (he is activities chairman and entertainment producer for the lodge). His favorite pickup joint is the Boom Boom Room at the Purple Pig Club, and in one episode he invested $10,000 in one of Ann and Francine's accounts—Georgette Jeans.

Ginny Wroblinki, Ann's sexy neighbor, is a waitress at the Alibi Room bar; Bob Morton is Barbara's friend; Kathryn Romano, Ann's mother, calls Barbara "Muffin". The telephone number of Connors and Davenport is 555-7974.

Relatives: Joseph Campanella (Ann's ex-husband, *Ed Cooper*), Nanette Fabray (Ann's mother, *Kathryn Romano*), Elizabeth Kerr (Ann's grandmother, *Helen Romano*), Jeff Corey (Ann's father, *Michael Romano*), Priscilla Morrill (Ann's mother-in-law, *Estelle Cooper*), Gretchen Corbett (Ann's *Cousin Sophie*), J. C. Dilley and R. J. Dilley; Beth and Heather Cooke; Paige and Lauren Maloney (Julie's daughter, *Annie Horvath*), Van Johnson (Francine's father, *Gus Webster*), Dick Van Patten (Ginny's ex-husband, *Frank*), Mark Hamill (Dwayne's nephew, *Harvey*), Darrell Larson (Dwayne's son, *Ronnie Baxter*), Claudette Nevins (Sam's ex-wife, *Marge Royer*), Elinor Donahue (Nick's ex-wife, *Felicia*), Glenn Scarpelli (Nick's son, *Alex*)

Theme: "One Day At a Time," written by Jeff and Nancy Barry

OPEN HOUSE

Fox, 8.27.89 to 7.21.90

"Open House" is a "Duet" spinoff in which Linda Phillips (Alison LaPlaca) and Laura Kelly (Mary Page Keller) become brokers with Juan Verde Real Estate in Los Angeles. Linda and Richard (Chris Lemmon) are still married at first; they later separate and divorce. Their daughter, Amanda (Ginger Orsi), appears in the first episode and is then said to be cared for by Geneva (Arleen Sorkin), the Phillips' housekeeper.

Laura, who had a catering business, gave it up when she and her husband, Ben, divorced. She lives at 13205 Ocean Avenue and has an account at the Happy Valley Bank. Laura is sweet, innocent, a bit naive and troubled by a drinking problem. She also has one regret: having had her address tattooed on her left breast (which she had done so she could remember where she lives when on a drinking binge). In the opening theme, Laura is seen reading a book called *Real Estate for Beginners*.

Linda is a high-powered sales agent and is continually engaged in a battle of wits with fellow agent Ted Nichols (Philip Charles MacKenzie) to make the most sales. Richard plays piano at Jasper's Bar-Restaurant; Margo Van Meter (Ellen DeGeneres), the receptionist, has a cat named Boris and wears a size seven ring; Roger McSwain (Nick Tate) is the agency's owner; Scott Babylon (Danny Gans) is an agent who uses celebrities' voices to make sales. The telephone number of Juan Verde is 555-1612.

Sherrie Krenn appeared as Roger's man-crazy daughter, Phoebe, and Marian Mercer played Ted's mother, Dorothy. In the first few episodes, John Greene (played by Jon Cypher) owned Juan Verde (he was bought out by McSwain). John Beasley and John Veiter composed the theme.

OUR HOUSE

NBC, 9.11.86 to 6.26.88

Principal Cast: Wilford Brimley (*Gus Witherspoon*), Deidre Hall (*Jessie Witherspoon*), Shannen Doherty (*Kris Witherspoon*), Keri Houlihan (*Molly Witherspoon*), Chad Allen (*David Witherspoon*), Gerald S. O'Loughlin (*Joe Kaplan*)

Trivia: Following the death of her husband, John, Jessie Witherspoon accepts help from her father-in-law, Gus, a widower who offers to let Jessie and her children (Kris, Molly and David) live with him at 14 Ashton Street in Los Angeles (his phone number is given as both 555-4680 and 555-4847). Gus, whose hobby is model railroading ("HO-Scale"), is a retired engineer (by the road names of his model equipment, Gus worked for the

Santa Fe Railroad). Gus and his friend Joe Kaplan are members of the Monona Service Club; Joe has a never-seen wife named Gladys.

Jessie was originally a models photographer for Cathcart Architects, then a photographer for the Los Angeles *Post-Gazette*. Kris, her eldest daughter, attends James K. Polk High School (in United School District 8). David, her middle child, is enrolled in Naismith Junior High and Molly, her youngest, attends Naismith Elementary School. Jessie and her family, who have a dog named Arthur, originally lived in Fort Wayne, Indiana.

Relatives: William Katt (Gus's estranged son, *Ben Witherspoon*), Rebecca Balding (Ben's wife, *Gail Witherspoon*), Laurie Burton (Jessie's sister, *Sheila*). Mentioned, but not seen, is Gus's wife, Mary (deceased).

Flashbacks: Patrick Duffy (Jessie's husband, *John Witherspoon*)

Theme: "Our House," written by Billy Goldenberg

OUT OF THIS WORLD

Syndicated, 9.87 to

Principal Cast: Donna Pescow (*Donna Garland*), Maureen Flannigan (*Evie Garland*), Joe Alasky (*Beano Froelich*), Doug McClure (*Kyle Applegate*), Christina Nigra (*Lindsey Selkirk*), Stephen Burton (*Chris Fuller*), Buzz Bellmondo (*Buzz*), Burt Reynolds (*voice of Troy*)

Trivia: An Earth woman (Donna) and an alien from the planet Anterias (Troy) meet during his mission on Earth, fall in love and marry shortly after (on July 27, 1974 at the Our Lady of the Strip Wedding Chapel in Las Vegas). As Troy completes his mission and returns to Anterias, Donna gives birth to a baby girl they name Evie. Stories, which begin when Evie is 13 years old, relate events in her life.

Half-Earthling and half-Anterian, Evie possesses several powers: freezing and unfreezing time (by placing her two index fingers together, she freezes time; placing her palms together unfreezes time) and gleeping (the ability to rearrange molecules by concentrating).

Evie, whose middle name is Ethel, attends Marlowe High School. Her hangout is the Goody Goody (a soda shop) and her stuffed cat doll is named Twinky. Evie is a member of the school's basketball team, the Fighting Hamsters, and the Marlowe Teenage Bowling Team. She communicates with her father via a crystal cube that allows voice transmission (Troy calls her his "Earth Angel").

Evie's birthday is whenever the new season begins. On her 13th birthday (1987) she received the power to freeze time; for her 14th birthday (9.88) she acquired the power of gleeping; on her 16th birthday (9.89; for unknown reasons her 15th birthday was skipped), Evie received the choice of the top 10 Anterian powers: (1) To read minds; (2) Make others obey your every command; (3) Reverse time; (4) A free face-lift (hardly ever chosen); (5) Levitation; (6) Ability to change shoes quickly; (7) Make someone else invisible; (8) Make oneself invisible; (9) A money tree; (10) See through walls. Evie chose none, feeling it would not be right for an Earth kid to have too many powers.

Evie lives with Donna in a spacious house at 17 Medvale Road in Marlowe, California (the home has a million-dollar view of the Pacific Ocean from the living room). Their phone number is 406–555–4669. Donna was originally the principal of Marlowe High (1987–88), then the owner of the catering service, Donna's Delights Planning and Catering (1988–90), and (as of 5.27.90) the mayor of Marlowe. Her car's license plate number is 2XHX 622.

Evie's Uncle Beano (Donna's brother) is the overweight owner of the Waist-A-Weigh Diet Clinic (later changed to Beano's Health Club). He has a stuffed bear doll named Sparky and lives next door to Donna.

Kyle Applegate, a former Hollywood movie and TV star, was the original mayor of Marlowe (1987–90). He lost in an election to Donna by one vote (500 to 501) and now serves as the police chief. In first-season episodes, Kyle was the star of two former TV series, "The Floridian" and "Mosquito Man." During the second season, Kyle was a movie star and the star of "Cowboy Kyle" feature films; those mentioned: *The Good, the Bad and the Unattractive; Gunfight at the Pretty Good Corral* and *A Six Shooter in My Shorts*. Third-season episodes find Kyle the star of a former TV series called "Cowboy Kyle" (his horse was named Myron and his sidekick was "Sheldon Moskowitz, the Frontier Dentist." Kyle was Marshal of Laramie Heights and wore fancy shirts with ruffles. Off the set he was called "The Ruffleman." Charlie Brill played Sheldon). Kyle has a dog named Buster.

Lindsey Selkirk is Evie's girlfriend (she has a dog named Mimi); Chris Fuller is Evie's on-and-off boyfriend; Buzz, who lives at 1412 Elm Street, has a frog named Farley and is Beano's assistant.

On Anterian Mother's Day (about the same time as Earth Mother's Day), Troy gives Donna a pair of Venutian Shades (sun glasses). (On Anterias, Anterians shop at Sears.) When Evie presents Troy with a problem he can't solve, he consults Professor Bob, who helps him ungleep Evie's gleeps. Troy's father, Grandpa Zelig, has an ancient space ship called the *Anterias I*.

Relatives: Betsy Palmer (Donna's mother, *Barbara*), Tom Bosley (Troy's father, *Zelig*), Susan Bugg (Lindsey's mother, *Paula Selkirk*), Jack Lynch (Lindsey's brother, *Spencer Selkirk*)

PAPER DOLLS

ABC, 9.23.84 to 12.25.84

High fashion models Taryn Blake (Nicollette Sheridan) and Laurie Caswell (Terry Farrell) are the "Paper Dolls" of the title. Morgan Fairchild plays Racine, the owner of the Racine Model Agency; Lloyd Bridges, Grant Harper, owner of the agency Harper World Wide; Lauren Hutton, Colette Ferrier, who owns Ferrier Cosmetics. Mark Bailey (Roscoe Born), is a reporter for *Newsbeat* magazine and David Fenton (Richard Beymer) owns Tempus Sportswear.

Relatives: Jennifer Warren (Laurie's mother, *Dinah Caswell*), Brenda Vaccaro

(Taryn's mother, *Julia Blake*), John Bennett Perry (Dinah's husband, *Michael*), Dack Rambo (Grant's son, *Wesley Harper*), Mimi Rogers (David's wife, *Blair Fenton*)

Mark Snow composed the theme.

In the TV movie pilot, *Paper Dolls* (ABC, 5.4.83), Joan Collins played Racine; Darryl Hannah, Taryn; Alexandra Paul, Laurie; and Joan Hackett played Julia Blake, Taryn's mother.

PAPER MOON

ABC, 9.12.74 to 1.2.75

Moses "Moze" Pray (Christopher Connelly) and his 11-year-old daughter, Addie (Jodie Foster), travel throughout the Midwest during the Great Depression selling bibles for the Dixie Bible company (a scam to make money). Moses's 1931 Roadster's license plate number is 68132; Addie was born in Ophelia, Kansas, on November 19, 1922 to Essie Mae MacLoggins, who lived at 47 Bridge Corner. Essie Mae, who is never seen, was born in Oak View, Kansas. (Addie ran away from home to be with Moses—whom she believes to be her father because she looks like him.) Harold Arlen wrote the theme. The series was based on the movie of the same name.

PARTNERS IN CRIME

NBC, 9.22.84 to 12.29.84

Principal Cast: Lynda Carter (*Carole Stanwyck*), Loni Anderson (*Sydney Kovak*), Eileen Heckart (*Jeanine Caulfield*), Walter Olkewicz (*Harvey Shain*)

Trivia: At the reading of the will of Raymond Dashell Caulfield, Carole Stanwyck and Sydney Kovak, his two ex-wives, inherit his mansion and San Francisco business, the Raymond Dashell Caulfield Detective Agency (also known as the Caulfield Detective Agency). They become "Partners in Crime" when they decide to become detectives.

Carole, a strikingly beautiful brunette who measures 38–25–37, was a debutante and teabag heiress from New York who lost her fortune through bad investments.

Now working as a freelance photographer, she was married to Raymond for three years (1972–75) and was owed $62,000 in back alimony. Carole, whose car's license plate reads IFL 896, wears a size medium dress.

Sydney, a stunning blonde ("not my natural color"), measures 36–24–36 and grew up in the Mission district of San Francisco where she learned all the tricks of the trade—from lock picking to picking pockets. She is now an aspiring but struggling musician (bass fiddle) who lived at 921 Hayworth Street (Apartment 3-C) before moving into Ray's mansion (address not given). Sydney, whose car license plate reads IPCE 467, wears a size small dress. She has a fake plaque that says "Sydney Kovak of the San Francisco Symphony Orchestra" (her dream is to play with the renowned orchestra). Sydney has been studying the bass for 20 years and has played professionally for 15 years. She was Ray's second wife (dates not given); he proposed to her at the Top of the Mark Restaurant (as he did Carole).

Jeanine, Ray's mother and Carole and Sydney's mutual mother-in-law, is an unpublished author (57 books written) and the owner of the Partners in Crime Book Store (later changed to Jeanine's Book Store). She lives in the mansion with Carole and Sydney. Harvey Shain is their housekeeper (whose claim to fame is that he met Rock Hudson at Fisherman's Wharf).

Relatives: Cameron Mitchell (Sydney's father, *Duke Kovak*)

Theme: "Partners in Crime," by Nathan Sassover and Ken Heller

THE PARTRIDGE FAMILY
ABC, 9.25.70 to 9.7.74

Shirley Partridge (Shirley Jones) and her children, Keith (David Cassidy), Laurie (Susan Dey), Danny (Danny Bonaduce), Tracy (Suzanne Crough) and Chris (Jeremy Gelbwaks; later Brian Foster) are the show business sensation, the singing Partridge Family, a pop group managed by

Reuben Kincaid (Dave Madden), but founded by Danny (who organized the family into a group and convinced Reuben to take a chance on them).

The Partridges, who put on no show-business airs, live at 698 Sycamore Road (also given as the 700 block on Vassario Road) in San Pueblo, California. They drive a psychedelic school bus with license plate NLX 590 (and a sign on the back that reads "Careful. Nervous Mother Driving"). The first song they performed on stage was "Together" in a Los Angeles show that was headlined by Johnny Cash. Keith, whose favorite foods are meatloaf and steak and potatoes, attends San Pueblo High School (as does Laurie, a teenage women's libber who sometimes feels bewildered and frustrated over all the attention girls bestow on Keith). Shirley, whose maiden name is Renfrew, worked at the Bank of San Pueblo before joining the group; the family dog is named Simone.

Relatives: Rosemary DeCamp (Shirley's mother, *Amanda Renfrew*), Ray Bolger and Jackie Coogan (Shirley's father, *Walter Renfrew*), Margaret Hamilton (*Reuben's mother*), Alan Bursky (Reuben's nephew, *Alan Kincaid*)

Performing Partridge Family Vocals: Shirley Jones, David Cassidy, Jackie Ward, John and Tom Bahler, Ron Hicklin

Themes: "When We're Singing," by Wes Farrell and Diane Hildenbrand; and "Come on Get Happy," by Wes Farrell and Danny Janssen

THE PATTY DUKE SHOW
ABC, 9.18.63 to 8.31.66

Principal Cast: Patty Duke (*Patty Lane* and *Cathy Lane*), William Schallert (*Martin Lane*), Jean Byron (*Natalie Lane*), Paul O'Keefe (*Ross Lane*), Eddie Applegate (*Richard Harrison*), Rita McLaughlin (*Patty* when Patty Duke is Cathy; *Cathy* when Patty Duke is Patty)

Trivia: Patty Lane, the typical American teenage girl, who has "only seen the sights a girl can see from Brooklyn Heights," and Cathy Lane, her sophisticated look-alike cousin, "who's lived most everywhere from Zanzibar to Berkeley Square," live at 8 Remsen Drive in Brooklyn Heights, New York. Cathy, who lived in Glasgow, Scotland, has come to live with Patty, her father (Martin), her mother (Natalie) and brother (Ross) to complete her high school education (her father, Kenneth Lane, is a foreign correspondent for the New York *Chronicle* whose assignments would uproot Cathy too often). The Lanes' phone number is 624–1098 and the family dog is named Tiger. The Lanes' home was built in 1720 by Adam Prescott, whose son, Jonathan, served under General George Washington and whose daughter, Jane, offered the home to General Howe and charmed him in order to give Washington and his troops time to rest and regroup.

Patty and Cathy attend Brooklyn Heights High School (they are sophomores in the first season) and the after-school hangout is the Shake Shop (later Leslie's Ice Cream Parlor). They were bitter rivals for the presidency of the Girl's League (both were beaten by Susan Baxter), and when Cathy was named temporary chemistry teacher, substituting for Miss Reilly, she gave Patty three demerits for talking in class. Together, they attempted to make money through Patty's harebrained business ventures: the Worldwide Dress Company (selling Catnip dresses designed by Cathy for $9.95 each; when a classmate came out with an $8.95 dress that featured boys' photos, Patty's company folded), Mother Patty's Preserves: "The Jam of Kings—King of the Jams" (based on an apricot jam recipe Cathy found in a book of recipes from Charles the Third and packaged in jars purchased from the Fleming Bottle Company); and Doctors Baby Sitting Service (too many kids and no sitters closed the company after one day in business).

Patty, who wears a size-five dress, was born in December (her birth sign is Sagittarius), and she wrote a book called *I Was a Teenage Teenager* ("love, war, poverty, death—and cooking recipes"). One hundred copies were published by Fyre Publishing Company (a vanity press). Patty once took a job at the Pink Percolater Coffeehouse as a waitress and singer (under the name "Pittsburgh Patty"). Seventy-five kinds of coffee were served and Patty's boyfriend, Richard, had a job as the coffee shop manager. She also attempted to play the tuba in the school band, and as editor of the high school newspaper, the *Bugle*, Patty patterned one issue after the New York *Query* (a paper that uses sensational headlines).

Cathy, who also wears a size-five dress, attended Mrs. Tuttle's of Mountain Briar Private School (where she was the debate champion) before coming to America. Her father calls her "Kit Kat" and her full name is Catherine Margaret Rollin Lane. She has a built-in lie detector: when she lies or tries to, she gets the hiccups. In one episode she received a marriage proposal from Kalimi, Prince of Buckanistan, who wanted her to be the first of many wives. Cathy is a member of the Literary Club at school.

Patty Duke also played Betsy Lane, Patty's other look-alike cousin from Atlanta, a Southern bombshell who took the boys of Brooklyn Heights by storm. While Patty called her a "Confederate Cleopatra," Betsy was, in reality, a lonely girl who desperately tried to get Cathy to leave so she could stay with the Lanes. Betsy's parents, Gaylord and Cissy, ship Betsy off to boarding schools (so they can build up their business) and ignore her feelings. Betsy's "security blanket" was her doll, Sara Jane.

Martin Lane, the managing editor of the New York *Chronicle*, was captain of his football team in college and married Natalie when she was 17 years old. They honeymooned in Lake George and have been married 20 years, according to first-season episodes. Ross, who attends P.S. 8, has a weekly allowance of 50 cents; his birthsign is Taurus. (Martin's is Virgo and Natalie's is Pisces.) The paper in direct competition with the *Chronicle* is the New York *Record*.

In the episode "Fiancée for a Day," it is mentioned that Patty and Richard have been dating for five years. It is also mentioned that Richard's father is a banker; in another episode, he is a highway construction engineer. Lane family ancestors include Joshua Lane, who founded the first general store in Vermont, and Lieutenant Noah Lane, who was the first Union Officer captured at Bull Run. The school song of Brooklyn Heights High is sung to the tune of "O Tannenbaum"; the school's football coach is Gilbert Tugwell (Sorrell Booke); the school colors are red and gold; and Coach Hanson of the high school faculty was fond of saying to his players, "Hit 'em high, hit 'em low, hit 'em again and go, go, go!!!" The football player who gave up a promising career in the sport to return to studying art (sculpture) was Rockwell Inkovich (Daniel J. Travanti).

Relatives: William Schallert (Cathy's father, *Kenneth Lane*; and Martin's *Uncle Jed*), Ilka Chase (Martin's *Aunt Pauline*; willed her money to a foundation for sailors' widows), George Gaynes (Betsy's father, *Gaylord Lane*), Frances Heflin (Betsy's mother, *Cissy Lane*), David Doyle (Richard's father, *Jonathan Harrison*), Amzie Strickland (*Richard's mother*)

Unseen Relatives: Martin's Uncle Ben; Martin's Aunt Martha; Martin's Cousin Fran; Martin's niece, Ann; Martin's Aunt Kay (sends him a basket of peaches every year from the farm); Martin's Cousin Clarence (used to have a car dealership; sold Jed a lemon—a 1932 Packard); Jed's wife, Ellen; Richard's cousin, Florence Lawrence

Theme: "Theme from the Patty Duke Show," by Sid Ramin and Robert Wells

PEACEABLE KINGDOM

CBS, 9.20.89 to 11.7.89

Rebecca Cafferty (Lindsay Wagner), a widowed mother of three, moves from New York to California to become the director of the Los Angeles Zoo. Courtney (Melissa Clayton), Sam (Michael Mansseri) and Dean (Victor DiMattia) are her children. Tom Wopat plays Rebecca's brother, Dr. Ted McFadden, the curator of mammals. The Cafferty kids' pet seal is named Rover, and Rebecca and Jed attended Madison High School as teenagers; Dean and Courtney attend Liberty High School (in New York they attended the Marquis Private School). In the original (unaired) pilot, Tom Wopat played Rebecca's love interest, not her brother. David McHugh composed the theme.

THE PEOPLE NEXT DOOR

CBS, 9.18.89 to 10.16.89

Walter Kellogg (Jeffrey Jones) is a cartoonist with the ability to make things appear just by imagining them. Mary Gross plays his wife, Abigail MacIntyre-Kellogg; Aurora (Jaclyn Bernstein) and Matthew (Chance Quinn) are his children from a previous marriage. Christina Pickles plays Abigail's sister, Cissy MacIntyre. Walter, who draws the comic strip "The People Next Door," and Abigail, a therapist, live in the town of Covington (where the major industry is eggs). Their address is 607 Sycamore Lane, and their phone number is 555-0098. Aurora and Matthew attend Covington High School. Cissy owns a beauty shop called Cissy's Hot Rollers. Dr. John performed the theme vocal, "The People Next Door."

PERFECT STRANGERS

ABC, 3.26.86 to

Principal Cast: Mark Linn-Baker (*Larry Appleton*), Bronson Pinchot (*Balki Batokomous*), Ernie Sabella (*Donald "Twinkie" Twinkacetti*), Melanie Wilson (*Jennifer Lyons*), Rebeca Arthur (*Mary Anne*), Belita Moreno (*Lydia Markham*)

Trivia: At 627 Lincoln Boulevard, Apartment 203 (later 711 Caldwell Avenue, Apartment 209) in Chicago live Larry Appleton, a Wisconsin-born American, and his cousin, Balki Batokomous, who was born on the Mediterranean Island of Mypos. On Mypos, whose national debt is $635, Balki was a shepherd; in Chicago he works with cousin Larry at the Ritz Discount Store. Later they both work at the Chicago *Chronical* (Larry as an assistant to the city editor, Balki in the mailroom). Larry and Balki are members of the paper's bowling team, the Strike Force. When they were volunteers at Chicago General Hospital, Balki was awarded the Bed Changer of the Month Award. Balki's favorite food is pig snout puffs and his favorite TV show is "Uncle Shaggy's Dog House." When someone lies, Balki fears the Gabuggies—the Myposian Fib Furies (Eva, Magda and Zsa Zsa. These spirits, whose god is Vertosh, punish those who lie). Balki, who attends night classes at Chicago Community College, has a pet parrot called Yorgi (named after his pet goat on Mypos; in Mypos, children are named after sheep) and was a member (by accident) of a motorcycle gang called the Psychos Bikers Club. When the Chicago Lotto hit $28 million, Balki played the following numbers: 15, 32, 52, 21, 27, 37; the winning numbers were 15, 32, 52, 21, 24, 34. He won $100.

Donald Twinkacetti, Larry and Balki's boss in the first season, lived at 2831 Garfield Street. Jennifer Lyons is Larry's girlfriend and Mary Anne is Balki's girlfriend (both are flight attendants and share an apartment in the same building as Larry and Balki). Lydia Markham works at the paper and writes the column "Dear Lydia" (she did a TV show based on her advice column called "Lydia Live"). In the original (unaired) pilot, Louie Anderson played Cousin Louie (the role that became Cousin Larry). Jo Marie Payton France's character, Harriette Winslow, the elevator operator, was spun off into the series "Family Matters" (see entry).

Relatives: James Noble (Larry's father, *Mr. Appleton*), Ted McGinley (Larry's brother, *Billy Appleton*), Sue Ball (Larry's sister, *Elaine Appleton*), Belita Moreno (Twinkie's wife, *Edwina Twinkacetti*), Matthew Licht (Twinkie's son, *Donnie Twinkacetti*), Erica Gayle (Twinkie's daughter, *Marie Twinkacetti*), Bronson Pinchot (Balki's *Cousin Bartok*), Robert King (Jennifer's father, *Mr. Lyons*)

Theme: "Nothing's Gonna Stop Me Now," vocal by David Pomerantz

PETE KELLY'S BLUES
NBC, 4.5.59 to 9.4.59

"This one's about Pete Kelly. It's about the world he goes around in. It's about the big music, the big trouble—and the big Twenties." The time is the Roaring Twenties; Pete Kelly (William Reynolds) is a cornet player and leader of the Big Seven, a band that plays regularly at 17 Cherry Street in Kansas City—a brownstone-turned-funeral parlor-turned-speakeasy. ("It's a standard speakeasy. The booze is cut and the prices aren't. The beer is good and the whiskey is aged—if you get here later in the day.") "We play here from 10 P.M. to four A.M.," says Pete, "with a pizza break at midnight. The hours are bad but the music suits us."

George Lupo (Phil Gordon) owns 17 Cherry Street (also referred to as Lupo's). "He was the only kid in Lanback County who got turned down for reform school. He later fought in the war with the 102nd Infantry and he pays scale—with a $5 kickback."

Savannah Brown (Connee Boswell) is Pete's friend. "She sings at Fat Annie's on the Kansas Side and she says it's easy to sing the blues—all you need to do is be born when there is rain on the roof."

"There's one other thing about 17 Cherry Street," says Pete, "and that is trouble. You can get it by the yard, the pound, wholesale and retail. Like on Thursday night . . . " (The episode would then begin).

Anthony Eisley plays Johnny Casino, an officer with the Kansas City Police Department; Dick Cathcart is the off-screen cornet player for Pete and the Matty Matlock Combo provides the music for the club scenes.

PETTICOAT JUNCTION
CBS, 9.24.63 to 9.12.70

Principal Cast: Bea Benaderet (*Kate Bradley*), Edgar Buchanan (*Joe Carson*), Jeannine Riley, Gunilla Hutton and Meredith MacRae (*Billie Jo Bradley*), Pat Woodell and Lori Saunders (*Bobbie Jo Bradley*), Linda

Kaye Henning (*Betty Jo Bradley*), Smiley Burnett (*Charley Pratt*), Rufe Davis (*Floyd Smoot*), Mike Minor (*Steve Elliott*), June Lockhart (*Dr. Janet Craig*)

Trivia: "Come ride a little train that is rollin' down the tracks to the junction . . . lots of curves, you bet, even more when you get to the junction, Petticoat Junction." In the sleepy little town of Hooterville, a farming community of 72 farms, stands the Shady Rest Hotel, a small inn owned by Kate Bradley, a widow with three beautiful daughters (Billie Jo, Bobbie Jo and Betty Jo). She is assisted by her uncle, Joe Carson, the town fire chief who believes the hotel is haunted by the ghost of Chester W. Farnsworth, who was a guest at the hotel 50 years ago. When there is work to be done, Joe fakes an attack of lumbago, and his favorite place at the hotel is the rocking chair on the front porch.

Billie Jo, the eldest of the Bradley girls, attends classes at the Pixley Secretarial School; her first job was as secretary to Oliver Fenton, an author whose books have been banned in Hooterville. Bobbie Jo and Betty Jo attend Hooterville High School. In one episode, the girls formed the singing group the Lady Bugs. Betty Jo, who married Steve Elliott, a pilot (in the fourth season), had her first crush on Orville Miggs—who was more interested in cars than in girls. (In second-season episodes, Mike Minor, who later played Steve, portrayed Don Plout, the son of Kate's archenemy, Selma Plout, played by Virginia Sale.)

Kate, who has a special recipe called "Bachelor Butter," was replaced as the mother figure on the show in 1968 by Dr. Janet Craig (Bea Benaderet's death that year ended the Kate Bradley character). Boy is the Bradley family dog (actually owned by Betty Jo, whom he followed home from school one day. Press releases refer to Boy as "The Shady Rest Dog," played by Higgins).

Neighboring communities to Hooterville are Pixley and Crabtree Corners. The Cannonball Express, an 1890s steam engine, coal car and combination car (mail and passenger coach), is owned by the C.

F. & W. Railroad. (Railroad vice president Homer Bedloe, played by Charles Lane, is Hooterville Valley's nemesis, as he seeks to scrap the Cannonball.) Charley Pratt is the engineer and Floyd Smoot is the conductor. Three toots of the Cannonball's whistle alert the Valley's children that it is time for their ride to school; Betty Jo's biggest thrill is driving the Cannonball.

The title refers to the Cannonball's stop at the Shady Rest Hotel—in front of the train's watering stop. The Bradley girls swim in the water tank on hot days—and their petticoats can be seen hanging over the top rim.

Steve, who later forms the Carson-Elliott Cropdusting Company with Kate's Uncle Joe, was born in Seattle, Washington, and became a cropduster when he was discharged from the Air Force. He crashed his plane in Hooterville when he saw the Bradley girls in the water tower, as he paid more attention to them than to where he was flying.

In the original (unaired) pilot, Sharon Tate was cast as Billie Jo, but she was dropped when the producers of the family-oriented show learned she had posed for a *Playboy* layout.

Relatives: Rosemary DeCamp (Kate's *Aunt Helen*), Shirley Mitchell (Kate's *Cousin Mae*), Don Ameche (Steve's *Uncle George*), Elaine and Danielle Hubbel (Betty Jo's daughter, *Kathy Jo Elliott*)

Theme: "Petticoat Junction," by Curt Massey

PHYL AND MIKHY

CBS, 5.26.80 to 6.30.80

"What a bright new world, what a wonderful beginning . . . from two different worlds two kids found each other . . . together and until forever, it's Phyl and Mikhy." Phyllis "Phyl" Wilson (Murphy Cross), a pretty American track star for Pacific Western University (Pac West U for short), and Mikhail "Mikhy" Orlov (Rick Lohman), a Russian track star, meet and fall in love during a track meet. Mikhy defects, and he and Phyl marry and

171

set up housekeeping in the home of Phyl's father, Max (Larry Haines), a coach at Pac West U.

Mikhy, a promising decathlon champion and a hope of the gold for Russia in the 1980 Olympics, calls Phyl "Phyliska" and Max "Dead" (actually "Dad"—but with his accent it comes out "Dead"). Phyl, who has a Creeping Charlie plant named Charlie, calls Mikhy "my Russian bear." Mikhy earns $85 a week caring for the lawn of the college president. When Mikhy upsets Max, Max goes on a milkshake binge.

Eugene "Truck" Morley (Jack Dodson), Max's friend, is president of the Alumni Association and "the number one distributor of fiber glass patio covers." Vladimir Gimenko (Michael Pataki) is the Russian agent seeking to return Mikhy to the Motherland; Gwyn Bates (Rae Allen) is widower Max's romantic interest. Hal Cooper and Rod Parker composed the theme.

PHYLLIS

see THE MARY TYLER MOORE SHOW

POLICE WOMAN

NBC, 9.13.74 to 8.30.78

Lee Ann "Pepper" Anderson (Angie Dickinson) is a police sergeant with the Criminal Conspiracy Division of the Los Angeles Police Department. Pepper, whose first name is also given as Suzanne, lives at 102 Crestview Drive; her phone number is 514-7915. Her car's license plate number is 635 CIN, and her sister Cheryl (Nicole Kallis) attends the Austin School for Learning Disabilities. Before becoming a policewoman, Pepper was a high fashion model who quit the business when she felt her life was getting boring.

Pepper's co-workers are Sergeant Bill Crowley (Earl Holliman) and Investigators Joe Stiles (Ed Bernard) and Pete Royster (Charles Dierkop). Bibi Besch appears as Bill's ex-wife, Jackie; Keenan Wynn and Bettye Ackerman as Pepper's Uncle Ben and Aunt Helen Fletcher. Kan-

di Keith appears as Joe's wife, Harriet, in several episodes. Morton Stevens composed the theme. In the original pilot, "The Gamble," which aired on "Police Story" (3.26.74), Angie Dickinson played Lisa Beaumont, a vice-squad detective, and Bert Convy played Bill Crowley.

THE POPCORN KID

CBS, 3.23.87 to 4.24.87

Lynne Holly Brickhouse (Faith Ford), Scott Creaseman (Bruce Norris), Gwen Stuthlemeyer (Penelope Ann Miller) and William Dawson (Jeffrey Joseph) run the popcorn concession at the Majestic Theater, a movie palace in Kansas City. The theater is located at 2222 Algonquin Parkway, and the biggest event in its history was an Ed Asner Film Festival in honor of Ed Asner's visiting the theater. Deborah May played Lynne's mother, Yvonne, and James Staley appeared as Scott's father, Beryl, a salesman at Patio City. Gary Portnoy and Judy Hart Angelo composed the theme.

PRISONER: CELL BLOCK H

Syndicated, 1980

Principal Cast: Peita Toppano (*Karen Travers*), Kerry Armstrong (*Lynnette Warner*), Val Lehman (*Bea Smith*), Carol Burns (*Franky Doyle*), Colette Mann (*Doreen Anderson*), Margaret Laurence (*Marilyn Mason*), Mary Ward (*Jeannie Brooks*), Sheila Florance (*Elizabeth Birdsworth*), Elspeth Ballantyne (*Meg Jackson*), Fiona Spence (*Vera Bennett*), Patsy King (*Erica Davidson*)

Trivia: A drama about life in the Wentworth Detention Center, a women's prison in Melbourne, Australia.

The Prisoners: Karen Angela Travers, also known as Karen Healey, was born in Melbourne on August 27, 1954. Karen, a Roman Catholic, has blue eyes, brown hair, weighs 119 pounds, and is five feet, three inches tall. She was a schoolteacher who is sentenced to life imprisonment for killing her husband (Karen, who is deeply religious, offered no defense at her trial, other than to claim her husband was brutal). Her distinguishing marks are burns on her back.

Lynnette Jane Warner, born September 7, 1959, is single, also a Roman Catholic, and has no distinguishing marks. Lynnette has blue eyes, brown hair, weighs 105 pounds, and is five feet, one inch tall. Her qualifications: nanny. Lynnette, a naive country girl (born in Melbourne) was sentenced to ten years for kidnapping and attempting to murder the child of her employer (she claims she is completely innocent).

Bea Alice Smith, also known as Bea Carruthers, is a widow born in Hobart on February 2, 1938. Bea, a Methodist, weighs 138 pounds, is five feet, six inches tall, has brown eyes and gray hair and no distinguishing marks. She is a qualified hairdresser and was convicted, initially, of murdering her co-worker. Released on parole after serving ten years, she was later recommitted after murdering her husband. The toughest of the women, Bea is the undisputed leader of the prison society and constantly at odds with Franky.

Freida "Franky" Joan Doyle is single and was born in Melbourne on April 17, 1948. She was sentenced to life for armed robbery and murder. Franky weighs 147 pounds, is five feet, six inches tall and has brown hair and green eyes. Her religion is Salvation Army and her qualifications read shop assistant. Franky, who has naked women tattooed on her breasts, is a lesbian with an unrequited passion for Karen.

Doreen May Anderson, also known as Debbie Raye, is unmarried and the mother of a young son. She was born in Melbourne on June 15, 1953, weighs 132 pounds, is five feet, five-and-one-half inches tall, has blue eyes, black hair and no qualifications. Her religion is also Salvation Army and she has tattoos on her arms. The sometimes childlike Doreen, who was a battered child, is weak in character and easily led into crime. She has many petty convictions, but was sentenced to four years for breaking and entering.

Marilyn Anne Mason, also known as

Mandy, is unmarried and the mother of one child. She has no distinguishing marks, is a qualified fashion model, and her religion is Church of England. Marilyn was born on March 3, 1956 in Melbourne, weighs 112 pounds, is five feet, four-and-a-half inches tall, and has blue eyes and blonde hair. Sentenced to 12 months for soliciting, Marilyn has many prior convictions for soliciting and stealing and is known to have worked in a porno movie.

Jeannie "Mum" Brooks, a widow, has two children, and is also known as Jeannie Bradley. She is Presbyterian, weighs 97 pounds, is five feet, two inches tall, has blue eyes and gray hair, and was born in Melbourne on May 7, 1918. Mum has no distinguishing marks and is qualified as a shop assistant. She received a life sentence for murdering her husband; she is well regarded by her fellow inmates and prison officials alike. Mum is a gentle soul who befriends the young newcomers to prison and spends much of her time tending the prison garden.

Elizabeth Josephine Birdsworth, also known as Lizzie Lee, was born in Perth on November 5, 1908 and has four grown children. She is the eldest of the inmates, has gray hair, green eyes, weighs 101 pounds and is five feet, two inches tall. Her religion is Other Christian. With no distinguishing marks, she was sentenced to life for mass murder (Lizzie is an alcoholic and a kleptomaniac with many convictions for theft. She was sentenced for "accidentally" killing four sheep shearers by poisoning their food "to teach them a lesson"). She is obsessed with escaping.

Other Characters: Meg Jackson is the sympathetic prison guard (called "Warder") and has a happy relationship with her husband, prison psychologist Bill Jackson (Don Baker).

Vera Bennett is the harsh and ruthless prison guard who hopes her rule of iron will get her the prison governorship. Vera, who is single, lives at home with her invalid mother, has no social life and lives for her job at the prison.

Erica Davidson is the prison governor, and has a secret personal life. She is capable of running the prison, but her approach keeps her remote and she fails to understand the frustrations of the prisoners.

Relatives: Kim Deacon (Mum's granddaughter, *Judith Anne*), Ben Gabriel (Lynnette's father, *Ted Warner*), Greg Stroud (Franky's brother, *Gary Doyle*), Anne Haddy (Doreen's mother, *Alice Hemmings*), Judith Dick (Lizzie's daughter, *Marcia Huntley*), Michelle Argue (Lizzie's granddaughter, *Josie Huntley*)

Theme: "On the Inside," vocal by Lynne Hamilton

PRIVATE SECRETARY

CBS, 2.1.53 to 9.10.57

Principal Cast: Ann Sothern (*Susie McNamara*), Don Porter (*Peter Sands*), Ann Tyrrell (*Vi Praskins*)

Trivia: Susie Camille McNamara is private secretary to Peter Sands, a theatrical agent who runs International Artists, Inc. Before working for Peter, Susie was a WAVE for three years (she has been working for Peter for eight years when the series begins). She takes 125 words per minute shorthand and types 65 words per minute. Susie, who has blue eyes, is a Libra, and was born in Mumford, Iowa (her ancestors came from Scotland). She lives in the Brockhurst Apartments on East 92nd Street in New York City, and on her first day at work Peter took her out to eat at the Penguin Club. When Susie prepares Peter's coffee, she measures the milk with an eyedropper.

Peter, whose office phone number is Plaza 5-1955, was in the Air Force for four years before founding International Artists. In high school, Peter was voted "Most Likely to Succeed," and in an early episode he referred to "a remarkable talent he discovered: Harriet Lake" (Ann Sothern's real name). Peter's birth sign is Aries. The agency is located on the 22nd floor (Suite 2201) of an unnamed Manhattan building.

Vi Praskins, the agency's receptionist, began working for Peter on October 23; her birth sign is Scorpio. In the closing theme, a Remington-brand typewriter is seen (later it is replaced by an IBM machine).

Relatives: Gloria Winters (Susie's niece, *Patty*), Alma Townsend (Peter's mother, *Mrs. Sands*), Marie Devaux (*Peter's grandmother*)

Unseen Relatives: Vi's Aunt Olive, Vi's grandfather (who was one-eighth Potawatomi Indian), Vi's Aunt Martha, Peter's Aunt Julie (who lives in Chicago)

Note: The show is also known as "Susie" and "The Adventures of Susie."

QUANTUM LEAP

NBC, 3.26.89 to

Quantum Leap, a secret government project hidden in the desert, is concerned with time travel. When the government threatens to cut off its funding, quantum physics professor Dr. Sam Beckett (Scott Bakula) takes matters into his own hands and steps into the unit's acceleration chamber to prove that a man can be sent into time—and vanishes. He is sent back in time but can travel only within thirty years of his own lifetime, beginning in 1953 (when he was born), until a systems malfunction traps Sam in time—where he must remain until he can be retrieved. Through brainwave transmissions, Sam receives holographic assistance from Al (Dean Stockwell), an Admiral who is a project observer (Al can only be seen and heard by Sam).

While bouncing around in time, Sam finds himself assuming the identities of people he never knew in order to correct mistakes they made and set history straight (that is, according to what a computer named Ziggy deems it should be). The audience sees Sam in the various roles but other characters see the person Sam has become (when Sam looks into a mirror, he too sees the person whose identity he has assumed). When a mission is completed, Sam is propelled (leaps) into another time period and the person—man or woman—is restored to his or her normal self.

Al, who carries a slightly defective,

174

miniature Ziggy, has known Sam for many years. Al grew up in an orphanage and had a pet roach named Kevin. He ran away from the orphanage to join a circus and later enlisted in the Navy. In 1969, he married a girl named Beth (Susan Diol), the only girl he really loved, he says. An ensign at the time, Al was sent to Vietnam and was soon missing in action and presumed dead. When he was found in 1973, Beth had remarried. Al never returned to her.

Sam was born and raised on a farm and developed a fear of heights at the age of nine (after seeing a Tarzan movie, he attempted and failed to swing from a homemade vine he rigged from the barn roof). Sam's romantic interest is a woman named Donna (Terri Hatcher), a fellow scientist on the Star Bright Project in 1972. Mike Post composed the theme.

RAGS TO RICHES

NBC, 3.9.87 to 1.15.88

Principal Cast: Joseph Bologna (*Nick Foley*), Bridget Michele (*Diane Foley*), Kimiko Gelman (*Rose Foley*), Tisha Campbell (*Marva Foley*), Blanca DeGarr (*Patti Foley*), Heidi Zeigler (*Mickey Foley*), Heather McAdam (*Nina Foley*), Douglas Seale (*John Clapper*)

Trivia: In an attempt to refine his flamboyant lifestyle, millionaire frozen-food king Nick Foley adopts six orphan girls (Diane, Rose, Marva, Patti, Mickey and Nina). The series, set in Los Angeles in 1962, features musical numbers as it relates the adventures of five street-smart girls who have vowed to remain a family (Nina was dropped after the first episode when her mother reclaimed her).

Nick, the son of a bricklayer, owns Foley Frozen Foods. His real name is Nicholas Folitini. He owns a mansion in Bel Air (address not given) and is a member of the Green Hills Country Club. His phone number is Klondike 5–4023 and his car's license plate number is RDH 352.

Before being adopted, the girls lived in Room 204 of the Margaret Keating Home for Orphan Girls. The names of the schools the girls attend are not given. Marva and Rose work on their high school newspaper, the *Cougar*; Patti hopes to become a writer; Marva seeks a career in the world of high finance; Diane drives a car with license plate EZP 374; and Mickey, the youngest, has a pet guinea pig named Herbert. The girls buy their snack foods at Crawley's Market.

Relatives: Gina Hecht (Patti's mother, *Gloria Lang*), Joe Cortese (Nick's brother, *Frankie Folitini*), Richard Grieco (Nick's godson, *Billy Galanto*)

Theme: "Rags to Riches," by Peter Robinson and Mark Mueller

RAISING MIRANDA

CBS, 11.5.88 to 12.31.88

She reads *Teen World* magazine and concludes each episode with an entry in her diary that reads "Confidentially, Miranda." Miranda Marshack (Royana Black) is a teenage girl who lives at 85 Muskeegan Road in Racine, Wisconsin, with her father, Don (James Naughton), a construction worker with the Big M Construction Company. (Miranda's mother deserted the family some time ago and is not seen.) Miranda and her friend Marcine Marie Lindquist (Amy Lynne) attend Racine High School; Lee Garlington appears as Marcine's mother, Helen. Martin Silvestri, Jeremy Stone and Joel Higgins composed the theme.

RAMONA

Syndicated, 9.88

Nine-year-old Ramona Quimby (Sarah Polley), her mother, Dori (Lynda Mason Green), her father, Bob (Barry Flatman), and her sister, Beezis (Lori Chodos), live in an unnamed town in Canada. Bob works for Frozen Foods, Inc.; their fussy cat is named Picky Picky; and the family station wagon's license plate number is YEW 576. Kirsten Bishop, an almost deadringer for Lynda, plays Dori's sister, Beatrice (after whom Beezis is named; when Ramona was learning to speak, "Beatrice" became "Beezis"). Bea's sedan's license plate number is 531 AJX. Fred Mollin composed the theme. The series is based on the books by Beverly Cleary.

THE RAY MILLAND SHOW

CBS, 9.17.53 to 7.15.54

Professor Ray McNutley (Ray Milland), who lives in a white frame house at 187 Maple Terrace in the town of Lynnhaven with his wife, Peggy (Phyllis Avery), teaches English at the Lynnhaven College for Women. His phone number is Lynnhaven 3325. His neighbor Pete "Petey" Thomson (Gordon Jones) is a real estate salesman and calls Ray "Ray Boy." They love fishing and together purchased a boat called the *Hesperus* (a used 32-foot fishing boat that sank twice and had an engine that blew up). Pete's phone number is Lynnhaven 2556 and he drives a green convertible with white walls and a locked trunk full of House for Sale signs. Jacqueline DeWit plays Pete's wife, Ruth, and Minerva Urecal, Josephine Bradley, the college dean.

The series, also known as "Meet Mr. McNutley," underwent a format change for its second season (9.16.54 to 9.30.55) in which Ray moves to California to become a drama professor at Comstock University, a co-educational college. Ray and Peggy's last name was changed to McNulty; Lloyd Corrigan played Dean Dodsworth and David Stollery appeared as Peggy's boy-genius cousin, Grover.

THE REAL McCOYS

ABC, 10.3.57 to 9.20.62
CBS, 9.24.62 to 9.22.63

Principal Cast: Walter Brennan (*Amos McCoy*), Richard Crenna (*Luke McCoy*), Kathleen Nolan (*Kate McCoy*), Lydia Reed (*Hassie McCoy*), Michael Winkelman (*Little Luke McCoy*), Tony Martinez (*Pepino Garcia*)

Trivia: "Want you to meet the family known as the Real McCoys. That's Grandpappy Amos, head of the clan; he roars like a lion but he's gentle as a lamb; and now here's Luke who beams with joy since he made Kate Mrs. Luke McCoy . . . " Following the death of Ben McCoy, his brother Amos inherits the McCoy Ranch in the San Fernando Valley. Amos, a widower and head of the family; his grandson, Luke; Luke's wife, Kate; and Luke's sister and brother, Hassie and Little Luke, leave their dirt-poor farm in West Virginia for California to begin new lives.

The McCoys' phone number is Valley 4276; Amos, who was born in 1894 in Smokey Corners, West Virginia, and his wife (now deceased) honeymooned in Wheeling, West Virginia, in "the best boarding house in town" (their bridal suite was next to the kitchen). He has a Model-T Ford he calls Gertrude, and he is a member of the Royal Order of the Mystic Nile Lodge. Luke, who calls Kate "Sugar Babe" ("Honey Babe" in the pilot) honeymooned at the Colonial Palms Motel, Room 204. "Margie" was the song to which Luke and Kate danced when they first met. Luke's parents are deceased; he and Kate care for his sister Hassie and his brother Little Luke (Luke's parents were so excited when the baby arrived they named him Luke—forgetting they already had a son named Luke).

Hassie, who attends Valley High School (as does Little Luke), belongs to the Alpha Beta Sigma sorority. She has her hair done at Armand's Beauty Shop and she was the first one in her school to wear the latest craze from France—the Bouffant Beehive (which cost her $3.50). Pepino, the McCoys' farmhand, calls Amos "Señor Grandpa." The McCoys' milk cow is named Bessie. In 1962, after Kate's death, Janet DeGore joined the cast as Louise Howard, a widow (and romantic interest for Luke) who purchases the farm next to the McCoys.

Relatives: Jack Oakie (Luke's uncle, "Rightly" Ralph McCoy), Nora Hayden (Amos's cousin, Elviry Goody), Butch Patrick (Louise's son, Gregg Howard), Joan Blondell (Louise's aunt, Winifred Jordan)

Theme: "The Real McCoys," by Harry Ruby

REMINGTON STEELE

NBC, 10.1.82 to 9.16.86

Principal Cast: Stephanie Zimbalist (*Laura Holt*), Pierce Brosnan (*Remington Steele*), Doris Roberts (*Mildred Krebs*), James Read (*Murphy Michaels*), Janet De-May (*Bernice Foxx*)

Trivia: Shortly after graduating from Stamford University, Laura Holt, a hopeful private investigator, becomes an apprentice detective with the Havenhurst Detective Agency. When she feels she is ready, she quits and opens Laura Holt Investigations. As her business begins to fail, she figures that perhaps a female private investigator is "too feminine," and invents a mythical male boss named Remington Steele. She changes the company's name to Remington Steele Investigations, and suddenly business is booming.

A suave and sophisticated thief who 12 years earlier was a boxer known as "The Kilkearney Kid" comes to Los Angeles to steal the Royal Lavulite Diamonds, which Laura has been hired to protect. On the case, Laura meets the thief, who assumes the identity of Remington Steele to get himself out of a jam and later talks Laura into making him her partner.

Remington Steele Investigations is located in Suite 1157 of an unidentified building. The agency phone number is given as 555-9450, 555-3535 and 555-9548.

Laura, who weighs 110 pounds, lives at 800 10th Street, Apartment 3A, in a building owned by the Commercial Management Corporation. Her phone number is 213-555-6235, and she has a cat named Nero. Laura's car's license plate number is JEL 1525 (also seen as 1E49463) and her car telephone number is T7328. In college, Laura and three girlfriends were known as "the Four East" (they shared a fourth floor dorm room); Laura is plagued by "the Holt Curse"—a craving for chocolate candy. Laura's nickname is "Binky" (not explained). As a kid "Atomic Man" was Laura's favorite TV show.

"The Mysterious Remington Steele" is just that—mysterious. Born in Ireland and apparently an orphan, he was taught the fine art of crime by Daniel Chalmers (Efrem Zimbalist Jr.), a master con artist. He now lives at 1594 Rossmore Street, Apartment 5A, and drives a 1936 Auburn, license plate R. STEELE, and a blue Mercedes with the license plate IDR 0373. His favorite TV show is "The Honeymooners" and he projects motion pictures onto real life, most often solving cases based on plots from old movies. On his living room wall are movie posters from *Casablanca*, *Notorious*, *Hotel Imperial* and *The Thin Man*.

Murphy Michaels was Laura's original assistant (first season) and Bernice Foxx (whom Steele called "Miss Wolf") was her receptionist. Mildred Krebs, a former IRS auditor, replaced both characters from the second season on. Michael Constantine played George E. Mulch, the "idea man" who complicates Laura's life; and James Tolkan, Norman Keyes, the Vigilance Insurance Company detective who plagues Steele (seeking to uncover his true identity). The show's gimmick is the use of "Steele" in every title (e.g., "You're Steele the One for Me" and "Etched in Steele").

Relatives: Beverly Garland (Laura's mother, *Abigail Holt*), Maryedith Burrell (Laura's married sister, *Frances Piper*), Michael Durrell (Frances's husband, *Donald Piper*), Albert Macklin (Mildred's nephew, *Bernard*)

Theme: "Remington Steele," by Henry Mancini

THE RENEGADES

ABC, 3.4.83 to 4.8.83

This series is a "Mod Squad" update about seven gang members who are recruited by Lieutenant Frank Marciano (James Luisi) to form a special undercover Los Angeles police unit called the Renegades.

The Renegades: Patrick Swayze (*Bandit*; of the Aces gang), Tracy Scoggins (*Tracy*; of the Satin Dolls gang), Randy Brooks (*Eagle*; of the Chiefs gang), Robert Thaler (*Dancer*; of the Bombers gang), Brian

Tochi (*Dragon*; of the Shanghai Sheiks gang), Fausto Bara (*Gaucho*; of the Wild Cats Gang) and Paul Mones (*J. T.*; of the Romans Gang)

In the two-hour pilot (ABC, 8.11.82), Cheryl Paris played Tracy, Philip Casnoff, Dancer, Peter Kwong, Dragon and Angel Granados Jr. played Gaucho. Barry DeVorzon and Joseph Conlon composed the theme.

RHODA

CBS, 9.9.74 to 12.9.78

Principal Cast: Valerie Harper (*Rhoda Morganstern*), Julie Kavner (*Brenda Morganstern*), David Groh (*Joe Gerard*), Nancy Walker (*Ida Morganstern*), Harold Gould (*Martin Morganstern*), Lorenzo Music (*voice of Carlton the Doorman*)

Trivia: "Rhoda" is a "Mary Tyler Moore Show" spinoff in which Rhoda Morganstern leaves Minneapolis and returns to New York City (she was born in the Bronx) for a two-week vacation. She moves into her sister Brenda's apartment (2-D) at 332 West 46th Street. Shortly afterward, her mother, Ida, arranges a blind date for her with Joe Gerard, the owner of the New York Wrecking Company. Joe, who is divorced and the father of a 10-year-old son, falls in love with Rhoda and he and Rhoda soon marry. They set up housekeeping in Apartment 9-B in Brenda's building and Rhoda begins her own decorating business, Windows by Rhoda.

Two years later, Rhoda and Joe divorce. Rhoda now lives in Apartment 6-G (also given as 4-G) and works for the Doyle Costume Company. Brenda, a bank teller, works at the First Security Bank, Midtown Branch, in Manhattan. Carlton, who is never seen, is the building doorman ("Hello, this is Carlton, your doorman . . . "). Rhoda's parents, Ida and Martin, live in the Bronx at 3517 Grand Concourse (near Fordham Road). Rhoda, who was born in December 1941, won the third-grade science fair with a model of the human brain; as a teenager she was an usherette at the Loewe's State Thea-

ter; and, before becoming slender, was a member of the Weight Loss Club.

Relatives: Joan Van Ark (*Joe's ex-wife, Marian Gerard*), Todd Turquand and Shane Sinutko (*Joe's son, Donny Gerard*), Robert Alda (*Joe's father, Paul Gerard*), Paula Victor (*Joe's mother, Ruth Gerard*), Ruth Gordon (*Carlton's mother*)

Theme: "Rhoda's Theme," by Billy Goldenberg

THE RIFLEMAN

ABC, 9.30.58 to 7.1.63

Following the death of his wife, Lucas McCain (Chuck Connors) and his son, Mark (Johnny Crawford), leave their home in "the Nations" and head west to begin new lives. In the town of North Fork, New Mexico, Lucas purchases the old Dunlap Ranch, a 4100-acre spread that is located four miles south of town.

In the Nations, Lucas was called "the Rifleman," the fastest man with a .44–40 hair-trigger action rifle with a special hoop lever (that allows normal firing when a special screw is loose; rapid firing when the screw is tightened). In the opening theme, Lucas fires twelve shots; the rifle can fire eight times in two-and-a-half seconds. Lucas's horse is named Razor; Mark's horse is Blue Boy.

Other Regulars: Paul Fix (*Marshal Micah Torrance*), John Harmon (*Eddie Holstead*, owner of the Madera House Hotel), Patricia Blair (*Lou Mallory*, the owner of the Mallory House Hotel), Bill Quinn (*Sweeney*, the Last Chance Saloon bartender), Joan Taylor (*Millie Scott*, owner of the General Store)

Relatives: Jerome Courtland (*Lucas's brother-in-law, Johnny Gibbs*), Thomas Gomez (*Artemis Quarles*, Lucas's cousin by marriage), Gloria DeHaven (*Eddie's daughter Lillian Holstead*), Cheryl Holdridge (*Millie's niece, Sally Walker*)

Herschel Burke Gilbert composed the theme.

RIPTIDE

NBC, 1.3.83 to 4.18.86
8.22.86 (1 episode)

Nick Ryder (Joe Penny), Cody Allen (Perry King) and Murray "Boz" Bozinski (Thom Bray) run Pier 53 Investigations (later called the Riptide Detective Agency), located at Slip 7, Pier 56 in King Harbor in southern California. Their houseboat (and office) is the *Riptide* and their telephone number is 555–8300. The trio, who frequent the Straightaways Restaurant, have a motorboat called *Ebb Tide* and a pink helicopter called the *Screaming Mimi* (I.D. number N698). Murray has a robot called "the Roboz" and their friend, Mama Jo (Anne Francis), owns the cruise ship, *Contessa*.

Ted Quinlan (Jack Ging, 1983–85) and Joanna Parisi (June Chadwick) are lieutenants with the King Harbor Police Department; Geena Davis appears as Boz's sister, Melba Bozinski. Mike Post and Pete Carpenter composed the theme.

THE ROPERS

ABC, 3.13.79 to 5.22.80

This is a "Three's Company" spinoff in which Stanley and Helen Roper (Norman Fell and Audra Lindley) sell their apartment house in Santa Monica and move to a condominium at 46 Peacock Drive in Chevia Hills, California. Their phone number is 555–3099 and they live in the Royal Dale Condominium Townhouse Complex. Their neighbors (at 44 Peacock Drive) are Jeffrey P. Brookes III (Jeffrey Tambor), a real-estate salesman, his wife, Anne (Patricia McCormack), and their son, David (Evan Cohan). Helen, who was a USO entertainer during the war, has a dog named Muffin and a parakeet named Stanley. Helen's mother calls Stanley "Herbert."

Relatives: Dena Dietrich (Helen's sister, *Ethel Armbruster*), Lucille Benson (*Helen's mother*), Dulcie Pullman (Helen's younger sister, *Hilda*), Rod Colbin (Ethel's husband, *Hubert*)

Joe Raposo composed the theme.

"The Ropers" is based on the British series "George and Mildred" (Brian Murphy and Yootha Joyce as George and Mildred Roper, a retired couple who live at 46 Peacock Crescent in Hampton Wick, Middlesex, England).

ROSEANNE

ABC, 10.18.88 to

Principal Cast: Roseanne Barr (*Roseanne Conner*), John Goodman (*Dan Conner*), Lecy Goranson (*Becky Conner*), Sara Gilbert (*Darlene Conner*), Michael Fishman (*D. J. Conner*), Laurie Metcalf (*Jackie Harris*)

Trivia: It was in Lanford High School that they met. Roseanne Harris had dreams of becoming a writer and penning the great American novel. Dan Conner was an athlete, a member of the school's football team, and had the nickname "Yor." They married and later set up housekeeping at 714 Delaware Street in Lanford, Illinois. She became a housewife and the mother of three children (Becky, Darlene and D. J.); he became the owner of the Four Aces Construction Company (his truck's license plate is 846 759C). Roseanne's jobs (from when the series began): assembly-line worker at Wellman Plastics; bartender at the Lobo Lounge; order taker at Divine Chicken; telephone soliciter for Discount House Magazines; clean-up lady at Art's Beauty Parlor. Roseanne and Dan both have accounts at the Greyrock Bank. Dan reads the girlie magazine *Girls, Girls, Girls*.

Becky, their eldest child (born March 15, 1975), attends Lanford High School. She is sweet and feminine, loves clothes and shopping at the mall and is closer to her mother than to Dan. Her allowance is $10 per week.

Darlene, the middle child, first attends South Elementary School, then Lanford High. She is a tomboy and nasty; she loves sports and helping her father put up dry wall. She is closer to her father than she is to Roseanne. Her allowance is $5 per week.

D. J., the youngest child, attends South Elementary School. Jackie Harris,

Roseanne's sister, lives in Apartment A (address not given) and is an officer with the Lanford Police Department. She did her six weeks' basic training in Springfield and, as children, she and Roseanne attended the Wild Oaks Summer Camp.

Relatives: John Randolph (Roseanne's father, *Al Harris*), Estelle Parsons (Roseanne's mother, *Beverly Harris*), Ann Wedgeworth (Dan's mother, *Audrey Conner*), Ned Beatty (Dan's father, *Ed Conner*)

Theme: "Roseanne," by Howard Pearl and Dan Foliart

ROUTE 66

CBS, 10.7.60 to 9.18.64

Tod Stiles (Martin Milner), the son of a wealthy father who is left penniless after his death, and Buzz Murdock (George Maharis), an employee of Tod's father (who was abandoned as an infant and grew up in an orphanage in New York's Hell's Kitchen), pool their resources and purchase a 1960 Chevrolet (license plate 20-7876). Their experiences as they wander across the highway of U.S. Route 66 are related. (In 1963–64 episodes, Tod's partner is Linc Case, a Vietnam war veteran, played by Glen Corbett.)

Tod, whose birthday was given as March 12, 1936, married a woman named Mona (Barbara Eden) in the last episode. His parents (not seen) are Lee and Martha; Beatrice Straight appeared as his aunt, Kitty Chamberlain (his father's sister). Buzz, who was born in September 1937, has social security number 100-20-0853. Linda Watkins appears as his mother; his father, Thomas, is not seen. His parents' phone number in Landor, Texas, is (311) Klondike 5–2368. Nelson Riddle composed the theme.

ROXIE

CBS, 4.1.87 to 4.8.87

Roxanne "Roxie" Brinkerhoff (Andrea Martin) is the program director of WNYV, Channel 66, a financially troubled UHF station in New York City. The station's slogan is "Pictures That Fly Through the Air." Mitchell Lawrence is Roxie's husband, Michael, a teacher, and Jack Riley is Leon Buchanan, the star of "The Larry the Lizard Show." Jerry Stiller played the role of Leon in the original, unaired pilot.

The series was originally titled "Andrea Spinelli-Brinkerhoff" and actually had its beginnings as the "Stage Mother" episode of "Kate and Allie" (12.1.86), in which Andrea Martin played Eddie Gordon, the slightly dizzy manager of Channel G, a cable TV station in Manhattan.

THE ROY ROGERS SHOW

NBC, 10.4.51 to 6.9.57

Roy Rogers, "King of the Cowboys," and his wife, Dale Evans, "Queen of the West," own the Double-R-Bar Ranch in Mineral City. Their foreman, Patrick "Pat" Aloysius Brady (Pat Brady) has a temperamental jeep named Nellybelle. Roy's horse is Trigger; Dale's horse is Buttermilk; Pat's horse is Phineas; Roy's dog is named Bullet. Roy Rogers and Dale Evans sing the theme, "Happy Trails to You," which was composed by Dale Evans.

SALVAGE 1

ABC, 1.29.79 to 11.11.79

Harry Broderick (Andy Griffith) owns the Jettison Scrap and Salvage Company in California, an antique Rolls Royce with license plate NNT 516 and the *Vulture*, a homemade 30-foot by 10-foot rocketship he uses to recover items for clients. Harry's mobile number is 546-2144.

He has two partners: Melanie "Mel" Slozar (Trish Stewart), an explosives expert who developed the special fuel, Mono-hydrozyne, that powers the *Vulture* (in ABC's 1.20.79 pilot episode, Mel becomes the first woman on the moon when she and Skip salvage moon junk); and Addison "Skip" Carmichael (Joel Higgins), a "crazy" ex-astronaut who wrote a book, *The Trans-Linear Vector Principal* (describing a way of traveling to the moon using reduced speed and special fuel), and worked as a used-car salesman (company name not given) before joining Harry.

Richard Jaeckel plays Jack Klinger, the FBI agent (Department of Justice) who keeps tabs on Harry and his illegal flights; Jacqueline Scott is Lorene, Harry's ex-wife; and Heather McAdam is Michelle Ryan, the orphan Mel adopts. Walter Scharf composed the theme.

THE SANDY DUNCAN SHOW

see FUNNY FACE

SARA

NBC, 1.23.85 to 5.29.85

Sara McKenna (Geena Davis) is an idealistic lawyer with the Bay Area Legal Group (later changed to Cooper & Associates Law Firm) in San Francisco. The firm is located at 3600 Bay Street (same building for both firms). Sara, a statuesque beauty, lives at 46 Willow Place and her telephone number is 555–3436. Alfre Woodard plays attorney Roz Dupree, Bill Maher plays attorney Marty Lang and Bronson Pinchot portrays lawyer Dennis Kemper.

K Callan appears as Sara's mother, Claire McKenna; Jill Schoelen as Sara's cousin, Emily; and Arthur Lessac as Dennis's grandfather. Tom Scott composed the theme, "You've Got What It Takes."

SAVED BY THE BELL

NBC, 8.20.89 to

Students Jesse Spano (Elizabeth Berkley), Kelly Kaposki (Tiffani-Amber Thiessen), Lisa Turtle (Lark Voorhies), Zack Morris (Mark-Paul Gosselaar), Screech Powers (Dustin Diamond) and A. C. Slater (Marco Lopez) attend Bayside High School in the fictional town of Palisades, California. Their after-school hangout is the Max, a hamburger joint.

Kelly, the prettiest girl in the school, loves windsurfing and volleyball, and was voted "Bayside High Homecoming Queen." Although her teeth appear perfect, she fears someone will discover she wears a retainer at night. Jesse, the tallest one of the group, is sensitive about her height, very pretty, studious, very smart and an excellent dancer (she attended dance camp as a kid). Lisa, a stunning black girl, was the first of the group to get her own credit card (and misuse it). She has locker number 118 and is the object of Screech's affections (a situation that makes her cringe).

Screech, who lives at 88 Edgemont Road, was fifth runner-up in an ALF look-alike contest and has a robot named Kevin. He named his first zit Murray and invented Zit-Off, a blemish cream that removes zits—but later turns the area on which the cream was used maroon. Zack, the "preppy" student, is a natural con artist; and A. C., the school "hunk," is Zack's rival for Kelly's affections. The school principal, Richard Belding (Dennis Haskins), served with the 55th National Guard in Indianapolis and won the 1963 Chubby Checker Twist-Off. Scott Gale composed the theme.

The series had its beginnings as the NBC pilot "Good Morning, Miss Bliss" (7.11.87), in which Hayley Mills played Carrie Bliss, a sixth grade schoolteacher in Indianapolis (a school name is not given). Oliver Clark played the principal, Gerald Belding, and students were Wendy (Samantha Mills), Bradley (Gabriel Damon), Bobby (Jaleel White) and George (Matt Shakman).

In 1988, the Disney Channel presented a series called "Good Morning, Miss Bliss" (11.30 to 12.21.88) that eventually became "Saved By the Bell" on NBC. Hayley Mills plays Carrie Bliss, an eighth grade teacher at J.F.K. Junior High, and the students are Lisa (Lark Voorhies), Karen (Carla Gugino), Zack (Mark-Paul Gosselaar), Screech (Dustin Diamond), Nicole (Heather Hopper) and Mickey (Max Battimo). Dennis Haskins plays Mr. Belding; the hangout is a hamburger place called the Cosmos; the kids are in Homeroom 103; and Carrie (who was dropped for the NBC series) has been teaching for 11 years.

SCARECROW AND MRS. KING

CBS, 10.3.83 to 9.10.87

While being pursued by enemy agents, Lee Stetson (Bruce Boxleitner), a U.S. government secret agent (who operates under the code name "Scarecrow") for the Agency, runs into Amanda King (Kate Jackson), a divorced housewife, and gives her a package to deliver. Amanda takes the package, which is being pursued by the agents, and leaves. Later, Lee tracks her down and, with Amanda's help, plugs a security leak in the Agency.

Because Lee is a professional, and Amanda is an idealistic, unknown (and out-of-work) amateur, she is teamed with him by Billy Melrose (Mel Stewart), the head of the Agency, to form a unique team of undercover agents.

Amanda, the mother of two children, Philip (Paul Stout) and Jamie (Greg Morton), lives at 4247 Maplewood Drive in Arlington, Virginia (the Agency is located in Washington, D.C.). Amanda's telephone number is 555-3100, her children attend Calvin Elementary School; at the Agency, her security level is Fourth Level, 6SA. Lee, who lives at 46 Hamblin Boulevard, and whose car's license plate is 3N6 105, married Amanda on February 13, 1987. The Agency, which was founded by Captain Harry V. Thornton (Howard Duff) in 1954, operates under the cover of International Federal Film.

Beverly Garland plays Amanda's mother, Dotty West; Martha Smith, Agent Francine Desmond; and Arlen Dean Snyder appears as Lee's uncle, Colonel Robert Clayton. In flashback sequences, Bruce Boxleitner played Lee's father, Major Stetson, and Wendie Malick, Lee's mother, Jennie Stetson. Arthur B. Rubinstein composed the theme.

SHEENA, QUEEN OF THE JUNGLE

Syndicated, 1956 to 1957

A young American girl orphaned in Kenya is raised by a noble tribe. The girl (Irish McCalla), who is given the name Sheena, becomes a feared (by evil-doers), white jungle goddess who protects her adopted homeland from evil. Sheena, who has a pet chimpanzee named Chim, is assisted by Bob Rayburn (Christian Drake), a white trader who has made Kenya his home (he gets his supplies at the Evans Trading Post, which is run by Howard Evans, played by John Lang). Sheena uses a horn to summon help from the animals and most often helps Chief Logi (Lee Weaver) of the Inoma Tribe. The series is filmed in Mexico and, according to Irish McCalla, Sheena is 28 years old, 141 pounds, five feet, nine-and-a-half inches tall and measures 39½–24½–38. Anita Ekberg was first chosen to play the role and Mexican acrobat Raul Gaona performed the stunts when Irish injured her arm.

Eli Briskin composed the theme.

THE SIMPSONS

Fox, 1.14.90 to

"The Simpsons" is an adult cartoon about an outrageous family called the Simpsons, who live in the town of Springfield, U.S.A. (which was founded by Jebediah Springfield in the 1840s). Thirty-four-year-old Homer J. Simpson (voice by Dan Castallaneta) is the father, a 239-pound safety inspector in Sector 7G of the Springfield Nuclear Power Plant. His favorite food is pork chops. Marge (voice by Julie Kavner) is his wife, a seemingly content blue-haired housewife who is 34 years old and wears a size 13AA shoe. Their children are Bartholemew J. (voice by Nancy Cartwright), Lisa (voice by Yeardley Smith) and baby Maggie.

"I'm Bart Simpson, who the hell are you?" and "Don't have a cow, man," are but two of the 10-year-old Bart's wisecracking remarks that have made him every parent's nightmare and "the bad boy of TV." Bart, who is in the fourth grade at the Springfield Elementary School, has a pet frog named Froggie and spends more time in detention hall and the principal's office than he does in class. (He is seen in the opening theme writing his punishment on the blackboard for something he did in class; e.g., "I Shall Not Call My Teacher Hot Cakes," "Garlic Gum Is Not Funny" and "I Shall Not Draw Naked Ladies In Class.")

Bart, the undefeated champ of the video game "Slugfest," is also a practical joker and finds amusement in annoying Moe, the bartender at Moe's Tavern, with telephone pranks (e.g., asking Moe to page Al Coholic. Moe would say, of course, "Is there an alcoholic here?"). His favorite TV show is "Krusty the Clown" (a nasty TV clown on whom Bart has based his whole life).

Lisa, who is in the second grade (at the same school as Bart), is a budding saxophone player and precociously intelligent; baby Maggie is the most content of all, calmly observing life while sucking on her pacifier. The kids' favorite video cassette movie is *The Happy Little Elfs* (which Bart can't stand to see anymore). Danny Elfman composed "The Simpsons" theme. (The program originally began as a series of filler sketches on "The Tracey Ullman Show" by cartoonist Matt Groening.)

SMALL WONDER

Syndicated, 9.85 to 9.89

Principal Cast: Tiffany Brissette (*Vicki Lawson*), Dick Christie (*Ted Lawson*), Marla Pennington (*Joan Lawson*), Jerry Supiran (*Jamie Lawson*), Emily Schulman (*Harriet Brindal*), Edie McClurg (*Bonnie Brindal*), William Bogert (*Brandon Brindal*)

Trivia: "She's fantastic, made of plastic, microchips here and there; she's a small wonder, and brings love and laughter everywhere." Voice Input Child Identicate—Vicki for short—is the secret creation of Ted Lawson, a robotics engineer at United Robotronics, who developed Vicki, a very pretty robot, as part of an experiment to help handicapped children.

To conceal Vicki's true nature, and to be able to monitor her learning experiences in a suitable atmosphere, Ted passes her off as his adopted ten-year-old

daughter. Ted lives at 16 Maple Drive with his wife, Joan ("Joanie"), a substitute school teacher, and his son, Jamie; their phone number is 555-6606. Vicki's logic box code number is ML5500; her evil twin robot (prototype) is Vanessa (also played by Tiffany Brissette); and Ted's sophisticated computer program for Vicki is called LES. Vicki sleeps standing up in a closet ("Vicki's Closet") in Jamie's room and she and Jamie attend Washington Grammar School (where Joan also teaches in later episodes). Jamie is a member of the Fearless Five Club and Vicki won first runner-up in the "Little Miss Shopping Mall" contest (although Vicki was the most talented, Ellen Sue Beasley, the daughter of the mall owner, won).

The annoying Brindals are the Lawsons' neighbors. Harriet, who has a crush on Jamie, attends the same school and has a parrot named Polly (later called Waldo); her nosy mother, Bonnie, holds the title of "Miss Lettuce-Head of the San Joaquin Valley"; and Harriet's obnoxious father, Brandon, is Ted's wimpy boss.

Relatives: Jack Manning (Ted's father, *Bill Lawson*), Peggy Converse (Ted's mother, *Evelyn Lawson*), Alice Ghostley (Brandon's sister, *Ida Mae Brendal*), Leslie Bega (Harriet's *Cousin Mary*), David Glassner (Harriet's *Cousin Norman*)

Theme: "She's a Small Wonder," by Rod Alexander and Howard Leeds

THE SMOTHERS BROTHERS SHOW

CBS, 9.17.65 to 9.9.66

Two years after drowning ("lost at sea without his water wings"), Tom Smothers returns to earth as Probationary Angel Agent 009, a wingless apprentice angel who is assigned the eleven western states and Alaska. His assignment is to help people in trouble in order to earn full angel status. Tom takes up residence at the Los Angeles apartment (at 452 Vista Del Mar) of his brother, Dick, an executive with Pandora Publications in Beverly Hills (Dick's car's license plate is PGL 175). Roland Winters plays Dick's boss,

Leonard J. Costello, and Marilyn Scott, Leonard's daughter, Diane. Tom's superior, who is not seen but contacts Tom by phone, is named Ralph—the Temporary Assignment Angel.

In the original, unaired pilot version, Dick was assistant administrative assistant at Amalgamated Consolidated, Inc. The boss, Leonard J. Costello, was played by Alan Bunce, and Julie Parrish played his daughter, Diane. In the series, Tom's first assignment was to spring a jailed Marine so that he could marry his fiancée. In the unaired pilot, Tom's assignment was to break up a gambling ring of old ladies. Tom and Dick Smothers sing "The Theme from the Smothers Brothers Show."

SO THIS IS HOLLYWOOD

NBC, 1.1.55 to 8.19.55

Kim Tracy (Virginia Gibson), an aspiring actress, and Queenie Dugan (Mitzi Green), a stuntwoman, live together in an apartment at the La Paloma Courts on Sweeter Street in Hollywood, California. Queenie, who earns $70 a stunt and is frequently paired with her boyfriend, stuntman Hubie Dodd (Gordon Jones), works for Imperial Artists Studios (the phone number is Hollywood 2211). Their claim to fame is that Queenie once doubled for Jeanette MacDonald and Hubie, a slight bumbler, once doubled for Nelson Eddy.

Kim, who acquires small roles in films, got her first big break when she was screen tested for the role of the younger sister in the film *Dark Rapture* (the publicity department changed her name to Dale Vale for the project).

James Lydon plays Kim's agent, Andy Boone; Raymond Hatton, Mr. Sneed, the women's landlord; Paul Harvey, J. J. Carmichael, head of the studio (who plays golf at the Lakeside Golf Club); and Victor Moore portrays Oliver Hampton, the retired actor who lives next door to Kim and Queenie (there are no numbers on the individual apartment doors). He drives a 1934 Rolls Royce, earns $350 a week as a stock performer and appeared in such films as *Wander Lust, Flight Commander* and *The Last Chance*. William Lava composed the theme, "So This Is Hollywood."

SPACE PATROL

ABC, 3.13.50 to 2.26.55

"High adventure in the wild, vast regions of space. Missions of daring in the name of interplanetary justice. Travel into the future with Buzz Corry, commander-in-chief of the Space Patrol." Buzz Corry (Ed Kemmer) is commander of the Space Patrol, a 30th-century, Earth-based organization that is responsible for the safety of the United Planets (Earth, Mars, Venus, Jupiter and Mercury). The United Planets measure seven-and-one-third billion miles in diameter (it would take light, which travels at 186,000 miles per second, 11 hours to travel from one end of the galaxy to the other). Cadet Happy (Lyn Osborn) is the co-pilot (and famous for his catch phrase "Holy smokin' rockets"—which indicates to Buzz that something is wrong); Tonga (Nina Barra) is a Space Patrol ally; Carol Carlisle (Virginia Hewitt) is the daughter of the Secretary General of the United Planets; and Major "Robbie" Robertson (Ken Mayer) is the security chief of the Space Patrol.

The Space Patrol is based in the man-made city of Terra. Buzz's first ship was the *Battle Cruiser 100*; his second ship was the *Terra IV*, and finally, he commands the *Terra V* (equipped with a time drive and a paralyzer ray, it uses Star Drive to travel in deep space). The rocket ship *XRC* (Experimental Rocket Ship), also known as the Rocket Cockpit Ship, is the only other patrol ship equipped with time travel (via a magnetic time drive). When Cadet Happy was chosen to pilot the *XRC*, his first trip into time was to the New Mexico desert in 1956 at the site of an atomic bomb test. Space cadets vacation at Lake Azur; they wear Space Patrol wrist watches; and Space Patrol flashlights are shaped like the *Terra V*. The Evil Prince Bacarrati (Bela Kovacs) and Agent X (Norman Jolley) were two of Buzz's most diabolical enemies.

In 1950, when the series was seen locally in Los Angeles (over KCEA-TV), Kitt Corry (Glenn Denning), Buzz's brother, was head of the Space Patrol. In 1953, at the height of the 3-D craze, "Space Patrol" became the first series to present an episode in 3-D. In the episode "The Theft of the Rocket Cockpit," Carol mentions that the first Earth-to-Moon flight occurred on October 23, 1966 — an insignificant piece of dialogue that missed the actual date by less than three years.

STINGRAY

NBC, 3.11.86 to 7.31.87

"Sixty-five black Stingray for sale. Barter only. Call 555-7687." A newspaper ad that means help to people in deep trouble; an ad that runs only on Fridays, an ad placed by a mysterious man known only as Stingray (Nick Mancuso). Stingray, sometimes called Ray, drives a 1965 black Corvette Stingray with license plate EGW 769 (later, STINGRAY). He will accept no money for his fee; he asks only to be repaid by a favor when he needs it. Mike Post and Pete Carpenter composed the theme.

SUGAR AND SPICE

CBS, 3.30.90 to 5.25.90

"Sugar and Spice" is the story of two sisters, Vickilyn (Vickilyn Reynolds) and Loretta (Loretta Devine) and their efforts to raise their niece, Toby (LaVerne Anderson). Stephanie Hodge and Gerritt Graham play their neighbors, Bonnie and Cliff Buttram; Dana Hill is Toby's friend, Ginger. Dorian Harewood played Vickilyn's ex-husband, Hank, in one episode.

Vickilyn and Bonnie run a curio shop called Small World Miniatures and Loretta, who was a singer with the group the Chevelles, is a hostess at Café Jacques. Bonnie, an Elvis fan, calls her husband Cliff "Bunny Lips," and is president of the Truckers' Wives Auxiliary. Cliff, a truck driver, calls his 18-wheeler "Jolene" and Bonnie, "Cuddle Buns" and "Prairie Blossom." Toby and Ginger attend Edison High School in Ponca City, California;

Ginger has a pet fish named Freddie. Leslie Pearl, Paul Solovay and Susan Spiegel Solovay composed the theme.

SUGARTIME

ABC, 8.13.77 to 9.3.77
4.10.78 to 5.29.78

Maxx Douglas (Barbi Benton), Diane Zuckerman (Didi Carr) and Maggie Barton (Marianne Black) are three starry-eyed singers who form the group Sugar and perform regularly at the Tryout Room nightclub.

Maxx, born in Texas, is the prettiest of the girls and teaches exercise classes at a club called the Health Spa. Diane, who was born in the Bronx and whose favorite dessert is chocolate cake, is a dental assistant to Dr. Paul Landson (Mark Winkworth). Maggie, the most logical one of the group, teaches dancing to children at the Willow Dancing School. Charles Fleischer plays Lightning Jack Rappaport, a struggling comedian at the Tryout Room, and Wynn Irwin plays Al Marks, the club owner. Barbi Benton, Didi Carr and Marianne Black sing the theme, "Girls, Girls, Girls."

SUNSET BEAT

ABC, 4.21.90 to 4.28.90

The show ABC dropped before most people even knew it was on relates the exploits of a special unit of Los Angeles Police Department undercover cops who pose as rugged bikers (on Harley-Davidsons). The cops are based in an abandoned fire house called the L.A. Hose Company, and their favorite eatery is Tail o' the Pup.

Officer Chic Chesbro (George Clooney) has the bike code X-Ray 4309 and plays guitar in a band called Private Prayer. Officer Bradley Coolidge (Markus Flanagan) teaches at Selmar City College in his spare time; Officer Tim Kelly (Michael DeLuise) is a medical school dropout who hides the fact that he is a cop from his parents; and Officer Tucson Smith (Erik King) had a bit part in the porno flick *Hot*

Coed Fever when he went undercover to bust a porno producer. James Tolken plays their superior, Captain Ray Parker.

Arlene Golonka played Ray's ex-wife, Harriet, and Kathy Karges and Mark Hembrow play Tim's mother and father. The "Sunset Beat" theme was composed by Mike Clink Productions.

SUPERTRAIN
NBC, 2.7.79 to 3.14.79

Engineer Harry Flood (Edward Andrews), nurse Rose Casey (Nita Talbot), social director Dave Noonan (Patrick Collins), chief porter George Boone (Harrison Page) and Dr. Dan Lewis (Robert Alda) are the crew of Supertrain, an atomic-powered, ultramodern streamlined train designed by the TransAllied Corporation to improve passenger service (at speeds of 200 mph, it can travel from New York to Los Angeles in 36 hours). It consists of a sleek engine and nine double-decker passenger coaches. In the revised version of the show (4.7.79 to 5.5.79), Ilene Graff played Penny Whitaker, the social director, and Harrison Page received a promotion to Passenger Relations Officer. Bob Cobert composed the theme.

SYDNEY
CBS, 3.21.90 to 8.6.90

Twenty-five-year-old Sydney Kells (Valerie Bertinelli) is beautiful, single, a sloppy housekeeper and a private investigator for the law firm of Fenton, Benton and Sloane in Century City, Los Angeles. Her private investigator's license number is M83456; the license lists her height as five feet, five inches, her weight, 110 pounds, with eyes and hair, brown (her right thumbprint appears on the left side of the license). Sydney's favorite sandwich is Hershey Bars with almonds on white bread and her favorite drink is chocolate milk. She has a cat named Calvin and has dinner with her mother on Thursday nights. Her favorite hangout is the Blue Collar Bar and she first cried as a child when they replaced Dick York with Dick Sargent on "Bewitched." In the 4.25.90 episode, Valerie was reunited with her former "One Day At a Time" co-star, Pat Harrington Jr., in a story that found Sydney working with a 1940s-style private eye named George Garrity. The Los Angeles *Tribune* printed a story on Sydney called "A Week in the Life of Sydney Kells."

Sydney's friend, Jill (Rebeccah Bush), is a fashion model for Contemporary Fashions. She "likes to lounge around in a bathrobe and sew and wears a lacy push-up bra under her pajama tops." At age 12, she shared her first secret with Sydney—that her hero was Mighty Mouse.

Other Characters: Matthew Perry (Sydney's brother, police officer *Billy Kells*, whose favorite candy is Lemon Heads); Craig Bierko (Sydney's boss, *Matt Keating*); and Barney Martin (*Ray O' Shaughnessey*, the owner of the Blue Collar Bar). Georgia Brown appeared as Sydney's mother, Linda Kells, and Jane Milmore played Matt's girlfriend, Claire (who believes Sydney is "a fat, middle-aged, bald man").

Valerie Bertinelli selected the theme, "Finish What Ya Started," by Eddie Van Halen (her husband).

TABITHA
see BEWITCHED

TAKE FIVE
CBS, 4.1.87 to 4.8.87

Andy Kooper (George Segal) is a divorced public-relations man with the New York firm of Davis and Son. To find solace from the aggravation of his work, he plays banjo with a Dixieland band called the Lenny Goodman Quintet. David Frank composed the theme. The series was originally titled "Kooper with a K."

TALES OF WELLS FARGO
NBC, 3.18.57 to 9.8.62

"Dust over the prairie, dust everywhere, dust covers your face and your hair. Gold is what we carry, stop we don't dare, for Wells Fargo must get it there." James "Jim" Whitcomb Hardy (Dale Robertson) is an agent-troubleshooter for Wells Fargo, Incorporated, a gold transporting business based in the town of Gloribee, near San Francisco, during the 1860s. Shipments are made via Wells Fargo stages; the Overland Stage Lines and the Denver and Rio Grande Railroad service the area. Jim is also the owner of the Haymaker Farm, a cattle ranch near Salt Canyon.

Jebediah "Jeb" Ganés (William Demerest) is the ranch foreman; Beau McCloud (Jack Ging) is Jim's assistant; and the Widow Ovie (Virginia Christine) is Jim's neighbor. The Widow's two beautiful daughters, Miss Tina (Lory Patrick) and Mary Gee Ovie (Mary Jane Saunders) buy their clothes at the Dress Shop in Gloribee. Mary Gee, the younger of the two girls, has a crush on Jim and riles Jeb by using the ranch as a riding stable. Jeb's prize palomino is named Snowball. Steven Darnell plays the town sheriff, Hal Humphrey. Harry Warren composed the theme, "Tales of Wells Fargo." The pilot, "A Tale of Wells Fargo," aired on "The Schlitz Playhouse of Stars" on 12.14.56.

TAMMY

ABC, 9.17.65 to 7.15.66

"Tammy" is an adaptation of the movie series, with Debbie Watson playing TV's Tammy, the pretty Louisiana Bayou girl who was raised by her grandfather after her parents' death. TV changed the last name of Tammy from Tyree to Tarleton, and gave Tammy's grandfather, Mordecai Tarleton (Denver Pyle), another relative who is said to have helped raise her—Uncle Lucius Tarleton (Frank McGrath).

While Tammy still lives on the river boat, the *Ellen B* (named after her grandmother), and has a pet goat Nan and a cow named Beulah, she is said to have completed special courses at Seminole College (as in the movie, *Tammy Tell Me True*). When the series begins, Tammy is seen returning home from secretarial school and shortly afterward securing a job at Brent Enterprises as personal secretary to John Brent (Donald Woods), a wealthy widower. Tammy's ability to type almost 200 words a minute causes friction when she is offered the job over another applicant, Gloria Tate (Linda Marshall). Gloria's mother, Lavinia (Dorothy Green), had hoped that Gloria would get the job and thus increase her chances of marrying Gloria's new boss.

While the series deals with Lavinia's efforts to discredit Tammy (in the hope of getting her fired), it also retains a key element of the feature films: Tammy's ability to overcome adverse situations through her philsophy of love and understanding.

Relatives: Dennis Robertson (Tammy's *Uncle Cletus*), Jeanette Nolan (Tammy's *Aunt Hannah*), Jay Sheffield (John's son, *Stephen Brent*), David Macklin (Lavinia's son, *Peter Tate*), Sal Ponti (Lavinia's cousin, *Beauregard Bassett*), Jeff York (Lavinia's outcast cousin, *Grundy Tate*), and Bella Bruck (Grundy's wife, *Sybelline Tate*)

Jay Livingston and Ray Evans composed the theme.

THE TAMMY GRIMES SHOW

ABC, 9.8.66 to 9.29.66

Tammy Grimes in a ten-episode (only four were aired) series about a beautiful heiress named Tamantha "Tammy" Ward and her elaborate attempts to finance her expensive tastes. Tammy, the customer service relations girl at the Perpetual Savings Bank, lives at 365 Central Park West in New York City (her phone number is 476-7671). She is prohibited from touching her multi-million dollar inheritance until she reaches the age of thirty—a condition of her parents' will that her guardian, her uncle, Simon Grimsley (Hiram Sherman), the president of the Perpetual Savings Bank ("The Bank with a Heart"), strictly enforces. Dick Sargent plays Tammy's twin brother, Terence Ward, and Johnny Williams composed the "Theme from the Tammy Grimes Show."

TAXI

ABC, 9.12.78 to 6.10.82
NBC, 9.30.82 to 7.13.83

Principal Cast: Judd Hirsch (*Alex Reiger*), Marilu Henner (*Elaine Nardo*), Tony Danza (*Tony Banta*), Danny DeVito (*Louie DePalma*), Christopher Lloyd (*Jim "Iggie" Ignatowski*), Jeff Conaway (*Bobby Wheeler*), Andy Kaufman (*Latka Gravas*), Carol Kane (*Simka Gravas*), Rhea Perlman (*Zina Sherman*)

Trivia: 212-555-6382 is the phone number of the Sunshine Cab Company, a Manhattan-based taxi service whose rates are 90 cents for the first mile and 10 cents for each additional mile (later one dollar for the first mile and 15 cents each additional mile). The cabs are washed at Cars-a-Poppin' (located at 23rd Street between 5th and 6th Avenues) and a notice is posted in the garage: "Dayline drivers must report or phone in by 6 A.M. Nightline drivers must report or phone in by 3 P.M." Cab 804, driven by virtually every cabbie, holds the record of half a million miles; Cab 413 is known as "the Widow Maker" and Cab 704 as "the Memory Cab." And, according to Louie DePalma, the nasty dispatcher (whose office is called "the Cage"), all his drivers are losers, people who will never amount to anything. The only cabbie to make it out without returning was James Caan—"But he'll be back. They all come back." The cabbies' hangout is Mario's (a bar-restaurant). The vending machine in the garage dispenses hot coffee, chocolate or soups for 25 cents.

Louie, who lives for his job at the company, has been working there for 15 years—first as a driver, then as a dispatcher. Of all the words in the English language, he most hates the word "accident." He worships money. Although lecherous and mean, he considers himself a ladies' man and will pursue any woman he feels is worthy of him. He had a brief romance with Zina Sherman, the candy vending-machine delivery girl.

Alex Reiger, the eldest of the cabbies and the one the others turn to for help and advice, lives in Apartment 2A (address not identified) and has a dog named Buddy.

Elaine Nardo, the divorced mother of two children (Jennifer and Jason), works part time in an art gallery (name not given) and part time as a cabbie. The only female cabbie with a speaking part (others are seen lingering in the background), she is a natural target for Louie's lecherous ways (he refers to her breasts as "headlights" and has even made a peephole so he can watch Elaine undress in the ladies' room). Elaine, whose maiden name is O'Connor, attended Eastside High School and lives with her kids in Apartment 6A (address not given); Jennifer and Jason attend P.S. 33 in Manhattan.

Tony Banta, the cabbie who aspires to become a world champion boxer, is a middleweight boxer (who loses most of his matches). He served in Vietnam and has two goldfish named George and Wanda.

Bobby Wheeler, the aspiring actor, made his TV debut on the soap opera "For Better, For Worse" as "Skip"; he also made a TV series pilot (title not given) but didn't win the role. (The producers told him he wasn't sexy enough.)

Latka Gravas, the alien (country not identified) with strange customs and speech, is the garage mechanic. He marries Simka, a girl from his homeland, and has an alter ego named Vic Ferrari, a playboy who speaks perfect, unaccented English. Latka's attempt to make money was the ill-fated Grandma Latka's Cookies (which tasted great—but were laced with drugs). While Simka is normally very romantic and very moody, she becomes a beast when her monthly "*crimpka poosh*" time arrives.

Jim "Iggie" Ignatowski, the cabbie who still lives in the 1960s, was a studious, intelligent Harvard man before he turned to drugs (via "funny brownies") and ruined his life. He changed his name from James Caldwell to Jim Ignatowski because he thought Ignatowski was "Star Child" spelled backwards. His heroes are St. Thomas Aquinas, Alan Alda and Louie DePalma. *Star Wars* and *E.T.* are Jim's favorite movies; he was arrested at the 1968 Democratic convention for stealing decorations. Jim bought a racehorse he named Gary for $10,000 and lives in a condemned building in Manhattan. When the building was torn down, Jim went to live with Louie. Jim left a bean bag on the stove, the apartment burned and it cost Jim's wealthy father $29,542 to replace Louie's "stuff." When Jim inherited his father's money, he bought the hangout, Mario's, and changed the name to Jim's Mario's. Jim was also ordained as a minister in the Church of the Peaceful in 1968 and he is sometimes called Reverend Jim.

In the episode "On the Job," the Sunshine Cab Company temporarily goes broke and the cabbies are forced to look for other work. The jobs they found were: a stockbroker on Wall Street (Louie); night watchman in an office building (Alex); secretary for an unnamed company (Elaine); collector for a bookie (Tony); party entertainer for kids (Bobby); and door-to-door encyclopedia salesman (Jim—although he thought he was selling vacuum cleaners).

Relatives: Jack Gilford (Alex's father, *Joe Reiger*), Joan Hackett (Alex's sister, *Charlotte*), Louise Lasser (Alex's ex-wife, *Phyllis Reiger*), Talia Balsam (Alex's daughter, *Cathy Reiger*), Melanie Gaffin (Elaine's daughter, *Jennifer Nardo*), David Mendenhall (Elaine's son, *Jason Nardo*), Julie Kavner (Tony's sister,*Monica Douglas*), Donnelly Rhodes (Tony's father, *Angie Banta*), Richard Foronjy (Louie's brother, *Nick DePalma*), Julia DeVito (Louie's mother, *Gabriella DePalma*), Victor Buono (Jim's father, *Mr. Caldwell*), Walter Olkewicz (Jim's brother, *Tom Caldwell*), Barbara Deutsch (Jim's sister, *Lila Caldwell*), Susan Kellerman (Latka's mother, *Greta Gravas*), Mark Blankfield (Simka's *Cousin Zifka*), Camila Ashland (Zina's mother, *Beth Sherman*), John C. Becker, (Zina's father, *Nathan Sherman*)

Theme: "Theme from Taxi," by Bob James

THE TED KNIGHT SHOW

see TOO CLOSE FOR COMFORT

TENSPEED AND BROWN SHOE

ABC, 1.27.80 to 7.11.80

E. L. "Tenspeed" Turner (Ben Vereen) and Lionel Whitney (Jeff Goldblum) are private detectives and partners in the Los Angeles-based Whitney Investigations. E. L., who says the "E. L." stands for "Early LeRoy," is a street-wise con artist who was born in a taxi cab and studied law at Yale before he was expelled for rigging student elections. Lionel, who attended Pomona College, was a stockbroker with the firm of Gray, Johnson and Smith before he became a detective in order to live the life of adventure he always dreamed about. His favorite reading matter is "A Mark Savage Mystery" novel by Stephen J. Cannell (the show's producer). E. L. calls Lionel a "Brown Shoe—a guy in a three-piece suit with brown shoes, a square, a Dow Jones." Lionel, who was in the pistol club at college, was engaged to marry Bunny LaCrosse (Simone Griffeth); her parents were Herman and Ruth LaCrosse (Robert Webber and Jayne Meadows). Dana Wynter and John Hillerman appear as Lionel's parents, Harriet and William Whitney. Mike Post and Pete Carpenter composed the theme.

THAT GIRL

ABC, 9.8.66 to 9.10.71

Principal Cast: Marlo Thomas (*Ann Marie*), Ted Bessell (*Don Hollinger*)

Trivia: Her dream is to purchase the rights to the book *A Woman's Story* by Joseph Nelson and star in the movie version of it (every actress's dream). She was a member of her college drama club; a member of the Brewster Community Playhouse; and, as a kid, she won a medal for best actress at Camp Winnepoo. She's young, pretty and alive with a dream that somehow, some way, she'll become a star. She's Ann Marie, a small-town girl (from Brewster, New York) who moves to New York City to fulfill her dream.

Ann lives at 344 West 78th Street (Apartment 4D; sometimes mentioned as

2C); later at 627 East 54th Street. She is a member of the Benedict Workshop of the Dramatic Arts, and to support herself between acting jobs she takes whatever work she can find—from perfume sales-girl (at Macy's) to door-to-door shoe sales-girl (for Smart and Stunning Shoes) to waitress (diner not named). She was a meter maid in Brewster before deciding to come to Manhattan.

Ann made her TV debut on an un-named show (she played a bank teller who gets killed; her end credit read "The Girl . . . Ann Marie"). She under-studied famous Broadway actress Sandy Stafford (Sally Kellerman) (the name of the play was not given). Her most embar-rassing moment occurred when, on live TV, she played a corpse—and opened her eyes on camera.

Don Hollinger, born in Toledo, Ohio, is her boyfriend, a reporter for *Newsview* magazine; his home phone number is Bryant 9-9970, and he and Ann dine fre-quently at Nino's Italian Restaurant.

Ann's father, Lou Marie (Lew Parker) is a Shriner who owns the La Parisienne Restaurant in Brewster; her mother's name is Helen (Rosemary De Camp) and Frank Faylen and Mabel Albertson played Don's parents, Bert and Mildred Hol-linger.

Ann is represented by the Gilliam and Norris Theatrical Agency; her agents are: Sandy Stone (played by Morty Gunty), George Lester (George Carlin), Harvey Peck (Ronnie Schell) and Seymour Schwimmer (Don Penny). Cloris Leach-man appears as Don's sister, Sandi. Billy DeWolfe plays Jules Benedict, Ann's dra-ma coach (the sign on his office door reads "Never Enter Here"). In one episode, Ann, who was told she "had a rotten name for an actress" (most producers ask Ann Marie Who?), contemplated chang-ing her name to Marie Brewster, combin-ing her last name and her hometown; she never changed it.

In the original, unaired pilot (produced in 1965), Marlo Thomas played Ann Marie; Ted Bessell, her boyfriend Don Bluesky, a writer for *Newsview* magazine;

and Harold Gould and Penny Santon played Ann's father and mother.

THIS IS ALICE
Syndicated, 1958

"Being that little girl's father is the greatest adventure of my life," says Chester "Chet" Holliday (Tommy Farrell), the father of Alice Holliday (Patty Ann Ger-rity), a pretty, bright and bubbly nine-year-old girl.

Alice lives in the town of River Glen, New Jersey, with her father, Chet; her mother, Clarissa Mae (Phyllis Coates); Clarissa's father, Colonel Dixon (Lucien Littlefield); and her infant brother, Jun-ior (not credited). She lives at 857 Elm Street and attends River Glen Elementary School (her classes are held in Room 4B). She is a member of the All For One Club (their slogan is "Friends to the End") and is allowed to have as many pets as she wants—as long as she keeps them out of the house. She will help people she be-lieves are in trouble—whether they want it or not.

Clarence "Soapy" Weaver (Stephen Woolton), Susan Gray (Nancy DeCarl), who is vice president of the All For One Club—Alice is the president—and Stingy Jones (Jimmy Baird) are Alice's friends. Alice's father works for the local newspa-per, the *Star Herald*. Clarissa Mae, who was born in Georgia, is a southern belle whose father owns a peanut plantation.

Although Alice has a lot of pets—from frogs to lizards to flies (she is perhaps the only kid in the history of television to have pet flies)—only a few are named: Pegasus (a pony), Rudolph (a frog) and Madeline and Henry (flies). She also has a pet elephant named Cuddles, which she bought from a bankrupt carnival for 55 cents.

The population of River Glen, "A Good Place to Live," is 24,695, and its altitude is 322 feet. Benny Baker plays Soapy's father, Henry Weaver; Russell Arms, Su-san's father, John Gray; and Amy Doug-las, Susan's grandmother, Mrs. Porter. E. C. Norton is credited as music supervisor; no credit is given to the "This Is Alice" theme composer.

THREE'S A CROWD/ THREE'S COMPANY, TOO

ABC, 9.18.84 to 9.17.85

This is a "Three's Company" spinoff which focuses on Jack Tripper (John Ritter), the owner of Jack's Bistro, a small restaurant, and his live-in girlfriend, Vicky Bradford (Mary Cadorette), a flight attendant for TransAllied Airlines. Jack and Vicky live over the Bistro in Apartment 203 at 834 Ocean Vista Avenue in Ocean Vista, California. Robert Mandan plays James Bradford, Vicky's father and their landlord. He is also the owner of Allied Waste Disposal, the company that removes the Bistro's trash. Jessica Walter portrays Vicky's mother, Claudia (divorced from James), and Billie Bird appeared as Jack's Aunt Mae. Although she is not seen, it is mentioned that James has a sister named Agnes. The theme, "Side By Side," was composed by Al Kasha, Joel Hirschhorn, Don Nicoll and Michael Lloyd. The series is also syndicated as "Three's Company, Too" (which uses the "Three's Company" theme song).

THREE'S COMPANY

ABC, 3.15.77 to 9.18.84

Principal Cast: John Ritter (*Jack Tripper*), Joyce DeWitt (*Janet Wood*), Suzanne Somers (*Chrissy Snow*), Jenilee Harrison (*Cindy Snow*), Priscilla Barnes (*Terri Alden*), Richard Kline (*Larry Dallas*), Norman Fell (*Stanley Roper*), Audra Lindley (*Helen Roper*), Don Knotts (*Ralph Furley*)

Trivia: Following a wild going-away party for their roommate, Eleanor Garvey (Marianne Black), Janet Wood and Chrissy Snow find Jack Tripper, a guy who came to the party with a friend who knew one of the gate crashers, sleeping in their bathtub. Jack, a cooking student staying at the Y.M.C.A., can't afford an apartment of his own; Janet and Chrissy, who can neither cook nor afford the $300-a-month rent, agree to let Jack rent

Eleanor's old room (the one to the right of the living room) for $100 a month. To convince their landlords, Stanley and Helen Roper, that theirs will be a platonic relationship, Janet tells Stanley that Jack is gay—a charade Jack must live out in order to stay at the Ropers' apartment house (Apartment 201) in Santa Monica, California (in some episodes, the locale is given as Los Angeles).

After graduating from the Los Angeles Technical School, Jack becomes a chef at Angelino's Italian Restaurant, then opens his own eatery called Jack's Bistro (located at 834 Ocean Vista in Los Angeles; slightly altered in the spinoff series, "Three's a Crowd").

Janet, who was born in Massachusetts, is a salesgirl (later manager) of the Arcade Florist Shop (locale not given). Christmas "Chrissy" Snow is a beautiful but naive secretary who is sweet and very trusting; her company's name is not given (she works for C. J. Braddock, played by Emmaline Henry, in one episode). She also takes a job selling Easy Time Cosmetics door-to-door.

Cindy Snow, Chrissy's cousin (who replaces her character on the show) is a student at UCLA and earns money both as a secretary and by hiring herself out as a maid. Terri Alden, who was born in Indiana, is a nurse at Wilshire Memorial Hospital (her character replaced Cindy's). Larry Dallas, Jack's playboy friend, is a rather dishonest used-car salesman (company not named) who is always in need of money. Ralph Furley becomes the trio's landlord in 1978 when his rich brother, Bart, buys the Ropers' apartment house and hires him to manage the building.

The gang's hangout is the Regal Beagle, a bar styled after a British pub. Greedy Gretchen (Teresa Ganzel) is the girl of Jack's dreams (mentioned many times but seen only once). The show is based on the British series "Man About the House" (with Richard O'Sullivan as Robin Tripp, a male cookery student who lives with two girls—Sally Thomsett as Jo and Paula Wilcox as Chrissy. Their hangout is the Mucky Duck Saloon and Robin later opens a restaurant called Robin's Nest).

Relatives: Dick Shawn (Jack's father, *Jack Tripper Sr.*), Georgann Johnson (*Jack's mother*), Edward Andrews (Jack's *Grandpa Tripper*), John Getz (Jack's brother, *Lee Tripper*), John Ritter (Jack's brother, *Tex Tripper*), Peter Mark Richman (Chrissy's father, *Reverend Luther Snow*), Priscilla Morrill (*Chrissy's mother*), Jay Garfield (Chrissy's cousin, *Daniel Trent*), Paula Shaw (Janet's mother, *Ruth Wood*), Devon Erickson (Janet's sister, *Jenny Wood*), Macom McCalman (Janet's father, *Roland Wood*), Mina Kolb (*Terri's mother*), Jennifer Walker (Terri's sister, *Samantha Alden*), Alan Manson (*Terri's father*), Sue Ane Langdon (Cindy's aunt, *Becky Madison*), Lucinda Dooling (Larry's sister, *Diane Dallas*), Hamilton Camp (Ralph's brother, *Bart Furley*), Brian Robbins (Ralph's nephew, *Marc Furley*), Cristina Hart (Stanley's niece, *Karen*), Irene Tedrow (Helen's *Aunt Martha*)

Theme: "Three's Company," vocal by Julia Rinker and (The Other) Ray Charles

Spinoff Series: "Three's a Crowd" and "The Ropers" (see entries)

THREE'S COMPANY, TOO

see THREE'S A CROWD

THE THUNDERBIRDS

Syndicated, 1968

Principal Cast (voices for marionettes): Peter Dyneley (*Jeff Tracy*), Shane Rimmer (*Scott Tracy*), David Holliday (*Virgil Tracy*), Matt Zimmerman (*Alan Tracy*), David Graham (*Gordon Tracy*), Ray Barrett (*John Tracy*), Sylvia Anderson (*Lady Penelope*), Christine Finn (*Tin Tin Kyrano*), Ray Barrett (*the Hood*)

Trivia: "The Thunderbirds" relates the exploits of International Rescue (I.R.), a global organization dedicated to rescuing people trapped in unusual predicaments; their base is a remote Pacific island.

The Team: Jeff Tracy, the head of I.R., is a former astronaut, and has named all five of his sons—all members of I.R.—after American astronauts.

Scott Tracy, the eldest son, pilots *Thun-*derbird I; he is fast-talking and quick-thinking.

Virgil Tracy, reliable and steady, is the pilot of *Thunderbird II*, a freighter that handles the priceless rescue equipment.

Alan Tracy, the most romantic of the sons, is the pilot of *Thunderbird III*.

Gordon Tracy, young, enthusiastic and a joker, operates *Thunderbird IV*, the underwater vehicle.

John Tracy, the youngest of the brothers, commands *Thunderbird V*, the satellite base of I.R.

Lady Penelope Creighton-Ward, I.R.'s glamorous London agent, is adventurous and daring—a female James Bond. She owns an exotic wardrobe and a shocking-pink Rolls Royce with license plate FAB I.

The Hood, their enemy, is dedicated to discovering the secrets of I.R. He lives in an exotic eastern temple and practices "hoodoo" (a spell that controls people for his means).

The Equipment: *Thunderbird I* is primarily a fast scout vehicle that speeds to the crisis area. It can reach speeds of 7,000 miles an hour and take off vertically for speed. It also has retractable wings, booster and downward-firing rockets, which allow it to land vertically without the need for wheels.

Thunderbird II, the transport unit, has rollers instead of wheels to allow the craft's body to land on the ground. Hydraulic legs then lift the fuselage off the ground so that the rescue equipment can be lowered. It is the only armed craft (being slower, it is more prone to attack).

Thunderbird III, which is capable of space flight, possesses laser radio scanners that alert the base of its location. It is capable of sending high-powered signals.

Thunderbird IV, the underwater craft, is contained in a pod in *Thunderbird II*.

Thunderbird V, the space station, possesses the most advanced scientific equipment, the most ingenious of which is the Interpreter, which can immediately translate any language into English.

Lady Penelope's Rolls Royce's wheels rotate sideways so that it can be parked crab-wise; all wheels have retractable studs for snow and ice; and, at the press of a button, pointed end rods shoot out to form a tire slasher. A machine gun is hidden in the radiator, and the car can reach speeds up to 200 miles per hour. Besides a bullet-proof, glass and steel canopy, its back seat has retractable handcuffs and a chestband to subdue prisoners.

Theme: "The Thunderbirds," written by Barry Gray

TIMMY AND LASSIE

see JEFF'S COLLIE and THE NEW LASSIE

T. J. HOOKER

ABC, 3.13.82 to 5.4.85
CBS, 9.25.85 to 6.8.86

T. J. Hooker (William Shatner) is a sergeant with the Academy Precinct of the L.C.P.D. His badge number is 115 (also given as 141) and he lives in a messy room at the Safari Inn. His car code is 4-Adam-30 and he wears a Magnum Body Armor bulletproof vest. Hooker, whose favorite pie is rhubarb, holds the police record for the most damaged and/or destroyed police cars. Fran, T. J.'s ex-wife (who calls him Hooker—as does everybody else) is a nurse at Memorial Hospital. (What the T. J. in Hooker's name stands for is not given. In some episodes, background signs indicate that the community Hooker is protecting is L.C. City; what the L.C. stands for, however, is not revealed).

Officer Stacey Sheridan (Heather Locklear), whose badge number is 280, lives in an apartment at the Marina Club; she and her partner, Officer Jim Corrigan (James Darren), who was born in San Francisco, ride in a car with the code 4-Adam-16. Officer Vince Romano (Adrian Zmed), Hooker's partner, was born in South Philadelphia and as a kid had a dog named Bear.

In ABC episodes, the hangout is the Mid-City Bar; in CBS episodes, it's Sherry's Bar. Vince's favorite after-hours hangout is Adrienne's Bar.

Relatives: Leigh Christian and Lee Bryant (Hooker's ex-wife, *Fran Hooker*), Nicole Eggert and Jenny Beck (Hooker's daughter, *Chrissy Hooker*), Susan McClung (Hooker's daughter, *Cathy Hooker*), Andre Gower (Hooker's son, *Tommy Hooker*), John McLiam (Hooker's father, *John Hooker*), Richard Herd (Stacey's father, *Captain Dennis Sheridan*)

Mark Snow composed the theme.

TOM CORBETT, SPACE CADET

CBS, 10.2.50 to 12.29.50
ABC, 1.1.51 to 9.26.52
NBC, 7.7.51 to 9.8.51
DuMont, 8.29.53 to 5.22.54
NBC, 12.11.54 to 6.25.55

"Space Academy, U.S.A. in the world beyond tomorrow . . . Here the Space Cadets train for duty on distant planets. In roaring rockets they blast through the millions of miles from Earth to far-flung stars and brave the dangers of cosmic frontiers, protecting the liberties of the planets, safeguarding the cause of universal peace in the age of the conquest of space." The year is A.D. 2350. War as we know it no longer exists; guns are outlawed; men no longer wear suits (their everyday clothes are made in one piece); women wear short skirts "with the well-formed feminine knee in full view." Navigators have been replaced by astrogators and nucleonics have replaced engineers. The planets Earth, Mars, Venus and Jupiter have all been colonized and now form the Solar Alliance—a group of planets protected by the Solar Guards, a celestial police force that is based at Space Academy, U.S.A.—a training school for aspiring Solar Guards.

Frankie Thomas plays Cadet Tom Corbett; Jan Merlin, Cadet Roger Manning; Astro, the Venusian, is played by Al Markim; and Margaret Garland (later Patricia Ferris) plays Dr. Joan Dale.

Tom's ship is the *Polarius*; other Space Academy ships are the *Vega*, the *Orion*, the *Sirius*, the *Hydro* and the *Falcon*. The most common weapon is the Paralo-Ray (which causes temporary paralysis) and is only used when Solar Guards set out to explore new areas of the universe. Mercury, the smallest of the planets, has not yet been explored and is not part of the Solar Alliance. Pilots use Tele-Transceivers for visual communication with Space Academy and Strato-Screen for visual space exploration. As Tom says in early episodes of the series, "So long for now and spaceman's luck to all of you."

TOO CLOSE FOR COMFORT

ABC, 11.11.80 to 9.15.83
Syndicated, 4.84 to 3.86

Principal Cast: Ted Knight (*Henry Rush*), Nancy Dussault (*Muriel Rush*), Deborah Van Valkenburgh (*Jackie Rush*), Lydia Cornell (*Sarah Rush*), JM J Bullock (*Monroe Ficus*), Deena Freeman (*April Rush*)

Trivia: The story of over-protective parents (Henry and Muriel Rush) who rent the downstairs apartment of their two-family home to their daughters (Jackie and Sarah) in an effort to keep tabs on them.

Henry and Muriel own a red Victorian home on Buena Vista Street in San Francisco (it was once a famous brothel) and charge Jackie and Sarah $300 a month for rent. Henry, the creator and artist of the comic strip "Cosmic Cow" (a space-crime fighter), first worked as an artist by painting turtles. "Cosmic Cow" is published by Random Comics, a division of Wainwright Publishing. Henry gives Muriel $150 a week to run the house. Muriel, whose maiden name is Martin, is a freelance photographer; before marrying Henry, she was a singer with Al Crowler and His Orchestra. Henry and Muriel honeymooned at the Golden Pines Hotel and in each episode Henry is seen wearing a different college sweatshirt.

Jackie, the elder sister (22 years old), is first a teller at the Bay City Bank, then a salesgirl at Balaban's Department Store and finally a fashion designer. She wears a size 32A bra, is excessively neat and jealous of women with fuller figures.

Sarah, a freshman at San Francisco State College, takes various part-time jobs to earn her half of the rent money. Her first job was as a "wench waitress" at the Fox and Hound Bar (she got the job because she has a figure that fit the available uniform). She then became a teller at Jackie's bank, the local weather girl for KTSF-TV's "Dawn in San Francisco" program and a businesswoman who attempted to market Cosmic Cow Cookies. Sarah, who considers herself a "ten," wears a size 36C bra, is somewhat lazy and a sloppy housekeeper.

Monroe Ficus was originally a friend of Sarah's who attended State College also. His major was communications with a minor in journalism; he later became a security guard at the Riverwood Shopping Mall. He earns $200 a week, rents a converted attic apartment upstairs from Henry for $300 a month and was once named Security Guard of the Month (Officer April) for catching a lady taking pantyhose out of the egg; he has a pet hamster named Spunky.

April Rush, Henry's niece, appeared for one season and was a free-spirited musician who hung out with a character named Moonbeam.

In April 1986, the series became "The Ted Knight Show." Henry and Muriel relocate to Marin County, California, after Jackie and Sarah move away. Henry becomes co-owner (49%) of the weekly paper, the *Marin Bugler*, with Hope Stinson (Pat Carroll), who owns 51%. Norris J. Stinson (not seen), Hope's late husband, founded the paper 35 years ago. Brutus is the name of the dog on the paper's masthead. Monroe is now Henry's assistant at the paper. He hopes to become a stand-up comic and performs as Buddy Ficus at the Comedy Shack. Henry and Muriel's son, Andrew, is now five years old and played by Joshua Goodwin. Lisa Antelli plays their maid, Lisa; and Leah Ayres appeared as Hope's niece, Jennifer. The series was resyndicated as "Too Close for Comfort" after its initial run.

Relatives: Audrey Meadows (Muriel's mother, *Iris Martin*), Ray Middleton (Henry's father, *Huey Rush*), Robert Mandan (Henry's brother, *Bill Rush*), Pat Paulsen

(Monroe's father, *Benjamin Ficus*). Twins Eric and Jason Wells and William and Michael Cannon played Henry and Muriel's infant son, Baby Andrew.

Theme: "Too Close for Comfort," by Johnny Mandel

TOP OF THE HILL

CBS, 9.21.89 to 12.7.89

Political drama about Thomas Patrick Bell (William Katt), a newly elected congressman in Washington, D.C. Tom, whose hometown is Eureka, California (in the pilot) and Hopkins Bay (in the series), is assigned to office number 2467 in the Rayburn Building; his license plate number is 2PCE 096. Dick O'Neill plays Tom's father, Pat Bell, and Jordan Baker and Tony Edwards, Tom's office aides, Susan Pengilly and Link Winslow. Michael Green appears as Susan's father, Harris Pengilly. Mike Post composed the theme.

TOPPER

CBS, 10.3.52 to 9.30.55

While on a skiing trip in Switzerland for their fifth wedding anniversary, George and Marian Kerby (Robert Sterling, Anne Jeffreys) are killed in an avalanche—along with a booze-consuming St. Bernard that Marian names Neil (after George's cousin, whom the dog resembles). Three months later in New York, the henpecked Cosmo Topper (Leo G. Carroll) and his wife, Henrietta (Lee Patrick), purchase the $27,000 Kerby home (at 101 Maple Drive) for $16,000. Along with it he inherits the fun-loving ghosts of George, Marian and Neil, who try to bring some joy into his dull life.

Topper, a bank vice president (with a bank account of $3,500.27), does his business entertaining at Club 22. Over the course of the series, Topper is associated with the following banks: National Security Bank, City Bank, Gotham Trust Company and City Trust and Savings Bank. Humphrey Schuyler (Thurston Hall) is the bank president and Kathleen Freeman (1953–54) and Edna Skinner (1954–55) are

the Toppers' maids, Katie and Maggie. Neil was played by two St. Bernards raised by Beatrice Knight of the Sanctuary Kennels in Oregon.

On April 19, 1973, NBC aired the pilot, "Topper Returns," in which Cosmo Topper Jr. (Roddy McDowall), Cosmo's nephew, inherits his uncle's possessions, including the ghosts of George and Marian (John Fink, Stefanie Powers). Another unsold pilot, "Topper" (ABC, 11.9.79), found Cosmo Topper (Jack Warden) as a lawyer who inherits the ghosts of George and Marian Kerby (played by Andrew Stevens and Kate Jackson) after they are killed in a car crash. Rue McClanahan played Cosmo's wife, Clara; the Kerby's dog was named Sam. The series was based on the feature film of the same title.

THE TORTELLIS

NBC, 1.22.87 to 5.5.87

This series is a "Cheers" spinoff in which Nick Tortelli (Dan Hedaya), Carla's ex-husband, and his second wife Loretta (Jean Kasem) move from New Jersey to Las Vegas to begin new lives. Together with Nick's son, Anthony, and Anthony's wife, Annie (Timothy Williams, Mandy Ingber), Nick and Loretta move in with Loretta's sister, Charlotte Cooper (Carlene Watkins) and her young son, Mark (Aaron Moffett). The somewhat dizzy but beautiful Loretta was a singer with the Grinning Americans (later the Lemon Sisters) and is now struggling to become a Las Vegas showgirl. Nick, who ran Nick's Talent Emporium in New Jersey, now operates Tortellis' TV Hospital from Charlotte's garage. Nick's business telephone number is 555-4768 (his New Jersey phone number was 609-555-4397). Charlotte is a substitute teacher for the Nevada Public School System. Perry Botkin composed the theme.

TRUE BLUE

NBC, 12.3.89 to 2.16.90

The series follows the rescue exploits of Officers Frankie Avila (Eddie Velez), Bobby Traverso (John Bolger), Jessica "Jessy" Haley (Ally Walker), Casey Pierce (Grant Show) and Sergeant Skiboss "Ski" Wojeski (Timothy Van Patten)—all members of the E.S.U. (Emergency Service Unit) of the New York Police Department.

The team is attached to the Truck One Station, based on Bleeker Street in Manhattan. The unit's dog is Bird and the E.S.U. Standard Automated Robot is nicknamed Sam. Jessy, chosen from 287 applicants, is a registered nurse with psychological training. Mike's E.S.U. truck code is Boy-1. Elya Baskin plays Yuri, the amateur news photographer who drives a cab (license plate number T48611T) and frequently plagues the team in his attempts to capture rescues on tape.

Suzanne Gregard plays Bobby's ex-wife, Tess; Brit Hammer, Ski's wife, Judy; Victor Arnold, Chief Lou Servino (of the Manhattan 8th Precinct); and Mimi Cecchini portrays Sophie Zackalakis, the old lady who lives across the street from Truck One. Shawnee Jackson sings the theme, "True Blue."

TUCKER'S WITCH

CBS, 10.6.82 to 5.5.83

A beautiful apprentice witch named Amanda Tucker (Catherine Hicks) and her mortal husband Rick Tucker (Tim Matheson) are the owners of Tucker and Tucker, Inc., a Los Angeles-based private detective agency, and part-time investigators for the Sandrich Insurance Company. They live on a farm in Laurel Canyon's Mill Valley, where Amanda has a Siamese cat named Dickens (after Charles Dickens, her favorite writer) and a goat named Myra. Their office phone number is 213-555-6111; their home phone number is 555-4616; and Amanda's mobile car phone number is 555-8734. Barbara Barrie plays Amanda's mother, Ellen Hobbs. Ellen is not a witch; though witchcraft runs in her family, it skips every tenth generation. Girls born in the "off generation" do not inherit the powers of witchcraft. Brad Fiedel composed the theme. In the original, unaired pilot, "The Good Witch of Laurel Canyon," Kim Cat-

trall played Amanda and Art Hindle played Rick.

TWO GIRLS NAMED SMITH

ABC, 1.20.51 to 10.13.51

Frances "Fran" Smith (Peggy French) and her cousin Babs Smith (Peggy Ann Garner; later Marcia Henderson) are two small-town girls from Omaha, Nebraska, who move to New York to further their careers: Babs as a singer and Fran as a fashion designer. The girls live together in a small Manhattan apartment at 514 East 51st Street (their phone number is Plaza 3-0707). Jeffrey Carter (Kermit Kegley) is a lawyer and Fran's boyfriend; Mr. Basmany (Joseph Buloff) is their "friend, companion and philosopher." In the final episode, Babs, who has taken jobs from detective's assistant to stenographer, gets her big break replacing Janice Avery (Gloria Stroock) as the lead in the Broadway play *Stairway to Venus*. Jacques Press composed the theme.

VALERIE/THE HOGAN FAMILY

NBC, 9.21.87 to 6.11.90
3.1.86 to 9.14.87 (as "Valerie")

Principal Cast: Valerie Harper (*Valerie Hogan*), Sandy Duncan (*Sandy Hogan*), Josh Taylor (*Michael Hogan*), Jason Bateman (*David Hogan*), Danny Ponce (*Willie Hogan*), Jeremy Licht (*Mark Hogan*), Edie McClurg (*Patty Poole*)

Trivia: Valerie Hogan, manager of an art auction house called Forman-Lydell Antiques, is married to Michael, an airline pilot who is seldom at home, and the mother of three sons (David, Willie and Mark). They live in Oak Park, Illinois (a suburb of Chicago) at 46 Crescent Drive; her phone number is 555-4656 and her maiden name was Verone. The family dog (first season) is named Murray.

When a contract dispute between series star Valerie Harper and the show's producers could not be resolved, Valerie's character was killed in a car crash. Unable to raise his sons alone, Michael asks his sister, Sandy, to come and live with him and help bring them up. The show was then renamed "The Hogan Family." Sandy was first a guidance counselor, then the vice principal of Colfax High School. The eldest son, David, first attended Colfax, then Northwestern University. Willie and Mark attend Colfax High. Mark's first job was order taker at Bossy Burger. For a college project, David produced "Mrs. Poole's Kitchen," a cooking show for WZIN-TV, Channel 29. Patty Poole, the Hogans' neighbor, has a dog named Casey and a parrot named Tweeters.

Relatives: Nan Martin (Valerie's *Aunt Josephine*), Francine Tacker (Mike's sister, *Caroline Hogan*), Gretchen Wyler (*Mike's mother*), Robert Rockwell (*Mike's father*), Anne Haney (Mike's *Aunt Mildred*), Steve Vinovich (Sandy's ex-husband, *Richard*), Willard Scott (Patty's husband, *Peter Poole*), Kathleen Freeman (Patty's *Mother-in-Law Poole*), Dylan Shane (Patty's nephew, *Paulie Poole*)

Theme: "Together Through the Years," vocal by Roberta Flack

VOYAGERS!

NBC, 10.3.82 to 3.22.83

Principal Cast: Jon-Erik Hexum (*Phineas Bogg*), Meeno Peluce (*Jeffrey Jones*)

Trivia: Phineas Bogg is a 17th-century pirate who was "plucked out of time" to become a Voyager (a traveler in time who helps history along). Bogg travels through time with the aid of his Omni, a compass-like device inscribed with the words, "Time Waits for No Man." When the Omni flashes a red light, it indicates that history is wrong; a green light indicates that the historical period he is in is correct.

Following the death of his parents (Bill and Cathy) in a car accident, 11-year-old Jeffrey Jones is sent to live with his Aunt Elizabeth (Janie Bradley) in Manhattan. As Bogg is traveling in time, his Omni, which had only been programmed up to 1970, malfunctions and sends him to 1982. Bogg "falls to earth" on the window ledge of Jeffrey's high-rise apartment building bedroom. Bogg breaks the window and enters the room. Jeffrey's dog, Ralph, grabs Bogg's guidebook and a struggle ensues. As Jeffrey is attempting to get the book from Ralph, he accidentally falls out of the window. Bogg jumps out after him. He grabs Jeffrey, touches his Omni and the two are sent to safety in 1450 B.C. Egypt. Now, unable to return Jeffrey to his time, Bogg becomes his guardian.

Bogg, who attended Voyager School, was more interested in watching the girls in his class than in learning about history, and is therefore lost without his guidebook. Fortunately, Jeffrey, destined to become a Voyager, is a history buff and becomes Bogg's "guidebook." Together they set out to correct history's mistakes. (A split second before Bogg and Jeffrey met, the camera showed two books on Jeffrey's shelf—*Pirates and History* and *The Man Out There*—both of which refer to Bogg.)

Bogg, who has an eye for the ladies of the eras he visits, calls Jeffrey "Kid" and remarks, "Smart kids give me a pain." He uses the catch phrase "Bats' Breath" when something goes wrong. Jeffrey, whose father was a history professor, calls Phineas "Bogg" and poses as his son or his nephew depending on the situation. Tracy Brooks Swope plays Voyager Olivia Dunn (Class of '97) and Stephen Liska, Drake, the renegade Voyager (he has a model 31650 Open-Time Calibrated Omni). Anne Lockhart and John O'Connell appeared as Jeffrey's great-grandparents, Amy and Steven Jones, in the episode "Merry Christmas, Bogg." Jerrold Immel composed the theme.

In 1985, MCA Home Video released *Voyager from the Unknown* and everything changed:

"Far out in the cosmos there exists a planet known as Voyager, where the mystery of travel into space and through time has been solved. It is inhabited by a race who call themselves Voyagers. Their purpose is to keep constant surveillance on history . . . These people have a time-machine device, the Omni, which will take them into the past, present or future. As each Voyager graduates . . . he is given an Omni and a guidebook. One such graduate was Phineas Bogg, who was assigned as a field worker to operate in certain time zones . . . " (The History Surveillance Unit, a computer complex, keeps track of Voyagers during their assignments.)

The 91-minute movie was re-edited from the pilot and the "Voyagers of the Titanic" episodes of the series. The year that Jeffrey and Bogg met has been changed to 1984; the Omni now buzzes when opened (instead of sounding a bell); and they now travel through time in computer-guided space hoops (instead of the quasi-free flight through space in the series).

WAR OF THE WORLDS

Syndicated, 10.8.88 to 9.30.89

Principal Cast: Jared Martin (*Dr. Harrison Blackwood*), Lynda Mason Green (*Dr. Suzanne McCullough*), Richard Chaves (*Colonel Paul Ironhorse*), Philip Akin (*Norton Drake*), Rachel Blanchard (*Debbie McCullough*)

Trivia: "War of the Worlds" is an adaptation of the 1953 feature film about a Martian invasion of Earth. While mankind seemed doomed in its battle against the aliens, it was the smallest of things—the bacteria in the air, to which humans are immune—that killed the Martians.

In 1988, it is learned that the aliens' remains are stored in metal containers. A small group of aliens are revived by a nuclear accident when radioactive waste contacts one of the storage containers. To protect themselves from earthly viruses, the aliens must inhabit human bodies. Their leaders (now from the planet Mortex, not Mars) are called the Advocacy. When the U.S. government learns what has happened, it suppresses the information and creates the Blackwood Project, a secret army to battle the aliens. Dr. Harrison Blackwood is the leader; Dr. Suzanne McCullough, Colonel Paul Ironhorse and Norton Drake are his principal assistants.

Blackwood's team is based in a secret government safehouse (Cottage 348) on 25 secured acres of land. Blackwood's army is called the Omega Squad; Suzanne, who is divorced (her maiden name is Baxter), lives on the base with her teenage daugher, Debbie (who has a dog named Guido). Norton Drake, a crippled computer expert, calls his voice-activated wheelchair Gertrude. Harrison's aunt is Sylvia Van Buren, the girl who witnessed the original 1953 invasion and can now sense when the aliens are near (because of a traumatic shock she suffered, she now resides at the Westwood Mental Health Center). Before a dramatic storyline change, Elaine Giftos was introduced as Katara, the Synth from the planet Qar'to. Katara, a beautiful killing android, was sent to Earth to aide Blackwell, destroy the Mortex, and save mankind for Katara's people's more sinister plan—to use Earth as a food source.

When the series returned for its second season (10.89 to 9.90), the format was revamped in an effort to improve the show. It is now set in a time called Almost Tomorrow. When the planet Morthrai is destroyed, survivors journey to Earth and take over the war begun by the Mortex—with a goal of making the Earth their new Morthrai. In a fierce battle between the three different life forms, the Mortex are destroyed and the Earth is heavily damaged. Surviving Earthlings unite in an effort to defeat their new enemy. Adrian Paul as John Kincaid joins Suzanne, Debbie and Blackwood when Ironside and Drake are killed in the battle. The aliens are led by the Eternal; Catherine Disher (Mana) and Denis Forest (Malzor) are the two Morthrai aliens who serve the Eternal.

Relatives: Ann Robinson (Harrison's aunt, *Sylvia Van Buren*), Michael Parks (Suzanne's ex-husband, *Cash McCullough*)

Theme: "War of the Worlds," by Bill Thorpe

WATERFRONT

Syndicated, 1954

"Hello, I'm Preston Foster coming your way with another exciting episode of 'Waterfront.' " John Herrick (Preston Foster), who works for the Wellington Towing Company, is captain of the tugboat *Cheryl Ann* (docked in Berth 14 of the San Pedro, California, harbor). John, who was born in San Pedro (and lived at 91 Surf Street in an area called the Wharf), married his first and only sweetheart, Mae (Lois Moran), whom he calls "Mom" and who is famous for her lemon pies. John, whose telephone number is Terminal 5-6741, buys his gear from a store called Bailey's, and does his fishing off Bell Point.

John's son, Carl Herrick (Douglas Dick), is captain of the tugboat *Belinda* (docked in Berth 5). His friend, Dan Cord (Ramon Vallo) captains the tugboat *Isabel* (all tugs owned by Wellington are named after women), and his friend Max Benson (George Chandler) runs the Lobster Claw Restaurant.

Ralph Dumke plays John's boss, Zachary Morgan; and Kathleen Crowley, Carl's fiancée, the wealthy Terry Van Buren (who lives on Crown Hill). Carl Betz plays John's eldest son, Dave Herrick, a San Pedro police detective; Frank Wilcox and Frieda Inescourt portray Terry's parents, Henry and Emily Van Buren. Alexander Laszlo composed the theme.

WHIRLYBIRDS

Syndicated, 1954 to 1957

Chuck Martin (Kenneth Tobey) and P. T. Moore (Craig Hill) operate Whirlybirds, Inc., a helicopter charter service based at Longwood Field in California. They fly Bell Ranger Helicopters with the I.D.'s N975B and N2838B; their air code is Seven-Five Bravo. Nancy Hale plays their assistant, Helen Carter (originally Sandra Spence as Janet Culver), and Joe Perry, Al, their mechanic. Other than music supervision by Ed Norton, no credit is given for the show's theme, "The Whirlybirds Theme."

THE WHIZ KIDS

CBS, 10.5.83 to 6.2.84

Richie Adler (Matthew Laborteaux), Alice Tyler (Andrea Elson), Hamilton "Ham" Parker (Todd Porter) and Jeremy Saldino (Jeffrey Jacquet) are teenage computer whizzes who use their skills to help authorities solve crimes. They attend Canyon High School and help Lew Farley (Max Gail), a reporter for the Los Angeles *Gazette*, Carson Marsh (Dan O'Herlihy), the head of the Athena Society, an intelligence agency, and Neal Quinn (A Martinez), a Los Angeles Police Department lieutenant.

Richie has a "home-brewed" 64-K computer named Ralph, a roving robot called Herman and a dog named Rabies; Alice works after school as an order taker at the Burger Bar; Richie, Alice, Ham and Jeremy are members of the Canyon High School Computer Club.

Madelyn Cain plays Richie's divorced mother, Irene Adler, and Melanie Gaffin plays Richie's younger sister, Cheryl.

Relatives: Jim McMullan (Richie's father, *Don Adler*), Michael Boyle (Alice's father, *Dave Tyler*), Wayne Norton (Ham's father, *Lew Parker*), Barbara Brownell (Ham's mother, *Aggie Parker*)

Paul Chihara composed the theme.

WHO'S THE BOSS?

ABC, 10.4.84 to

Principal Cast: Tony Danza (*Tony Micelli*), Alyssa Milano (*Samantha Micelli*), Judith Light (*Angela Bower*), Katherine Helmond (*Mona Robinson*), Danny Pintauro (*Jonathan Bower*)

Trivia: At the summer camp Camp Cataba, Tony Micelli and a girl named Ingrid became friends and shared their first kiss at Kissing Rock. Unknown to Tony, the girl, who was afraid to use her real name, was Angela Robinson, who would years later become Angela Bower—and Tony's boss when he becomes her live-in house-keeper.

Tony, the widowed father of a young daughter (Samantha), tends house for Angela (a divorcée), her son Jonathan and Angela's mother, Mona Robinson. They live at 3344 Oak Hills Drive in Fairfield County, Connecticut (also given as 3334 Oaks Hills Drive); their phone number is KL5-6218. Tony, whose middle name is Morton, played second base for the St. Louis Cardinals and had the nickname "the Batman." Before moving to Connecticut, Tony and Samantha lived on Pitkin Avenue in Brooklyn, where Tony drove a fish truck. Tony has a '67 Chevy van with the license plate number 780 AGN and attends night courses (in business) at Ridgemont College. He plays golf at the Longridge Golf Club (with a ten handicap), is a member of a bowling team (Dr. Whittier's Drill Team) and posed as Mr. November for a calendar.

Angela, formerly the president of the Wallace and McQuade Ad Agency in New York City, later opened her own agency – the Angela Bower Agency at 323 East 57th Street in Manhattan. Angela attended the Montague Academy as a kid and, later, Harvard Business School. In high school, Angela was (as she calls herself) a geek and jealous because she was not as well-developed as the other girls in her class. She attempted to become one of "the Cool Kids" by stuffing kleenex in her bra, but was still rejected. So she drowned her sorrows in food (in other words, three chocolate puddings with lunch) and became slightly overweight before she "cleaned up her act" and learned to accept herself as she is.

Samantha, affectionately called Sam, attends Fairfield Junior High, then Fairfield High School, and receives $15 a week allowance. Sam, a tomboy in early episodes, is a member of the Bulldogs Baseball Team and had her first job experience as Angela's Girl Friday at Wallace and McQuade. Her after-school job is as a waitress at the Yellow Submarine (a hamburger joint) and Sam's car (a '68 Olds) has a license plate that reads SAM'S CAR.

Mona, Angela's ultra-sexy mother, works as Angela's assistant at her agency. She is very proud of her well-developed chest and is forever reminding Angela that she lacks cleavage. Mona, who seems to have countless affairs, appeared in a sexy pose on the cover of *Mature Woman* magazine. Her maiden name is Rockwell. She has a dog named Grover and when Angela was a kid she discouraged Angela from playing the cello (Angela played so badly that Mona discouraged her by hiding the cello in the attic).

Jonathan, who has a pet snake named Wilbur, first attends Oak Valley Grammar School, then Fairfield High School. He has a complete Lawrence Welk record collection and loves the accordian (which he is attempting to learn to play).

Relatives: James Naughton (Angela's ex-husband, *Michael Bower*), James Coco (Tony's father-in-law, *Nick Milano*), Ana Obregon (Tony's *Cousin Anna*), Vito Scotti (Tony's *Uncle Aldo*), Richard Grieco (Tony's *Cousin Maurio*), Tony Danza (*Tony's grandfather*), Antonia Rey (Tony's *Aunt Rosa*), Gordon Jump (Mona's brother, *Archie Rockwell*), James B. Sikking (Mona's brother, *Cornelius Rockwell*), Efrem Zimbalist Jr. (Mona's late husband, *Robert Robinson;* ghost sequence)

Flashbacks: Danny Geuis (*Tony as a boy*), Kenny Morrison (*Tony as a teenager*), Lani Golay (*Angela as a girl*), Candace Cameron (*Mona as a girl*)

Theme: "Brand New Life," vocal by Rick Riso

Spinoff Series: "Living Dolls" (see entry)

WILD JACK

NBC, 1.15.89 to 7.9.89

Following the death of his friend Winston Fielding (Mel Ferrer), "Wild" Jack McCall (John Schneider), an Alaskan wilderness guide, inherits Fielding's multi-million-dollar broadcasting empire, FCI Communications in Los Angeles.

Jack leaves his home in Skagway and moves to California where, as chairman of the board, he gives Winston's daughter, Constance Fielding (Carol Huston), the power to run the company. To feel more at home, Jack starts up a side business—Tracking Unlimited—where, with his pet wolf Dinale (the Great One), he helps people in trouble. Jack's GMC 4x4 van's license plate is 2LK G497; and Constance's birthday was given as August 27, 1957. Phil Marshall composed the theme. The series is also known as "McCall of the Wild" and "McCall."

WINGS

NBC, 4.19.90 to 5.24.90

Brothers Joe (Timothy Daly) and Brian (Steve Weber) Hackett run Sandpiper Air, a one-plane airline based at the Tom Nevers Field on Nantucket, a rustic island off the coast of Massachusetts. Their plane, a Cessna 402, has the I.D. number N121PP and their radio call letters are Sandpiper 28.

Helen Chappel (Crystal Bernard), the gorgeous airport lunch-counter operator, has hopes of becoming a musician (she plays the cello) with the Cambridge Symphony Orchestra. She was born in Texas, and wears Dusty Roads eye blush and Tahitian Rose lip gloss. As kids, Joe, Brian and Helen were friends when they all lived in Boston. Joe accidentally saw Helen in the nude when she was ten years old (how was not mentioned) and they didn't speak to each other for two years afterwards. Although it is hard to believe, Helen says she "was once as big as a whale." When she lived in Boston, her hangout was the South Bay Fudge Factory; she was such a good customer that for one Christmas, the staff made a life-size statue of Helen out of fudge; she ate it in a half hour.

David Schramm plays Roy Biggins, the owner of the six-plane Aeromass Airline, and Rebecca Schull, Faye Evelyn Cochran, the reservations clerk. Kim Ulrich appeared as Brian's ex-wife, Carol; and Joe and Brian mention that they have an Aunt Fern (not seen). Franz Schubert composed the theme.

WKRP IN CINCINNATI

CBS, 9.17.78 to 9.20.82

Principal Cast: Gary Sandy (*Andy Travis*), Loni Anderson (*Jennifer Marlowe*), Gordon Jump (*Arthur Carlson*), Jan Smithers (*Bailey Quarters*), Howard Hesseman (*Dr. Johnny Fever*), Richard Sanders (*Les Nessman*), Frank Bonner (*Herb Tarlek*), Tim Reid (*Venus Flytrap*)

Trivia: "Baby, if you've ever wondered, wondered whatever became of me, I'm living on the air in Cincinnati, Cincinnati WKRP . . ." WKRP is the number 16 station in an 18-station market. It is a 5,000 watt (50,000 watt in the first few episodes) AM radio station whose phone number is 555-WKRP. Its broadcast studios are located in Suite 1412 on the ninth floor of the Flem Building in downtown Cincinnati, Ohio. Its "mascot" is a fish (a carp) and its staff's favorite watering hole is Snooky's Bar. The first rock song played on it was "Queen of the Forest" from the *Stranglehold* album by Ted "The Sledge" Nugent.

Arthur Carlson has been the manager of WKRP since 1955 (his forbidding mother, "Mama Carlson," owns the station) and he has been married to his wife Carmen for 27 years. As a ballplayer Arthur had the nickname "Moose" and he is called "Big Guy" by some of his current staff. He once ran for city council with the slogan "A Big Guy for a Big Job." Though a family man and active in his church, Carlson is prone to shunning station responsibility and resorts to playing with toys and practicing golf or fishing in his office. His favorite reading matter is the magazine *Ohio Fisherman*.

Jennifer Elizabeth Marlowe, the ultra-sexy receptionist, is the highest-paid employee at WKRP. She earns $24,000 a year and will not take dictation or make coffee. Jennifer, who wears tight skirts and low-cut blouses, knows she is, as she says, "a very sexy and desirable woman"; other women describe Jennifer as "the best-looking woman I have ever seen." She dates wealthy, older men because she feels safer and more secure with them.

She won't lend money to or do any favors for men, yet men buy her things: "cars, acoustical ceilings, microwaves and appliances. Men love to give me appliances." Jennifer, who was born in Rock Throw, West Virginia, lives in a gorgeous apartment (number 330; address not given) that is overrun with appliances. Her doorbell plays the song "Fly Me to the Moon" and she has box seats to the Cincinnati Reds' games (season tickets). In later episodes, Jennifer moves to a Victorian house in the town of Landersville (its location is given as across the lake) for which she paid $125,000. Her former boyfriend from Rock Throw, T. J. Watson, was played by Hoyt Axton.

Bailey Quarters, the only other female employee at the station, majored in journalism in college and first did continuity work before becoming a member of the news staff (she does two of the ten daily "WKRP News Roundup" broadcasts).

Les Nessman is the news director of WKRP. He is a graduate of Xavier University and uses his motor scooter as the WKRP mobile news unit. Les is the proud owner of the Silver Sow Award (for his hog reports) and has also won the Buckeye Newshawk Award for his news broadcasts. In his youth (born in Dayton, Ohio), Les took up the violin and was pretty handy around the house until he tried to make a footstool and blew out the back of the garage. Les, the self-proclaimed "Information Beacon of the Ohio Valley," has a nasty dog named Phil, and only one record in his collection—"Chances Are," by Johnny Mathis. His favorite topic as chairman and speechmaker at the Cricket Club is "The Red Menace in Our Backyard." His favorite music is Beethoven's Ninth Symphony and, while he works in a large room with Bailey and Herb Tarlek, he has imaginary walls and an office door which all the staff respect. Les's news shows begin with a deep-voiced announcer saying: "London! Madrid! Bangkok! Moscow! Cincinnati! From the four corners of the world; from the news capitals at home and abroad; the day's headlines brought into focus. The issues and events that shape our times. WKRP, information bureau of the Ohio Valley, presents Les Nessman and the News." He ends each news broadcast with, "Good day and may the good news be yours."

Dr. Johnny Fever, whose real name is Johnny Caravella, is the spaced-out disc jockey who earns $17,500 a year. He was fired from a Los Angeles radio station for using the word "booger" on the air, and has a photo of himself taken with Mick Jagger.

Venus Flytrap, whose real name is Gordon Simms, is the night disc jockey. He went AWOL after serving ten months and 29 days in the Army and has been in hiding ever since. Though it is against the rules, he makes the most of his job by romancing his many women friends with candlelight and wine in the broadcast booth.

Herb Tarlek, the obnoxious sales manager, has been married to his wife Lucille for 12 years and is the father of two children, Herb III and Bunny. Although he has "the hots" for Jennifer, she won't give him the time of day. Herb's catch-phrase is "O.K., fine."

Andy Travis, the station's program director, has a dog named Pecos Bill (he found him on Mount Baldy) and is the only one at WKRP who realizes the station will never do any better than becoming number 14 (which it did achieve in one ratings period). The love of Andy's life is Linda Taylor, a singer played by Barrie Youngfellow.

The show's gimmick was a bandage that Les wore in each episode—but in a different location (it was a reminder of an injury Sanders received on the first day of shooting). The weather director was the unseen Skivvy Nelson; Carlson once hired Sparky Anderson (in a guest role) to do a sports show called "In the Bullpen"; and the three singers heard during the Sunday morning religious programming are the Three Merciful Sisters of Melody.

Relatives: Sylvia Sidney and Carol Bruce (Arthur's mother, *Mama Carlson*), Allyn Ann McLerie (Arthur's wife, *Carmen Carlson*), Sparky Marcus (Arthur's son, *Arthur*

Carlson Jr.; "Little Big Guy"), Ruth Silviera (Johnny's ex-wife, *Paula*), Patrie Allen (Johnny's daughter, *Lori Caravella*), Allison Argo (Andy's sister, *Carol Travis*), Edie McClurg (Herb's wife, *Lucille Tarlek*), Stacey Heather Tolkin (Herb's daughter, *Bunny Tarlek*), N. P. Soch (Herb's son, *Herb Tarlek III*), Bert Parks (Herb's father, *Herbert Tarlek Sr.*)

Theme: "WKRP in Cincinnati," by Tom Wells

WOMEN IN PRISON

Fox, 10.11.87 to 4.2.88

"Poor little girls, now you're trapped in this cruel, crazy world . . . While other girls make dates, you make license plates . . . Now you're in jail." A comical look at life in a women's prison as seen through the eyes of Vicki Springer (Julia Campbell), a beautiful, pampered, naive rich girl who is set up on shoplifting charges (by her husband) and sentenced to Cell Block J of the Bass Women's Prison in Wisconsin.

Vicki can't type or file, but she can cross her legs and show a little bit of thigh, and receives the job of secretary to the prison warden, Cliff Rafferty (Blake Clark), who majored in hotel management in college. Vicki, who believes she is "very sexy and the most attractive woman in captivity," was voted "Most Likely to Be Pictured Running Naked in Slow Motion on a Beach." She held the title of Miss Dairyland in 1984 and 1985 and her resumé lists "soft, mysterious and feminine" as her qualifications. Vicki, who wears a size 34B bra and a size seven shoe, will only allow her hairdresser, "Mr. Joey," to cut "her gorgeous hair." Vicki's prison number is 659142 (a.k.a. 689055).

Other Prisoners: Eve Shipley (Peggy Cass), a gun moll serving a life sentence for murder and robbery (prison number 000023; a.k.a. 628524); Bonnie Harper (Antoinette Byron), a coquettish lesbian, arrested for soliciting (prison number 563478; a.k.a. 856095). She wears a size seven shoe, has eyes for Vicki, and wears a streetwalker-style wardrobe that makes Vicki cringe.

Dawn Murphy (C. C. H. Pounder), a street-wise murderer, is the toughest of the women and commands respect through fear (prison number 447210; a.k.a. 526482). Pam Norwell (Wendie Jo Sperber) is a computer whiz who was arrested for embezzling (prison number 519731; a.k.a. 596085). While Vicki, Bonnie, Eve and Dawn share a cell, Pam has her own cell, complete with computer, a shade for privacy and furnishings.

Meg Brando (Denny Dillon) is the nasty prison guard who delights in tormenting the girls, especially Vicki. Her favorite pastime is going down to Death Row and fiddling with the dimmer switch. Thomas Calloway appears as Vicki's low-life husband, Philip Springer; Arlen Dean Snyder plays Eve's husband, Charlie. Ray Colcord and Phyllis Katz composed the theme, "Women in Prison."

WONDER WOMAN

ABC, 11.7.75 (pilot)
ABC, 3.31.76 to 7.30.77
CBS, 9.23.77 to 2.19.79

Principal Cast: Lynda Carter (*Diana Prince/Wonder Woman*), Lyle Waggoner (*Steve Trevor/Steve Trevor Jr.*), Richard Eastham (*General Philip Blankenshipp; ABC episodes*), Beatrice Colen (*Yeoman Etta Candy; ABC episodes*), Normann Burton (*Joe Atkinson; CBS episodes*)

Trivia: In the year 200 B.C., the rival gods Mars and Aphrodite ruled the earth. When Aphrodite failed to defeat Mars, she created a race of superwomen called Amazons and established a home for them on a still uncharted land mass called Paradise Island. There, the goddess Hippolyte became their queen. As the battle continued, Mars resorted to skullduggery and used Hippolyte's own weapon of love to defeat her. To receive forgiveness, Hippolyte fashioned a small statue and offered it to Aphrodite. Aphrodite brought the statue to life as the baby Diana.

A plane flown by U.S. fighter pilot

Steve Trevor is hit by enemy gunfire and crash lands on Paradise Island (located in the Bermuda Triangle). There, Steve is found by the Princess Diana (now a grown woman) and nursed back to health. When Diana learns from Steve that there is a world war (II) on, and that the Allies are battling a fierce enemy called Nazis, she approaches her Queen Mother and asks for permission to use her great abilities to help America.

From her Queen Mother, Diana receives a red, white and blue costume to signify her allegiance to freedom and democracy, a gold belt to retain her cunning and strength away from Paradise Island, a magic lariat (which compels people to tell the truth) and her gold bracelets, which are made of the metal Feminun and are capable of deflecting bullets.

Steve is given a special drug from the Hybernia Tree that erases all memory of Diana and Paradise Island. Diana flies Steve back to Washington, D.C., in her invisible plane and leaves him at the hospital. After acquainting herself with the American way of life, she adopts the alias Diana Prince and secures a position as a Navy yeoman. She is assigned to the War Department as Major Steve Trevor's secretary. When the need arises for Diana to use her superpowers, the plain-looking Diana does a twirling striptease that transforms her into the gorgeous Wonder Woman. The ABC version ended with Diana and Steve battling Nazism in 1945. It is assumed that Diana returned to Paradise Island when the war ended. General Philip Blankenshipp is Steve's superior and Etta Candy is Philip's secretary. This ABC version of the show was based on the "Wonder Woman" comic strip.

The CBS Version: In 1977, a sabotaged plane lands on Paradise Island. By coincidence, Steve Trevor Jr., the son of the major Diana helped 32 years ago, is aboard. When Diana learns that the modern world is threatened by evil, she again receives permission from her Queen Mother to save the free world from its enemies. Diana uses her invisible plane to guide the jet back to Washington, D.C.

There, she again adopts the disguise of Diana Prince and acquires a job as Steve's assistant at the I.A.D.C. (Interagency Defense Command). The I.A.D.C.'s computer (voiced by Tom Kratichzil) is named IRA; addresses and phone numbers are not given for the regulars. Joe Atkinson is their superior. When Diana is Wonder Woman, she can be seen in high-heeled boots. During a running sequence, the boots have flat heels; they switch back to high heels when the running sequence is over. The series is also known as "The New, Original Wonder Woman" (ABC) and "The New Adventures of Wonder Woman" (CBS).

On March 12, 1974, Cathy Lee Crosby played Diana Prince/Wonder Woman in an unsold pilot film called "Wonder Woman" (set in modern times with the character somewhat changed from that in the original comic strip). Kaz Garas played Steve Trevor and Charlene Holt, the Queen Mother. Ellie Wood Walker, the first choice to play Wonder Woman, appeared as Wonder Woman in a four-minute, 45-second presentation pilot for ABC that has never aired.

Relatives: Debra Winger (Diana's sister, *Drusilla*; a.k.a. Wonder Girl), Cloris Leachman and Carolyn Jones (Diana's *Queen Mother* on ABC), Beatrice Straight (Diana's *Queen Mother* on CBS)

Theme: "Wonder Woman," vocal by the Charles Fox Singers

THE WONDER YEARS

ABC, 1.31.88 to

Principal Cast: Fred Savage (*Kevin Arnold*), Dan Lauria (*Jack Arnold*), Alley Mills (*Norma Arnold*), Olivia D'Abo (*Karen Arnold*), Jason Hervey (*Wayne Arnold*), Danica McKellar (*Winnie Cooper*), Josh Saviano (*Paul Pfeiffer*), Crystal McKellar (*Becky Slater*), Daniel Stern (*Narrator*)

Trivia: "The Wonder Years" presents a nostalgic look at life in the late 1960s and early 1970s, as narrated by the adult Kevin Arnold, but seen from his pre-teen (age 12 when the series begins) and teenage viewpoint.

Kevin first attended Hillcrest Grammar School, then Robert F. Kennedy Junior High School. He was born on March 18, 1956 and hopes to become either a center fielder for the San Francisco Giants or an astronaut (and a member of the first manned flight to Mars). Kevin, a member of the rock band the Electric Shoes in one episode, keeps a picture of Raquel Welch on his locker door at school, and wears a New York Jets football jacket. He is also a member of the Kennedy Junior High Glee Club (for the 1970 Spring Sing, they sang "Stouthearted Men").

Gwendolyn "Winnie" Cooper, the pretty girl next door, is Kevin's on-and-off girlfriend. At Kennedy Junior High, Winnie is a member of the field hockey and cheerleading teams, and starred in the school's production of *Our Town* (for which Kevin worked the spotlight). She and Kevin shared their first kiss while sitting on a rock in Harper's Woods. When Kevin and Winnie have a falling out, he turns to classmate Becky Slater to fill the void left by Winnie. When he broke up with Becky (who punched his lights out), Kevin had a "Star Trek" dream in which he was Captain Kirk and Winnie was a beautiful alien with long hair and a short skirt ("Hey, it's my fantasy. I figured I might as well do it right"). Even as Kirk, Kevin still couldn't understand girls.

In the episode of May 16, 1990, Winnie moves to a new home (only four miles away) and enrolls in a new school (Lincoln High). During the summer of 1969, when Kevin and his family spent their vacation in Ocean City, Kevin met "an older woman," a 15-year-old girl named Teri (Holly Sampson). She called him "Brown Eyes" and it appeared they had a crush on each other. When it came time to part ways, and she returned to New Mexico, she said she would write. She wrote only once ("I keep that letter in an old shoe box now").

Jack Arnold, Kevin's father, gets up at five o'clock in the morning, fights traffic, "busts his hump all day," comes home and pays taxes. He is manager of distribution and product support services for Norcom Enterprises, a government com-

pany. His ritual the night before paying income taxes is to watch the news on TV hoping to see someone else worse off than he is. His Chevrolet Impala's license plate number is GPE 385 and the family station wagon's license plate number reads XDH 975.

Norma Arnold, Kevin's mother, is the woman who keeps the family together. Jack and Norma married in 1949 and spent their honeymoon in Ocean City. They have lived in their current house (address not given) for 17 years. As a teenager, Norma was sent to the principal's office for smoking and dreamed of becoming a singer after high school (she even auditioned for a radio show).

Karen, Kevin's rebellious 16-year-old sister, attends Kennedy High School and is a typical "flower child" of the late 1960s.

Wayne, Kevin's obnoxious older brother, also attends Kennedy High and delights in annoying Kevin (whom he calls "Butthead").

Paul Pfeiffer is Kevin's best friend and, like Winnie, has attended the same schools. He finds schoolwork a breeze and suffers from a number of allergies (e.g., to fish).

Relatives: David Huddleston (Jack's father, *Albert Arnold*), Lynn Milgrim (*Winnie's mother*), H. Richard Greene (*Winnie's father*), John C. Moskoff (Paul's father, *Al Pfeiffer*), Stephanie Sitie (Paul's mother, *Ida Pfeiffer*), Torry Ann Cook (Paul's sister, *Debbie Pfeiffer*), Philip Sterling (Paul's *Grandpa Pfeiffer*)

Flashbacks: Zachary Benjamin (*young Kevin*), Jodie Rae (*young Karen*), Benjamin Daskin (*young Paul*)

Theme: "With a Little Help from My Friends," vocal by Joe Cocker

---

WORKING GIRL

NBC, 4.16.90 to 7.30.90

A TV adaptation of the Melanie Griffith feature film about career girl Tess McGill and her struggle up the ladder of corporate success. Tess (Sandra Bullock) works for Trask Industries in Manhattan. She had been a secretary in accounting before acquiring the position of Junior Marketing Executive to Bryn Newhouse (Nana Visitor), the marketing head. (Feeling she had the qualifications for the job, but lacking a college degree, Tess submitted a report to Bryn under the name Fred MacDonald. The marketing report impressed Bryn and got Tess the job.) Bryn, a Yale graduate, was a member of the Kappa Gamma sorority. Tess, born on Staten Island on January 25, 1965, began working for Trask Industries on April 13, 1989. Her favorite perfume is Adorable.

Tess and her girlfriend Lana (Judy Prescott), a secretary in Accounting at Trask, shoot pool at Nick's Pool House. Tess's parents, Joe (David Schramm) and Fran (B. J. Ward) McGill, run McGill's Deli on Staten Island, where Tess also lives in Apartment 210 (address not given). Carly Simon wrote the theme, "Let the River Run."

In the original, unaired pilot (produced in 1989), Nancy McKeon played Tess and Holly Fulger, Lana.

YOU CAN'T TAKE IT WITH YOU

Syndicated, 9.87 to 9.88

The series relates life with an eccentric family: Martin Vanderhoff (Harry Morgan), a retired advertising man; Penelope "Penny" Sycamore (Lois Nettleton), his daughter, a writer; Paul Sycamore (Richard Sanders), Penny's husband, an eccentric toy inventor; and Alice (Lisa Aliff) and Essie (Heather Blodgett), Penny's daughters. Their address is 121 Liberty Lane, Staten Island, New York; Essie attends Island High School. Penny's cats are named Kate and Alley Cat. In the original, unaired pilot, Elizabeth Townsend played Essie and Teddy Wilson, who plays Durwood Pinner, Paul's assistant, played Mr. DePinna, Paul's co-worker.

THE YOUNG PIONEERS

ABC, 4.2.78 to 4.16.78

With a dream of becoming homesteaders, newlyweds (married April 8, 1873) Molly Beaton (Linda Purl), age 16, and her husband David (Roger Kern) age 18, leave Indian Falls, Iowa, and head for Dakota in their horse-drawn wagon (pulled by their Morgan horses, Whitefoot and Star). In Yankton, Dakota, David files a claim (it costs $18.00: $14 down and the balance to be paid after homesteading for five years) for 160 acres of farmland (on which they plant wheat and corn) plus five acres for planting trees. Through Molly's narration (from her diary—which she keeps in a seashell-decorated box David gave her) their struggles are chronicled.

While they lived alone in the wilderness when they first homesteaded, they were closest to the town of Wildrose and eventually acquired some neighbors: Dan Gray (Robert Hays) and the pioneering Peters family—a father (Robert Donner) and his children, Nettie (Mare Winningham), Flora (Michelle Stacey) and Charles (Jeff Cotler). The Peters family owns the claim next to the Beatons'; Mr. Peters is not given a first name and is a widower. During the harsh winter months, David earns money working as a hauler for the Chicago and Northwestern Railroad or as a hand at the Roslyn Feed Mill.

In the first pilot (ABC, 3.1.76) Shelly Jutner played Nettie and a son, Little Davy, was born to Molly on January 18, 1874 (the infant was not credited). In the second pilot, "Young Pioneers' Christmas" (ABC, 12.17.76), Kay Kimler played Nettie, Sherri Wagner, Flora and Brian Melrose, Charlie. (In this story, Molly and David lose Little Davy to disease and struggle to put aside their grief to extend a gift of friendship at Christmastime.) Charles Tyner played David's father, Mr. Beaton, in the first pilot. Laurence Rosenthal composed the theme.

THE ZOO GANG

NBC, 7.6.75 to 8.6.75

The exploits of four World War II resistance fighters, known as "the Zoo Gang," who reunite in 1975 to battle crime in Europe.

The Zoo Gang: Brian Keith as Steve Halliday (an antique dealer), known as the Fox; Lilli Palmer as Manouche Roget (the owner of the Les Pêcheurs Bar in France), known as the Leopard; John Mills as Tom Devon (a jeweler), known as the Elephant; and Barry Morse as Alec Marlowe (a mechanic), known as the Tiger.

Seretta Wilson plays Tom's niece, Jill Barton, and Michael Petrovitch plays Manouche's son, Police Lieutenant Georges Roget. Paul and Linda McCartney composed the theme.

About the Author

Vincent Terrace, a native New Yorker, is a graduate of the New York Institute of Technology and holds a bachelor's degree in Fine Arts. He is the author of *The Complete Encyclopedia of Television Programs, 1947–1979; Radio's Golden Years, 1930–1960; Television 1970–1980;* the three-volume *Television: Series, Pilots & Specials, 1937–1984; 50 Years of Television: A Guide to Series and Pilots, 1937–1988* and the two-volume *Complete Actors' Television Credits, 1948–1988* with James Robert Parish. Mr. Terrace has also been a research associate on numerous books, including *The Television Book, The Great Science Fiction Pictures* and *The Great Detective Films* and has co-authored supplements two and three of *Actors' Television Credits* with Mr. Parish.